D1411726

REBUILDING AMERICA'S LEGACY CITIES

REBUILDING AMERICA'S LEGACY CITIES

New Directions for the Industrial Heartland

Alan Mallach, Editor

published by

Summary: For America's Legacy Cities—cities losing population and their economic base—this book puts forth strategies to create smaller, healthier cities. Creative strategies for using vacant land need to be matched with successful efforts to stabilize the local economy and re-engage residents in the workforce, and to reinvigorate the city's still-viable neighborhoods. This volume offers a broader discussion which recognizes the complex relationships between today's problems and their solutions.

The rich material contained in this volume provides thought-provoking reading for anyone concerned with the transformation of America's older industrial cities, either with respect to a specific city or from a broader perspective, whether the reader is a policymaker, practitioner, or concerned layperson. These chapters do not suggest that that the process of change will be an easy one. They do offer a robust collection of ideas and directions that can help animate local action or state policy and help practitioners and policymakers take the steps that may indeed lead to the smaller, stronger, and healthier city that the authors believe is possible.

Typeset in Adobe Garamond.

Designed by Mark Swindle.

Printed by Createspace, An Amazon.com company.

Cover photograph: Close-up of the "Spirit of Detroit," sculpted by Marshall Fredericks.

Contents

Foreword

Our nation's well-being is substantially tied to the strength of our metropolitan areas and the central cities around which they grew. The cities and their metro area can be the country's economic drivers in the 21st century, and our overall national economic strength will be directly correlated to their well-being.

While many cities in America are doing far better than thirty years ago, when mayors and city managers were confronting economic decline, rising crime, and abandonment amidst widespread sentiment that cities no longer mattered, other cities are still struggling to define their role in the 21st century. These cities are searching for their future as they seek to transition from their historic role as the manufacturing centers of the industrial revolution and the arsenal of America during World War II.

These cities—called Legacy Cities in this book—are the places that have continued to lose population, see their neighborhoods decay and which must grapple with high unemployment and poverty. This book of thoughtful, informed essays edited by Alan Mallach will make a major contribution in helping business, civic, and political leaders of these cities understand the dimensions of what is occurring in our country and elsewhere, and offers valuable ideas and suggestions on how to confront the challenges these cities face.

The recovery of the nation's legacy cities is important not only to the people and businesses in them but to our nation as a whole, for many reasons. First, these cities contain centuries of accumulated infrastructure, an investment that the nation cannot afford to allow to go to waste through neglect. That infrastructure goes far beyond roads, highways, sewer and water lines. It includes the historic neighborhoods and downtowns that were the glory of American urban life at the end of the 19th, and for much of the 20th century. It includes many of the nation's greatest academic institutions and medical research centers, such as the Cleveland Clinic or Johns Hopkins. All of these represent powerful economic assets that need to be harnessed for these cities' revitalization and for the nation's growth.

Second, these cities have critical resources needed to accommodate the millions of additional people that will live in our country. We are likely to see population growth occurring in places where natural resources have already become a constraint on growth. In much of the Southwest and West, the water supply is simply not sufficient to accommodate the fifty million additional people expected to be added to the nation by 2050. Revitalizing legacy cities that have plentiful water and other natural and built resources so that some of that population growth can be attracted to these places is sound national policy.

Both of us have been mayors of major American cities. As mayors, we came personally to understand how important it is that the actions taken to mold our cities' futures be based on thoughtful analysis and sound planning principles. The essays in this volume, which offer thoughtful insight and suggestions on not only the physical, but also the economic and social dimensions of the process of re-building our legacy cities, will be of great value for everyone wrestling with this critical and timely public policy issue.

The Hon. Henry G. Cisneros
Executive Chairman
CityView
Former Mayor
City of San Antonio

The Hon. Gregory S. Lashutka
Senior Consultant
Findley Davies
Former Mayor
City of Columbus

Preface

The revitalization of many U.S. cities from their nadir of two or three decades ago is one of America's major success stories. While these cities have developed healthier downtowns, safer neighborhoods, and vibrant local economies, other cities, inside and outside the industrial heartland, face daunting challenges as they struggle with prolonged demographic and economic downturns. All too often, these material difficulties are complicated by political, psychological, and legal challenges. There is little accepted language for talking about a city experiencing severe population loss and few policy frameworks that do not revert to talk about growth.

If they are to thrive once again, this group of American cities must find strategies that manage their realities and that result in stabilization and reinvention rather than continued decline. Identifying those strategies was the challenge The American Assembly took on in the fall of 2009, as it began planning the activities that culminated in the 110th American Assembly and in this edited volume. The Assembly remains conscious of building on the important work of many others—including its own earlier projects on urban policy in formulating language and policy recommendations adequate to the challenge. Yet, the time has come for more deliberate and focused attention to these problems, lest we lose the rich historical heritages and valuable resources of these cities. Documenting these challenges and charting practical paths through them is the central purpose of this volume.

Many people contributed to this process. Urban policy scholar and advocate Paul C. Brophy, of Brophy & Reilly LLC, guided the project from its early planning meetings to the final report from the Assembly. Mr. Brophy was involved in or led most of The American Assembly's urban policy projects. The project benefited greatly from the cosponsorship of The Center for Sustainable Urban Development at Columbia University's The Earth Institute, directed by Elliott D. Sclar, who served as project co-director with Mr. Brophy and The

Center for Community Progress of Flint, Michigan and Washington D.C., led by Daniel T. Kildee.

Henry G. Cisneros, the Executive Chair of CityView and the former Secretary of Housing and Urban Development and Gregory S. Lashutka, Senior Consultant, Findley Davies and former Mayor of Columbus, Ohio served as co-chairs. They were assisted by a distinguished national steering committee whose names and affiliations are listed in the appendix.

Alan Mallach, non-resident senior fellow at the Brookings Institution and senior fellow at The Center for Community Progress, conceived and structured this volume. As its editor, he was nothing short of remarkable in guiding his writing team through various drafts and producing this important and much-needed contribution to U.S. urban policy.

The chapters in this volume were first used as background for the 110th American Assembly held in Detroit, Michigan on April 14-17, 2011. Eighty representatives of government, business, law, labor, academia, nonprofit organizations, and the media came together to discuss the harsh realities facing these "legacy cities"—as the Assembly participants chose to call them—and develop policy frameworks for addressing them. In their fifty-page report of findings and recommendations, the participants agreed these legacy cities can be placed on a trajectory for long term recovery. The participants' names and affiliations as well as the final report are included in the appendix of this volume.

In 1997 Mr. Brophy directed an Assembly project called "Community Capitalism: Rediscovering the Markets of America's Urban Neigborhoods" that helped launch a redefinition of inner city communities as viable investment opportunities. It is our hope that the land use strategies, creative financing approaches, improved civic capacity, and stronger partnerships presented in The Assembly report and in this new volume will make a similar contribution. We want to ensure that our nation acknowledges the historic contributions of its legacy cities, and that the immense value in skills, institutions, and hard resources that these cities hold are assets for America's future.

We gratefully acknowledge the generous support of, the Ford Foundation, the Kresge Foundation, the Mott Foundation, Bank of America, and Ally Financial. Without their invaluable help, this project could not have been undertaken.

The chapters in this volume reflect the opinions and positions of their authors, and do not represent positions of the American Assembly, the Center for Community Progress, or the Center for Sustainable Urban Development.

David H. Mortimer
The American Assembly

Introduction

Alan Mallach, Editor

With the end of World War II, an era of urban disinvestment in the United States began. Suburban flight, deindustrialization, and the southward movement of the nation's population to the Sun Belt led to massive population and job loss in the cities that had driven America's economic growth for the preceding century. While some cities have rebounded in recent years, others—including iconic American cities like Detroit, St. Louis, and Cleveland, as well as many smaller cities and towns—have not, and they continue to decline. As the population of these legacy cities, as we term them, has declined, lack of demand for their land and buildings has created a new urban landscape dominated by vacant lots and empty buildings. Their remaining population has become poorer, with many residents lacking the skills, labor-force attachment, or mobility to compete in the regional or national labor markets. Recent trends, including the rise and fall of subprime lending, the Great Recession, and the crisis in the automotive industry, have hit these cities with particular force, making their already difficult conditions worse.

Today, many of these cities are in crisis. While some may have begun to stabilize in recent years, most continue to hemorrhage jobs and people. All share debilitating problems of vacant land and buildings, unemployment, and poverty. Today, more than ever before, they share even more crippling fiscal problems, as declining incomes and property values, coupled with shrinkage of the one-time state and federal safety net, have drastically cut municipal revenues, while expenditures for public services, debt service, health benefits, and pensions continue to skyrocket. Layoffs have become endemic, while the once-unthinkable subject of municipal bankruptcy has become a matter of serious discussion.

Legacy cities, as we call them in this volume, are far smaller cities—not in land area, but in population and economic activity—than they were in their heyday. Even if they emerge from the current crisis, they will continue to be smaller cities. That is not a matter of speculation, but reality. Some will continue to lose population for years to come, while others may stabilize their population and begin to grow once more, but they will still remain smaller than they were fifty or sixty years earlier. How to address this reality is the central challenge for these cities. How they reconfigure their physical environment and repurpose their surplus buildings and vacant land, how they stabilize their economies and utilize their human capital, and how they capitalize on their man-made and natural assets may determine whether their future will be one of continued decline or that of regained vitality as smaller but stronger cities.

These Cities Matter

The future of America's legacy cities is not a minor matter. In 2000, 45 million people—15 percent of the nation's population—lived in these cities and their surrounding metropolitan areas. This in itself should be enough to make the question of what will happen to them a matter of national importance, and make their efforts worthy of careful attention. There are other reasons, though, why the future of America's legacy cities should be seen as important, not only for the people who live there but for all of us.

Disproportionately concentrated as these cities are in the nation's Northeast and near Midwest, the so-called Rust Belt, their course will affect not only themselves and their immediate surroundings but also the future vitality of states like Michigan, New York, Pennsylvania, and Ohio. Legacy cities offer both resources for and impose burdens on the larger economy. They contain untapped resources of human capital, and billions of dollars in sunk infrastructure investment in roads, transit, sewer and water facilities, parks, and other public facilities. They contain major networks of educational and medical facilities, including such renowned centers as Johns Hopkins, Carnegie-Mellon, and the Cleveland Clinic, while they continue to serve as regional and national centers of culture, art, sport, and entertainment. These assets and resources are of critical importance for a nation struggling with rebuilding its economy and finding its course in the twenty-first century.

In their present condition, these cities are also weighty burdens on public resources, due to the municipal and school aid they need to provide public services and due to transfer payments to their residents, who are disproportionately poor, elderly, and disabled. In 2009, the state of New Jersey spent over $400 million to support Camden's city and school budgets, or over five thousand dollars per city resident. Continued deterioration and impoverishment in central cities also act as a drag on suburban economies, which are, even after decades of sprawl and decentralization, still closely interwoven with the fates of their central cities. The revival of America's older industrial cities will add value to the regional and national economy while reducing the burden that these cities impose in their present condition.

Defining A New Paradigm

The challenge of sustained population loss is not a new one. For most of the cities under consideration, shrinkage has been a reality since the 1950s or 1960s. It is a challenge, however, that cities have only recently begun to take up. When the idea of addressing urban population loss was raised in the past, its advocates were shouted down. Roger Starr's 1976 call for the "planned shrinkage" of parts of New York City ignited a polemical firestorm, while when Detroit's city ombudsman proposed in 1993 that the city "mothball" severely blighted areas, demolishing properties and suspending city services to those areas, her proposal was greeted with a mixture of controversy and ridicule.

This has changed dramatically. More and more public officials and civic leaders have acknowledged that their cities are, in fact, smaller cities, and that the way they plan and allocate their resources must recognize that reality. Cleveland, Dayton, Detroit, and Rochester, among others, have all incorporated the reality of sustained population loss into their plans, recognizing that the future shape of their cities will be very different from what it was fifty or a hundred years earlier. What has begun to emerge is a new planning paradigm, which confronts the reality of population loss by offering a vision of a city that is a smaller but healthier place. That paradigm recognizes that with a smaller population, the face of the city will change in ways still hard to predict, a subject addressed by Terry Schwarz in Chapter 6.

The growing acceptance of this paradigm does not mean that it is no longer a matter of controversy. To some, the mere idea of acknowledging shrinkage still seems to be a declaration of failure or an abdication of responsibility, as is the case with the usually thoughtful *New York Times* columnist Bob Herbert, who has characterized it as an example of "the same pathetic lack of creativity and helpless mind-set that now seems to be the default position of Americans in the 21st century."

I would argue the opposite, an argument that is borne out by the rich variety of ideas, suggestions, and proposals that will be found in the chapters of this volume. To address the reality of smaller cities is to recognize that times have indeed changed, that the great days of steel and coal are gone, but that rather than passively surrender, cities are not helpless in the face of change. Rather than either wallowing in fantasies of silver bullets that will bring about the return of the good old days or assuming that continued decline and shrinkage are inevitable, cities can chart a new course to make them vital participants in today's economy and society. The many individuals and organizations that have embraced this idea, and are working to rebuild their communities, need the active support and engagement not only of the state and federal governments but of private business and community leadership, and of the public at large.

The mission of the April 2011 American Assembly was to build that engagement by reshaping the policy conversation about America's legacy cities at the local, state, and federal levels. As part of that goal, this volume plays a critical role. It tries to answer a central, salient question: How can change best be brought about? What attitudes and past practices need to be changed and what concrete steps need to be taken in order to put these cities on the path to regeneration as smaller, healthier cities? First, though, it is worth offering some thoughts on what we mean by smaller, healthier cities.

Visualizing Smaller, Healthier Cities

Restoring vitality to older industrial cities that have experienced decades of population and job loss will not be a simple matter, and it will not happen overnight. It will be a complex, gradual process involving change to these cities' social, economic, and physical features, a task rendered even more difficult by the severe fiscal constraints facing not only the cities themselves but the state and federal governments to which they might hope to turn for help. It also demands that we try to visualize what should be the end of this process; in other words, what does it mean to be a smaller, healthier city?

While the smaller, healthier city of the future will still contain poor people and distressed areas, it will be a very different place from today's shrinking older industrial city. It will be a city in which the local and regional economy offers a pool of jobs commensurate with the size of the area's workforce, along with the education, training, and mobility options that will enable any willing resident of the city not only to find a job but to have opportunities for upward mobility without having to leave the community. The city's population will be stable, and may even grow slightly, as more people choose to stay rather than leave. It will accommodate a variety of healthy, stable neighborhoods that will have become communities of choice for different segments of the regional market; while distressed and disinvested areas may still exist, they will be outnumbered by the city's stronger, vital neighborhoods. Downtown will once again be a center of life and activity for the city and region, although perhaps at a more modest level and within a smaller geographic compass than in the city's heyday.

The great majority of the city's businesses and residents will now occupy a land area considerably smaller than the total contained within the city's boundaries, but the city will have far fewer vacant, derelict buildings than before, in part because of demolition and in part because of reuse. Since reuse and upgrading of existing buildings will have met most of the city's demand, little of the city's vacant land will have been redeveloped with new buildings. Most of that land will be reused instead for non-development purposes such as wetlands, forests, or farming—thereby providing visually attractive and environmentally sustainable areas that will enhance the city's quality of life.

Local government will deliver good-quality and cost-effective public services, and work closely with CDCs and other nonprofit organizations, colleges and hospitals, businesses, and residents to sustain healthy neighborhoods and reuse vacant land. The cities and towns within the region will cooperate with one another and with the private sector to build the regional economy and increase opportunities for the region's residents.

This is not a utopian dream, but an achievable vision. It will not, however, be an easy one to achieve, nor will it come unbidden. Such a vision demands that people change how they think about their communities, how they distribute their resources, and how they form relationships with one another. Above all, it will only be realized through deliberate, systematic action by all of those who have a stake in the future of their city or region.

Setting The Course

While we may not yet know enough to offer a road map to create the smaller, healthier city described above, we can begin to put the pieces together to help build that map for cities ready to make the effort to get there. The first step is to acknowledge that change will require not a single step, but many separate, parallel steps along many different paths in order to address the complex and interrelated issues that have led to and that perpetuate the current condition of the nation's legacy cities. While much of the "shrinking city" discussion—and much of the media attention it has received—has focused on what to do about these cities' large and growing inventory of vacant land and buildings, that is only part of the picture and it cannot be addressed in isolation. Creative strategies for using vacant land in heavily abandoned areas will not in themselves restore a city to health unless they are matched with successful efforts to stabilize the local economy and re-engage residents in the workforce, and to reinvigorate the city's still-viable neighborhoods. We need a shrinking city discussion that is broader in scope than the debate over demolishing buildings and using vacant land, and which recognizes the complex relationships between today's problems and their solutions.

The object of the eleven chapters that make up this volume is to contribute to this discussion. The first three chapters frame the discussion; Bob Beauregard provides an overview of urban population loss in the United States, while Ned Hill, Hal Wolman and their colleagues examine the factors, both internal and external, that are likely to affect a city's growth or decline. I contribute a chapter that looks at the forces that have created the surplus property inventory in older industrial cities, and the implications of this surplus for the future of these cities.

The next group of chapters explores a series of specific topics, each of which will play a critical role in the process of building a strategy for change. Since planning practice has historically been about managing growth, Margie Dewar and Hunter Morrison open this section with their ideas on how planning practices can be reframed to address the future of shrinking cities. David Boehlke addresses the ways in which strong neighborhoods can be preserved, and others regenerated, while Terry Schwarz looks at the growing arsenal of ways to think about the reuse of vacant urban land, the "places in between." Bob Giloth and Jillien Meier look at these cities' underutilized human capital and address how shrinking cities can integrate workforce development with economic development strategies, while June Manning Thomas looks at how public policy should address the critical but often neglected intersection between race, class, and ethnicity in America's older industrial cities.

The final section of this volume looks more broadly at the role of policymaking and governance in creating a better future for older industrial cities in the United States. Paul Brophy and I explore the need for reforming local government practices, while Lavea Brachman looks at the role the states and the federal government must play in providing the support that these cities need if the opportunity for change is to be a real rather than an illusory one. Finally, Jörg Plöger draws on the rich body of experience in Europe, with its older industrial cities, in order to draw lessons for American cities.

Interspersed among these chapters, each of which offers an extended discussion of an issue or question, are a number of shorter essays or "sidebars," illustrating the themes of the chapters with short, descriptive case studies drawn from the experience of specific cities. The case studies include descriptions of existing conditions—like Saginaw's fiscal problems or Detroit's vacant land inventory—and of changes and new initiatives—such as Pittsburgh's high-tech revival or the innovative Youngstown 2010 planning process.

The rich material contained in this volume offers thought-provoking reading for anyone concerned with the transformation of America's older industrial cities, either with respect to a specific city or from a broader perspective, whether the reader is a policymaker, practitioner, or concerned layperson. These chapters do not suggest that that the process of change will be an easy one. They do offer a robust collection of ideas and directions that can help animate local action or state policy and help practitioners and policymakers take the steps that may indeed lead to the smaller, stronger and healthier city that the authors believe is possible.

1

Growth And Depopulation In The United States

Robert A. Beauregard, Columbia University

Since this country's European settlement, unrelenting national growth and a continuous geographic concentration of people have meant that the great majority of the country's urban places have grown without interruption. At the same time, numerous villages, towns, and cities have failed to keep pace with their peers or have actually become smaller as they have lost out to regional competition. Others were too small to survive and disappeared. In the United States, a decrease in population growth and decline that results have been inseparable.

This chapter provides a general overview of the complex mix of population expansion and contraction that has characterized urban development in the United States. It also includes a more detailed investigation of the phenomenon of shrinking cities in the late twentieth century. In considering both, I treat shrinkage as a matter of depopulation. My assumption is that a city experiences decline (that is, multiple dimensions of incapacity) when it is no longer attractive to households, a condition that occurs almost always because it has become less attractive to investors. A drop-off in investment capital diminishes a city's economic activity and constricts job opportunities, powerful deterrents to living there. Disinvestment, a signal of a problematic future, makes matters worse.

Central to my approach is the recognition that shrinkage is not new. Rather, it is a novel way of thinking about the failure of places to maintain their social and economic value. Shrinking, or legacy, cities have become a prominent topic in academic and policy circles for three reasons. One is that urban decline, a condition that has been in ample evidence at least since the early twentieth century, has become entrenched in cities like Buffalo, Philadelphia, and Detroit, places that were once the powerhouses of the national economy and seemingly invincible.[1] Second, although political and corporate elites have resisted and attempted to reverse decline for decades, they have done so with only limited success; they have pursued growth but failed to attract it. Consequently, since the 1990s, civic leaders in a number of shrinking cities have entertained the possibility that these cities might never recapture their glory days.[2] The most realistic and likely future is that these cities will become smaller. Civic leaders must therefore embrace policies that make a city viable and livable even as it shrinks. Third, city planners, neighborhood activists, and elected officials have embraced a new combination of policy tools—demolition, land banking, and "green" initiatives—that has engendered the hope that these cities can be stabilized and made desirable once again. "Smaller" is not only becoming acceptable but seems to be manageable.

This chapter has three substantive sections, all of which rely on population data published by the U.S. Census. (*See Research Note on page 23*). The first section takes a national perspective and looks to the country's past. It assesses population growth in the United States at various spatial scales: the nation, the four census regions, metropolitan areas both as a whole and disaggregated into the central cities and the suburban periphery, and cities in different size categories. What we see through this lens is nearly uninterrupted expansion both in population size and in the number of urban places. The second section shortens the time frame to the last half of the twentieth century and considers places that have lost population. Despite a background of growth, a number of metropolitan areas, central cities, suburbs, and neighborhoods have become smaller. The third and last section compares three shrinking cities with three growing cities in order to convey a sense of the disadvantages that residents and local governments experience when their cities shrink. Population loss is accompanied by fewer job opportunities, deterioration in the condition of neighborhoods and the market value of housing, and local governments constrained to provide quality public services.

National Expansion

In 1790, the federal government undertook its first census; it recorded just shy of four million people living in the country. Since then, the population of the United States has risen without interruption, climbing to just over 308 million people in 2010. Between 1790 and 1850, in fact, the population expanded by about one-third every ten years. Thereafter, the rate of growth fell steadily until the 1960s and has hovered around 10 percent for each decade since that time. Yet the population continues to increase by significant numbers. Interestingly, some of the largest absolute increases have occurred recently. In the 1990s and in the first decade of the twenty-first century, approximately sixty million residents were added to the population; much of this increase is due to a renewed and robust immigration.

Regional Growth

The four major regions—the Northeast, Midwest, South, and West—of the United States have each experienced unbroken demographic expansion throughout the twentieth century (*See Figure 1*). The regions, though, have not expanded at similar rates, and significant regional variation exists (*See Figure 2*). In 1890, the Midwest was the largest region, with 22.5 million inhabitants, followed by the South's 20 million residents. At that time, the West was sparsely populated, with just over three million people. By 2010, the Midwest had lost its numerical dominance to both the South and the West. Over the last one hundred years or so, the South and West have experienced the fastest growth, while the Midwest and the Northeast have lagged behind. In fact, the South now overshadows the other three regions in population size, being home to one out of every three U.S. inhabitants. The West is over twenty times larger in population than it was in 1890, whereas the Northeast, in contrast, has had a mere threefold increase. In 1890, almost three out of every five residents lived in the Northeast or Midwest. By 2010, that ratio had fallen to one of every three residents. Although no region

Figure 1: *Census Regions and Divisions of the United States*

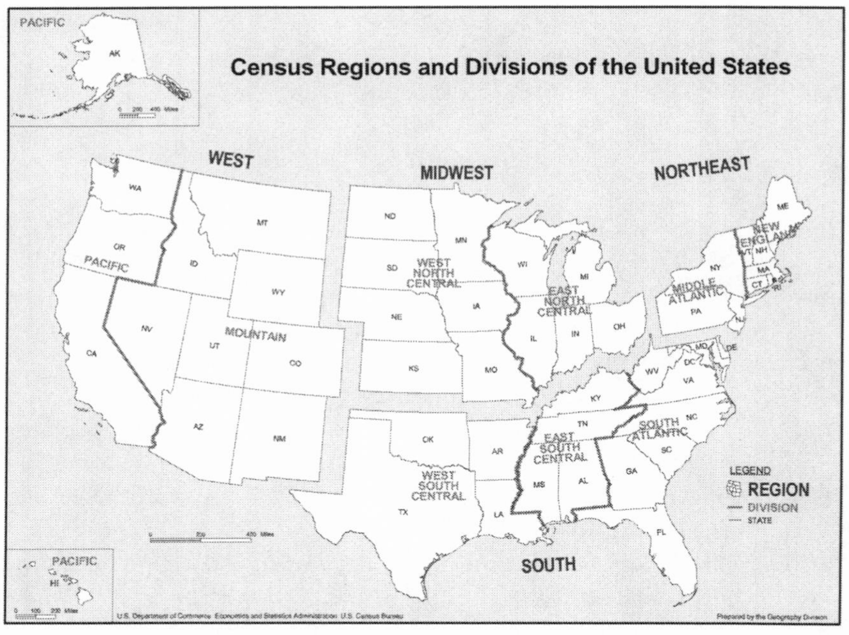

Figure 2: *Regional Population Change: 1890-2010*

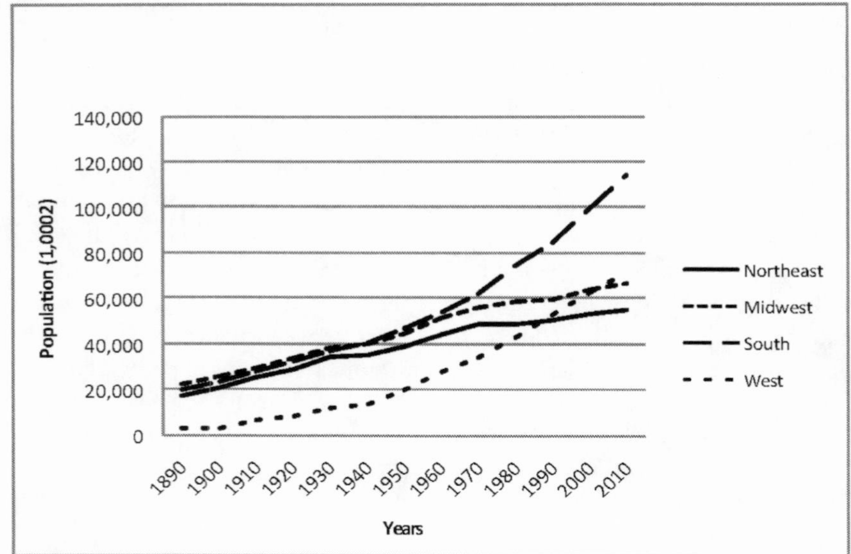

Although no region has declined in population, where people live has changed dramatically. Proportionately, fewer and fewer people are living in the Northeast and Midwest, the two regions whose nineteenth century prosperity was built on manufacturing, a point to which we will return.

Metropolitan Growth

Growth continues to be the dominant condition when we drop down in scale to the metropolis, the integrated urban sub-regions where work and commuting are spatially concentrated. Since the late nineteenth century, the number of people residing in these regions has risen from 14 million to over 250 million. By the beginning of the twenty-first century, approximately eight out of every ten residents of the United States lived in a metropolitan area. The number of these places, moreover, has steadily increased. As of 2009, there were over 366 such urban regions, ranging from Sandusky (OH) and Corvallis (OR), with fewer than 100,000 residents, to New York City and Los Angeles, with over 22 million and 18 million people, respectively.

When one looks within metropolitan areas, growth is pervasive, although one also encounters circumstantial evidence of shrinkage. For example, consider the simple but widely-used distinction between the central cities and the suburban peripheries. Central cities once anchored their metropolitan areas economically, politically, culturally, and demographically; they were dominant within the metropolis. Whereas the number of people living in central cities throughout the twentieth century has risen steadily, mainly due to the growth of metropolitan areas in the South and West, the central city share of metropolitan population has fallen from about three-quarters to approximately one-third. Since the end of World War II, most growth in metropolitan areas has been in the suburban periphery, not in the central cities. From 1950 to 2000, the number of suburbanites went from 35 million to over 140 million, while the number of those living in central cities failed even to double, going from 49 million to 85 million (*See Figure 3*). This has meant a loss of demographic dominance for the central cities. St. Louis, for example, had over 80 percent of the area's residents in 1910; by 2010, it had 13 percent. Among others, the cities of Providence, Milwaukee, Pittsburgh, and Kansas City also witnessed a relative (if not absolute) decline in their metropolitan position. Moreover, emerging metropolitan areas like Las Vegas, Phoenix, and Austin grew not in the center but on their edges, quite unlike the early twentieth century metropolises.

Figure 3: *Metropolitan Population Growth: 1890-2000*

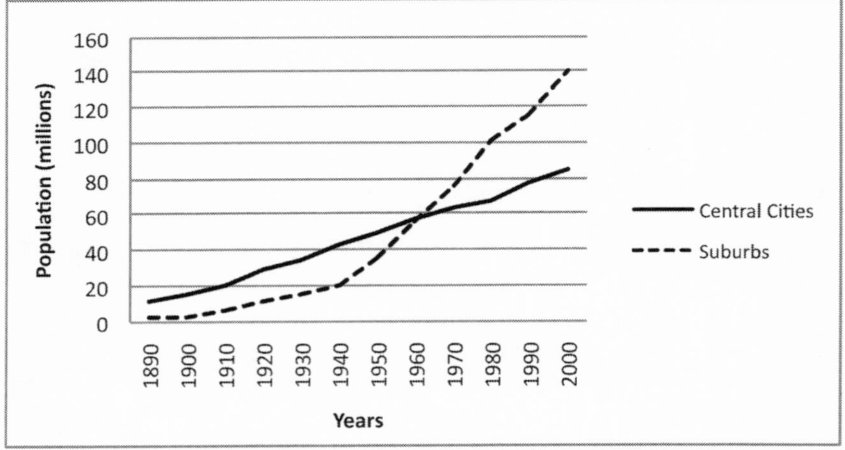

Growth of Cities

Our last look from the national level considers the growth of cities of different sizes. The U.S. Census Bureau aggregates population data for places ranging from fewer than 2,500 inhabitants (non-urban places) to those over a million inhabitants. Most places—over 90 percent in the early twentieth century and still well over 80 percent in the early twenty-first century—have fewer than 25,000 residents. Places with populations from 25,000 to 250,000 make up the great majority of the remainder. Relatively few cities exceed this size. In 2009, the United States had nine cities with over a million residents, with New York City, Los Angeles, Chicago, and Houston leading the way. Another twenty-five cities (places like Denver and Jacksonville) had between 500,000 and 1 million residents, and forty-two cities (for example, Anaheim [CA]and Omaha [NE]) had between 250,000 and 500,000 people. In almost all of these city-size categories—with few exceptions—the numbers of cities have increased since 1790. The largest city, New York in 1790 had only fifty thousand or so residents and the country did not have a single city with one million inhabitants until the population of New York reached that number in 1880. Prior to 1820, no cities exceeded 100,000 residents. The city which did so first was New York, and it has sat atop the nation's urban hierarchy ever since.

Throughout its history, the United States has extended its land area from the East to the West and South (and to Alaska and Hawaii in 1959) and experienced continuous population expansion. Regionally, growth has also been uninterrupted, although the regions themselves have shifted in demographic importance. Further down in scale, metropolitan areas have grown in number and expanded, with four out of every five Americans now living in either a central city or a suburb. Most important, investors and households continue to create new places and make existing places larger. Except for the loss of metropolitan dominance of some central cities, a national perspective reveals little evidence of shrinkage. For this, one must turn to a more detailed analysis of metropolitan areas, cities, and neighborhoods for the decades after World War II.

Postwar Urban Shrinkage

During the early postwar period and into the 1980s, three large migratory shifts and a new round of industrial restructuring established the conditions for the shrinkage of cities. The worst of the consequences fell on the industrial cities of the Northeast and Midwest.[3] One of these migrations occurred just after World War II. It involved working-class and middle-class residents leaving their urban neighborhoods for the suburbs. Pushed from the central cities by the lack of housing and the ensuing over-crowding, they were attracted to the suburbs by newly built single-family homes. At the same time, African-Americans from the South were traveling to the industrial cities in search of decent jobs and relief from discrimination. There, they were channeled into the older, less costly, and more deteriorated neighborhoods, making their presence both obvious and politically contentious. The third migration was the movement of people away from the Northeast and Midwest. This trend had begun during the war, but did not gain full momentum until the 1980s, when a collapse of heavy manufacturing in the country's industrial areas sent people in search of jobs in the South and West. This further drained population from the older, central cities.

These migratory shifts were amplified by a restructuring of the country's industrial base, a change that had originated during World War II. One dimension of this restructuring was spatial: the growth of manufacturing in the South and

West, whereas it had previously been concentrated in the Northeast and Midwest. Textile and shoe manufacturing industries, for example, prior to moving overseas, fled the pro-labor union states of the Northeast and Midwest for the right-to-work, lower-wage states of the South. War mobilization, moreover, had established new centers of shipbuilding and aircraft production on the West Coast. After the war ended, the plant and public infrastructure that had been built there enabled the growth of domestic industries. Equally important were the decline of heavy manufacturing (for example, shipbuilding and steel production) and the decentralization of light manufacturing (such as food production) from the industrial Northeast and Midwest. Decentralization of plants, foreign competition, and the shift to new products (for example, to plastics and away from steel) favored the growing regions of the country. As manufacturing declined, business, social, and personal services—insurance, business consulting, higher education, fast food retailing, and health care, among others—became more economically important. The national economy shifted from manufacturing to services, and this disadvantaged the cities and regions whose prosperity had been based on the production of goods.

Together, industrial restructuring and these three migrations had a profound impact on older, industrial cities, their neighborhoods, and the metropolitan areas in which they were located. As large-scale heavy manufacturing declined, unemployed workers left for the suburbs or regions where jobs were on the rise. Too few people moved to the cities to overcome this out-migration and neighborhoods subsequently emptied. In fact, most of the in-migrants (primarily African-Americans) were steered into slums or lacked the income to maintain the neighborhoods in which they were allowed to live. African-Americans who came to the cities in search of well-paying manufacturing jobs were, more often than not, unsuccessful, not just because the industries offering these jobs were leaving or disappearing but also because they encountered prejudice and discrimination in job and housing markets. Denied the opportunity to benefit from upward mobility, they ended up economically and culturally marginalized in deteriorating urban neighborhoods. The shrinkage of manufacturing also hit industrial suburbs like McKeesport, outside Pittsburgh and Pawtucket, adjacent to Providence. They, too, declined, often causing the metropolitan area to falter and people to move to growing metropolises in the South and West. Shrinking cities emerged because of these conditions.

Metropolitan Shrinkage

We begin with the postwar flight of residents from metropolitan areas. Despite the promise of suburbanization and the rise of business, retail, and other services in the metropolitan periphery, a number of metropolitan areas have shrunk in population size, mostly, but not wholly, driven by the depopulation of their central cities.

According to the celebratory wisdom of postwar suburbanization, metropolitan areas are not designed to lose population and decline.[4] The suburbs are a unique form of American urbanism, one encased in a growth ideology that has constant spatial expansion as one of its defining characteristics. The growth of the metropolis is seen by many as relentless and unstoppable. And this has been more or less true. Throughout most of the twentieth century, the number of urban regions and the number of people living in them has steadily increased. Central cities declined, but they did so due to factors heretofore alien to the suburbs: crime, physical decay, political incompetence, poor schools, racial tensions, and obsolete industries. Suburbs were their opposites and ostensibly slated for uninterrupted prosperity.

Yet, in the 1970s, a number of metropolitan areas did lose residents. During that decade, the largest of them in the Northeast and Midwest experienced a collective loss of population—an almost 10 percent deficit.[5] On the whole, all other metropolitan areas in the United States grew, with those in the South and West doubling and even tripling the rate of expansion in the other two regions. The metropolitan areas of New York, Philadelphia, Detroit, Cleveland, St. Louis, Pittsburgh, and Milwaukee all had smaller populations in 1980 than in 1970. Pittsburgh's metropolitan area, moreover, had also shed residents in the 1960s and it, along with the metropolitan areas of Detroit and Cleveland, lost population in the 1980s, as well.[6]

In fact, instances of metropolitan decline extend back to the 1940s. Then, of the metropolitan areas of more than 250,000 residents, five of them experienced depopulation: Scranton, Wilkes-Barre, and Johnstown, Pennsylvania; Wheeling, West Virginia; and Duluth, Minnesota. Moreover, metropolitan decline has persisted; fifteen of the large metropolitan areas suffered population loss between 2000 and 2009. The 1980s represented the worst decade—population-wise—for metropolitan areas. Then, twenty-one of them—compared to nineteen in the 1970s—were smaller at the end compared to the start of the decade. All of these metropolitan areas—with the exception of Beaumont (TX), Shreveport (LA), and New Orleans—are located in the Northeast and Midwest and, furthermore, are geographically concentrated in the states of New York, Pennsylvania, and Ohio.

Most relevant is the number of metropolitan areas that have shed residents over multiple and even consecutive decades. A one-decade population decline might be simply an anomaly—or a harbinger—but a string of losses is a clear sign of chronic and debilitating conditions and bodes ill for the central city and its older suburbs. Scranton and Wilkes-Barre lost residents in the 1940s and 1950s. Then, combined into a single metropolitan area by the Census Bureau, they did not lose population again until the 1980s. Growth was only temporary, however. Detroit and Cleveland both declined in the 1970s and 1980s and again in the 2000s. Buffalo's metropolitan area has been losing population continuously since 1980 and Pittsburgh's since 1970.

Almost all this metropolitan decline (with the exception of Duluth, Johnstown, and Wheeling in the 1940s) has been accompanied—even driven—by central city population loss. The city of Trenton (NJ) was one-third smaller in 2000 than it had been in 1950, while one of its bedroom communities—Ewing Township—had doubled. Yet, in many of these metropolises, the municipalities in the suburban periphery lost residents, as well. Buffalo, Cleveland, and Detroit, for example, experienced suburban shrinkage in the 2000s; Pittsburgh and Scranton/Wilkes-Barre in the 1990s; Gary (IN), Erie (PA), and Pittsburgh and Scranton/Wilkes-Barre again in the 1980s; and Pittsburgh, Newark (NJ), and Boston in the 1970s. For the most part, though, suburban losses in the aggregate have not exceeded central city losses. In the 1970s, Boston's suburbs decreased by nearly sixty thousand residents while the city itself lost nearly eighty thousand residents. Syracuse (NY) in the 1990s, Louisville (KY) in the 1980s, and Jersey City (NJ) in the 1960s had similar imbalances.

Only in rare instances did suburban losses overshadow central city losses. Rochester (NY) shed nearly five times as many residents from its suburbs than from its central city in the 2000s, in part because the city had been hemorrhaging population for decades. In the 1980s, Pittsburgh's suburban shrinkage was twice the central city's shrinkage—102,000 versus 54,000 residents. With both the central cities and the suburbs of these metropolitan areas losing residents, we have, as in Rochester, a situation in which shrinking cities are located in shrinking regions. There, attempts by city officials to resist decline or engender growth are more difficult than if the metropolitan region were expanding.

Shrinking Cities

The phenomenon of shrinkage, though, is popularly, politically, and primarily associated with central cities. This is due in part to the general sense that suburbs and metropolitan areas are immune from decline. The assumption, as we have just seen, is wrong for metropolitan areas and, as I will show below, for suburbs, as well. But first, we will consider the cities.

Since the late nineteenth century, central city decline has been a topic of public discussion in the United States.[7] One hundred years ago, the issue was not the disappearance of households and businesses. Rather, it was the consequences of rapid growth: overcrowded housing, precarious public health, and shortfalls in such public services as education, waste removal, and parks. After World War II, however, growth was no longer the culprit. Cities were shrinking. Racial tensions; the loss of residents, economic activity, and tax revenues; and the spread of slums and blight took center stage.

Figure 4: *Large City Population Loss, 1840-2010*

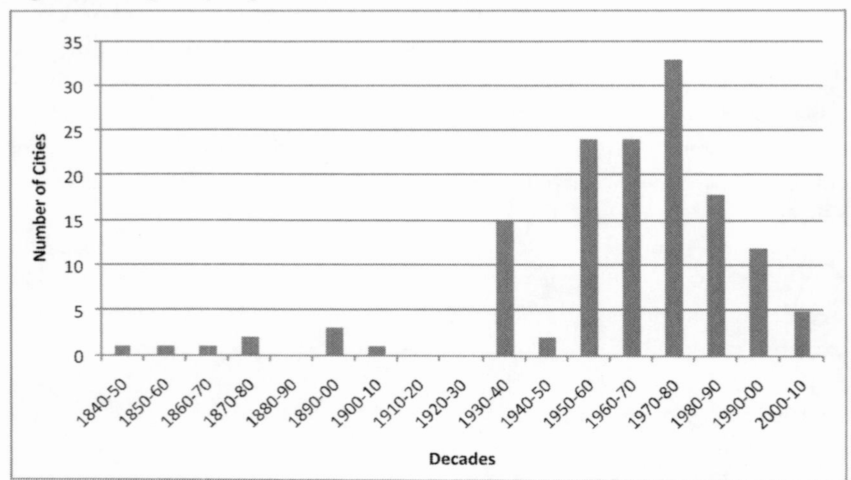

Prior to the postwar period, only infrequently did central cities lose population (*See Figure 4*). Between 1790 and 1930, very few large cities lost population in any decade, and only one city experienced multiple decades of loss—Charleston (SC) in the 1830s and 1850s.[8] In fact, only the 1830s had a significant number of depopulating cities, when five of the large cities (10 percent) struggled unsuccessfully to retain residents. Many decades witnessed no such occurrences, and most of the cities that lost population did so in a single decade and grew thereafter.Urban shrinkage prior to 1930 was an aberration, with some of the losses so small—seventeen fewer people for Trenton in the 1820s—as to be statistically suspect, given the crudeness of census surveys at the time. These shrinking cities were not just located, like Albany (NY), in the Northeast but were spread throughout the Midwest (for example, Omaha), as well as in the South (for example, Augusta [GA] and Mobile [AL]).

During the 1930s, though, fifteen of the fifty largest cities (30 percent of the total) lost residents.[9] The Depression had stifled migration to the cities and discouraged people from having babies. The result was depopulation in Grand Rapids (MI), Syracuse (NY), Toledo (OH), and Philadelphia, among other central cities. With war mobilization and the expansion of the national economy, people were attracted back to the cities. The Depression-era shrinking cities, with the exception of Jersey City, subsequently experienced population growth. In the 1940s, only Jersey City and Providence, of the large cities, failed to hold on to their residents.

Not until just after World War II did large numbers of large cities begin to shed residents and do so continuously.[10] The peak came in the 1970s, when thirty-three of the fifty largest cities shrank. Since then, the numbers have declined,

Table 1: *Population Change in Selected Cities by Size in 1950*

	Population in Peak Year	*Population in 2009*	*Absolute Change*	*Percent Change*
Large Cites (>500,000 residents):				
St. Louis, MO	856,796 (1950)	356,587	-500,209	-58.4
Buffalo, NY	580,132 (1950)	270,240	-309,892	-53.4
Cleveland, OH	914,808 (1950)	431,369	-483,439	-52.8
Detroit, MI	1,849,568 (1950)	910,921	-938,647	-50.7
Baltimore, MD	949,708 (1950)	637,418	-312,290	-32.9
Medium-Size Cities (250,000–499,999 residents):				
Rochester, NY	332,488 (1950)	207,294	-125,194	-37.7
Newark, NJ	442,337 (1930)	278,154	-164,183	-37.1
Louisville, KY	390,639 (1960)	256,231	-134,408	-34.4
Cincinnati, OH	503,998 (1950)	333,012	-170,986	-33.9
Toledo, OH	383,062 (1970)	316,179	-66,883	-17.5
Small Cities (100,000–249,999 residents):				
Syracuse, NY	220,583 (1950)	138,560	-82,023	-37.2
Camden, NJ	124,555 (1950)	78,788	-45,767	-36.7
Duluth, MN	107,312 (1960)	84,419	-22,893	-21.3
Bridgeport, CT	158,709 (1950)	137,298	-21,411	-13.5
Worcester, MA	203,486 (1950)	182,882	-20,604	-10.1

Source: U. S. Census Bureau's population reports for selected years.

Note: Population data for the 2010 census year were not available for all cities at the time this table was created.

in part because certain of these cities ceased to be large cities and dropped out of this size category. Only five large cities lost population between 2000 and 2009. Throughout this period, population loss has been devastating for the large manufacturing-based cities. Between 1950 and 2009, Detroit lost nearly 900,000 residents, approximately one-half its population; Philadelphia lost a half million people; Chicago, 700,000; and Pittsburgh, over 300,000. Left behind were empty factories and stores, swaths of uninhabited housing—much of it later abandoned—near-empty neighborhoods, a shrunken tax base, and fiscally stressed local governments. Moreover, these losses were not confined to large cities. In the 1970s, three out of every four cities with a population between 50,000 and 500,000 people cast off residents, and even though that ratio has decreased considerably, an alarming number of these cities continue to shrink (*see Table 1 for examples*).

Unlike the late nineteenth century and first half of the twentieth century, after World War II many of these cities shrank multiple times and even in consecutive decades. Of the large cities, Baltimore, Cleveland, Detroit, Pittsburgh, and St. Louis, among others, have been contracting continually since 1950. Persistent population loss has made it more and more difficult for city leaders to counter an image of decay. These cities are basically unable to attract and retain households and investors. Despite these traumas, many shrinking cities have prosperous neighborhoods with thriving retail districts, places like Rittenhouse Square in Philadelphia and the Central West End in St. Louis, as well as areas with substantial concentrations of jobs, such as the Oakland neighborhood in Pittsburgh where the University of Pittsburgh, Carnegie Mellon University, and a major hospital complex are located. Nevertheless, the overall reputation of these cities is one of decline, a characterization vividly supported by images of dilapidated waterfronts, derelict industrial areas, half-empty neighborhoods, and central business districts pockmarked with boarded-up storefronts. Seattle lost population in two postwar decades and then rebounded; Buffalo, with a persistent population loss over many more decades has had a much different, and less enviable, experience, and it has fewer prospects as a result.

Shrinking Suburbs

Suburban communities have not been immune from depopulation. Depopulation in the suburbs, though, seems to be confined to industrial communities, such as Lynn, outside of Boston, and Chester, south of Philadelphia and the first-tier or inner-ring suburbs of the early postwar period, such as Levittown (NY), whose population dropped nearly 20 percent between 1960 and 2000.[12] The industrial suburbs have suffered from the decline of manufacturing, while their inner-ring counterparts are constrained by a housing stock comprised of small homes with little aesthetic appeal, disadvantaged by the allure of newer and bigger homes on the suburban periphery, and unable to leverage the assets (for example, universities and hospitals) that many central cities still possess.

Much of the literature on suburban shrinkage focuses on decline as measured by a combined fall in household incomes, rising poverty, and population loss.[13] Typically, such research uses multiple variables to identify different types of suburbs. In one study[14], the number of suburbs experiencing extreme distress was arrayed by census region. The Washington, D.C.–Baltimore metropolitan area led the way in the South with 20 percent of its suburbs distressed. St. Louis and Chicago topped the list in the Midwest at 22 percent apiece, New York at 40 percent was first in the Northeast; and Los Angeles was on top in the West at 29 percent.

In places like Milwaukee and Providence, staunch manufacturing cities throughout the early twentieth century, relatively small percentages of their suburbs—3 and 2 percent, respectively—qualified for this dubious distinction.

The discussion of shrinkage here, though, focuses on depopulation and not "distress" as measured by income. In this regard, consider two shrinking cities: Buffalo and Pittsburgh. In 1950, the Buffalo urban area had approximately 800,000 people spread across eleven municipalities, ten of which can be considered suburban. Of those suburbs, only one—Lackawanna—had a net loss of population over the next fifty years. An industrial suburb of 28,000 people just after World War II, it was one-third smaller by 2000, having lost most of the steel industry, which in 1965 had employed nearly twenty thousand workers. The bulk of the metropolitan shrinkage, though, still came from Buffalo; it lost one-half of its 1950 population of 600,000 people. Compare this concentrated suburban decline with that occurring in Pittsburgh. Twice as big in population as Buffalo, it had fourteen times the number of suburban municipalities. Of these, close to six out of every ten of these communities shed residents between 1950 and 2000. Most of the losses were small compared to that from the central city, but McKeesport lost over one-half its 52,000 residents, while Aliquippa and Wilkinsburg experienced significant population declines. All of these losses were small relative to Pittsburgh's drop of over 300,000 people. Clearly, this is a much different picture than that for Buffalo. In Pittsburgh, suburban shrinkage has been prevalent and has spread across multiple municipalities, including industrial satellites as well as their bedroom communities. Nonetheless, metropolitan depopulation in both areas was dominated by the central city, not the suburbs.

By contrast, consider Boston, a metropolitan area that has never lost population and with a central city that shrank in the three decades between 1950 and 1980 but has grown ever since. Falling numerically between Buffalo and Pittsburgh, 30 percent of Boston's suburbs became smaller between 1950 and 2000. Many of these, like Lynn and Watertown, had been major manufacturing centers. None of them experienced the scale of depletion recorded in the Pittsburgh metropolitan area. The largest absolute suburban decline was Somerville, with 25,000 fewer residents, but as with Buffalo and Pittsburgh, once again, the central city accounted for the largest losses. Since other suburbs were attracting residents, the Boston metropolitan area grew.

Shrinking Neighborhoods

The public discussion of shrinking cities primarily addresses depopulating and distressed neighborhoods in shrinking cities. Neighborhoods in decline are often called "slums" and slums have existed in the United States since the nineteenth century, becoming the target of public health and other Progressive reformers in the early twentieth century.[16] After World War II, as the central cities began to falter, more generally, slums were addressed with redevelopment projects that relied on demolition to clear large sites for new construction. Often, public housing complexes were built to replace the housing that had been destroyed. As the central city became less attractive, though, slum-like conditions—overcrowding, unsanitary and unsafe buildings, and abandonment—spread. In the 1980s, a few of these run-down neighborhoods in a few of these cities began to experience an influx of middle-income residents. Places like Adams Morgan in Washington, D.C., the Lower East Side in New York City, and Northern Liberties in Philadelphia gentrified.[17] Nevertheless, in many gentrifying neighborhoods, the number of residents continued to fall as a result of the displacement of existing residents and the loss of housing units as developers and gentrifiers combined apartments to create larger living spaces. A declining population, however, did not always mean fewer households. Hoboken (NJ) is a prime example. Despite significant gentrification and real estate speculation in the late 1970s and 1980s that attracted new residents, the overall population declined through to 2000. At the same time, household size was shrinking and Hoboken actually had an increase in the number of households. Gentrification thus reminds us that population loss from neighborhoods is not always an indicator of a social problem, though it most often is.

Various studies have documented neighborhood decline in shrinking cities.[18] Their focus has been mainly on the economics and politics of this transition and the racial and class consequences that ensued. Moreover, they tend to investigate only specific neighborhoods. Our concern, though, is with all of the neighborhoods within a city and, specifically, with their depopulation. Enabling us to do this for two shrinking cities—Cleveland and Pittsburgh—are data sets created by the respective city planning departments. They display the population for each neighborhood in the city for the census years from 1940 to 2000.

In Cleveland, the planners have divided the city into thirty-six Statistical Planning Areas, each of which they consider "equivalent to a traditional neighborhood." Of the total, thirty-one neighborhoods were smaller in 2000 than in 1940, and even the five neighborhoods that grew experienced population losses in at least two decades. The neighborhoods with the biggest declines were places like Hough, which fell from 65,000 residents to 16,000, and Ohio City, which went from 28,000 to 9,000 residents. Moreover, whereas nineteen neighborhoods (over one-half the total) had lost population in the 1940s, thirty-five did so in the 1980s—only one neighborhood actually grew in those ten years. The 1990s offered a respite; six neighborhoods added population, up from that one neighborhood (Euclid-Green) in the 1980s. Neighborhood shrinkage was geographically pervasive and unrelenting, even though the rate of depopulation varied.

The story in Pittsburgh is similar. In the 1940s, over one-half of its ninety neighborhoods lost residents, and by the 1980s, that ratio exceeded 90 percent. The 1990s were an improvement; ten neighborhoods grew in population, compared to seven in the previous decade. Still, thirty-four neighborhoods lost population in all six decades and only eleven grew in size over the sixty years. Decade increases, though, were small and short-lived. Neighborhoods like Crawford and the South Side Flats had major losses; the former from 17,000 to less than 3,000 and the latter from 22,000 to less than 6,000. Crawford actually grew in the 1940s, before starting its decline. By contrast, the South Side Flats, Polish Hill, and Lawrenceville went steadily downward.

In sum, population change in the United States has been dominated by aggregate growth, but with numerous instances of shrinkage at finer geographical scales. Population growth and depopulation have coexisted, with growth, for most of the country's history, dominant. After World War II, though, the balance shifted, specifically in the metropolitan areas and central cities of the Northeast and Midwest. There, growth has become abnormal and depopulation the default condition.

City Comparisons

In the discussion of shrinking cities, one is likely to encounter the claim that losing residents could be desirable. In cities where serious overcrowding exists in the housing market, the flight of households might relieve this pressure and thereby dampen the high housing costs with which it is associated. Then there is an argument, implicit in the literature on shrinking suburbs, that population loss does not capture the change in the quality of life of a place. A suburb might experience a net loss of population, but this could involve low-income households leaving and being partly replaced in number by higher-income households, thus resulting in the suburb—Hoboken is an example—being better off.[20] Or depopulation might be an opportunity for the city government to make the city more environmentally sustainable.[21] While these are all theoretical possibilities, cities that experience large and often sustained population loss are more likely to have a lower quality of life for most residents, fewer opportunities to counter the loss, and a municipal government unable to provide high-quality services. Depopulation almost always leaves the city less desirable as a place to live and invest.[22]

In order to illustrate the hardships associated with shrinkage, I compare three shrinking cities to three growing cities. The three shrinking cities are Detroit, Pittsburgh, and Flint and their counterparts are San Diego, Arlington (TX), and Alexandria (VA). Each group has a large, medium-sized, and small central city. All of the shrinking cities are in the former manufacturing belt of the country and none of the growing cities is. For each of these cities, I have collected data on the indicators typically used to assess the multiple dimensions of urban growth and decline.

Table 2: *Demographic Change in Shrinking and Growing Cities*

	Shrinking Cities:			*Growing Cities:*		
	Detroit	*Pittsburgh*	*Flint*	*San Diego*	*Arlington*	*Alex-andria*
Population, 1950	1,849,568	676,806	163,143	334,387	7,692	61,787
Population, 2010	713,777	305,704	102,434	1,301,617	365,438	139,966
Absolute Population Change, 1950–2010	-1,135,791	-371,102	-60,709	967,230	357,746	78,179
Percent Population Change, 1950-2010	-61.4	-54.8	-37.2	289.3	4 ,650.9	126.5
Percent Foreign-Born, 2000	4.8	5.6	1.5	25.7	15.3	25.4
Percent African-American, 2005	82.1	28.8	55.8	6.8	16.9	20.1
Percent Hispanic or Latino Origin, 2005	5.6	1.8	2.3	25.9	23.8	13.8
Percent Asian, 2005	1.1	3.8	0.2	15.8	5.4	5.7

Sources: U.S. Census Bureau's population reports and County and City Data Book 2007 for data on race and ethnicity.

Clearly, the three shrinking cities and the three growing cities are on radically different developmental trajectories (*See Table 2*).

Between 1950 and 2000, the former lost between one-fifth and one-half of their residents, while the latter doubled, tripled, and, in the case of Arlington, expanded by over forty times in population. The differences seem to lie in the movement of people in and out of these places rather than with any natural increase (that is, excess of births over deaths).

Take immigration. Shrinking cities are much less likely to attract immigrants than growing cities, as measured by the percentage of residents born outside the United States. In the shrinking cities, these percentages are much smaller than they are in the growing cities. The sense that these cities are unable to attract immigrants is supported by metropolitan-level data. The metropolitan areas of all three growing cities attracted more immigrants than their shrinking counterparts. In the Arlington and Alexandria metropolitan areas—Dallas–Fort Worth and Washington, D.C., respectively—there was an increase of more than 250,000 immigrants between 2000 and 2008, whereas Flint's metropolitan area showed an increase of just over 1,000 immigrants and Detroit's immigrant population increased by fewer than 95,000.

Over the same time period, the three shrinking cities also had a net loss of domestic migrants from their metropolitan areas—that is, people moving to other places within the country. Detroit alone had 330,000 more people leave the metropolitan area than enter it. And while the San Diego and Alexandria metropolitan areas, too, had a deficit of domestic migrants, they more than compensated for this with immigration and natural increase. Only Arlington had a surplus of domestic migrants.

What is interesting about these population fluctuations is how it has sharpened racial differences between the two types of cities (see Chapter 8). These shrinking cities have much higher proportions of African-Americans and much lower proportions of Hispanics and Asians. African-Americans are, on the whole, poorer than non-African-Americans—their median household income in 2009 was $34,000 compared to $68,500 for Asians and $54,500 for Caucasians—and this suggests a lessened ability to invest in housing or pay higher rents, and an increased need for social and other public services. Their presence also conveys a racially charged image that has, throughout the history of the United States, contributed to residential segregation by race and class and the flight of white residents to the suburbs.[23] Second, the relative lack of Hispanics and Asians also raises concerns. These groups are likely to be immigrants and are associated (possibly stereotypically) with hard work, if not entrepreneurship, and these qualities often add economic activity to the city, thereby counteracting decline.

Table 3: *Economic Characteristics of Shrinking and Growing Cities*

	Shrinking Cities:			*Growing Cities:*		
	Detroit	*Pittsburgh*	*Flint*	*San Diego*	*Arlington*	*Alexandria*
Metropolitan GDP/ capita, 2008 ($)	45,404	48,700	26,898	56,081	60,285	73,587
Percent Metropolitan Job Growth, 2000-2008	-14.5	-2.6	-19.6	12.9	42.6	10.9
Percent Residents in Labor Force, 2000	56.3	58.5	58.5	65.7	74.0	74.4
Percent Residents With Graduate and Professional Degrees	4.7	15.1	4.3	16.1	8.1	28.2
Median Household Income, 2005 ($)	28,069	30,278	25,972	55,637	48,992	66,116

Sources: GDP data are from State and Local Government Finance Reports, U.S. Census Bureau; the job data are from *County Business Patterns* for selected years; the labor force data from the 2000 decennial census; and the educational and income indicators from the *County and City Data Book*.

In addition, shrinking cities are further challenged by being in poorly performing metropolitan economies (*See Table 3*).[24] For 2008, the gross domestic product (GDP) per capita for the metropolitan areas of shrinking cities was well below that for growing cities. Detroit, at $45,000 came close to San Diego, at $56,100, but Alexandria, at $73,590, dwarfed Flint, at $26,900. Moreover, the metropolitan economies in which shrinking cities exist are all growing much slower in GDP terms, or even declining, relative to the metropolitan economies of growing cities. Employment data reinforce these differences. The number of paid employees in the shrinking cities metropolitan areas declined between 2000 and 2008. In the growing cities, paid employment grew between 10 and 40 percent. Data on the number of business establishments show a similar pattern. Shrinking cities tend to be located in shrinking metropolitan economies.

One result of this is that fewer residents of shrinking cities have jobs. Just over one-half of all adults work in these shrinking cities, whereas two-thirds to three-quarters do so in the growing cities. In the former, more of the population is dependent on fewer workers. Their residents, with the exception of those in Pittsburgh, are also less likely to have graduate or professional degrees, thus disadvantaging them in the country's service and knowledge-based economy. The result—lower household incomes—is predictable. Median household incomes in the growing cities are twice and three times those in the shrinking cities. And although the cost of living is usually higher when growth and not decline is the backdrop, the lower values for the residents of shrinking cities provide few resources to migrate to better-performing economies where they might prosper.

Table 4: *Housing Characteristics of Shrinking and Growing Cities*

	Shrinking Cities:			*Growing Cities:*		
	Detroit	*Pittsburgh*	*Flint*	*San Diego*	*Arlington*	*Alexandria*
Housing Built Pre-1939 2000 (%)	29.9	50.7	23.0	7.7	0.7	10.4
Housing Vacancy Rate, 2005-2009 (%)	21.4	16.1	20.9	7.3	9.7	10.2
Median Value of Owner-Occupied Housing, 2005 ($)	88,300	74,000	64,600	566,700	121,700	490,700

Sources: U.S. Census Bureau reports plus *County and City Data Book* for 2005 median housing value data and the American Community Survey for the five-year estimates of housing vacancy rates.

All of these "negatives" associated with shrinking cities have implications for their housing markets.[25] For most cities, housing occupies the largest amount of land, its quality can influence people to migrate or stay, its value can stabilize neighborhoods or not, its maintenance can project a positive image of the city, and it can provide people with secure homes and even augment their financial assets. The housing markets of shrinking cities have none of these "positives" (*See Table 4*). First of all, much of the housing stock in shrinking cities was built prior to 1939, whereas that in growing cities is much newer. Older housing is usually smaller, lacks contemporary amenities, and is thus less desirable. Second, a significant proportion of units are vacant, with the percentages well above the two to four needed for a housing market to work smoothly. This suggests chronically vacant and possibly abandoned housing. Abandoned housing, in fact, is a key element in the discussion of shrinking cities.[26]

Lastly, stemming from the age and a likely lack of maintenance and upgrading, the median housing values in shrinking cities are well below those of the growing cities. In Detroit, the median owner-occupied house was estimated to be worth $88,300 in 2005; in San Diego, it was $566,700. The value for Detroit, moreover, is deceptive. It represents what homeowners declare their home to be worth and excludes renter-occupied housing. The number needs to be seen in relation to sale prices. In 2010, one local real estate reporting service (AOL Real Estate) estimated the average sale price at $41,000. Even more telling of the state of housing markets in shrinking cities is this statistic: of the 24,500 homes for sale in Detroit in 2010, 70 percent of them were vacant and only one was a new construction; the rest were existing homes. With so many homes vacant, it is not only difficult to sell in Detroit but, even if one could sell, what little one could earn from doing so would make it difficult to relocate to someplace with a stronger housing market.

Low and declining house values harm municipal governments. Highly dependent on their property tax base for revenues, governments in shrinking cities have to cut services, obtain more intergovernmental aid, or raise taxes, with the last being a desperate move and likely to make matters worse, given the low incomes of residents and the lack of highly profitable and growing businesses. Additionally, it is commonly accepted that local governments in shrinking cities suffer from revenue shortfalls, a lowered capacity to find new revenue sources, and an inability to pay good wages to city workers. The results are cuts in services and a diminishing capacity to plan and thereby address the city's problems.[27]

Using the Comprehensive Annual Financial Reports for each of the cities, one can calculate the "ending balances as a percentage of expenditures." This is the year's revenues plus the previous year's savings (or deficit) divided by the year's expenditures. The calculations indicate that the shrinking cities are financially weaker than the growing cities. When the ratio drops below 1.0, a shortfall is indicated. Both Detroit and Flint are well below that cutoff (0.78 and 0.81, respectively), and Arlington (1.06) and Alexandria (1.01) above it. Pittsburgh and San Diego are the exceptions, with the former above 1.0 and the latter slightly below it.

In short, the argument that depopulation might be good for cities does not apply to shrinking cities. Population loss is associated with, and partly a function of, lower home values, housing vacancy and abandonment, poorer residents, racial segregation, and a paucity of employment opportunities. On the whole, living in Flint confers few advantages. One would be better off in Arlington.

Conclusion

The shrinkage of cities in the United States is not a new phenomenon. Its prevalence and intensity increased after World War II, but it was hardly absent in the early twentieth century or in the nineteenth century. Its postwar manifestation, however, was not ubiquitous across the country. In fact, whether one talks of metropolitan, central city, or suburban shrinkage, each has been geographically concentrated in the famed "manufacturing belt" that spawned the country's industrial cities. There, the big industrial states—New York, Pennsylvania, Ohio, and Michigan—have a disproportionate share of shrinking cities.

Shrinkage, moreover, is not confined to cities; depopulation has occurred at other spatial scales. Certain types of suburbs have also become smaller, with shrinking cities having a higher proportion of them than growing cities. These cities and suburbs are also likely, though not necessarily, to be in metropolitan areas that are faltering, as well. The decline of nearby industrial suburbs with which the central cities were once economically connected casts an additional pall over their fortunes. And even though the regions in which shrinking cities are located are not suffering absolute losses of residents, these regions are falling behind the South and West as regards overall population growth.

Nevertheless, shrinkage has always unfolded against a background of growth. The United States has never declined in population and continues to add residents at a healthy pace. All of its major regions are growing, some admittedly more slowly than others, and not one of them is in such dire straits as to be labeled as "depressed." In the weaker regions, a good deal of prosperity remains. Boston, New York, and Chicago are vibrant cities, and many suburban communities—places like Stamford (CT) and Catonsville (MD), outside Baltimore—are faring well economically and demographically. This is particularly the case when the suburbs have developed significant office parks and regional shopping centers. Additionally, in many shrinking cities, certain neighborhoods—Squirrel Hill in Pittsburgh, the Central West End in St. Louis, and the Ironbound in Newark—remain attractive as places to live and shop.

Not all shrinking cities remain on a downward trajectory. Boston lost population in two consecutive decades and then rebounded. Oakland, Miami, Denver, and Atlanta have had periods of depopulation followed by growth. These cities have been resilient in the face of adversity; they have managed to weather shrinkage. Still, they are anomalies.

Many shrinking cities seem unable to overcome the forces causing depopulation. Nor are they able to deflect the burdens faced by their governments, households, and businesses. Opportunities are scarcer than in growing cities; metropolitan economies are not as robust, job growth is relatively anemic and fewer jobs are available, and less wealth is being generated. Immigrants who might occupy homes and open businesses are less likely to locate in shrinking cities, while these cities are more likely to have higher percentages of African-Americans. As a result, fewer people work in shrinking cities and household incomes are lower. These factors burden the local housing market, as well. Home values barely appreciate, chronic vacancy is prevalent, and an older housing stock is neither upgraded nor replaced. Here, housing is not a source of wealth. Moreover, the local governments can hardly be of much assistance, constrained as they are by diminishing tax bases and expanding demands to demolish abandoned housing, replace aged infrastructure, and offer services for an increasingly dependent population.

In sum, the depopulation of metropolitan areas, cities, suburbs, and neighborhoods poses significant challenges for policy makers at the local, state, and federal levels. For local government officials in these cities, shrinkage and its consequences are unavoidable and civic leaders struggle with how to respond. The pursuit of growth and past glory seems ill-advised. "Rightsizing" makes sense, but how to do it is neither obvious nor politically palatable. Therein lies the challenge.

Research Note

The population data used in this chapter came from the U.S. Census Bureau decennial censuses for various years. The data were accessed using both the paper census reports available in university libraries and the Census Bureau's web site (www.census.gov). The web site enables access to the population reports for each decade by state. In addition, it provides access to various compilations: *Statistical Abstract of the United States, County and City Data Book*, and *State and Metropolitan Area Data Book*. The data on immigration and domestic migration for the shrinking and growing cities are from the State and Metropolitan Area Data Book, accessed on the Census Bureau's web site.

Notes

1. Beauregard (2006), pp. 19–39.
2. Berkooz (2010), pp. 26-31.
3. Beauregard (2006), pp. 19-39.
4. Baxandall and Ewen (2000).
5. Frey (1988), p. 745, Table 1.
6. Frey (1988), p. 747, Table 2.
7. Beauregard (2003a).
8. Beauregard (2003b), pp. 672-690.
9. Beauregard (2006), Appendix A.
10. Beauregard (2009), pp. 514-528.
11. Ebner (1985), pp. 368-381.
12. Lucy and Phillips (2000), pp. 55-62, and Short, Hanlon, and Vicino (2007), pp. 641-656.
13. Hanlon (2008), pp. 423-456, and Short, Hanlon and Vicino, (2007), pp. 641-656.
14. Hanlon (2008), pp. 423-456.
15. Billiteri (2010), pp. 941-964.
16. Spain (2001), pp. 30–60.
17. Lees, Slater, and Wyly (2008).
18. for example, Gordon (2002)
19. Bradbury, Downs, and Small (1982), pp. 4–5, 18.
20. Hanlon (2008), pp. 432–433.
21. Schilling and Logan (2008).
22. Vey (2007), pp. 10–33.
23. Sugrue (1996).
24. Vey (2007), pp. 10–33.
25. McGovern (2006), pp. 529-570.
26. Gurwitt (2002), pp28-34.
27. Davey (2010), Judd and Swanstrom (1994), pp. 307–334, and Hoene and Pagano (2010).

Bibliography

Baxandall, R., and E. Ewen. 2000. *Picture Windows: How the Suburbs Happened.* New York: Basic Books.

Beauregard, R. A. 2003a. *Voices of Decline: The Postwar Fate of U.S. Cities.* New York: Routledge.

__________. 2003b. "Aberrant Cities: Urban Population Loss in the United States, 1820–1930." *Urban Geography* 24: 672–690.

__________. 2006. *When America Became Suburban.* Minneapolis: University of Minnesota Press.

__________. 2009. "Urban Population Loss in Historical Perspective: United States, 1820–2000." *Environment and Planning A* 41: 514–528.

Berkooz, C. B. 2010. "Repurposing Detroit." *Planning* 76: 26–31.

Billiteri, T. J. 2010. "Blighted Cities." *CQ Researcher* 20:941–964.

Bradbury, K. L., A. Downs, and K. A. Small. 1982. *Urban Decline and the Future of American Cities.* Washington, D.C.: Brookings Institution.

Davey, M. 2010. "Michigan Town Is Left Pleading for Bankruptcy." *The New York Times,* December 28.

Ebner, M. 1985. "Re-Reading Suburban America: Urban Population Deconcentration, 1810–1980." *American Quarterly* 37:368–381.

Frey, W. H., and A. Speare, Jr. 1988. *Regional and Metropolitan Growth and Decline in the United States.* New York: Russell Sage Foundation.

Gordon, C. 2008. *Mapping Decline: St. Louis and the Fate of the American City.* Philadelphia: University of Pennsylvania Press.

Gotham, K. F. 2002. *Race, Real Estate, and Uneven Development: The Kansas City Experience.* 1900–2000. Albany, NY: SUNY Press.

Gurwitt, R. 2002. "Betting on the Bulldozer." *Governing* 15:28–34.

Hanlon, B. 2008. "The Decline of Older, Inner Suburbs in Metropolitan America." *Housing Policy Debate* 19: 423–456.

Hoene, C. W., and M. A. Pagano. 2010. "City Fiscal Conditions in 2010." Washington, D.C.: National League of Cities, Research Brief on America's Cities.

Jackson, K. T. 1985. *Crabgrass Frontier: The Suburbanization of America.* New York: Oxford University Press.

Judd, D., and T. Swanstrom. 1994. *City Politics: Private Power and Public Policy.* New York: HarperCollins.

Kenyon, A. M. 2004. *Dreaming Suburbia: Detroit and the Production of Postwar Space and Culture.* Detroit: Wayne State University Press.

Lees, L., T. Slater, and E. Wyly. 2008. *Gentrification* New York: Routledge.

Lucy, W. H., and D. L. Phillips. 2000. "Suburban Decline: The Next Urban Crisis." *Issues in Science and Technology,* Fall: 55–62.

McGovern, S. J. 2006. "Philadelphia's Neighborhood Transformation Initiative," *Housing Policy Debate* 17:529–570.

Okrent, D., and S. Gray. 2010. "The Future of Detroit: How to Shrink a City." *Time* November 11.

Schilling, J., and J. Logan. 2008. "Greening the Rust Belt: A Green Infrastructure Model for Right Sizing America's Shrinking Cities." *Journal of the American Planning Association* 74:451–466.

Short, J. R., B. Hanlon, and T. J. Vicino. 2007. "The Decline of Inner Suburbs: The New Suburban Gothic in the United States." *Geography Compass* 1: 641–656.

Spain, D. 2001. *How Women Saved the City*. Minneapolis: University of Minnesota Press.

Sugrue, T. J. 1996. *The Origins of the Urban Crisis*. Princeton, NJ: Princeton University Press.

Vey, J. 2007. *Restoring Prosperity: The State Role in Revitalizing America's Older Industrial Cities*. Washington, D.C.: Brookings Institution.

Case Study: Fiscal Shrinkage In Saginaw, Michigan

Eric Scorsone, Michigan State University

The city of Saginaw and its surrounding areas have been one of the United States' most important regional trading and manufacturing centers over the past 150 years. For almost thirty years in the period following the Civil War, Saginaw was the leading lumber center for the growing country. This wealth became the basis for Saginaw's emergence as a regional trading center in the Midwest. By the turn of the century, local business and government leaders realized that Saginaw's lumber industry was dying and it was time to diversify. Saginaw became a hub of manufacturing plants for what ultimately became General Motors. In 1947, following the war, Saginaw built a sixty-five mile water pipeline that drew water from Lake Huron, in anticipation of huge growth. During its height in the 1950s, the city's population peaked at over one hundred thousand persons.

Beginning in the 1970s, Saginaw's auto industry began to falter. Over the next few decades, plant closings and layoffs decimated the local industry. In 1970, the city of Saginaw had over fifteen thousand auto-related jobs; by 2010, this had fallen to fewer than two thousand jobs. The city began to shrink dramatically. As of 2009, the city's population was estimated at 56,321 persons. Only 10 percent of those people had a college degree or greater, and this is less than half of the national average. Educational-attainment problems mirrored disparities in poverty and income. The city of Saginaw has nearly one in three residents living below the poverty level and the per capita income is below half the national average.

Along with a falling population have come vacant and abandoned buildings and homes. Out of a total of 26,000 housing units in the city, nearly 20 percent were vacant in 2009. These vacancies were particularly concentrated in the east side of the city. These vacant homes have become major problems not only for neighborhoods but for city services. Over half of the city's fire runs were to vacant buildings in 2009. Almost no new housing has been built since 1960. Thus, vacant buildings and a falling population continue to cause stress for both the city economy and city services.

The city of Saginaw is a home-rule city and has a city-manager form of government. Its most recent charter was approved in 1935. The city provides traditional municipal services, such as police, fire, code compliance, and neighborhood services, water and sewer services, and internal functions, including accounting, treasury, general management, and human resources. In 1978, a total of $23.8 million ($63.1 million in 2011 dollars) from the city's general fund was spent to provide core services. Of that amount, nearly $7 million went to police and fire protection. The total included $1 million for maintaining a civic center and $500,000 for park and recreation services, among other items.

There are two perspectives that can be taken with regard to the city of Saginaw's budget over the last three decades. By 2008, the city's general fund had a total budget of over $33 million. On the face of it, this represents a nearly 44 percent increase in total spending. In that same time frame, the state and local government inflation factor grew by 265 percent. Thus, accounting for inflation, real city spending was actually cut by more than half. At the same time, however, police and fire spending grew by over 85 percent (see *Table 1*), to become nearly 64 percent of the general fund (see *Table 2*). All other city services were squeezed by these two major categories. In fact, police and fire spending squeezed out nearly every other municipal service without a dedicated revenue stream.

Table 1: *City of Saginaw General Fund Spending (% change and inflation-adjusted budget)*

	1978 Actual Spending	*2008 Actual Spending*	*% Change (1978-2008)*	*Inflation–adjusted budget (2008 Dollars)*
General Govt.	$1,558,063	$1,946,613	25%	$4,128,866.95
Fiscal Services	$1,108,169	$ 2,570,150	132%	$ 2,936,647.85
Public Safety	$ 11,432,906	$ 21,165,083	85%	$ 30,297,200.90
General Services	$ 5,624,303	$ 4,000,317	-29%	$ 14,904,402.95
Community Services	$ 2,398,889	$ 1,771,819	-26%	$ 6,357,055.85
Capital	$728,563	$ 0	-100%	$ 1,930,691.95
Other	$ 192,246	$ 1,807,841	840%	$ 509,451.90
Total Spending	$ 23,043,139	$ 33,261,822	44%	$ 61,064,318.35

Table 2: *City of Saginaw General Fund Spending (% Share of Total Budget by Category)*

	1978 Share of Budget	*2008 Share of Budget*
General Govt.	7%	6%
Fiscal Services	5%	8%
Public Safety	50%	64%
General Services	24%	12%
Community Services	10%	5%
Capital	3%	0%
Other	1%	5%

In *Table 2* above, public safety spending increased from a 50 percent budget share in 1978 to over 64 percent in 2008. Despite that increase, the number of police officers dropped from over 135 in 1980 to 95 in 2008. There was a major increase in the cost per officer even as the number of officers dropped. Throughout this period, crime in the city remained high. In 1980, the violent crime rate was over 2,000 incidents per 100,000 residents, and it was just over 2,500 incidents per 100,000 residents in 2008.

Many other core services were reduced as public safety spending increased. The civic center and parks and recreation spending were eliminated (see *Table 2*). Spending on community services, which included areas such as the Civic Center, inspections, zoning, and economic development have been cut by nearly 30 percent, from $2 million in 1978 to $1.3 million in 2008. General public works spending has also fallen over the last thirty years, despite cost increases and essentially the same number of streetlights, sidewalks, cemeteries, and other basic public facilities to maintain. The net result has been a major decline in the quality of such facilities and infrastructure. In some limited cases, such as the Saginaw Dow Event Center, Dow Chemical of nearby Midland, Michigan, did provide funding to maintain a privately run facility.

Another view of the city's challenges is from the revenue side. City revenues have also grown at a pace far slower than the level of inflation, explaining the significant inflation-adjusted drop in general government spending. In fact, with city revenues growing on a long-term basis at a slightly lower rate than spending (43 percent vs. 44 percent), this explains the city's persistently slim to negative general fund balance and its inability to build up adequate rainy-day reserves.

Looking beyond the current economic crisis, city income tax growth at 61 percent, state revenue-sharing growth of 143 percent and license revenue growth at 169 percent have been the key to maintaining any revenue stability over the past three decades (see *Tables 3* and *4*). Federal revenue sharing and property tax revenues have stagnated or been eliminated over the same period. The necessity of higher tax rates to maintain revenues has likely had a negative impact on economic development efforts within city limits. The recent decline in income tax due to the Great Recession only reveals the long-term inability of income taxes to fund city services adequately.

Table 3: *City of Saginaw General Fund Revenues (% change, 1978 to 2008)*

	1978 Actual Revenues	*2008 Actual Revenues*	*% Change*
Property Taxes	$ 4,256,188	$ 3,992,722	-6%
Special Assessments	$ 0	$ 83,752	
City Income Tax	$ 7,023,842	$ 11,282,887	61%
State Shared Revenue	$ 4,047,553	$ 9,837,511	143%
Federal Revenue Sharing	$ 2,054,940	$ 0	-100%
Licenses, Permits & Fees	$ 158,798	$ 1,260,985	694%
Fines, Penalties & Forfeitures	$ 253,326	$ 389,753	54%
Grants & Contributions	$ 1,865,746	$ 576,472	-69%
Indirect Costs Charged Internally	$ 157,500	$ 2,737,821	1638%
Interest	$ 1,006,331	$ 509,325	-49%
Rent	$ 500,859	$ 104,073	-79%
Sale of Materials and Services	$ 626,674	$ 808,001	29%
Miscellaneous/Fund Equity	$ 107,455	$ 34,726	-68%
Loan Repayments	$ 0	$ 0	
Total Revenue	$ 22,059,212	$ 31,618,027	43%

On the face of it, the city of Saginaw's general budget has increased greatly over the past few decades, going from $20 million in 1978 to over $36 million at its peak in 2002. This budget increase has occurred in the context of a steadily dropping population; thus more money for fewer people. However, once inflation is taken into account, the story changes dramatically. In fact, in order to keep up with the cost of goods and service increases, the city budget should be over $60 million today.

In order to maintain a semblance of fiscal stability, the city has undertaken significant cuts. For example, street maintenance is not being undertaken except on major roads. Out of the three hundred miles of city streets, only one hundred miles of major roads and highways are maintained on a regular basis. Many of the other roads are in serious disrepair—near the point of gravel in some cases. Cultural and community services have been significantly cut and not replaced by the private sector in some cases. Finally, the number of police and fire personnel has dropped even as demand arguably remains at a high level. All of this even as the city has been unable to build or maintain an adequate fund reserve for emergencies.

Table 4: *City of Saginaw Share of Total Revenues by Category*

	1978 Revenue Share	*2008 Revenue Share*
Property Taxes	19%	13%
Special Assessments	0%	0%
City Income Tax	32%	36%
State Shared Revenue	18%	31%
Federal Revenue Sharing	9%	0%
Licenses, Permits & Fees	1%	4%
Fines, Penalties & Forfeitures	1%	1%
Grants & Contributions	8%	2%
Indirect Costs Charged Internally	1%	9%
Interest	5%	2%
Rent	2%	0%
Sale of Materials and Services	3%	3%
Miscellaneous/Fund Equity	0%	0%
Loan Repayments	0%	0%

Looking out over the next decade, the city faces a significant number of financial and service challenges. The biggest financial challenge is the legacy costs of pension and retiree health care. In the early 1980s, the city had to pay out over $3.3 million in pension contributions. By 2008, the number had grown to over $9 million in contributions. These changes occurred even as the total number of city employees went from 751 in the early 1980s to just 465 by 2008.

Even more troubling, the city faces a thirty-year accrued liability, based on existing benefit plans, of $215 million for retiree health care. Currently, the city has set aside zero funding for this unfunded liability. In order to pay this amount on a funded basis, the city would have to set aside another $12 million annually out of the city budget. For example, this would essentially mean eliminating the police department. Over time, the amount that has to paid out will grow and force budget reductions if money is not set aside or major retiree benefit reductions are not secured.

This story underlines the complexity of understanding the true needs, costs, and service-delivery challenges in a declining and shrinking city. Shouldn't a shrinking city simply need fewer police officers, firefighters, and other services? If so, one would expect that the budget would decline or grow slowly over time. At the same time, perhaps a shrinking city and those remaining residents actually require a greater level of services and spending to maintain the basic infrastructure and capacity of a place. These questions challenge the basic economic and fiscal foundations of a city and its municipal government in a shrinking environment.

2

Forces Affecting City Population Growth or Decline: The Effects of Interregional and Inter-municipal Competition

Edward W. Hill, Harold L. Wolman, Katherine Kowalczyk, and Travis St. Clair

About the authors:

Edward (Ned) Hill is the dean of the Maxine Goodman Levin College of Urban Affairs at Cleveland State University and a professor of economic development.

Harold (Hal) Wolman is the Director of the George Washington Institute of Public Policy and a professor of political science and public policy at the George Washington University.

Katherine Kowalczyk was a graduate research assistant at Cleveland State University and is currently a project engineer at AECOM.

Travis St. Clair is a doctoral candidate in the Trachtenberg School of public policy and public administration at the George Washington University.

Acknowledgments:

We thank Alan Mallach for superb editorial advice and guidance and Nick Matej for his design of Figure 1. Partial funding was provided to the Maxine Goodman Levin College of Urban Affairs at Cleveland State University by the What Works Collaborative, which is managed by the Urban Institute. Additional general support was provided to both the Levin College and the George Washington Institute of Public Policy through the John D. and Catherine T. MacArthur Foundation's Network on Building Resilient Regions.

The publication of the 2010 U.S. Census documents the continued population decline of a number of storied American cities. Declines that started between 1960 and 1970 continue. Central cities that at one time dominated their regional markets for business locations are now just one potential location among many in much less dense and much larger metropolitan areas. In fact, some of these metropolitan areas are themselves experiencing population decline.

To begin to understand why this is happening, critical questions need to be answered, first about the metropolitan region and then about the central city. What are the characteristics of the region's portfolio of products? How does that portfolio influence the way companies invest in the region and use regional resources? How is the region growing in terms of jobs and population? What is the economic purpose of the city? What is the central city's potential value to households and businesses relative to the rest of the region? What is its share of the regional market of households and businesses?

The purpose of this chapter is to analyze the causes of population decline in large U.S. cities and the implications of this decline for future urban stabilization and/or regeneration efforts. To accomplish this, we examine a variety of hypotheses that have been suggested about the causes of population shrinkage in central cities. Our method is to focus on cities that have lost population and compare them to those that have not, and then to examine cities that, after initially losing population, have rebounded and are now growing and compare them to cities that have continued to decline.

There are many reasons, reflecting implicit hypotheses, given for city population declines, and many approaches are being pursued to stem these declines based on the implicit acceptance of one or more of these hypotheses. In this chapter we make explicit these implicit hypotheses and examine the plausibility of each as a guide for assessing city policy. We do this by asking two questions: Which factors show a relationship to city population change? And, have the various development strategies worked in changing the population trajectories of declining central cities?

We begin by examining city population change over the past half century and identifying different types of shrinking and growing cities. We then set forth a variety of theories that might explain those changes. In the third section we form a series of testable hypotheses from these theories, as well from a number of widely accepted economic development strategies that are intended to bring about city regeneration. These hypotheses are tested in the fourth section to determine the extent to which they—and the various strategies that flow from them—are supported by data. Finally, we discuss the implications of these quantitative findings.

Central Cities In The United States: Growth And Decline

In this section we classify all major central cities in the United States according to their population dynamics from 1960 to 2010, identifying four major central city subsets: shrinking, growing, positive-turnaround and negative-turnaround cities. We also examine the distribution of these four city types and their distribution by Census Division (see appendix 1 for a map of the divisions).

The Universe of Major Central Cities in the United States

Three categories of city were included in our universe of major central cities. The first named central city, frequently called the primary central city, for each metropolitan statistical area (MSA) that existed in 2000 was included as long as it had 50,000 residents in 2000.[1] Additional central cities in a metropolitan area were included as long as they had populations of at least 150,000 in 2000. Those municipalities in the metropolitan area with populations less than 150,000 were also included if their population was at least half that of the primary central city in 1990 or in 2000.[2]

Data were collected on each of these municipalities from the 1960, 1970, 1980, 1990, and 2010 U.S. Censuses and were supplemented with data on Gross Metropolitan (Domestic) Product and employment by industry from 1970 to 2007 from the Moody's Analytics Economy.com county database.[3]

We first divided our universe of cities into two categories: all major central cities that gained population between 1960 and 2010 (these numbered 301) and all that lost population over that time period (94). However, this initial classification hides more than it reveals, for two reasons: changes in population dynamics that took place during the fifty-year time interval studied and the public policy implications of those dynamics. Therefore, both population-losing and population-gaining central cities can be meaningfully subdivided and, in one special case, combined for analytical purposes.

Our statistical analysis rests on four major categories, or subsets, of central cities: shrinking, growing, positive-turnaround, and negative-turnaround. The categories of shrinking and growing central cities are clear. Shrinking cities lost population from 1960 to 2010 and their lowest population level was reached in 2010; growing cities increased their population over that same time period and reached their highest population level in 2010. The category of positive-turnaround central cities consists of groups of cities that lost population during the first-part of the study period and then changed trajectory and began to grow. The negative-turnaround category consists of two groups of central cities that increased their population from 1960 to 2010 but experienced intercensus population declines toward the end of the period. We emphasize these latter two definitions because a

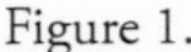

Figure 1.

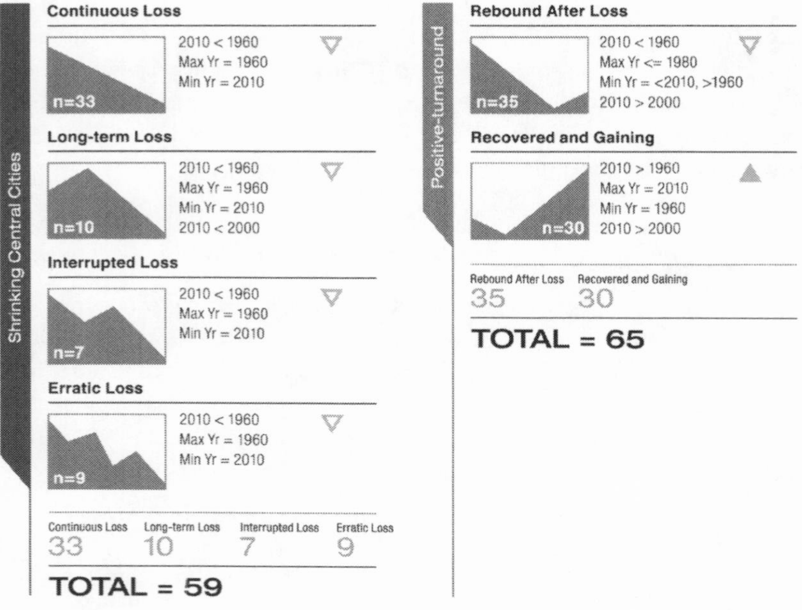

quick reading may cause confusion later in the chapter. We examine each of these four categories and their components below. Examining *Figure 1* should help in understanding the way the final four groups of central cities were composed.[4]

Shrinking Central Cities

Shrinking central cities are composed of four specific subsets of central cities. All lost population between 1960 and 2010, but they did so in different ways. Most experienced population loss decade after decade; some grew for a decade or two after 1960 and then entered a period of long-term decline; others declined from 1960, experienced a decade or two of growth, and then reentered decline. There are two characteristics common to all of the central cities that are in the shrinking central city category: They have lower populations in 2010 than in 1960, and they lost population from 2000 to 2010.

Shrinking cities can be divided into those that have experienced consistent population loss over each decade of the period 1960 to 2010 and those that have not but still lost population between 1990 and 2010. The thirty-three cities that continuously lost population in every decade after 1960 make up the largest number of places in this group. These include Detroit, Cleveland, Evansville, Illinois and Gary, Indiana, as well as Birmingham and New Orleans in the south.

Ten central cities experienced long-term population loss. The 2010 population of each is lower than their 1960 population, and population decline set in

Figure 1. *(cont)*

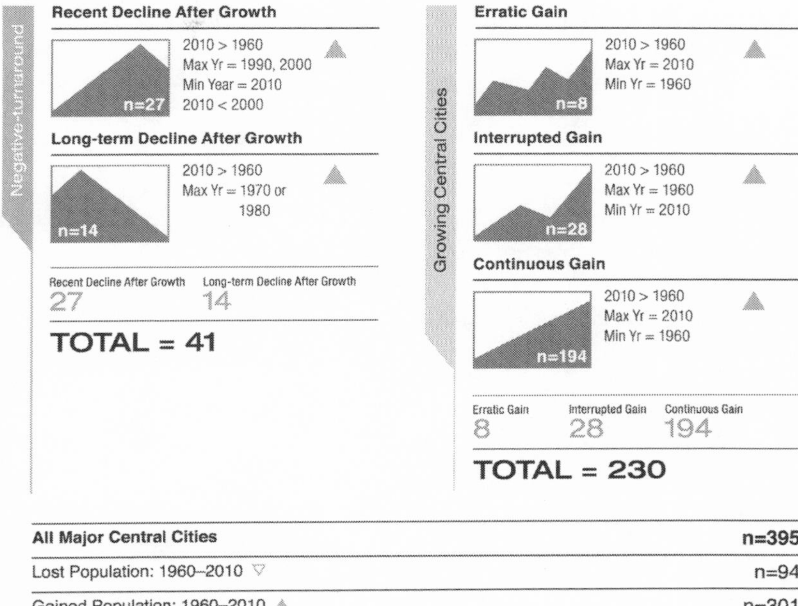

sometime between 1960 and 1980. This is where Kalamazoo, Michigan is found, along with Pensacola, Florida.

Seven cities lost population in each decade except one (they experienced interrupted population loss). Chicago is the largest city in this group. The others were manufacturing centers that rose and fell with their industry: these include South Bend, Indiana, where decline in the automotive sector could not be offset by growth in higher education; the oil-refining centers of Galveston and Port Arthur, Texas; and the former mill-towns of Fall River, Massachusetts and Pawtucket, Rhode Island.

Nine central cities experienced erratic population loss. Each had mild rebounds, but their overall trend was negative and population was lower in 2010 than in 1960. Mobile, Alabama is in this group, as is Wilmington, Delaware.

Positive-turnaround Central Cities

These central cities experienced population gains after at least a decade of decline. One set gained population over the fifty-year time period studies; the other reverse its trajectory of decline even though its population in 2010 was lower than it was in 1960. Together they are termed *positive-turnaround.*

Thirty-five central cities rebounded after losing population. Their populations declined from a peak in 1960, 1970, or 1980 and then experienced growth but did not reach the previous peak. Despite long-term population losses, the change in the population dynamic of these cities is significant. Boston, Philadelphia, and

Washington, D.C. are good examples, as are the central cities in New York City's orbit: Jersey City, Newark, and Bethlehem, Pennsylvania, which has experienced spillover from both Philadelphia and New York. Some cities outside the Northeast are in this set as well, such as Richmond, Virginia, and Salt Lake City.

A second group of central cities reversed population losses to the extent that they ended up with 2010 populations larger than their 1960 populations. Thirty central cities recovered from population losses and gained population. They fit our broad definition of growing central cities, but their change in trajectory led us to combine them with rebounding cities and call the combined group *positive-turnaround cities*. These include Denver, New York, and San Francisco, as well as smaller places such as Portland, Oregon, and Topeka, Kansas.

Negative-turnaround Central Cities

Two types of central cities may be considered growing in that their 2010 population is larger than their 1960 population, but they began to lose population toward the end of the fifty-year study period. These two subsets form a group that we call *negative-turnaround cities* due to these more recent changes in their population trajectories. As with the *positive-turnaround* group, this set of central cities may offer lessons for public policy.

Twenty-seven cities grew from 1960 until 1990 or 2000 and then experienced losses in population, though their 2010 population remains above 1960 levels. These cities may be the mirror image of the *positive-turnaround* central cities. While they are predominantly in the South, especially in Florida, five are in California, and several are in the Midwest. Ann Arbor, Battle Creek, and Grand Rapids in Michigan are part of this set, as are Tulsa, Memphis, and Honolulu.

An additional fourteen cities, while they experienced overall population growth from 1960 to 2010, had multi-decade population declines during the latter part of that period. The Ohio cities of Elyria and Mansfield join Lansing, Michigan, and Jackson, Mississippi, in this group. This is a set of central cities that are in long-term decline after experiencing a burst of growth after 1960. These places may have more in common with declining cities than with growing cities.

Growing Central Cities

Fifty-eight percent of America's central cities are members of this set. The great majority gained population without interruption over the fifty-year period, while a small percentage experienced some downturns along the way. Their common ground is that their populations were higher in 2010 than in 1960 and rose between 1990 and 2010. *Growing central cities* can be divided among those that continuously gained population over every decade of the study period (these number 194) and those that, while experiencing overall growth, had brief downturns before returning to their growth path (36).

Fewer than half of all major central cities in the United States are in the continuously gaining category, with populations in 2010 that are larger than in 1960 and gains in each decade. The list is heavily weighted toward cities in the South and West, but it includes some from the Midwest and East as well.

The twenty-eight cities that experienced one decade of population shrinkage between 1960 and 2000 were labeled interrupted gaining cities; these cities include Rockford and Joliet, Illinois, as well as Indianapolis and Fort Wayne Indiana. Eight cities experienced multiple population downturns over the period, and gained population erratically. These cities include Muncie, Indiana, and Chattanooga.

Table 1: *The Distribution of Population by Type of Central City in 1960, 2000, and 2010*

						Percent Distribution by Type of Central City			
	Number	*Central City Population*			*Percent*	*Central City Population*			*Share of 2010*
Type of Central City	*by Type*	1960	2000	2010	*by Type*	1960	2000	2010	*U.S. Population*
Growing	230	19158472	44155175	49862827	58.2	31.2	53.4	56.4	16.2
Shrinking	59	16966942	12255618	11116367	14.9	27.7	14.8	12.6	3.6
Negative-turnaround	41	3,977,714	5,746,809	5,591,941	10.4	6.5	6.9	6.3	1.8
Positive-turnaround	65	21250951	20538070	21826853	16.5	34.6	24.8	24.7	7.1
Total	395	61354079	82695672	88397988	100.0	100.0	100.0	100.0	28.6

Source: U.S. Census of Population, various years.

Table 1 presents summary statistics below on the number of cities and the total population in our four major subsets, or categories, of central cities: *growing, shrinking, negative-turnaround*, and *positive-turnaround.*

In 2010, 49.9 million Americans lived in central cities that grew consistently since 1960; contrasted with 11.1 million residing in shrinking central cities. The population living in these shrinking central cities is 34.5 percent smaller than it was in 1960. At the same time, 21.8 million Americans lived in positive-turnaround central cities, cities that experienced growth after decades of decline. In other words, more than seven percent of the nation's population, and nearly 24.7 percent of all central city residents, live in central cities that experienced positive population turnarounds.

The Distribution of Major Central Cities by Census Division

The distribution of central cities in each of the nine U.S. Census Divisions by their population classification and by Location Quotients (LQ), reflecting the share of cities by type in each division, is presented in Appendix 2. (An LQ over 1.0 indicates a higher-than-proportional share of population living in the region relative to the share in the nation as a whole, while an LQ under 1.0 indicates a lower share.) What do these data indicate about the geographic distribution of the various types of central cities?

While *shrinking* central cities are present in all Census Divisions, except the Mountain Division, they are disproportionately concentrated in the Middle Atlantic, East North Central, and West North Central regions. The LQ of population for the East North Central states is 4.34, and it is 2.04 for the West North Central states. If the metropolitan areas of upstate New York and central and western Pennsylvania were added to the East North Central Census Division, then the concentration would be stronger still. New York's upstate cities of Binghamton, Buffalo, Rochester, and Syracuse are classified as shrinking, as are Altoona, Erie, Pittsburgh, Scranton, and Wilkes-Barre in Pennsylvania.

The Middle Atlantic region, however, has a smaller proportion of the nation's shrinking city population than expected when compared to the percentage of people living in shrinking cities nationally. The Middle Atlantic region's central city population disproportionately lives in positive-turnaround cities.

The group of cities we term *negative-turnaround* reflects the negative aftereffects of recent shocks. In terms of the number of these cities, there were higher-than-expected concentrations in New England, the East North Central Division (predominantly cities that specialized in auto parts production), and the East South Central Division. The East South Central Division has a population LQ of 3.44, which means that the concentration of population in cities that are negative-turnaround is 244 percent higher than expected based on the region's share of central city population, a reflection of the impact of Hurricane Katrina on Biloxi and Gulfport, Mississippi. The other higher than expected concentration of negative-turnaround cities is in the Pacific Division, with six of California's central cities and Honolulu.

Positive-turnaround central cities are concentrated in New England and the Middle Atlantic states. This demonstrates the resurgent strength of the cluster of metropolitan areas anchored by Boston and New York City. However, as we noted earlier, positive-turnaround central cities exist in all Census Divisions.

Growing central cities are disproportionately concentrated in the West South Central Division, Mountain Division, and Pacific Division. This is true both in terms of the number of cities and in terms of the population LQ. There is a 12 percent higher concentration than expected in the South Atlantic Division in terms of population.

The LQ data demonstrates that while the four major types of central cities are regionally concentrated, geography alone does not explain central city performance. Market, institutional, and structural forces determine the fate of America's central cities. In the next section of this chapter we examine the hypotheses that have been suggested as causes of long-term population change in American central cities.

The Context of City Population Change: Theory and Expectations

Two broad sets of forces can put a city or a region on a downward population trajectory: loss in *interregional* competitive position and loss of *intraregional* competitive position (Beauregard, this volume). Underlying both is a simple premise: To be sustainable, a city must have an economic purpose, and it must be competitive—both with other regions and within its own region.

Loss of Interregional Competitive Position: Product Initiated Decline

The first of the two forces triggering population loss reflects changes in the competitive position of products that form a region's traditional economic base. It also emphasizes the close relationship between the economic and demographic fortunes of a city and of its region. If the entire region is experiencing economic decline, then the region's core city is virtually certain to be doing so, and city population is likely to decline as well.

An economic region can be seen as being made up of a portfolio of products, with each product having a position in the product life cycle and its associated S-curve.[5] The overall growth of the economy is then dependent on the growth and volatility of the elements of the portfolio weighted by its share of gross regional product.[6] Population decline can set in as the product moves through its life cycle and the locational requirements of production changes or when the product's market declines or collapses. Population decline can also occur because of institutional sclerosis, wage and income rigidities, and inflexible cost structures, such as overly rigid work rules that allow lower-cost competitor regions to gain market share. This is usually accompanied by population decline in the traditional production center, or headquarters city, of these corporations. [7]

Theoretically, decline in key parts of the region's product portfolio takes place when products that have been historically central to the region's output, or product, portfolio move along the product cycle and either enter the maturity stage, where growth slows, or into decline.[8] Decline is then transmitted through the cluster of economic activity that surrounds the product or industry, either through forward linkages (which are sales to customers) or through backward linkages (which are purchases made from the supply chain).[9]

Decline associated with the maturation of products that form a large part of a region's product portfolio is often associated with regional population decline or slow growth, since it can trigger population losses through the labor market. Less demand for the region's products leads to less demand for labor; less regional demand for labor, in turn, results in outmigration of those who have lost jobs and of younger adults who are searching for careers and paychecks. A second source of population loss can take place in cities that were industrial centers during the early 20th century: With a decline in job growth and, with it, a decline in perceived opportunity, the domestic and foreign immigrants that historically fueled these cities just stop coming. Moreover, population decline will be more concentrated in those cities and neighborhoods that house workers with occupational skills that are no longer in demand,[10] and in municipalities with tax bases that are most dependent on declining industries.[11]

If the root of the region's decline rests with a product portfolio dominated by mature or declining industries, then economic development solutions may include endogenous development strategies, such as encouraging entrepreneurship leading to new products; assisting in product revitalization (a form of technology-based development); lowering transaction costs that inhibit local firms from expanding; or engaging in import substitution through activities such as buy-local campaigns. A second set of strategies focuses on exogenous development by either encouraging external demand for local products through trade promotion or attracting external investment in the regional economy.

Loss of Intraregional Competitive Position

The second major force behind central city population decline is its competitive position relative to its neighboring municipalities, or its locational advantage. Cities compete for residents and businesses based on a combination of location, quality of services provided with an accompanying tax cost, quality and appropriateness of infrastructure, and quality and appropriateness of its building stock. This second set of forces can be thought of as the determinants of a city's market share of metropolitan area population and of business activity.

Somewhat different forces determine the value proposition (value obtained for the cost of the location both in terms of purchase price, operating costs, and tax cost) considered by businesses and households when it comes to intraregional locational decisions. Some forces pull users toward a city's land and others push users away from that land. Businesses evaluate these factors through their income statements; households do so through their utility functions.

Suburban pull factors for households include the positive aspects of suburban living, particularly more land at affordable prices and a lifestyle that is attractive to many households. Suburban pull factors for businesses are major changes in transportation, communication, and infrastructure that have reshaped the competitive position of land uses within the metropolitan area since the 1950s.[12] For the retail and service sectors, the growth of population and disposable income in suburban areas and their decline in the city provides additional incentive, or pull, to locate in the suburbs in order to be close to their customers.

Central city push factors for households include quality-of-life issues, such as crime, density, and the quality of services (primarily education); tax costs for services received; obsolescence of building stock; and racial or ethnic change. For businesses these include some of the household factors (crime, tax cost, obsolescence of building stock) but may also include congestion, deteriorated infrastructure, and a lack of local government responsiveness and transparency.

Companies choose locations (both intra- and inter-regionally) based on the impact the location has on gross income or sales (the top lines of their income statement) and/or on their operating costs (the middle lines). For most traded sectors of the economy, those that export their goods and services to customers outside the region, location within a metropolitan area should not affect gross sales; however, it can influence operating costs, as well as a company's ability to attract and retain scarce labor or talent.[13]

Factors Associated With City Population Decline: Hypotheses

What are the forces that can explain why some cities have experienced long-term population growth while others have suffered decline? Above we divided these forces into interregional and intraregional factors that affect the locational decisions of households and businesses. Here we present specific hypotheses and note which of these provide the intellectual foundation for specific types of economic development strategies. In the following section we test these hypotheses and policy strategies based on them to assess their validity.

Drawing on the above discussion, we offer several hypotheses on possible factors contributing to city population decline between 1960 and 2010. Since some of these potential explanations are implicitly embodied in city economic development strategies, the extent to which each is valid may have important implications for urban economic development policy.

We divide our hypotheses into those that relate to interregional competitive forces that might affect the entire metropolitan area and thus also affect city population growth or decline, and those that reflect possible intraregional forces that reflect the distribution of metropolitan area population between a central city and its suburbs.

Interregional Competitive Forces

At the base of any city or region's population growth is the health and vitality of its economy in relation to that of its competitor regions. In this section we present eight hypotheses that relate to interregional competitive forces, looking first at four hypotheses about the demand side of the market for the factors of production—land, labor, capital, and knowledge—followed by hypotheses about the performance of the supply side of those markets.

Hypotheses about the demand side of markets for metropolitan factors of production

Hypothesis 1: Low metropolitan area economic growth is expected to be associated with central city population decline. This reflects the observation that a region's economic success is necessary for it's central cities to remain viable.[14]

Hypothesis 2: Central cities whose residents were disproportionately employed in the manufacturing sector at the beginning of the period were likely to grow more slowly or decline over the course of the period. We hold this expectation for several reasons. First, these manufactured products are most likely to be old in terms of their position in the product cycle and, therefore, growing slowly or declining. Second, plants are likely to be old, built to accommodate outdated modes of transportation, and most likely difficult and expensive to modify. Third, if the manufacturing activity is abandoned, the building site will be expensive to adapt for alternative or new land uses. And fourth, we know that heavy industries with central city operations have declined. The quest to reinvigorate declining manufacturing is a major economic development strategy in many regions.

Hypothesis 3: Central cities that had a disproportionately high share of employment in the manufacturing sector in 2000 are expected to experience population decline over the period. U.S. manufacturing experienced severe difficulties from about a year and a half before the 2001 recession began through the 2007 recession. While the most dramatic set of losses revolved around the Detroit-based auto industry, U.S. manufacturing in general experienced a competitive onslaught from offshore competitors, especially for routine manufacturing production dominated by low-skilled and semiskilled jobs. We expect that declines in regional manufacturing employment will be associated with net outmigration from the region and from the central city.

Hypothesis 4: Central cities located in metropolitan areas that had a disproportionately high share of employment in the health sector in 2000 are expected to experience population growth over the period. One of the most dramatic changes in the modern U.S. economy has been the rise in the share of gross domestic product spent on health care and the growing importance of health care employment in central cities. We expect that the larger the share of health care jobs in the metropolitan economy, the greater the gain in central city population. This hypothesis underlies the "meds" part of an "eds and meds" economic development strategy.

Hypotheses about the supply-side of markets for metropolitan factors of production. Work and economic opportunity are attracted to a city and region due to the cost and quality of the factors of production, both in the economic region and in the city itself. There are four broad factors in modern production: land, labor, capital, and knowledge. Since most portions of the capital market are national or global, our investigation focused on the other three "sticky" factors of production that define the competitive and comparative advantages of regional economies.

Hypothesis 5: Central cities whose residents had lower levels of higher education attainment in 1960 were more likely to experience population decline from 1960 to 2010. This hypothesis directly addresses the role that advanced education plays in the labor market. As the economy has moved increasingly to producing traded services, managerial occupations and technical occupations that demand an educated workforce have grown. Many researchers argue that demand for workers with high skill levels and advanced education provides large central cities with a comparative advantage in the competition for the location of businesses that produce and trade services outside of their immediate market area. Robert Reich called people with these skills "knowledge workers and symbolic analysts."[15]

This hypothesis lies behind the efforts of many cities to pursue a "get smarter" economic development strategy, designed to improve the educational quality of their labor force. Such a strategy implies raising rates of educational attainment (degrees and certificates earned), deepening levels of educational achievement (improving soft skills, critical thinking, literacy, and numeracy), and developing pools of tradable knowledge. Education is seen as the root not only of increased labor productivity but also of increased multifactor productivity.

Hypothesis 6A: Increases in labor supply brought about by regional economic growth are expected to be associated with city population growth. Migration is a critical way in which cities and metropolitan economies augment and enhance their labor supplies. The supply of labor increases through several stages as regional labor markets tighten.[16]

In the very short run, unemployment rates go down as employers hire those who are not working and are actively seeking work. The second stage of an increase in the labor supply takes place when potential workers with reasonable skills believe that their chances of being employed at a wage above their reservation wage is improving.[17]

They then move into the labor force, either directly to work, or into unemployment; this is when the labor force participation rate increases and secondary workers are attracted into the regional labor market. In the next stage those with lower skills who were previously either unemployed or not participating in the labor market gain employment as labor markets tighten. The last stage of increasing the labor supply takes place when people are attracted into the regional labor market through migration in response to economic opportunity.

Hypothesis 6B: Regional amenities are likely to be associated with higher levels of city population growth. Cortright, Glaeser, Florida, and others have suggested that interregional migration is not wholly influenced by job and wage concerns but is also affected by a desire for regional amenities.[18] This hypothesis is the basis for the pursuit of amenity-based economic development strategies by cities and regions.

We could not collect data on the list of amenities frequently mentioned, with one prominent exception: mean July temperature. It is well known that the United States has experienced a long-term internal migration to the South and West, which has resulted in a broad deepening of the labor supply in those regions. It is assumed that this migration is in part stimulated by a search for warmer winter temperatures now that air conditioning has taken away the discomfort of hot, humid summers.

Hypothesis 7: Cities located in regions with better-quality and more modern infrastructure and with a more "business friendly" environment will likely be associated with greater population growth. The land market for business locations has two parts. The first is the cost, access, and other characteristics of the land itself. Unfortunately we do not have data on these characteristics. The second aspect of the cost of land is the cost and quality of public services and the public policy environment that is associated with a region. Economic activity, and the population associated with it, will gravitate toward regions whose land and other attributes provide a better operating environment. The cost and quality of public services is the basis for much local economic development policy, manifested in efforts to reduce costs through business tax incentives, through infrastructure improvements, and through regulatory reform to create a more business-friendly environment.

Hypothesis 8A: The presence of research universities in a metropolitan area is likely to be associated with greater central city population growth. This hypothesis directly addresses the knowledge portion of the new production function. The presence of a research university may lead to localized success in translating knowledge creation into viable new products, new industry formation, and, relocation.[19] Encouraging academic research is a popular economic development strategy.

Hypothesis 8B: Agglomeration economies and density are expected to be associated with central city population growth. There are two competing hypotheses with respect to city density and population size. Clarke and Gaile and Glaeser both hypothesize that a competitive advantage of central cities is their density, based on the traditional argument for "agglomeration economies."[20] Density facilitates the exchange of ideas and will—as Alfred Marshall argued in the late 1890s—enhance labor pooling, since central cities have enough density of people and of jobs that those with rare skills have a higher probability of finding work that matches their skills. This makes density a component of the knowledge base of a region. The dense co-location of different knowledge industries will create demand for skilled labor. Porter has also made this argument about the development advantages of central cities.[21] Agglomeration economies are the intellectual core for the economic cluster strategies that have been widely adopted in the past two decades. The opposing hypothesis is that density triggers a series of negative externalities in terms of congestion and accompanying noise, dirt, deterioration in safety, and other inconveniences and increased production costs, so that it provides an incentive to move to less dense regions.

Intraregional, or intrametropolitan area, competitive position

Central cities compete for residents with other jurisdictions within a metropolitan area. They may have had a historical advantage based on access to dense locations of work, but this advantage has eroded over time with the establishment of multinuclear metropolitan regions. Other locational factors include the tax cost associated with a residence, safety, quality of schooling, the ability to attract and acculturate immigrants, and the age and density of the housing stock. We collected data on many of these hypothesized relationships to see how much each was associated with change in central city populations from 1960 to 2010, first focusing on factors that are external to individual household decision-making about which municipality to live in and then moving onto factors that directly influence household choice.

Factors that are external to individual household locational choice.
Hypothesis 9: It is expected that greater increases in regional population will be associated with greater increases in central city population. This would be true even if the share of the regional increase is lower in the central city than in the rest of the region.

Hypothesis 10: The historical flow of international migration to a city is expected to be positively associated with population growth. This hypothesis is based on the expectation that existing foreign-born populations would be a foundation for subsequent chain migration. A number of central cities that have experienced sharp population losses have shown great interest in drawing international migrants as new sources of population. Part of this interest is based on the observation that Hispanic immigration has been critical to sustaining population levels in Chicago and in California's major central cities;[22] another part is based on the realization that international migration has the potential to offset suburban outmigration and an appreciation of the traditional role of central cities as the entry point for international migrants, who then move out as they move up the income ladder.[23]

Hypothesis 11: Cities that have the ability to annex land on their borders are expected to be able to increase their populations more rapidly than those that are unable or unwilling to do so. There are three reasons for this: First, the annexed land will contain existing residents who will immediately add to the city's population. Second, cities annex only land that is desirable. Third, the larger the portion of the metropolitan area contained within the municipal corporate limits, the better its ability to accommodate further population growth.[24]

Factors that directly bear on household locational choice.
People choose where to live within a metropolitan area by balancing a number of characteristics about their family, access to work and amenities, the full cost of living at a particular location, conditioned upon their wealth and income. Life-cycle stage and family structure play roles, as do the characteristics of the potential residence itself. While there is little that public policy can do to directly affect location decisions in the near term, it can influence important factors such as crime rates and the quality of education, which, over a longer time period, will affect those decisions.

Hypothesis 12: The quality of the city public school system is likely to be positively related to central city population change. A public school system seen to be poorly performing will lead middle-class families with children to migrate from the central city to suburbs with better schools. The process is self-reinforcing, since the reduction of middle-class students leaves the school system with a greater proportion of students from low-income families, whom research has shown are more expensive and difficult to educate.

Hypothesis 13: Higher rates of city crime are expected to be associated with population movement from the central city to suburbs and thus result in lower city population. Cities increasingly recognize that crime reduction is related not only to population out-migration but to their local economic development success because business owners understand that it is difficult to attract and retain employees in dangerous neighborhoods, customers are repelled by street crime, and operating costs (including insurance) are driven up by crime.

Hypothesis 14: A higher rate of poverty among central city residents is expected to be associated with city population decline. It is widely held that the larger the share of low-income families living in a central city, the lower will be the city's long-term population growth rate. One reason for this expectation is that low-income families cannot pay for the local public services that they consume, raising the tax burden on families that are not poor. The second concern is over the concentration of the poor. Much work has been done on tipping points and the impact of high densities of low-income families on social problems associated with poverty, including crime and educational achievement.[25]

Hypothesis 15: An observation commonly made during the time period studied is white residents frequently flee established residential neighborhoods following an influx of African-Americans; this is termed racial succession. Therefore, *it is hypothesized that rapid racial succession and negative attitudes among white residents toward African-Americans integrating neighborhoods added a propulsive force to suburbanization during the late 1960s through the 1970s.*[26] Our expectation is that the retention of the white population would be inversely associated with the percentage of African-Americans in the city population at the beginning of the period and that population loss would be associated with white flight. We also hypothesized that the frequency and intensity of racially identified riots or civil disturbances from 1964 to 1971 would be shown to have stimulated white flight and long-term population loss.

The above discussion has set forth the hypotheses that underlie many efforts to improve local economies and to reverse population decline (although we note that a review of these hypotheses suggests that many strategies to address population push factors depend on policies and practices that lie outside the purview of the economic development department and require improving the operating conditions of the city). The extent to which these hypotheses are supported by the analysis we present below should clarify whether the policies and strategies are well grounded.

Factors Associated With Central City Population Decline: Testing The Hypotheses

The goal of the statistical portion of the chapter is to test a set of variables that reflect, or operationalize, the specific development hypotheses set forth above. Each of these variables reflects a social, demographic, or economic factor that is held to be associated with population change in American central cities from 1960 to 2010, the period covered by this study, or is the outcome of a public policy strategy designed to influence population change. Because we are interested in population change over this time period we selected variables at the start of the time period, or as close to 1960 as possible, to shed light on what caused subsequent population movements.

We use three analytic methods. *Correlation analysis* shows how closely each of these variables is individually associated with the percent change in central city population between 1960 and 2010. *Multiple regression analysis* allows us to estimate the effect of a variable on central city population change while controlling for the effects of other variables. *Difference in means* tests show the difference in the mean value of a particular variable between two groups of cities, such as the difference in the average poverty rate between growing and shrinking cities.

To interpret the results of a correlation analysis we must first determine whether the sign of the coefficient (positive or negative), corresponds to what our hypothesis would predict. The sign indicates the direction of the relationship between the two variables. Second, we must determine whether the correlation between the two variables is statistically different from zero or whether there is no statistical association.[27]

The results are given in *Table 2* which contains the correlation coefficients, the critical values for each type of central city based on the number of observations in each group (this indicates the value required for the correlation to be deemed to be statically significant given the size of the subset or group), and the probability that the result is statistically significant. In addition to this information Jacob Cohen suggests that qualitative statements can be made about the association between the two variables based on the size of the correlation coefficient, where values above 0.5 are considered large or strong, between 0.3 and 0.5 moderate, between 0.1 and 0.3 small or weak, and less than 0.1 trivial or insubstantial.[28] The results are presented in *Table 2* for all major central cities in the nation as well as for each of the nine Census Divisions. The data are arrayed by the size of the correlation coefficients for the national set of central cities, moving from the largest positive correlation to the largest negative correlation.[29]

Correlation analysis is limited. It does not determine causation, nor can it measure the independent effects of each variable on population change. This is because all of the variables we are investigating influence the percent change in central city population simultaneously. To assess the independent effect of each of the variables while controlling for the other variables requires multivariate analysis. Thus our second approach is to test a multiple regression model for which the dependent variable is percent change in central city population from 1960 to 2010. (*See Appendix 3 for the presentation of the model and results*).

Our third approach is to utilize difference in means tests to compare the means of the independent variables for the four different subsets of central cities: growing, shrinking, positive-turnaround from decline, and negative-turnaround from growth. This supplements our correlation analysis and allows us to better understand what leads to either successful growth or positive economic transition among central cities. There are very large differences in population growth rates across the four groups of central cities, and we expect that a close examination of differences in the independent variables can help explain why or how those differences occurred.

The results from the difference in means tests are displayed in *Table 3*. This table presents the mean values for the variables for the four subsets of central cities. The mean for each variable for each subset is tested to determine whether it is statistically different from the mean of the other groups, and is reported in the section on the left side of *Table 3*. The results from the tests are reported on the right-hand section of the table, along with the statistical significance of the test. The variables are ordered according to their association with central city population growth rates as displayed in *Table 2*.

Four horizontal lines divide *Table 3*. The four variables above the first (solid) line had strong positive correlations with city population change that were statistically significant at the 99 percent confidence interval for the universe of major central cities, as depicted in *Table 2*. The variable between the solid line and the following dashed line (Annexation) was positively correlated with population change and was significantly different from having no association at the 95 percent confidence interval. The two variables between the lower dashed line and the lower solid line had statistically significant negative correlations with population change at the 95 percent confidence level. The six variables below the second solid line had correlations that exceeded the 99 percent critical value.

In the following section we present the findings derived from an analysis of our full set of cities.[30] We refer to findings within individual regions only when relevant. A more systematic presentation of within-region results is presented in Appendix 4.

Interregional Competitive Forces

Hypotheses about the demand-side of markets for metropolitan factors of production

Hypothesis 1: Low metropolitan area economic growth is expected to be associated with central city population decline. There is a strong statistical association between the employment growth rates of metropolitan areas from 1970 to 2007 and population growth rates of their central cities from 1960 to 2010. This reinforces the observation that regional economic success is necessary for central cities to remain viable. The correlation coefficient is 0.302 among the universe of central cities, the second-highest correlation coefficient. Controlling for the other variables in the multivariate model, we found that an increase of one percentage point in the typical metropolitan area's employment growth from 1970 to 2007 was associated with a 0.98 percentage point increase in central city population from 1960 to 2010.

Metropolitan population and employment growth rates distinguish the performance of shrinking central cities from growing central cities, shrinking central cities from central cities that have experienced a positive-turnaround from decline, and those that have gone through a negative-turnaround from growing central cities. Metropolitan area population growth rates in positive-turnaround cities (i.e., cities that first suffered declines in population after 1960 but then began grow-

Table 2.

Correlations with Percent Change in Central City Population from 1960 to 2010 Sorted from the highest national correlation statistic to the smallest

Hypothesized Causal Variables	*United States*	*New England*	*Middle Atlantic*
Percent change in MSA population from 1980 to 2000[1]	0.380 ***	0.195	0.620 ***
Percent change in MSA employment from 1970 to 2007[2]	0.302 ***	0.269 *	0.094
Average July temperature	0.204 ***	-0.069	0.595 ***
Percentage of MSA population that is Hispanic in 2000	0.192 ***	0.115	0.685 ***
Right-to-work state in 1960	0.164 ***	.	.
Annexation: percent change in land area from 1990 to 2000	0.099 **	0.101	-0.043
Percentage of central city population that is Hispanic in 1970	0.066	-0.209	0.654 ***
Percentage of central city population age 25+ with 4 or more years of college in 1960	0.065	-0.022	0.189
Percentage of MSA population age 25+ with bachelor's degree or higher in 2000	0.030	0.356 **	-0.056
Percentage of central city families with incomes below $3,000 in 1960	0.022	-0.365 **	-0.210
Number of Universities in MSA that are high or very high in research activity[3]	0.008	-0.144	0.305 *
Percent change in MSA GDP per capita from 1980 to 20002	-0.039	0.376 **	0.006
Percentage of central city population that was foreign born in 1970	-0.064	-0.281 *	0.274 *
Intensity of central city civil disturbances from 1964 to 1971[4]	-0.083 **	-0.265 *	-0.130
Percentage of central city population that was African-American in 1960	-0.100 **	-0.177	-0.187
Percentage of MSA jobs in the manufacturing sector in 2000	-0.127 ***	-0.006	0.043
City age[5]	-0.128 ***	-0.226	-0.004
Percentage of employed central city residents working in manufacturing in 1960	-0.181 ***	0.205	0.141
Central city robberies per 100,000 residents in 1992	-0.189 ***	-0.367 **	-0.061
Central city population density in 1980[6]	-0.197 ***	-0.512 ***	0.107
Percentage of MSA jobs in health care sector in 2000	-0.219 ***	-0.406 **	-0.187
Number of central cities	395	28	30
Critical value, one-tail test 90% confidence *		0.250	0.241
Critical value, one-tail test 95% confidence **	0.073	0.317	0.306
Critical value, one-tail test 99% confidence ***	0.103	0.437	0.423

Notes:

1 A common Metropolitan Statistical Area (MSA) definition was used for all years based on the 2003 MSA definitions of the U.S. Office of Management and Budget. Data were provided by the Building Resilient Regions Network.

2 Data obtained from Moody's Analytics' Economy.com data service. MSAs were based on 2003 definitions and were constructed from Economy.com's county data files.

3 Research university: Number of universities in the MSA classified by the Carnegie Foundation as having either "high" or "very high" research activity.

Table 2. *(cont)*

Census Division						
East North Central	*West North Central*	*South Atlantic*	*East South Central*	*West South Central*	*Mountain*	*Pacific*
0.496 ***	0.541 ***	0.157 *	0.616 ***	0.293 **	0.649 ***	0.115
0.434 ***	0.778 ***	-0.020	0.326 *	0.205 *	0.654 ***	0.093
0.320 ***	-0.106	0.083	-0.418 **	0.174	0.644 ***	-0.004
0.152	-0.271	0.085	0.764 ***	0.033	0.083	0.162
.	-0.023	0.141	-0.646 ***	0.074	0.379 **	.
0.426 ***	0.484 ***	0.142	-0.018	-0.033	-0.064	0.089
-0.062	-0.286 *	-0.029	0.148	-0.072	-0.100	0.011
0.377 ***	0.705 ***	0.030	0.057	-0.039	-0.188	-0.064
0.308 ***	0.521 ***	0.008	0.136	0.273 **	-0.159	-0.095
-0.483 ***	-0.069	-0.140	0.450 **	-0.103	0.151	0.080
0.179 *	-0.081	0.099	0.033	0.392 ***	0.164	-0.084
0.453 ***	0.135	-0.203 *	-0.099	0.211 *	0.138	0.043
-0.218 **	-0.054	-0.010	0.239	-0.026	-0.134	-0.131
-0.270 **	-0.312 *	-0.095	-0.255	-0.102	-0.192	-0.099
-0.527 ***	-0.385 **	-0.363 ***	-0.042	-0.063	0.142	-0.219 **
-0.014	-0.265 *	-0.093	0.151	0.042	0.062	0.054
-0.115	-0.710 ***	-0.069	-0.162	0.124	0.095	-0.115
-0.246 **	-0.635 ***	-0.241 **	-0.132	0.235 **	0.136	-0.048
-0.505 ***	-0.491 ***	-0.285 ***	-0.416 **	-0.256 **	-0.063	-0.264 **
-0.382 ***	-0.301 *	-0.264 **	-0.526 ***	-0.191 *	-0.468 ***	-0.208 *
-0.383 ***	0.288 *	-0.073	-0.158	-0.222 *	-0.369 **	-0.116
68	27	72	21	51	35	63
0.157	0.255	0.153	0.291	0.183	0.222	0.164
0.201	0.323	0.195	0.369	0.233	0.283	0.209
0.282	0.445	0.274	0.503	0.325	0.392	0.293

4 Civil disturbance: Riot severity index from Collins and Margo (2004a).

5 City age: Number of years from the Census decade in which the central city reached a population of 50,000 to 2010.

6 Population density: City data are primarily from 1980; 1990 data were substituted for 12 central cities where 1980 data were unavailable. Two cities were omitted because 1980 and 1990 data were unavailable.

Degrees of freedom for the significance test is (n-2); that is two less than the number of central cities in the group or subset.

Table 3.

Difference in Means Between Shrinking, Growing, Positive-Turnaround, and Negative-Turnaround Central Cities

Dependent Variable	*Mean growing*	*Mean shrinking*	*Mean negative turnaround*
Percent change in central city population from 1960 to 2010	522.37	-28.30	160.33
Hypothesized Causal Variables			
Percent change in MSA population from 1980 to 20002	47.36	6.22	24.38
Percent change in MSA employment from 1970 to 20073	182.43	47.32	99.19
Average July temperature	77.67	74.29	75.88
Percentage of MSA population that is Hispanic in 2000	16.67	5.00	11.09
Annexation: percent change in land area from 1990 to 2000	26.02	1.24	12.00
Percentage of central city population that is Hispanic in 1970	7.99	2.15	4.89
Percentage of central city population age 25+ with or mote 4 years of college in 1960	11.12	6.28	10.32
Percentage of MSA population age 25+ with bachelor's degree or higher in 2000	24.82	22.12	24.30
Percentage of central city families with incomes below $3,000 in 1960	19.19	17.81	17.43
Number of Universities in MSA that are high or very high in research activity4	1.08	1.10	1.90
Percent change in MSA GDP per capita from 1980 to 20003	48.58	44.33	48.33
Percentage of central city population that was foreign born in 1970	3.90	4.63	5.69
Intensity of central city civil disturbances from 1964 to 19715	0.0039	0.0294	0.0034
Percentage of central city population that was African-American in 1960	9.10	14.40	11.53
Percentage of MSA jobs in the manufacturing sector in 2000	11.46	15.47	13.95
City age6	63.11	108.64	86.58
Percentage of employed central city residents working in manufacturing in 1960	19.94	33.97	26.70
Central city robberies per 100,000 residents in 1992	265.36	485.82	352.11
Central city population density in 19807	5.67	7.23	6.07
Percentage of MSA jobs in health care sector in 2000	9.30	11.37	10.06

Significance level or confidence intervals: * 90% confidence; ** 95% confidence;

*** 99% confidence.

Notes:

1 Differences in means are calculated by subtracting the mean value of the second set of central cities from the mean value of the first named set.

2 A common Metropolitan Statistical Area (MSA) definition was used for all years based on the 2003 MSA definitions of the U.S. Office of Management and Budget. Data were provided by the Building Resilient Regions Network.

3 Data obtained from Moody's Analytics' Economy.com data service. MSAs were based on 2003 definitions and were constructed from Economy.com's county data files.

Table 3. *(cont)*

Difference between[1]						
Mean positive turnaround	*Shrinking & growing*	*Shrinking & positive turnaround*	*Positive-turnaround & growing*	*Negative-turnaround & growing*	*Negative- turn-around & posi-tive- turnaround*	*Shrinking & negative-turnaround*
18.15	-550.67***	-46.45***	-504.22***	-362.04*	142.18**	-188.63***
21.91	-41.15***	-15.69***	-25.45***	-22.98***	2.47	-18.16***
90.25	-135.10***	-42.93***	-92.17***	-83.24***	8.93	-51.86***
75.66	-3.38***	-1.37*	-2.005**	-1.79	0.22	-1.59
8.69	-11.67***	-3.69***	-7.98***	-5.58**	2.40	-6.09***
24.48	-24.78**	-23.24	-1.54	-14.02	-12.48	-10.76***
3.82	-5.85***	-1.67**	-4.17**	-3.10	1.07	-2.74**
7.97	-4.83***	-1.69***	-3.15***	-0.80	2.35*	-4.04***
26.21	-2.70***	-4.09***	1.39	-0.51	-1.91	-2.19*
18.47	-1.39	-0.66	-0.72	-1.76	-1.04	0.37
2.02	0.02	-0.914*	0.932***	0.819**	-0.11	-0.801*
55.60	-4.25	-11.26**	7.01	-0.25	-7.26	-4.01
5.84	0.73	-1.20	1.94***	1.79**	-0.15	-1.05
0.0203	0.0255	0.01	0.0164***	0.00	-0.0169*	0.026**
12.73	5.30***	1.67	3.63**	2.44	-1.19	2.86
11.50	4.01***	3.96***	0.04	2.49**	2.45*	1.52
111.38	45.53***	-2.74	48.27***	23.47***	-24.80**	22.06**
25.74	14.03***	8.23***	5.81***	6.77***	0.96	7.27***
493.81	220.46***	-7.99	228.44***	86.74*	-141.70*	133.72*
7.68	1.56	-0.46	2.02	0.40	-1.62	1.16
10.48	2.06***	0.89**	1.18***	0.76*	-0.42	1.31***

4 Research university: Number of universities in the MSA classified by the Carnegie Foundation as having either "high" or "very high" research activity.

5 Civil disturbance: Riot severity index from Collins and Margo (2004a).

6 City age: Number of years from the Census decade in which the central city reached a population of 50,000 to 2010.

7 Central city population density: City data are primarily from 1980; 1990 data were substituted for 12 central cities where 1980 data were unavailable. Two cities were omitted because 1980 and 1990 data were unavailable.

ing again) were nearly 16 percentage points higher from 1980 to 2010 than in shrinking cities. The clear lesson is that the economy is regional, as are population dynamics that are derived from economic performance.

Hypothesis 2: Central cities whose residents were disproportionately employed in the manufacturing sector at the beginning of the period were likely to grow more slowly or decline over the course of the period. This variable has the fourth largest negative association with change in central city population nationally (-0.181). That association is strongest in the Midwest, the historic industrial heartland of the United States.

There were large differences in the share of employed central city residents who worked in manufacturing in 1960 among the four groups of central cities. The largest share was in the group of shrinking cities, 34.0 percent, and the smallest in growing cities, 19.9 percent; with the mean for the positive-turnaround central cities being 25.7 percent. The differences between all these means were statistically significant. Cities whose residents were historically disproportionately employed in the manufacturing sector were likely to experience greater population decline.

Hypothesis 3: Central cities that had a disproportionately high share of employment in the manufacturing sector in 2000 are expected to experience population decline over the period. The correlation between employment in the manufacturing sector in 2000 and population change from 1960 to 2010 is negative, as the hypothesis suggests, but the result is only weakly statistically significant. We also correlated employment in the manufacturing sector in 2000 with population growth from 2000 to 2010, which showed a slight increase in the relationship.

The difference in means tests also suggests a modest negative relationship. The highest percentage, 15.5 percent, was in regions with shrinking central cities; the lowest was in regions with growing central cities, 11.5 percent, which was the same as that of central cities that experienced positive-turnaround. The difference in the proportion of people employed in manufacturing was statistically meaningful between shrinking central cities and the other two groups of cities. The rate of employment in the manufacturing sector in 2000 in shrinking central cities was than more than four percentage points higher than in positive-turnaround cities.

Hypothesis 4: Central cities located in metropolitan areas that had a disproportionately high share of employment in the health sector in 2000 are expected to experience population growth over the period. We found the opposite to be true. This result is very strong. The correlation between the share of regional employment in the health care sector in 2000 and the percent change in central city population for both 1960 to 2010 and 2000 to 2010 is negative. In fact, it has the largest negative relationship with population change from 1960 to 2010 among the universe of central cities. The multivariate analysis in Appendix 3 supports this finding.

This surprising result persists in the difference in means analysis. Growing central cities had the lowest share of employed workers in the MSA working in the health care sector in 2000, 9.3 percent of jobs; the mean for the group of shrinking central cities was the highest, at 11.4 percent, with positive-turnaround central cities at 10.5 percent. The differences are statistically meaningful. How could this be true when cities are focusing on higher education and health care, the "eds and meds," as engines for both job and community development? These results call for taking a deeper look at the role that the regional health care sector plays in local economic and community development.

Three speculative explanations about this relationship come to mind. First, the health care sector, with the exception of metropolitan areas with major research institutions and hospitals that draw significant patient revenue from outside the metropolitan area is largely a local service sector. As such, the share of employment in the sector (other than that which is exported) is likely to be much the same, whether the city is growing or declining. Indeed, as decline sets in across the economy and jobs and population leave, health care jobs may not disappear at the same rate, due to the fact that health care is a nontraded sector of the regional economy and its major institutions are relatively immobile. In fact, it is rare to see a major health care anchor move, although one may close as its suburban competition captures its paying customers.

Second, as a city's population declines the share of elderly among those who remain could increase, requiring relatively more health care services, which can be supported through public health insurance and public and retiree health care plans. Third, most new health care jobs may be suburban, following migration of the population with money and medical insurance.

Hypotheses about the supply-side of markets for metropolitan factors of production

Hypothesis 5: Central cities whose residents had lower levels of higher education attainment in 1960 were more likely to experience population decline from 1960 to 2010. There were clear differences among the four types of cities in their shares of adults with four years or more of college, and the differences are consistent with our expectations. The mean share of the adult population of shrinking central cities with four or more years of college in 1960 was 6.3 percent; it was 11.1 percent for growing central cities and nearly 8 percent for positive-turnaround cities. The differences between these types of cities were all statistically significant at the 99 percent confidence level.

The share of adult workers with advanced education grew substantially between 1960 and 2000, so we also examined the relationship between the percentage of adults with higher education in the metropolitan area in 2000 and city population change. The positive-turnaround central cities were in metropolitan areas with the highest mean level of advanced educational achievement in 2000, 26.2 percent, followed by growing central cities at 24.8 percent; the lowest mean attainment level (22.1 percent) was in the metropolitan areas of shrinking central cities. There was a statistically meaningful difference of more than four percentage points between the educational levels of residents of metropolitan areas with positive-turnaround central cities compared with those of shrinking central cities. There were also statistically significant differences between shrinking and growing central cities.

Hypothesis 6A: Increases in labor supply brought about by regional economic growth are expected to be associated with city population growth. We employ the growth rate in gross metropolitan product between 1980 and 2000 to examine this hypothesis.[31] While there was no statistically significant correlation between regional economic growth and city population change at the national level, there was a strong and significant positive correlation in the East North Central states (0.453) and in New England (0.376). In these states, there was a substantial and statistically significant difference between growth in regional economic output in turnaround cities and shrinking cities, with the latter having output growth 11 percentage points than the former between 1980 and 2000.

Hypothesis 6B: Regional amenities are likely to be associated with higher levels of city population growth. There are many types of amenities and people hold widely varying preferences for them. Here we focus only on one amenity, climate, testing the common observation that internal migration is shifting people toward warmer locations. The variable we use is July average temperature, and we expect a positive relationship between that and central city population growth. Indeed, the correlation between the two over this fifty-year period is very high. In the multivariate analysis, an increase in one degree of average July temperature was associated with a 8.7 percentage point increase in central city population from 1960 to 2010.

The relationships among the regional Census Divisions suggest a somewhat different dynamic: a search for less extreme climates, rather than simply for the warmest climate. In the Mountain Division the association between long-term population growth rates and temperature is a very strong 0.644. We note that the Mountain states run the length of the nation, from north to south and cover a wide range of temperatures. In the Middle Atlantic Division the correlation is 0.595, making the July temperature the fourth largest positive correlation for that region. The relationship is reversed in the four East South Central states. These range from Mississippi and Alabama in the Deep South to more temperate Tennessee and Kentucky to the north. The coefficient is a moderately strong negative one, indicating that central city population change in this region is inversely associated with the temperature in midsummer. The true search may be for moderate temperatures, not just pure heat.

Growing central cities have an average July temperature 3.4 degrees above that of the average shrinking city, while positive-turnaround cities have a July temperature 1.4 degrees above that of shrinking cities. The U.S. population appears to be heat-seeking, to the benefit of the supply side of regional labor markets in warm-weather regions of the nation. There is nothing, however, that local and state government can do about their average July temperature.

Hypothesis 7: Cities located in regions with better-quality and more modern infrastructure and with a more "business friendly" environment will likely be associated with greater population growth. We use city age, measured as the number of years between 2010 and the census year when the central city first reached a population of 50,000, as the proxy for city infrastructure quality. A city's age is directly tied to the age of its infrastructure and the cost of maintaining and modernizing that infrastructure, the ability to accommodate modern forms of transport, and the ability of the existing building stock to accommodate modern modes of production and housing. There may also be an indirect association between the economic age of the central city and the composition of its product portfolio. Our expectation was that city age is negatively associated with central city population growth over this time period, which is indeed the case, and the relationship is statistically significant.

In terms of our four types of cities, growing cities are the youngest and therefore presumably have the highest-quality infrastructure. Their mean age is 63.1 years. Shrinking cities are much older, with a mean age of 108.6 years. But the oldest group of cities is the one that is composed of places that are reversing their decline, the positive-turnaround central cities, with a mean age of 111.4 years. The 2.7-year difference in the mean age of shrinking cities and positive-turnaround cities is not statistically significant; the differences between both shrinking and positive-turnaround central cities and growing central cities are large and statistically meaningful.

Regarding business-friendly environments, we use the right-to-work status of the state in which the central city is located as a proxy for the "business friendliness" of a state, as well as for the value some employers place on locating in a regional labor market where the costs of an organized workforce can be avoided. Our expectation was that location in a right-to-work state would be positively associated with central city population growth. The right-to-work state variable was positively associated with central city population growth, as expected, and is statistically significant.

Hypothesis 8A: The presence of research universities in a metropolitan area is likely to be associated with greater central city population growth. We expected a positive correlation between the number of universities in a metropolitan area that the Carnegie Foundation rated "high" or "very high" in terms of their research activity and the city population growth rate. In the multiple regression equation the relationship was statistically significant, at the 90 percent confidence level. If a metropolitan area were able to increase the number of research intense universities by 1, the fifty-year population growth rate would increase by 36 percentage points.

Moreover, those central cities that have experienced a positive-turnaround have, on average, more research universities than do the other groups of central cities. They have, on average, two such universities, compared with 1.08 for the average growing central city, and 1.10 for the average shrinking central city. This finding, combined with that on educational attainment, suggests that research universities have played a role in the turnaround of formerly shrinking central cities.

This expectation was not met in the correlation analysis. While the correlation between the two variables was positive, it was not statistically significant.

Hypothesis 8B: Agglomeration economies and density are expected to be associated with central city population growth. This expectation could not be supported by our statistical findings. Central city density, as measured by population per acre in 1980, was negatively correlated with the growth rate of central city populations from 1960 to 2010. In the multivariate analysis, city density is statistically significant from having no effect: For every additional person per acre in 1980, central city populations declined from 1960 to 2010 by 20.5 percentage points. Mean density in growing central cities was 5.67 people per acre, which is much lower than the density of 7.23 people per acre in shrinking cities. What muddies the waters a bit is the fact that in Table 3 the differences in the mean number of people per acre between each of the groups of cities were not statistically different from each other. We interpret the different results between the regression equation and the difference in means tests as indicating that at very high levels of density the costs of congestion outweigh the benefits of intense economic interaction.

Intraregional, or intrametropolitan area, competitive position

Hypothesis 9: It is expected that greater increases in regional population will be associated with greater increases in central city population. This would be true even if even if the share of the regional increase was lower in the central city than in the remainder of the area. The strongest statistical association between any independent variable and the percent change in central city population is the percent change in metropolitan area population from 1980 to 2000, where the correlation coefficient is 0.380. This is followed closely by the correlation between metropolitan area employment growth from 1970 to 2007 and central city population growth.

Of all of the factors studied, these two regional variables have the most consistent impact of all of the factors studied on differences in the central city population growth rates. The mean regional population and employment growth rates distinguish the performance of shrinking central cities from growing central cities, shrinking central cities from central cities that have experienced a positive-turnaround from decline and those that have gone through a negative-turnaround from growing central cities. Repeating our earlier statement: The lesson is that the economy is regional, as are population dynamics that are derived from economic performance.

Hypothesis 10: The historical flow of international migration to a city is expected to be positively associated with population growth. We found no statistical association between overall immigration and central city population growth. Given the importance of Hispanic immigration, we looked just at the percent of central city population that is Hispanic in 1970 with the expectation that chain migration would play an important role in attracting further waves of Hispanic residents to central cities. However, the percent of the central city population that was Hispanic in 1970 was not correlated with central city population growth rates from 1960 to 2010 nationally; the only statistically positive relationship was in the Middle Atlantic region, where the coefficient was a very strong 0.654.

However, there are statistically significant differences in the means of this variable between shrinking and growing cities—the 1970 mean for city Hispanic population was nearly 6 percentage points higher in growing central cities and 1.7 percentage points higher in positive-turnaround central cities when compared with shrinking central cities.

We also introduced the percent of a metropolitan region's population that was Hispanic in 2000 to capture the association with more current migration chains. The regional share of the population that was Hispanic in 2000 had the fourth-highest positive relationship with central city population change from 1960 to 2010. The correlation between the percent of a metropolitan region's population that was Hispanic in 2000 and population change from 2000 to 2010 was even higher.

Growing central cities had a much higher share of Hispanic residents in their metropolitan area population than did any other type of central city in 2000. The difference was nearly 12 percentage points higher for growing central cities compared with shrinking cities. The positive-turnaround cities had, on average, 3.7 percentage points more Hispanic residents in their metropolitan area than did shrinking cities. This difference also appears for cities that we termed negative-turnaround. It is, of course, difficult to determine the chronological or causal relationships involved: Does attracting Hispanic immigrants lead to growth and turnaround, or are Hispanic immigrants attracted to the economic opportunities that exist in growing and positive-turnaround cities?

The ability to take advantage of new and emerging sources of international chain migration allows central cities to continue their historical function as gateways to the U.S. economy and social integration. Migrants, however, are economically rational, heading toward work and job opportunities. While there are information lags and imperfections that will direct migrants to long-established gateways, this should dissipate over time. We note that migrants are increasingly choosing to live outside central cities if work opportunities are located elsewhere in the metropolitan area.

Hypothesis 11: Cities that have the ability to annex land on their borders are expected to be able to increase their populations more rapidly than those that are unable or unwilling to do so. The correlation analysis found that, across the national set of central cities, the association between the percentage of land area a central city added between 1990 and 2000 and its percent change in population from 1960 to 2010, while positive, as expected, and statistically significant, was trivial. This may be because the public policy variable covers only a ten-year time span (consistent data from before this point in time could not be found). The mean percent change in the land area of growing central cities from 1990 to 2000 was 26 percent; compared with 1 percent for shrinking cities. The mean percent change in the land area of positive-turnaround cities was 24.5 percent. Despite the size of the difference between shrinking cities and positive-turnaround cities, the difference was not statistically significant.

Factors that directly bear on household locational choice

Hypothesis 12: The quality of the city public school system is likely to be positively related to central city population change. Unfortunately, we could not test this important hypothesis, since we were unable to locate consistent data on K to 12 educational performance at the municipal level for the start of the time period examined.

Hypothesis 13: Higher rates of city crime are expected to be associated with population movement from the central city to suburbs and thus result in lower city population. Our measure of crime was the number of reported robberies in 1992 per 100,000 residents of the central city. We expected the variable to be negatively associated with central city population growth over the time period examined.

The crime variable was both negative and large; it had the third-highest negative association with population change (-0.189) and was highly statistically significant. Using the multivariate analysis to control for other variables we find that an increase of 100 robberies per 100,000 residents in 1992 was associated with a decline of 0.355 percentage points in central city population from 1960 to 2010. The correlation between crime and city population change was significant in seven of the nine Census Divisions, the exceptions being the Middle Atlantic and Mountain Divisions.

There were major differences in 1992 crime rates between the different groups of central cities. The lowest rate was for growing central cities, with a rate of 265 per 100,000 residents, while the crime rate for shrinking central cities was 486. Surprisingly, the rate was highest for the positive-turnaround cities, at 494 per 100,000 people, and not significantly different from that for shrinking cities.

That raises the question of whether crime rates have dropped for the positive-turnaround cities since 1992 and whether this decline was associated with the turnaround. To evaluate this, we examined the crime rate for the four types of cities in 2007. The mean reported rate was 319 per 100,000 residents in positive-turnaround cities compared with 383 per 100,000 residents in shrinking cities, a statistically significant difference at the 90 percent confidence level. This indicates that over the 1992 to 2007 period positive-turnaround cities increasingly distinguished themselves from shrinking cities in terms of crime reduction. The correlation coefficient between the crime rate in 2007 and the long-term central city population growth rate was the highest negative correlation we observed.

Hypothesis 14: A higher rate of poverty among central city residents is expected to be associated with city population decline. We included the percentage of families living in central cities with incomes below $3,000 in 1960 as the measure of poverty with the expectation that it would be negatively associated with the long-term city population growth rate. At the national level there was no statistical association between the family poverty variables and the percent change in central city populations from 1960 to 2010. There were only very small differences in 1960 poverty among the four types of cities, none of which were statistically significant. To the extent that there are significant differences in poverty level today among the four city types, they are likely to be the product of other forces.

Hypothesis 15: It was hypothesized that rapid racial succession and negative attitudes among white residents toward African-Americans integrating neighborhoods added a propulsive force to suburbanization during the late 1960s through the 1970s. Our expectation was that the retention of the white population would be inversely associated with the percentage of African-Americans in the city population in 1960 and that population loss would be associated with white flight. We also hypothesized that the frequency and intensity of racially identified riots or civil disturbances from 1964 to 1971 would stimulate white flight and long-term population loss.

Our expectation was correct in that the percentage of the central city's population defined as African–American in 1960 is negatively associated with the central city population growth rate from 1960 to 2010 at the 95 percent confidence interval. The association is weak, however, with a correlation coefficient of -0.100. The negative associations between these variables are much stronger, however, in three of the Census Divisions: East North Central (-0.527), West North Central (-0.385), and South Atlantic (-0.363).

We also hypothesized that the frequency and intensity of racially identified riots or civil disturbances from 1964 to 1971 would stimulate white flight and long-term population loss. Collins and Margo provided the index for our use. [32] The results for this variable are similar to those of the African-American share of 1960 city population. There is a negative association, but it is weak, with a correlation coefficient of -0.083 for the universe of central cities. The only Census Division where the variable had an impact that was significant at the 95 percent confidence level was the East North Central Division, where the correlation coefficient was a modest -0.270. This division contains Ohio, Michigan, Indiana, Illinois, and Wisconsin, where intense race riots took place.

Shrinking central cities had higher shares of African-American residents in their population in 1960 (14.4 percent) than did growing central cities (9.1 percent) and positive-turnaround cities (12.7 percent). There is a statistically meaningful difference between shrinking and growing cities in terms of the racial makeup of their populations in 1960, but not between shrinking and positive-turnaround cities.

Summary and Implications

We have examined a variety of hypotheses related to the population growth or decline of central cities over the past half century. Many of these hypotheses underlie, although usually implicitly, widely used or proposed local economic development policies. What can we learn from these results?

Correlation analysis

Our correlation analysis indicated that city population change is associated with the following at various levels of strength:

Strongest Positive Association

- Long-term metropolitan area population growth rate; i.e., slow-growing regional population growth is associated with slow-growing or declining city population.
- Long-term metropolitan area employment growth rate, i.e., slow-growing regional employment growth is associated with slow-growing or declining city population.

Moderately Strong Positive Association

- Amenities as measured by average July temperature: Extreme climates, particularly cold climates, are associated with declining central city population. We saw signs that population movements may be toward moderate temperature rather than toward pure heat.

- Hispanic share of the metropolitan area population in 2000; i.e., cities in regions with higher proportions of Hispanic households are likely to grow faster than those with lower, though the direction of this association is uncertain—that is, Hispanic migration may be leading job and native population growth into the metropolitan area or following it.
- Business-friendliness as measured by the existence of state right-to-work legislation. Cities in states with such legislation experience greater population growth; those in states without it are more likely to suffer population declines.

Moderate Negative Association

- Employment in the health care sector: Cities in metropolitan areas with a greater proportion of employment in health care jobs in 2000 were more likely to experience population decline.
- City crime rate: Cities with higher crime rates are more likely to experience population decline.
- City population density in 1980: Dense central cities had lower population growth rates than did less dense central cities.
- Employment in the manufacturing sector: Cities with a higher percentage of employed city residents working in manufacturing in 1960 were more likely to experience population decline.
- Infrastructure quality as measured by city age: Older cities, with presumed lower infrastructure quality, were more likely to experience population loss between 1960 and 2010.

Weak Negative Association

- Racial succession and white flight. Cities with a higher proportion of the city population that was African-American in 1960 and those that experienced more intense central city civil disturbances from 1964 to 1971 had slower population growth.

Differences between positive-turnaround cities and shrinking cities

We are particularly interested in the differences between shrinking central cities and positive-turnaround central cities, which declined immediately after 1960 but whose 2010 population was greater than its population in 2000. We find that, compared to shrinking cities, positive-turnaround cities were more likely to:

- be located in metropolitan areas whose population, employment, and gross metropolitan product were more rapidly increasing;

- have had a lower proportion of their residents employed in the manufacturing sector in 1960;
- have slightly older infrastructure;
- have lower crime rates;
- have a greater number of research universities in the metropolitan area; and
- have a higher proportion of residents with higher education

In many respects the positive-turnaround cities were from the beginning of the period midway between shrinking cities and growing cites, in the sense that their conditions for the factors related to population change were not as good as those in growing cities nor as poor as those in shrinking cities. The result was that these cities declined for a period and then bounced back.

There are, however, a few positive-turnaround cities whose conditions were as bad as or worse than those of many shrinking cities in earlier years. Philadelphia, a positive-turnaround central city, had a four percentage point higher poverty rate in 1980 than did Pittsburgh, a shrinking city, and more of Philadelphia's 1960 employed population worked in manufacturing than Pittsburgh's (33.2 percent versus 26.1 percent), In 1960, Newark's poverty rate nearly equaled that of Detroit (18.9 percent versus 19.0 percent) and its share of manufacturing workers in its population was similar—36.2 percent and 37.4 percent. Newark is a turnaround story, and Detroit is the poster child for population loss, prompting one to speculate about the effect of the former's proximity to the economic dynamo that is New York City. The positive-turnaround central cities certainly are worth further investigation to determine the reasons for their turnaround.

What are the implications for city and regional economic development policies? Clearly some of the factors that distinguish growing from shrinking cities, and particularly shrinking from positive-turnaround cities, are beyond the control of cities, and others are beyond their control in at least the short term. For example, cities cannot change their climate, nor can they escape their historical legacy as manufacturing centers. The educational attainment of their labor force is subject to change, but only slowly.

There is much, however, in our analysis that can inform city action. First, city economic and population performance is highly conditioned upon population, employment, and overall growth of the region as a whole. As noted elsewhere,[33] there are hardly any examples of growing cities in slow-growing or declining regions. This stark conclusion should emphasize the importance of focusing on regional growth as opposed to simply city growth. Regional growth may not necessarily ensure city growth or health, but city growth and health are not likely to occur without regional growth.

Implications of our findings for City Economic Development Strategies

Human Capital Strategies

Our findings, as well as other research, indicate that these strategies are well founded, although the evidence from our analysis was rather modest. Nonetheless, positive-turnaround cities had a higher percentage of residents with higher education than did shrinking cities and also were in metropolitan areas with a higher percentage of such residents than were shrinking cities. What is not clear is how the increase occurred. Were the additional highly educated adult workers locally grown? Or were they attracted to the region by career opportunities, lifestyle amenities, or local higher educational institutions and found jobs in the regional economy?

Eds and Meds Strategies

The evidence here was mixed. The presence of research universities in the metropolitan regions mattered for central city population growth, and the more there were, the more it mattered. This certainly suggests that cities should do whatever they can to take advantage of this presence to assist in translating knowledge creation into viable new products, company relocations, and new industry formation. It also suggests that encouraging existing universities that are not heavily engaged in research to do so could be productive. In this context, the research arms of major health care complexes are more like the "eds" than the "meds," because they are primarily research organizations and their products are traded services.

The "meds" part of the strategy is more problematic. We found no evidence that the percentage of workers in the health care sector of the average city has any positive effect on population growth. Fostering a city or region's health care sector as an economic development strategy may make sense only if that sector includes a strong health care research component or if it provides substantial services to people from outside the metropolitan area for treatment—that is, it functions as an export industry or traded service rather than as part of the local service sector.

We recognize that the medical sector generates large numbers of jobs across a very broad range of skills and occupations in nearly all central cities. The "meds" in central cities where the medical industry does not export its services beyond the region can be an anchor institution, but its existence depends on the continued ability of health care institutions located in the central city to defend their market shares against competing suburban institutions. In these cities staffing medical facilities is both a workforce and anti-poverty strategy and a community development issue.

Improving Infrastructure as a Means of Increasing Productivity

Our evidence supports this strategy. We approximate the infrastructure quality in a city by estimating its economic age; while nothing can be done to change city age, older cities can renew their infrastructure and increase its quality. While shrinking cities are much older than growing cities, positive-turnaround cities are just as old as shrinking cities, which suggests the possibility that one factor in their turnaround was that these cities improved their infrastructure more than shrinking cities.

Agglomeration Effects

Our correlation analysis shows a strong negative relationship between agglomeration economies as measured by density at the city level and central city population growth. The multivariate analysis, which controls for other variables, also found a negative relationship. This is contrasted with a body of existing research that demonstrates that agglomeration economies at the regional level are positively related to economic growth primarily at the regional level. While density at the level of the central city may not be the best indicator of agglomeration economies, our use of it does not support the observation of density's positive effect on central city population growth.

Improving City Public services as an Economic Development Strategy: Crime Reduction and Education Quality

The evidence shows that crime rates are strongly associated with population decline and that cities that have experienced a positive-turnaround have reduced their crime rates below those of shrinking cities. While we were unable to analyze data on the quality of education provided by the public school system, a substantial body of existing research links perceived poor school quality with decisions by families with children to move to the suburbs.

Conclusion

We conclude by returning to the question posed at the start of this chapter: Have the various development strategies worked in achieving urban regeneration, or at least in changing the development trajectory of central cities? The answer is a qualified yes.

Our key finding is that nothing supports central city population growth better than being in a fast-growing region with growing employment. In other words, economic opportunity promotes population growth. People and businesses are attracted to regional economies that provide economic opportunity. Regional growth in residential and business locations is then distributed across the region according to the value propositions offered by competing jurisdictions. The interregional competitive position of the region and of its central cities is hypothesized to depend in large part on the competitive position of its products and of its factors of production. The intraregional distribution of people and work then takes place as jurisdictions compete for regional market shares of population and business activity based on services provided, amenities, and cost.

At the heart of any central city's ability to retain population or not to shrink are two central propositions: Successful metropolitan areas have an economic purpose and through that purpose income and opportunity are generated, and successful central cities offer competitive residential services within the context of the broader regional economy. In other words, cities should cooperate with the metropolitan region on economic development but compete with other jurisdictions in the region on community development.

The ability of the region to reload its product portfolio and to overcome the challenges that economic age brings to both the built environment and the product portfolio is fundamental to its economic success. Buildings must be recycled, and the economy must promote flexibility, especially in the labor market.

In conclusion, while some population loss and economic hardship was probably all but inevitable for cities that were perilously positioned in 1960, continued decline is not inevitable, as shown by those cities that had a positive-turnaround after a period of decline. Our findings should be useful in helping to better understand both the forces that contributed to those turnarounds and the economic development strategies and activities that can promote similar turnarounds elsewhere.

Notes

1. The 2007 definitions of Metropolitan Statistical Areas (MSA) were used throughout. Naming conventions were in accordance to the Metropolitan Statistical Area designation of the U.S. Office of Management and Budget. Due to data limitations, the central cities of Puerto Rico were not included.
2. This set of selection criteria is similar to that used by Wolman et al. (2008).
3. We decided to begin this investigation in 1960 for three reasons. First, population patterns in 1950 were an aberration. Cities were extremely crowded, and the twenty-year hiatus in building caused by the Great Depression and World War II was just beginning to end in 1950. Second, the great social and technological innovations that allowed the suburbanization of population and industry in America were just being unleashed—the nationwide spread of limited- access highways, popularly priced and financed automobile consumption, and the acceptance of low- down- payment, declining- balance mortgages with the express purpose of promoting single-family home ownership—were just being unleashed. Third, 1960 predates three major political and legal events that changed the structure of urban America: the passage of the Civil Rights Act in 1964, the series of summer race riots that took place from 1964 to 1970, and the spread of busing to promote school desegregation outside of the American South during the early 1970s. White flight began in many cities with the escalation in racial tensions associated with the civil disturbances of the mid- to late-1960s and frequently accelerated with court-ordered busing and the integration of public schools.
4. The complete list of central cities and their assigned status are posted in a searchable database on the Levin College of Urban Affairs Web site: http://urban.csuohio.edu/research/. It is also available on the Web site of the George Washington Institute of Public Policy: http://www.gwu.edu/~gwipp/
5. The S-curve is derived from the product-cycle and incorporates the incubation, take-off, and maturation phases of the cycle. See Christensen (1992) and Skinner (1996).
6. This is a variation of the hypothesis posed by Benjamin Chinitz in his 1961 article, where he posited that industry organizational structure and market power of a region's dominant industries influences the path and composition of development.
7. Markusen (1985).
8. Cantwell (1995), pp. 155-174, and Vernon (1966, 1979), pp. 190-207, 255-267.
9. Hill and Brennan (2000), pp. 65-96.
10. Hill and Bier (1989), pp. 123-144
11. Baumol (1963, 1967) showed how residents who place a high value on city services may move as services are cut to match a declining tax base and others may move in response to higher tax payments for diminished service provision.
12. Beauregard (2006) and Hill and Brennan (2005), pp. 65-96
13. Push factors are at work on the regional level as well. Businesses can be attracted to locations with business-friendly operating environments. That is, those with low business taxes, responsive bureaucracies, cooperative labor-management relations systems, right-to-work legislation, and comparatively low operating costs (Blumenthal et al., 2009). Since the 1960s the U.S. population has also been showing signs of being attracted to metropolitan areas that are warmer in the winter.
14. This is a conclusion we reached in an earlier article (Hill, et al., 1995).
15. Reich (1991).

16. Hill and Wolman (1997), pp. 558-582.
17. The reservation wage is the lowest wage that a person is willing to accept to begin work.
18. Cortright (2002), pp. 3-16; Glaeser (2010); Florida (2002).
19. Hill and Lendel (2007), pp. 223-243.
20. Clarke and Gail (1998), and Glaeser (2010).
21. Porter (1995, 1997), pp. 55-71, 11-27.
22. Singer (2004).
23. Singer (2008).
24. Rusk (1995, 1999).
25. Berube and Kneebone (2008); Jargowsky (1997).
26. Collins and Margo (2004b); Massey and Denton (1993)
27. This is done by examining the size of the coefficient relative to the number of observations in the sample.
28. Cohen (1988).
29. Strictly speaking, the association between the two variables in the correlation analysis is not one of independence and dependence, because correlations determine only association—the degree to which the levels of the two variables move together. Despite this fact, the term dependent variable is used in the rest of the chapter as a shorthand way of identifying the percent change in central city population from 1960 to 2010, because that variable measures what is of interest in the public policy discussion about the viability of central cities. Similarly, we use the term independent variable to describe the variables in the left-most column of Table 2 because theory, observation, or policy intent identifies them as being part of a simultaneous set of social and economic forces that result in population change in central cities.
30. Critical values for levels of statistical significance are listed in Tables 2 and 3 rather than presented in the text.
31. The first year for which data are available by consistent metropolitan areas is 1980.
32. Collins and Margo (2004a, 2004b).
33. Wolman (2008), pp. 151-178.

Bibliography

Baumol, W. 1967. "Macroeconomics of Unbalanced Growth: The Anatomy of the Urban Crisis." *American Economic Review*. 57 (3): 415—426.

———. 1963. "Urban Services: Interactions of Public and Private Decisions." *Public Expenditure Decisions in the Urban Community*. ed. H. Schaller (ed.). Washington, DC: Resources for the Future, pp.1—18.

Beauregard, R. 2011. "Growth and Depopulation in the United States." *Defining a Future for American Cities Experiencing Severe Population Loss*. ed. Alan Mallach. New York: American Assembly.

———. 2006. *When America Became Suburban*. Minneapolis: University of Minnesota Press.

Berube, A. and Kneebone, E. 2008. *The Enduring Challenge of Concentrated Poverty in America*. Washington, DC: The Metropolitan Policy Program of the Brookings Institution.

Blumenthal, P., Wolman, H., and Hill, E. 2009. "Understanding the Economic Performance of Metropolitan Areas in the United States." *Urban Studies*. 46 (3): 605—627.

Cantwell, J. 1995. "The Globalization of Technology: What Remains of the Product Cycle?" *Cambridge Journal of Economics*. 19 (1): 155—174.

Chinitz, B. 1961. "Contrasts in Agglomeration: New York and Pittsburgh." *American Economic Review, Papers and Proceedings*. 51 (2): 279—289.

Christensen, C. 1992. "Exploring the Limits of the Technology S-Curve." *Production and Operations Management*. 1 (40): 334—357.

Clarke, S. and Gaile, G. 1998. *The Work of Cities*. Minneapolis: University of Minnesota Press.

Cohen, J. 1988. *Statistical Power Analysis for the Behavioral Sciences*, 2nd ed. Hillsdale, NJ: Lawrence Erlbaum Associates.

Collins, W. and Margo, R. 2004. "The Economic Aftermath of the 1960s Riots: Evidence from Property Values." Cambridge, MA: NBER Working Paper W10493.

———. 2004. "The Labor Market Effects of the 1960s Riots." Cambridge, MA: NBER Working Paper W10243.

Cortright, J. 2002. "The Economic Importance of Being Different: Regional Variation in Tastes, Increasing Returns, and the Dynamic of Development." *Economic Development Quarterly*. 16 (1): 3—16.

———. 2005. *The Young and the Restless in a Knowledge Economy*. Chicago: CEOs for Cities.

Florida, R. 2002. *The Rise of the Creative Class*. New York: Basic Books.

Glaeser, E. 2010. *Triumph of the City*. New York: Penguin.

Hill, E. and Bier, T. 1989. "Economic Restructuring: Earnings, Occupations and Housing Values in Cleveland." *Economic Development Quarterly*. 3 (2): 123--144.

Hill, E. and Brennan. J.. 2005. "America's Central Cities and the Location of Work: Can Cities Compete with their Suburbs?" *Journal of the American Planning Association*. 71 (4): 411—432.

———. 2000. “A Methodology for Identifying the Drivers of Industrial Clusters: The Foundation of Regional Competitive Advantage.” *Economic Development Quarterly*. 14 (1): 65—96.

Hill, E. and Lendel, I. 2007. “The Impact of the Reputation of Bio-Life Science and Engineering Doctoral Programs on Regional Economic Development,” *Economic Development Quarterly*. 21 (3): 223—243.

Hill, E. and Wolman, H. 1997. “City-Suburban Income Disparities and Metropolitan Area Employment: Can Tightening Labor Markets Reduce the Gaps?” *Urban Affairs Review*. 32 (4): 558--582.

Hill, E., Wolman, H. and Ford, C. 1995. “Can Suburbs Survive Without Their Central Cities? Examining the Suburban Dependence Hypothesis.” *Urban Affairs Review*. 31 (2): 147—174.

Jargowsky, P. 1997. *Poverty and Place*. New York: Russell Sage Foundation.

Markusen, A. 1985. *Profit Cycles, Oligopoly, and Regional Development*. Cambridge: MIT Press.

Massey, D. and Denton, N. 1993. *American Apartheid: Segregation and the Making of the Underclass*. Cambridge: Harvard University Press.

Porter, M. 1995. “The Competitive Advantage of the Inner-City,” *Harvard Business Review*. May/June: 55—71.

———. 1997. “New strategies for inner-city economic development.” *Economic Development Quarterly*, February 11(1): 11-27.

Reich, R. 1991. *The Work of Nations*. New York: Vintage Press.

Rusk, D. 1995. *Cities Without Suburbs*. Washington, DC: Woodrow Wilson Center Press.

———. 1999. *Inside Game/Outside Game*. Washington, DC: The Brookings Institution Press.

Singer, A. 2004. *The Rise of New Immigrant Gateways*. Washington, DC: The Metropolitan Policy Program of the Brookings Institution.

Singer, A., Hardwick, S. and Bretell, B. 2008. *Twenty-First-Century Gateways*. Washington, DC: The Brookings Institution Press.

Skinner, W. 1996. “Manufacturing Strategy on the ‘S’ Curve.” *Production and Operations Management*. 1 (4): 334—357.

Vernon, R. 1966. “Investment and International Trade in the Product Cycle.” Quarterly Journal of Economics. 80 (2): 190—207.

———. 1979. “The product cycle hypothesis in a new international environment.” *Oxford Bulletin of Economics and Statistics*. 41 (4): 255—267.

Wolman, H., Hill, E., Blumenthal,P. and Furdell, K. 2008. “Understanding Economically Distressed Cities.” *Retooling for Growth*. ed. McGahey,R. and Vey, J. Washington, DC: The Brookings Institution Press: 151—178.

Appendix 1.

U.S. Bureau of the Census Regions and Divisions

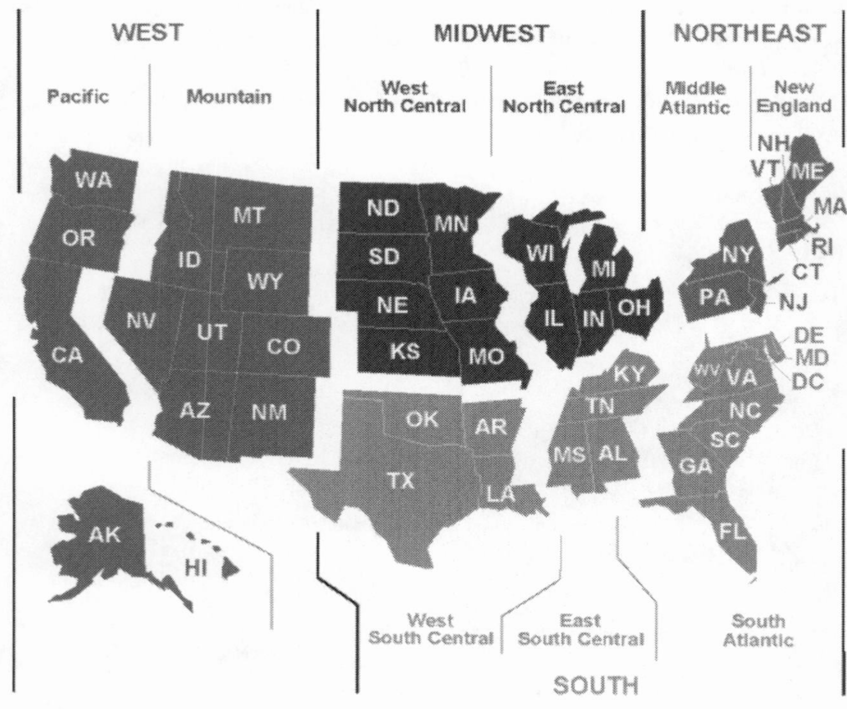

Source: U.S. Bureau of the Census

Appendix 2: Location Quotients for City Type by Census Division

The distribution of central cities in each of the nine Census Divisions by their population classification and the relevant Location Quotients (LQ) are displayed in Tables A-1 and A-2. The data in Table A-1 are sorted by Census Division and include the counts of central cities by type or subset; the population in 1960, 2000, and 2010; and the percent change in population from 1960 to 2000, 2000 to 2010, and 1960 to 2010. The data are rearranged in Table A-2 to make it easier to see whether the subsets of central cities are heavily concentrated in specific Census Divisions. The upper section of Table A-2 contains the data: counts of cities by type (or subset) and by Census Division, and the total population in each city type by Census Division. The percent distribution of each type of city and 2010 population by region are in the middle section of the table. This is the regional distribution of the counts of central cities and population for each city subset. The last section of Table A-2 displays the LQ for each division, reflecting the share of cities by type in each region. What does this data indicate about the geographic distribution of the various types of central cities?

The LQs are calculated by dividing a Census Division's share of the count of a particular subset of central cities by the same Census Division's share of all central cities in the nation. As an example, in the Middle Atlantic Division, the LQ for the number of shrinking cities is 2.90; 43.3 percent of the central cities in the region are shrinking, while shrinking cities constitute 14.9 percent of all major central cities in the nation. The LQ is calculated by dividing 43.3 percent by 14.9 percent, yielding an LQ of 2.90. The LQ indicates that the Middle Atlantic Division has 190 percent more shrinking central cities than expected if the composition, or percent distribution, of central cities in the region mirrored that of the nation as a whole. In terms of the number of central cities, the Middle Atlantic states could be thought of as specializing in shrinking cities and cities experiencing a positive-turnaround in population loss.

Similarly, the LQ for population among shrinking central cities in the Middle Atlantic Division is 0.89. The region's share of central city population living in shrinking cities is 11.2 percent, while the nation's share of the total central city population living in shrinking central cities is 12.6 percent. Therefore, the Middle Atlantic region has a smaller proportion of its central city residents living in shrinking central cities than expected compared with the percentage of central city residents living in shrinking central cities nationally. This means that the Middle Atlantic Division's central city population disproportionately lives in a different type of central city, and they do; they live in positive-turnaround cities.

Table A-1.

The Number of Central Cities and Their Population 1960, 2000, and 2010 by Census Division and Percent change from 2000 to 2010, and 1960 to 2010

Type of Central City	Number of Cities	Population			Percent Population Change		
		1960	2000	2010	1960 - 2000	2000 - 2010	1960 - 2010
United States							
Shrinking	59	16,966,942	12,255,618	11,116,367	-27.8%	-9.3%	-34.5%
Negative-turnaround	41	3,977,714	5,746,809	5,591,941	44.5%	-2.7%	40.6%
Growing	230	19,158,472	44,155,175	49,862,827	130.5%	12.9%	160.3%
Positive-turnaround	65	21,250,951	20,538,070	21,826,853	-3.4%	6.3%	2.7%
Total	395	61,354,079	82,695,672	88,397,988	34.8%	6.9%	44.1%
New England Division							
Shrinking	3	228,023	208,120	201,191	-8.7%	-3.3%	-12.1%
Negative-turnaround	4	242,795	330,306	326,244	36.0%	-1.2%	34.8%
Growing	7	376,254	525,968	546,983	39.8%	4.0%	43.8%
Positive-turnaround	14	2,306,654	2,047,066	2,120,183	-11.3%	3.6%	-7.7%
Total	28	3,153,726	3,111,460	3,194,601	-1.3%	2.7%	1.3%
Middle Atlantic Division							
Shrinking	13	2,433,486	1,523,656	1,436,217	-37.4%	-5.7%	-43.1%
Negative-turnaround	2	334,297	345,308	342,175	3.3%	-0.9%	2.4%
Growing	1	37,685	56,271	60,724	49.3%	7.9%	57.2%
Positive-turnaround	14	11,349,895	10,749,867	10,976,313	-5.3%	2.1%	-3.2%
Total	30	14,155,363	12,675,102	12,815,429	-10.5%	1.1%	-9.4%
East North Central Division							
Shrinking	22	9,782,110	7,108,720	6,369,293	-27.3%	-10.4%	-37.7%
Negative-turnaround	13	734,517	934,265	901,422	27.2%	-3.5%	23.7%
Growing	31	2,447,867	3,846,256	4,263,897	57.1%	10.9%	68.0%
Positive-turnaround	2	144,854	120,304	123,262	-16.9%	2.5%	-14.5%
Total	68	13,109,348	12,009,545	11,657,874	-8.4%	-2.9%	-11.3%
West North Central Division							
Shrinking	6	1,814,107	1,258,636	1,224,295	-30.6%	-2.7%	-33.3%
Negative-turnaround	1	56,606	57,686	57,637	1.9%	-0.1%	1.8%
Growing	16	1,342,519	2,068,189	2,299,755	54.1%	11.2%	65.2%
Positive-turnaround	4	883,678	836,594	867,473	-5.3%	3.7%	-1.6%
Total	27	4,096,910	4,221,105	4,449,160	3.0%	5.4%	8.4%
South Atlantic Division							
Shrinking	7	1,351,955	973,053	924,341	-28.0%	-5.0%	-33.0%
Negative-turnaround	7	393,066	810,602	792,893	106.2%	-2.2%	104.0%
Growing	45	2,228,462	6,396,226	7,599,169	187.0%	18.8%	205.8%
Positive-turnaround	13	2,757,776	2,601,227	2,765,087	-5.7%	6.3%	0.6%
Total	72	6,731,259	10,781,108	12,081,490	60.2%	12.1%	72.2%
East South Central Division							
Shrinking	2	543,666	441,735	407,348	-18.7%	-7.8%	-26.5%
Negative-turnaround	4	716,203	956,127	932,250	33.5%	-2.5%	31.0%
Growing	13	826,459	1,800,807	2,002,087	117.9%	11.2%	129.1%
Positive-turnaround	2	525,032	457,799	946,860	-12.8%	106.8%	94.0%
Total	21	2,611,360	3,656,468	4,288,545	40.0%	17.3%	57.3%
West South Central Division							
Shrinking	5	813,595	686,494	523,794	-15.6%	-23.7%	-39.3%
Negative-turnaround	3	470,094	648,279	640,300	37.9%	-1.2%	36.7%
Growing	36	4,766,900	10,042,174	11,420,814	110.7%	13.7%	124.4%
Positive-turnaround	7	690,007	807,285	866,499	17.0%	7.3%	24.3%
Total	51	6,740,596	12,184,232	13,451,407	80.8%	10.4%	91.2%
Mountain Division							
Growing	32	1,745,029	6,692,794	7,684,648	283.5%	14.8%	298.4%
Positive Turnaround	3	726,846	789,390	846,064	8.6%	7.2%	15.8%
Total	35	2,471,875	7,482,184	8,530,712	202.7%	14.0%	216.7%
Pacific Division							
Shrinking	1	0	55,204	29,888		-45.9%	-45.9%
Negative-turnaround	7	1,030,136	1,664,236	1,599,020	61.6%	-3.9%	57.6%
Growing	49	5,387,297	12,726,490	13,984,750	136.2%	9.9%	146.1%
Positive-turnaround	6	1,866,209	2,128,538	2,315,112	14.1%	8.8%	22.8%
Total	63	8,283,642	16,574,468	17,928,770	100.1%	8.2%	108.3%

Table A-2.

Distribution and the Location Quotients of the Number Central Cities and Population Living in Central Cities by Type and Census Division

	Number of Central Cities by Type					*2010 Population by Type of Central City*				
Census Division	Shrinking	Negative-turnaround	Growing	Positive turnaround	Total number of central cities	Shrinking	Negative-turnaround	Growing	Positive turnaround	Total central city population
Nation (total)	59	41	230	65	395	11116367	5,591,941	49862827	21826853	88,397,988
New England	3	4	7	14	28	201,191	326,244	546,983	2,120,183	3,194,601
Middle Atlantic	13	2	1	14	30	1,436,217	342,175	60,724	10976313	12,815,429
East North Central	22	13	31	2	68	6,369,293	901,422	4,263,897	123,262	11,657,874
West North Central	6	1	16	4	27	1,224,295	57,637	2,299,755	867,473	4,449,160
South Atlantic	7	7	45	13	72	924,341	792,893	7,599,169	2,765,087	12,081,490
East South Central	2	4	13	2	21	407,348	932,250	2,002,087	946,860	4,288,545
West South Central	5	3	36	7	51	523,794	640,300	11420814	866,499	13,451,407
Mountain			32	3	35			7,684,648	846,064	8,530,712
Pacific	1	7	49	6	63	29,888	1,599,020	13984750	2,315,112	17,928,770
	Percent Distribution of Central Cities by Type by Division					*Percent Distribution of 2010 Population by Type of Central City*				
Census Division	Shrinking	Negative-turnaround	Growing	Positive turnaround	Percent of US central cities	Shrinking	Negative-turnaround	Growing	Positive turnaround	Percent US central city population
Nation (total)	14.9%	10.4%	58.2%	16.5%	100.0%	12.6%	6.3%	56.4%	24.7%	100.0%
New England	10.7%	14.3%	25.0%	50.0%	7.1%	6.3%	10.2%	17.1%	66.4%	3.6%
Middle Atlantic	43.3%	6.7%	3.3%	46.7%	7.6%	11.2%	2.7%	0.5%	85.6%	14.5%
East North Central	32.4%	19.1%	45.6%	2.9%	17.2%	54.6%	7.7%	36.6%	1.1%	13.2%
West North Central	22.2%	3.7%	59.3%	14.8%	6.8%	27.5%	1.3%	51.7%	19.5%	5.0%
South Atlantic	9.7%	9.7%	62.5%	18.1%	18.2%	7.7%	6.6%	62.9%	22.9%	13.7%
East South Central	9.5%	19.0%	61.9%	9.5%	5.3%	9.5%	21.7%	46.7%	22.1%	4.9%
West South Central	9.8%	5.9%	70.6%	13.7%	12.9%	3.9%	4.8%	84.9%	6.4%	15.2%
Mountain	0.0%	0.0%	91.4%	8.6%	8.9%			90.1%	9.9%	9.7%
Pacific	1.6%	11.1%	77.8%	9.5%	15.9%	0.2%	8.9%	78.0%	12.9%	20.3%
	Location Quotient: Number of Central Cities by Type					*Location Quotient: Population by Type of Central City*				
Census Division	Shrinking	Negative-turnaround	Growing	Positive turnaround		Shrinking	Negative-turnaround	Growing	Positive turnaround	Percent US central city population
Nation (total)	0.72	**1.38**	0.43	**3.04**		0.50	**1.61**	0.30	**2.69**	
New England	**2.90**	0.64	0.06	**2.84**		0.89	0.42	0.01	**3.47**	
Middle Atlantic	**2.17**	**1.84**	0.78	0.18		**4.34**	**1.22**	0.65	0.04	
East North Central	**1.49**	0.36	*1.02*	0.90		**2.19**	0.20	0.92	0.79	
West North Central	0.65	0.94	*1.07*	*1.10*		0.61	*1.04*	*1.12*	0.93	
South Atlantic	0.64	**1.84**	*1.06*	0.58		0.76	**3.44**	0.83	0.89	
East South Central	0.66	0.57	**1.21**	0.83		0.31	0.75	**1.51**	0.26	
West South Central			**1.57**	0.52				**1.60**	0.40	
Mountain	0.11	*1.07*	**1.34**	0.58		0.01	**1.41**	**1.38**	0.52	
Pacific	1.6%	11.1%	77.8%	9.5%		0.2%	8.9%	78.0%	12.9%	

Notes:

Bold type indicates the LQ is greater than 1.20, meaning that the number of cities or population is at least 20% larger than expected based on the Division's proportionate share of population or the number of cities.

Italics type indicates that the LQ is between 1.00 and 1.20, meaning the number of cities or population in the category is above its proportionate share but less than 20 percent greater.

Appendix 3.

Multivariate Model of Central City Population Change from 1960 to 2010

Dependent variable			
Percent change in central city population from 1960 to 2010			
Independent Variables	*Coefficient*	*Significance Level*	*Standard Error*
Percent change in MSA employment from 1970 to 2007	0.98	**	0.39
Average July temperature	8.70		8.11
Percentage of MSA population that is Hispanic in 2000	3.13		2.72
Right-to-work state in 1960	19.51		101.34
Annexation: percent change in land area 1990-2000	0.31		0.53
Percentage of MSA population age 25+ with bachelor's degree or higher in 2000	-0.36		7.09
Percentage of central city families with incomes below $3,000 in 1960	-1.83		6.17
Number of Universities in MSA that are high or very high in research activity	36.09	*	21.74
Percent change in MSA GDP per capita from 1980 to 2000	0.02		1.59
Intensity of central city civil disturbances from 1964 to 1971	684.91		736.59
Percentage of central city population that was African-American in 1960	-1.58		4.70
Percentage of MSA jobs in the manufacturing sector in 2000	0.46		7.33
City age	0.77		1.09
Percentage of employed central city residents working in manufacturing in 1960	-2.54		3.77
Central city robberies per 100,000 residents in 1992	-0.36	**	0.16
Central city population density in 1980	-20.47	*	12.06
Percentage of MSA jobs in health care sector in 2000	-30.73	**	13.40
Number of observations	357		
R2	0.18		

Notes:

Significance levels: *** $p<0.01$, ** $p<0.05$, * $p<0.1$

Variables are defined in Tables 2 and 3.

Appendix 4: Within-Region Correlations

There were interesting regional variations in the pattern of associations, each of which provides insights on economic development strategies. The strongest correlates of central city population growth from five of the Census Divisions are presented below. We included all that were statistically significant at the 0.95 percent confidence interval.

Northeast Region

New England	*Correlation Coefficient*
Percent change in MSA GDP per capita from 1980 to 2000[2]	0.376
Percentage of MSA population age 25+ with bachelor's degree or higher in 2000	0.356
Percentage of central city families with incomes below $3,000 in 1960	-0.365
Central city robberies per 100,000 residents in 1992	-0.367
Percentage of MSA jobs in health care sector in 2000	-0.406
Central city population density in 1980	-0.512
Number of central cities: 28	
Middle Atlantic	
Percentage of MSA population that is Hispanic in 2000	0.685
Percentage of central city population that is Hispanic in 1970	0.654
Percent change in MSA population from 1980 to 2000[1]	0.620
Average July temperature	0.595
Number of central cities: 30	

Midwest Region

East North Central	*Correlation Coefficient*
Percent change in MSA population from 1980 to 2000[1]	0.496
Percent change in MSA GDP per capita from 1980 to 2000[2]	0.453
Percent change in MSA employment from 1970 to 2007[2]	0.434
Annexation: percent change in land area from 1990 to 2000	0.426
Percentage of central city population age 25+ with 4 or more years of college in 1960	0.377
Average July temperature	0.320
Percentage of MSA population age 25+ with bachelor's degree or higher in 2000	0.308
Percentage of central city populaiton that was foreign born in 1970	-0.218
Intensity of central city civil disturbances deom 1964 to 1971	-0.270
Central city population density in 1980[3]	-0.382
Percentage of MSA jobs in health care sector in 2000	-0.383
Percentage of central city families with incomes below $3,000 in 1960	-0.483
Central city robberies per 100,000 residents in 1992	-0.505
Percentage of central city population that was African-American in 1960	-0.527
Number of central cities: 68	

West North Central	*Correlation Coefficient*
Percent change in MSA employment from 1970 to 2007[2]	0.778
Percent city population (25+) with 4 or more years of college 1960	0.705
Percent change in MSA population from 1980 to 2000[1]	0.541
Percent MSA population (25+) with bachelor's degree or higher 2000	0.521
Annexation: percent change in land area from 1990 to 2000	0.484
Percentage of central city populaiton that was African-American in 1960	-0.385
Central city robberies per 100,000 residents in 1992	-0.491
Percent employed city residents working in manufacturing 1960	-0.635
City age[5]	-0.710
Number of central cities: 27	

South Region

South Atlantic	*Correlation Coefficient*
Percent change in MSA GDP per capita from 1980 to 2000[2]	-0.203
Percentage of employed central city residents working in manufacturing in 1960	-0.241
Central city population density in 1980[3]	-0.264
Central city robberies per 100,000 residents in 1992	-0.285
Percentage of central city population that was African-American in 1960	-0.363
Number of central cities: 72	
East South Central	
Percentage of MSA population that is Hispanic in 2000	0.764
Percent change in MSA population from 1980 to 2000[1]	0.616
Percentage of central city families with incomes below $3,000 in 1960	0.450
Central city robberies per 100,000 residents in 1992	-0.416
Average July temperature	-0.418
Central city population density in 1980[3]	-0.526
Right-to-work state in 1960	-0.646
Number of central cities: 21	
West South Central	
Number of Universities in MSA that are high or very high in research activity4	0.392
Percent change in MSA population from 1980 to 20001	0.293
Percentage of MSA population age 25+ with bachelor's degree or higher in 2000	0.273
Percentage of employed central city residents working in manufacturing in 1960	0.235
Central city robberies per 100,000 residents in 1992	-0.256
Number of central cities: 51	

West Region

Mountain	*Correlation Coefficient*
Percent change in MSA employment from 1970 to 2007[2]	0.654
Percent change in MSA population from 1980 to 2000[1]	0.649
Average July temperature	0.644
Right-to-work state in 1960	0.379
Percentage of MSA jobs in health care sector in 2000	-0.369
Central city population density in 1980[3]	-0.468
Number of central cities: 28	
Pacific	
Percentage of central city population that was African-American in 1960	-0.219
Central city robberies per 100,000 residents in 1992	-0.264
Number of central cities: 63	

Notes:

1. A common Metropolitan Statistical Area (MSA) definition was used for all years based on the 2003 MSA definitions of the U.S. Office of Management and Budget. Data were provided by the Building Resilient Regions Network.
2. Data obtained from Moody's Analytics' Economy.com data service. MSAs were based on 2003 definitions and were constructed from Economy.com's county data files.
3. Population density: City data are primarily from 1980; 1990 data were substituted for 12 central cities where 1980 data were unavailable. Two cities were omitted because 1980 and 1990 data were unavailable.
4. Research university: Number of universities in the MSA classified by the Carnegie Foundation as having either "high" or "very high" research activity.
5. City age: Number of years from the Census decade in which the central city reached a population of 50,000 to 2010.

Case Study: Pittsburgh Goes High Tech

Sabina Deitrick, University of Pittsburgh

In August 2009, the White House announced Pittsburgh as the site for the next G20 meeting. For many, the Steel City was an odd choice, but the selection was not based on the smokestack view of Pittsburgh. A new picture of Pittsburgh had taken shape. In the twenty-five years since the steel industry had collapsed, the Rust Belt relic revealed impressive gains in advanced technology, health care, life sciences, education, financial services, green building, and, indeed, manufacturing, now of specialized production with tightly linked services and engineering. Pittsburgh's revitalization in the face of economic restructuring was the appeal of its location.

The Pittsburgh case provides an interesting comparison to Youngstown and Cleveland in understanding shrinking cities. It suggests a stock but probably accurate rhetorical question: Is the glass half-empty or half-full? Is Pittsburgh a model of a resilient city in the Rust Belt? Is Pittsburgh distinguished from other shrinking cities? And what can be learned about the changes taking place?

Pittsburgh stands with Cleveland and Youngstown on a number of indicators, starting at or near the top on the defining measure of shrinking cities—population loss. The number of residents today is less than half what it was in the city's peak period in the middle of the twentieth century, with another expected decline, though slower, with the 2010 population figures. The city's population was once 45 percent of the central county population (Allegheny County), down to 25 percent today, in a county that has also lost population over half a century.

Pittsburgh's decline preceded that of other industrial places. By the middle of the twentieth century, regional analysts already recognized the difference in population change in the Pittsburgh region compared to that in other cities in the country: "Pittsburgh's sluggish population growth stands out as almost unique among metropolitan areas."[1]

The built environment and urban landscape mirror the image of the shrinking city. Slow growth for the first half of the twentieth century, coupled with depopulation over the latter half, means that Pittsburgh's housing stock is, on average, nearly a century old. Depopulation and aged housing have resulted in surplus land and buildings. A fifth of the city's taxable parcels, or over 25,000 parcels, were tax-delinquent in 2009, with delinquency in some neighborhoods at or above 50 percent. Eleven percent of residential properties were vacant or estimated to be vacant in 2009, with some neighborhoods experiencing over 20 percent vacancy rates. Impacts extend further. Since just 2005, twenty-two schools have been shuttered by the city's school district.

Largely African-American neighborhoods in what is still a racially segregated city have the oldest housing and highest levels of abandonment, conditions also mirrored in nearby former mills towns. The post-World War II pace toward "smaller, poorer, older populations dramatically quickened" in working-class communities and neighborhoods with the steel shutdowns of the 1980s.[2] Twenty-five years later, many of these neighborhoods have become even smaller, poorer, and older. Many have relatively high concentrations of elderly residents and little turnover of housing units, contributing to neighborhood housing falling further into decline. The problem is particularly acute in some African-American neighborhoods, where residents over sixty-five years old make up a third or more of the neighborhood population, property vacancy tops 40 percent, and owners have little prospect of marketing their properties.

There has been a fiscal toll from decline, as well. In 2003, Pittsburgh became an Act 47 community under the state's Financially Distressed Municipalities Act, one of twenty communities under a state oversight committee. The city remains in fiscal distress and faces a pension crisis. The current mayor has sought revenue from new sources—most recently proposing to tax college students and to sell parking garage assets. Though neither found support from city council, the city has yet to solve its fiscal woes, along with other older industrial cities in the state.

Another side of Pittsburgh, however, makes the glass half-full. Typically, population change and employment change are highly correlated, as in Pittsburgh's steel days, "[i]t [w]as no surprise that in jobs as well as in people Pittsburgh lagged behind the country and behind other large metropolitan areas."[3] In the twenty-first century, Pittsburgh strays from its former self. Not that employment growth in Pittsburgh surpassed the U.S. average over decades, but in recent years, the markers of downturn have not hit as hard in Pittsburgh as other places. Decades of economic restructuring place the region is a different position from that of many older industrial regions.

First, the number of jobs in the Pittsburgh region, although down slightly from 2000, at 1.1 million, is greater today than at any point during its heyday as an industrial center. Over the 2000s, the manufacturing sector has declined by one-third, to approximately 85,000 workers in 2010, representing just 8.4 percent of the regional economy (and the fewest number of manufacturing workers since 1880). Because the economy is less concentrated in manufacturing, unlike most previous downturns, Pittsburgh's unemployment rate fell below the nation's. Nonetheless, not surprisingly over this recent recession, virtually no major manufacturing sector gained in employment over the 2000s. Most sectors employed fewer workers before the recession began in 2006 than in 1990, with an exception of the computer and electronics sector, which gained 9.2 percent workers between 1990 and 2006, a sector closely linked to the region's educational institutions and research base.

These totals, however, tend to understate the importance of manufacturing in the region, as knowledge and skill sets extend to technology-based clusters. For instance, the Steel Technology Cluster, comprising steel suppliers, research and educational institutions, equipment makers, machinery repair, engineering, raw materials, and support organizations, employs more workers than does the primary metals sector in the region; while Pittsburgh lost much of its steelmaking capacity, it has retained and expanded its steelmaking expertise.[4]

The city of Pittsburgh has also retained its share of the region's workers. Though the city's population made up just 13 percent of the region's population, the nearly 320,000 workers in the city represented almost 31 percent of total regional employment in 2001.[5] Despite shrinking city population loss, the city has retained its working population over the decades.

Women's labor force participation today is at or above U.S. average rates, except for the oldest working age cohort, another important post-industrial shift. In the region's steel days, women in Pittsburgh, whether white or black, exhibited significantly lower rates of labor force participation compared to other urban areas and put overall labor force participation at the bottom in the country.[6] Today, women make up nearly half the region's workers, marking one of the most significant changes in the post-steel era.

Finally, education has played a central role in the region's resilience. The education sector is vitally important to the regional economy, and higher-education institutions serve important anchor roles in the region. Students add to the fabric of the city and the employment base. More important, the level of educational attainment among young workers today in the Pittsburgh region marks a stark contrast to its steel days. In 2009, in the Pittsburgh region, workers between the ages of twenty-five and thirty-four were among the most educated in the country, with 48.1 percent with a bachelor's degree or higher, compared to the U.S. average of 34.7 percent for the cohort. Nearly 22 percent had a graduate or post-baccalaureate professional degree, also among the top percentage in the nation. Today's young workers are well-educated for the demands of a more diversified economy than former cohorts.

The regional economy has been buoyed by employment growth in the education sector, and, along with health services, employed nearly 233,000 workers in 2009, marking an increase of 17.6 percent since 2000. Other sectors adding employment over the recent decade include professional and business services and leisure and hospitality activities. Along with financial services, the Pittsburgh economy today reflects national and global growth.

In 2004, Governing magazine categorized the city's fiscal distress, coupled with its economic vitality, as "the Pittsburgh Paradox."[7] In 2011, the paradox stubbornly persists. Nonetheless, the half-full glass shows a place of remarkable resilience in the face of regional restructuring. Though Pittsburgh retains many of the challenges facing shrinking cities, its revitalization in the post-steel era and its economic success in recent years mean that rebuilding regional economies, though difficult and prolonged, is critical in regenerating shrinking cities as vibrant and attractive urban centers.

Notes

1. Hoover (1963), pg. 2.
2. Lubove (1996), pg. 10.
3. Hoover, (1963), pg. 2.
4. Treado (2008).
5. U.S. Department of Housing and Urban Development (2005).
6. Hoover (1963).
7. Sostek (2004).

Bibliography

Hoover, E.M. 1963. Economic Study of the Pittsburgh Region. Vol.1, *Region in Transition.* Pittsburgh: University of Pittsburgh Press.

Lubove, R. 1996. *Twentieth Century Pittsburgh.* Vol. 2, The Post Steel Era. Pittsburgh: University of Pittsburgh Press.

Sostek, A. 2004. "The Well That Dried Up." *Governing* 17:

Treado, C. 2008. *Sustaining Pittsburgh's Steel Cluster.* Pittsburgh: Center for Industry Studies, Department of Economics, University of Pittsburgh.

3

Depopulation, Market Collapse and Property Abandonment: Surplus Land and Buildings in Legacy Cities

Alan Mallach, Center for Community Progress

America's legacy cities have been losing population and jobs steadily for fifty years or more. Although these cities have demolished thousands of buildings over the past fifty years, sharply reducing both the residential and non-residential supply,[1] demand has declined even faster. Demolition has not stabilized the market, instead, it has increased the amount of vacant land as more buildings continue to be abandoned. As a result, these cities are confronted with vast inventories of surplus vacant land and buildings for which no apparent market demand exists. How to address this issue is a critical question for those trying to frame realistic strategies for these cities' future.

This chapter will begin by looking at housing market trends in legacy cities and the implications of those trends for the near and mid-term future of these cities. That is followed by a discussion of how these trends are changing the landscape of these cities, and how those changes in turn, are affecting the vitality of the cities and their neighborhoods. The chapter concludes by presenting a framework for future public policies in legacy cities that recognize both the reality of shrinkage and the opportunities that it offers for rethinking and reconfiguring urban land use patterns.

Market Collapse in Shrinking Cities

As legacy cities have torn down houses that have become vacant, the number of vacant houses has grown even faster. *Table 1* compares the number of total and vacant housing units in six of these cities in 1990 and in 2010. While demolition led to significant reductions in each city's housing inventory during that period,[2] the decline from continued net loss in the number of households living in the city exceeded the reduction in the inventory, while the number of vacant units increased both as a percentage of the housing stock and in absolute numbers, although to varying degrees in different cities. Since the number of units removed was consistently much greater than the number added, the number of vacant lots grew, as well as the number of vacant structures.

Table 1: *Change in Housing Inventory and Utilization in Six Cities 1990-2010*

City		*1990*	*2010*	*% Change 1990-2010*
Detroit	Total Units	410,017	349,170	-14.6%
	Vacant Units	36,170	79,725	+120.4
	% Vacant	8.8%	22.8%	
Dayton	Total Units	80,370	74,065	-7.8%
	Vacant Units	7,700	15,661	+103.4
	% Vacant	9.6%	21.1%	
Cleveland	Total Units	224,311	207,536	-7.5%
	Vacant Units	24,524	40,046	+63.3
	% Vacant	10.9%	19.3%	
Youngstown	Total Units	40,885	33,123	-19.0%
	Vacant Units	3,763	6,289	+67.0
	% Vacant	9.2%	19.0%	
Pittsburgh	Total Units	170,159	156,165	-8.3%
	Vacant Units	16,676	19,948	+19.6
	% Vacant	9.8%	12.8%	
Scranton	Total Units	35,357	33,853	-4.3%
	Vacant Units	2,720	3,784	+39.1
	% Vacant	7.7%	11.2%	

Source: U.S. Bureau of the Census

All of this is a function of lack of demand. Demand for housing in these cities is far less than the supply; while demolition has reduced that supply, demand has dropped even faster. This data reflects a long-term trend that has been going on in most of these cities since the 1960s or even earlier. Between 1960 and 2000,

Detroit removed 178,000 dwelling units, or 32 percent of its 1960 housing stock, while the number of vacant houses and vacant lots steadily increased.

The Supply/Demand Imbalance

To better understand the relationship between housing supply and demand and the extent of the market collapse taking place in legacy cities, it is important to move away from examining broad historical trends and take a closer look at the way the market is actually working in these cities today. That is facilitated by identifying and analyzing measures of market activity or indicators—that is, key data sets that indicate the features and direction of the market. Four separate housing market indicators are readily available at the census tract level—which roughly corresponds to the neighborhood level in smaller cities:

- Level of sales transactions, as a ratio of sales to properties
- Level of home-purchase mortgage originations, as a ratio of originations to properties
- Average sales price per transaction
- Percentage of properties vacant or abandoned[3]

Two of these indicators can be combined to create a fifth indicator:

- Ratio of sales transactions to purchase mortgage originations

Since most owner-occupant buyers obtain mortgages, while the great majority of absentee buyers use cash or nonmortgage capital sources, such as investment pools, the number of mortgage originations roughly reflects the number of buyers for owner-occupancy. The ratio of total sales to mortgages, therefore, is a surrogate for the ratio of absentee buyers to owner-occupant buyers, something which no data source tracks directly.

These indicators can be studied individually or can be combined to form a composite index of market activity in a city or neighborhood. In the next few pages, we will examine what these indicators say about housing demand and supply in legacy cities by looking at two small cities, both of which have lost a large part of their population in recent years: Saginaw, Michigan, and Youngstown, Ohio.

Since normal housing turnover typically runs between 6 and 7 percent per year,[4] a rule of thumb suggests that under normal market conditions a ratio of properties to sales should be fifteen to one or less; that is, if a city contains thirty thousand single-family properties, sales should be in the vicinity of two thousand per year to ensure that all properties coming onto the market are absorbed. Total sales in Saginaw in 2009 thus fell 350 to 400 properties short of fully absorbing

Table 2: *Saginaw, MI, 2009 Market Indicators*

Indicator	*Metric*	*Source*
Total sales	1004	Boxwood Means Data from PolicyMap
Ratio of Properties to Sales	21 to 1	
Purchase Mortgage Originations	153	Home Mortgage Disclosure Act
Ratio of Sales to Mortgage Originations	6.6 to 1	
Average Sales Price	$48,700	Boxwood Means (aggregate sales amounts divided by number of sales transactions)
Percentage of Addresses Vacant ninety or More Days on Abandoned	19%	U.S. Postal Service

the available supply. The weakness of market demand is reinforced by the finding that nearly one out of every five addresses in the city was either vacant over ninety days or abandoned.

The ratio between mortgage originations and sales, however, shows that the great majority of sales were most probably to absentee buyers, rather than to owner-occupants. It is likely that 70 to 80 percent of the house sales in Saginaw in 2009 were to absentee buyers. Many of these sales took place at extremely low prices; while the average sales price for the city was under $50,000, the average price in six of the city's nineteen census tracts was under $25,000.

The number of vacant and abandoned properties in Saginaw is gradually increasing, as the demand is inadequate to absorb the supply of housing coming onto the market, let alone make inroads into the already-large supply of vacant housing. Since the lion's share of what demand exists is coming from absentee buyers, including most probably many short-term speculators drawn by the city's low housing prices, owner-occupancy is declining as well. Low sales prices and large numbers of vacant properties mean not only that no new market-rate housing is being constructed but also that home owners and absentee owners alike are likely to hesitate to put money in their properties.

Sobering as this picture is, it *understates* the severity of the problem. Saginaw contains widely varying housing market conditions, including not only areas that have experienced widespread abandonment but also attractive, well-maintained neighborhoods. *Table 3* shows the market indicators for Saginaw by census tract.

Saginaw is a sharply divided city. Sales ratios in roughly half of the tracts (12 through 21) are at or close to absorption levels, while sales ratios in the other half (1 through 11) are so far from absorption levels as to suggest that houses coming on the market in this half of the city may be more likely to be abandoned than find a buyer. These two areas correspond to the division of the city by the Saginaw River; tracts 12 through 21 are west of the river, while tracts 1 through 11 are east

Table 3: *Saginaw Market Indicators by Census Tract*

	Sales Ratio	*Mortgages*	*Sales/Mortgage Ratio*	*Price ($000)*	*Vacant 90+ Days or Abandoned*
1	228.0	No mortgages	NA	14.2	39%
2	31.5	No mortgages	NA	37.7	12
4	39.9	No mortgages	NA	13.2	30
6	40.5	425	10.5	27.6	22
7	79.2	No mortgages	NA	16.9	31
8	65.8	1580	24.0	17.4	19
9	57.1	No mortgages	NA	22.4	18
10	42.2	No mortgages	NA	37.4	19
11	76.4	993	13.0	22.0	16
12	15.9	166	10.4	28.5	16
13	15.6	452	29.0	31.6	23
14	13.4	107	8.0	45.9	8.1
15	11.5	47	4.1	56.6	7.4
16	11.9	140	11.8	29.2	16
17	18.3	155	8.5	38.2	21
18	18.2	401	22.0	30.0	27
19	17.7	90	5.1	32.7	18
20	13.2	63	4.9	53.5	9.8
21	12.9	34	2.6	66.5	4.7

of the river. These two areas also correspond to Saginaw's racial divide, with the great majority of the city's African-American population living east of the river and most of the city's white population west of the river. Seventy-eight percent of all sales that took place and *all but 4 of the 153 mortgages* were made west of the river (*Figure 1*).

This does not mean that the area west of the river shows consistently strong market conditions; in fact, only a small part of this area can be seen as having a healthy market, even by the modest standards of a distressed Rust Belt community. While tract 18 showed a moderately high level of sales in 2009, only two mortgages were made in that entire tract during the year, while its low sales prices and high vacancy rates indicate severe distress. This area is in serious trouble. Nearly all of the sales in this tract were to speculative absentee buyers. Indeed, the only part of the western half of Saginaw to show even moderately strong market conditions—as reflected in high sales volumes, sales prices and mortgages, and low vacancy rates *relative to the citywide average* are the three census tracts in the city's northwest corner (15, 20, and 21), with tract 14 having what one might call borderline conditions. These three tracts, with 22 percent of the city's single-

Figure 1: *Map of Market Conditions in Saginaw Michigan*

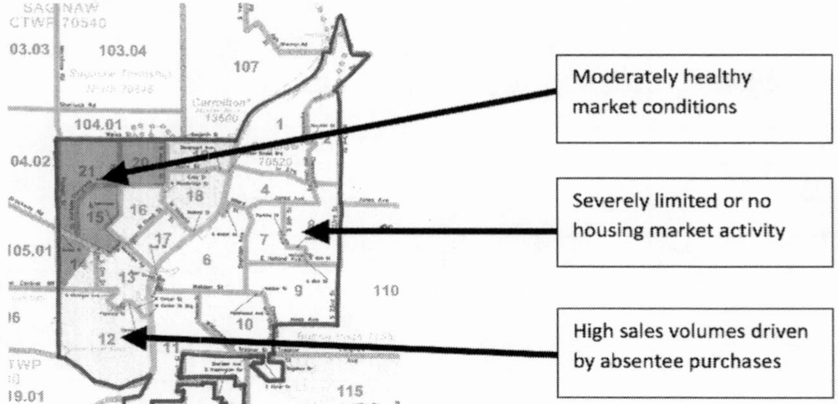

family homes, accounted for 36 percent of all sales and 68 percent of all home purchase mortgages in 2009. House prices in these three tracts were above the citywide average (the only tracts of which that was true), while long-term vacancy rates were less than half the citywide average.

Two central points flow from this analysis. First, *no effective home buyer demand exists in half or more of the census tracts in Saginaw*. A house that becomes vacant whether in the normal course of household transition or through deliberate abandonment in any of these tracts has so little likelihood of finding a buyer that for most houses, vacancy is tantamount to abandonment. With neither short nor long-term prospects for reuse, many of these properties will soon deteriorate beyond repair.

Second, *in all but the strongest census tracts in these cities, homebuyer demand may be too weak to ensure productive reuse of all available houses*. Even the strongest tracts have sales prices that are well below replacement cost, or the cost to restore a house to good condition once it has been abandoned. Vacant, boarded-up houses can be found in the most desirable neighborhoods. In Detroit's once-elite Palmer Woods neighborhood, the boyhood mansion of presidential hopeful Mitt Romney was recently demolished after years of sitting abandoned and derelict. Conditions in most of the remaining tracts suggest that despite relatively high sales volumes, the combination of high vacancy rates, low sales prices, and little or no demand from prospective home owners, has severely destabilized these areas. These areas may not be doomed, but they are seriously at risk of further decline unless effective interventions strengthen their housing markets.

Market conditions in Youngstown are worse than in Saginaw. The sales ratio at thirty-two to one is less than half of what may be needed to absorb the available supply; the annual shortfall in demand may be as high as one thousand sales in a city with fewer than thirty thousand total houses. Reflecting low demand, the

Figure. 2: *Map of Market Conditions in Youngstown Ohio*

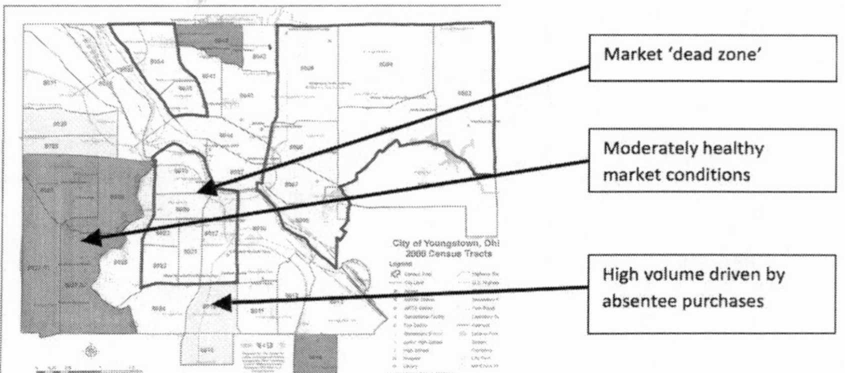

citywide average sales price was $27,560, little more than half the average price in Saginaw. Prices in over half of the city's census tracts were under twenty thousand dollars, and in five tracts under ten thousand dollars. Vacancies were over 20 percent in twenty of the city's tracts, and over thirty percent in eleven tracts.

Figure 2 illustrates salient market conditions in Youngstown. An area containing roughly half of the city's land area and 30 percent of its one- and two-family housing stock can be considered a housing market "dead zone" (shown in heavy outline), in which even absentee buyer activity is minimal. This area accounted for only 8 percent of all sales and 4 percent of all home purchase mortgages in the city in 2009. On the other side of the ledger, a few areas combine at least moderately high sales volumes with continuing home buyer activity and relatively low vacancy rates (gray areas), all of which are located at the city's borders with its suburban neighbors.

This is the grim reality of many legacy cities today, a reality that is critically different in its economic underpinnings and its relationship to the larger trends in the national economy from the superficially similar conditions widely observed in the 1970s in areas such as New York City's South Bronx that prompted Roger Starr's controversial call for "planned shrinkage."[6] Mass abandonment was part of a nearly universal urban condition in the 1970s, when almost every older American city was hemorrhaging jobs and population, driven by social and economic forces they were powerless to influence. That is no longer the case. Since then, American attitudes toward cities and urban living have changed significantly.[7] Many once-distressed cities have experienced market revival, while others have seen population losses reversed by immigration, particularly in the Northeast. *Table 4* shows a number of cities that lost population during the period from 1950 to 1980 at rates that paralleled today's shrinking cities but that regained population between 1980 and 2000. At least two additional major cities, Philadelphia and Milwaukee, have seen their population stabilize since 2000.

Table 4: *Population Trends in Selected Formerly Shrinking Cities*

City	*Population Loss 1950-1980*		*Population Gain*		
	Number	*% Loss*	*Period*	*Number*	*% Gain*
Providence	- 91,870	- 36.9%	1980-2000	+ 16,814	+ 10.7%
Boston	- 238,450	- 29.8	1980-2000	+ 26,147	+ 4.6
Minneapolis	- 150,767	- 28.9	1990-2000	+ 14,255	+ 3.9
Jersey City	- 75,485	- 25.2	1980-2000	+ 16,523	+ 7.4
Chicago	- 615,890	- 17.0	1990-2000	+ 112,290	+ 4.0
New York	- 820,328	- 10.4	1980-2000	+ 936,639	+ 13.2

Source: U.S. Census Bureau

While urban population and job loss during the 1960s and 1970s were driven by large-scale forces of change affecting almost every older city in the United States, the cities that continue to register losses today are doing so *despite* major changes in urban market conditions nationally. They are the cities that have not benefited from those changes and, for many reasons, are unlikely to do so in the future. This is not to suggest that *no* revitalization activities are taking place in these cities. Many legacy cities contain areas, such as Over-the-Rhine in Cincinnati, that are seeing dramatic transformation. No number of heartwarming anecdotes of small victories, of artists buying and fixing up old houses, however, should divert attention from the overarching reality that these cities have a vast oversupply of housing and other buildings relative to demand.

Those victories, however desirable, are one-off efforts incapable of absorbing more than a minute fraction of the oversupply; as the Youngstown data cited earlier suggests, the excess of available housing supply over demand in a city of less than seventy thousand people may be as much as one thousand housing units *per year*. For an older industrial city located in an economically weak region, oversupply is likely to be a long-term condition. It is for these reasons that there is no real debate among on-the-ground practitioners over whether these cities should engage in large-scale demolition. While there are important issues to address, such as which buildings should be demolished, which areas should be targeted, and what role deconstruction[8] should play in the process, the need to further reduce the supply of housing in older industrial cities, coupled with the sheer impossibility of trying to maintain thousands of vacant houses in sound condition indefinitely, dictates that demolition will continue to be an important part of the cities' response to their condition.

House Prices

The lack of market demand in shrinking cities is not a function of price, since houses that come on the market in these cities already sell for prices so low that affordability, as such, is no longer an issue. The median Multiple Listing Service asking price for houses in zip code 48602, which closely parallels the economically-stronger part of the city of Saginaw west of the Saginaw River, in which nearly all the market demand in the city is concentrated, was $44,900. Nearly a quarter of the listings were for prices under $24,900.[9] A more extreme case is zip code 48505, largely coterminous with the northern part of the city of Flint, although it includes a small part of an adjacent suburban township. The median listing price in this zip code was $9,900, with nearly 80 percent of the homes listed below $25,000.[10] The average *selling* price of houses in Detroit for the first ten months of 2010, according to the Detroit Board of Realtors, was $16,036.

Prices this low actually depress demand rather than increase it. While some may see low house prices as an asset, by making home ownership affordable to a larger spectrum of potential buyers, they actually create more problems than they solve. When existing houses sell for less than their replacement cost and have little likelihood of appreciating over time, developers have no incentive to build new houses on vacant land, and home buyers have no incentive to rehabilitate houses that have fallen into disrepair. Except for housing built or rehabilitated with public subsidies, the use of which in these cities raises serious public policy issues, little or no replacement housing is being built in most shrinking cities. The small amount of market-driven housing that is built is located in a handful of prime locations, principally the downtowns of larger cities such as Pittsburgh or St. Louis or emerging near-downtown areas such as Over-the-Rhine or Philadelphia's Northern Liberties. Existing housing in many other parts of these cities—with owners having little incentive to upgrade it—continues to deteriorate.

Despite low prices, prospective home buyers are few and far between. Many prefer to buy in nearby suburban communities—where house prices are slightly higher but still highly affordable—because of the greater likelihood of appreciation as well as real or perceived benefits in terms of safety and school quality. That, in turn, further depresses the demand for houses in urban neighborhoods and reduces home ownership rates, as more houses are bought by investors or speculators rather than by families planning to occupy the home they buy.[11] Between 1970 and 2006, Youngstown's home ownership rate dropped from 68 percent to 60 percent. With homebuyer demand weak, most sales at present in legacy cities are to absentee buyers, many of whom are short-term speculators likely to leave their properties worse in a few years than when they bought them.

It is hard to imagine any change in economic conditions likely to take place in the near future at a scale that will materially affect aggregate housing demand in older industrial cities and their metropolitan areas, although shifting consumer preferences and determined neighborhood revitalization efforts may improve demand in selected areas within some cities. Most legacy cities are located in regions that are economically weak and showing little growth. With regional demand weak as a whole, strategies to build market demand by increasing the city's share of the regional market, while desirable, can have only a modest effect, and is most likely to largely benefit only a few of the city's neighborhoods. The ability of these localities or regions to build new economic drivers to replace their lost manufacturing bases is uncertain, and at best likely to be a slow process, with significant effects visible only after many years. This is particularly likely if, as many economists believe, the United States is entering an extended period of sluggish economic growth. In that case, little growth may trickle down to the nation's economically weaker regions, and market conditions there may not improve in the foreseeable future.

The New Urban Landscape[12]

The collapse of market demand and the resulting widespread abandonment of properties is creating a new urban landscape in legacy cities. As these cities grew during the late nineteenth and twentieth centuries, in contrast to today's automobile-oriented "leapfrog" development, their growth was continuous, with nearly all properties within the urban sphere being utilized for activities linked to the urban economy: homes, stores, factories, or urban amenities such as public parks. In keeping with the classic density gradient model of urban form,[13] the highest density uses were in the center, with a gradual decrease in density as one moved farther away from the heart of the city. Within the city's boundaries, a continuous and largely interconnected functional network of streets and sewer and water lines was laid down, again in contrast to the more fragmented branching networks that emerged in more outlying areas developed since World War II.

While cities varied in their density and layout, reflecting regional variations in settlement forms and housing types, from Boston triple-deckers to Philadelphia and Baltimore row houses and the more dispersed Midwestern pattern of single-family detached housing in Detroit and Cleveland, the underlying pattern was largely consistent and distinctively urban in character. Even where the typical housing unit was a detached single-family house, as in Detroit, houses were sited close to one another and usually within walking distance of a major street where retail services were offered.

This pattern can be seen clearly in *Figure 3*, which shows the population-density distribution in Detroit in 1950, and shows clearly how closely the city's 1950 population distribution fit the classic density gradient model. *Figure 4* shows the city's population distribution in 2000. While in ancient times, depopulation of a city would have led the remaining population to converge around the center, the pattern of urban shrinkage in older industrial cities is radically different. Central-city depopulation, rather than reinforcing the center, has undone it. Although density has declined throughout Detroit, the central area, extending roughly two miles in all directions from the city's core, has seen the greatest population loss.

Figure 3: *Population Density by Census Tract in Detroit, 1950*

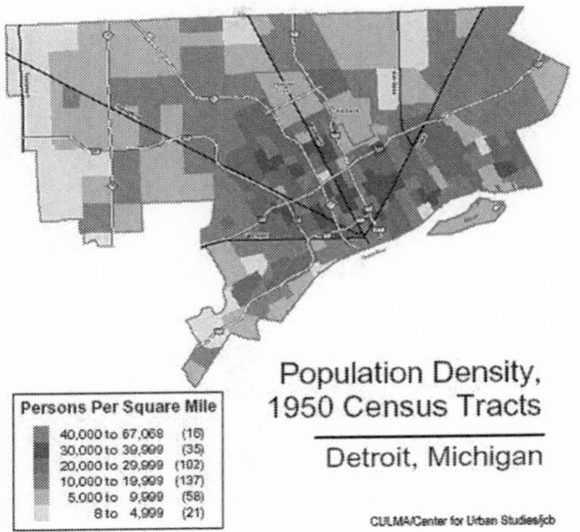

Source: U.S. Census Bureau data, Wayne State University

Figure 4: *Population Density by Census Tract in Detroit, 2000*

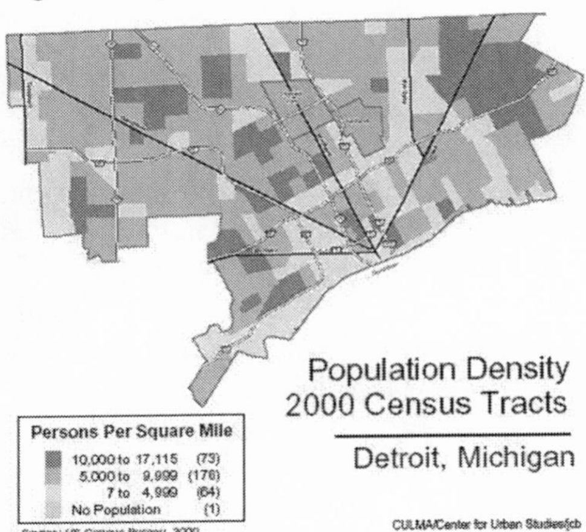

Source: U.S. Census Bureau data, Wayne State University

The depopulation of urban areas has created a new urban landscape. The formal subdivision of blocks and lots remains, but instead of the consistent, compact fabric that arose from the initial subdivision of land and development of individual lots, a city block in a disinvested area is now likely to contain four distinct types of property:

- Vacant lots, where houses once stood and have been demolished after having been abandoned

- Vacant and abandoned houses, often fire-damaged and likely sooner or later to be demolished
- Absentee-owned occupied houses, usually in poor repair and likely to be abandoned by their owners as soon as the cost of operation exceeds the rental cash flow
- Owner-occupied houses, generally in somewhat better repair than the absentee-owned properties, but often in poor condition after years of deferred maintenance

Many blocks in cities like Buffalo or Gary contain far more vacant lots than lots on which structures still exist, and more vacant structures than occupied buildings. In such areas, reflecting the absence of home buyer demand, the remaining owner-occupants are often disproportionately elderly; in some parts of Youngstown, nearly half of the home owners are over sixty-five years old. Many of these houses are likely to be abandoned when the current owner either moves or dies, while others may be bought by an absentee owner, who will milk the property for a few years and then abandon it.

The division of properties between these four property types on the block reflects the degree of depopulation and abandonment on that block. Whether the process of depopulation is reversible, or how fast it may move toward an ultimate outcome of near-total abandonment, will depend on the level of housing market demand that exists or that can be stimulated. Concerted efforts may be able to reverse the cycle in some areas by drawing demand from other parts of the city or from the rest of the city's region. Ultimately, however, the sheer lack of effective market demand means in most cases that once a house deteriorates beyond a certain point, it will not be restored, and once it is torn down, nothing will be built on the site.[14] Similarly, limited aggregate demand means that only some of a city's neighborhoods, not all, can realistically be candidates for revitalization.

This landscape does not describe the entire city. Legacy cities contain many different areas, falling along a continuum of densities and economic activity levels. Most cities contain an economic core, which includes the city's downtown, along with other areas that contain strong economic anchors, such as Detroit's Midtown, with the Detroit Medical Center and Wayne State University; West Philadelphia, with the University of Pennsylvania and Drexel University; and University Circle in Cleveland, home of Case Western Reserve University and most of the region's major cultural facilities. Cities like Cleveland and Pittsburgh still contain substantial downtown employment bases. Most cities still contain *strong neighborhoods* with strong market demand, such as Detroit's Boston-Edison and Indian Village neighborhoods, as well as others where signs of deterioration and abandonment are visible but where decline is still likely to be reversible. The Youngstown Neighborhood Development Corporation has achieved some success in revitalizing that city's Idora neighborhood, an area with relatively high levels of vacancy and abandonment but also with important physical assets and engaged residents.[15]

All of these cities, however, also contain areas where market failure and abandonment have reached levels where they are unlikely to be reversed and where market demand is likely to be too weak to prompt market-driven revival. In Detroit, where 27 percent of all residential parcels are vacant, the continuum of areas is clearly visible on a map of the city (*Figure 5*). In much of the city, particularly on the east side, over half of all residential parcels are vacant lots. There are also large areas, however, principally in the city's northeast and northwest, where there are few vacant lots and the residential fabric remains intact. While it is easy enough to identify the places at the ends of the continuum—the strong neighborhoods and the most heavily abandoned areas—many places fall in between, showing some degree of strength and some of weakness.

Figure 5: *Percentage of Residential Parcels That Are Vacant Lots in Detroit, 2010*

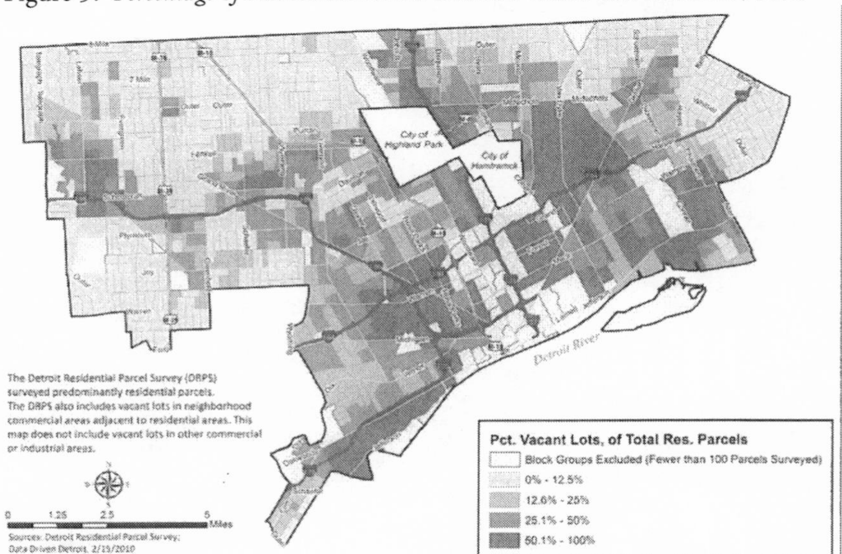

Source: Detroit Vacant Parcel Survey

A similar mix of land uses exists in all cities that have lost a large part of their population since their peak, but with important variations in their distribution. In cities like Youngstown or Buffalo which have lost half or more of their peak population, large areas show little market activity and extensive abandonment, and fewer areas retain market vitality and a strong urban fabric. In cities like Philadelphia or Baltimore, where population loss has been more modest, although still substantial, the ratio tends to be reversed. The heavily disinvested areas tend to be more localized, while a much larger part of the city retains both market and physical vitality.

The continuous texture of the historical city is giving way to a fragmented texture, in which areas that retain a strong physical fabric are interspersed with places that have lost most of their population and their historic character, and in which large tracts of land may be reverting to nature. John Gallagher, in his book *Reimagining Detroit*, describes how beavers, red foxes, and ring-necked pheasants have recolonized parts of that city.[17] The pattern, however, is a messy one. To imagine the future shrinking city as an English countryside in miniature, with its central town and peripheral villages set in a bucolic green landscape, is to fail to acknowledge the complex and untidy reality of urban population loss and property abandonment. Detroit may contain hundreds of city blocks on which vacant properties outnumber occupied ones, but few blocks that have become *completely vacant*. While few people may live on any one largely-abandoned city block, the sum total of those who live on all of the blocks that contain more vacant lots than houses is likely to be substantial. Since it would be ethically unacceptable, politically unsupportable, and financially untenable to uproot them against their will, the residual areas of shrinking cities will continue to contain *some* population for many years to come; indeed, some may ultimately be restored to vitality as low-density quasi-rural residential areas. Urban reconfiguration demands a scalpel, not a sledgehammer.

Toward A Strategic Framework For Reusing Urban Land

The goal of every legacy city with respect to its land inventory should be to achieve a balance of supply and demand to ensure a productive use—whether through development or green uses such as open space or farming—for every parcel in the city, and that those uses complement the city's overall strategy for revitalization. In pursuing that goal, two options, pursued separately or in combination, are available to cities faced with the supply/demand imbalance described above. They can reduce supply, either permanently through demolition or temporarily through "mothballing" or other holding actions. In addition, they can attempt to increase demand, either by stimulating greater demand for housing or other traditional building uses or by identifying new uses for land and buildings for which demand may potentially exist or can be created. These strategies are not mutually exclusive, but complementary; indeed, as the foregoing discussion would suggest, any strategy that focuses on reducing supply without building market demand may ultimately be self-defeating. This basic framework is illustrated in *Table 5*.

Reducing Supply

While demolition may be necessary to deal with hazards and nuisance conditions, as a strategy *in itself* to reduce the supply of housing and bring it into balance with

Table 5: *Strategic Framework for Reusing Urban Land*

Strategy	*Approach*	*Examples*
Reduce Supply	Permanently reduce housing supply	Demolition or deconstruction
	Temporarily reduce housing supply	Stabilize or "mothball" significant properties for future restoration
	Reduce surplus land supply	Hold vacant land and put to temporary use
		Sell vacant lots to adjacent homeowners
Increase Demand	Increase demand for housing in urban neighborhoods	Undertake market-oriented neighborhood revitalization strategies
		Insure owners against loss of equity from declines in market value
		Provide financial incentives for buying and restoring vacant properties
	Create new uses for land or buildings	Create an urban agriculture system
		Create parks and greenways
		Offer buildings to artists

demand, it has largely been unsuccessful. While reducing the supply of housing, it fails to keep pace with the continuing decline in demand. Moreover, in the process of reducing the supply of housing, it has increased the supply of vacant land parcels, something for which there is arguably even less market demand than for housing. It is doubtful that a strategy that focuses on reducing supply, without a parallel effort to build demand, can *ever* be successful.

Demolition serves purposes other than reducing supply. It eliminates properties that have become blighting influences on their surroundings or that represent hazards to health and safety. In heavily disinvested areas, it fosters potential reuse opportunities by creating larger areas of open space that may potentially lend themselves to a variety of future greening uses. Not all properties can or *should* be demolished, however; not only are resources for this purpose limited but not all vacant properties should be demolished.

As with other public resources, funds for demolition need to betargeted on the basis of a rational framework such as that illustrated in *Table 6*, reflecting not only the aesthetic or historic value of the building and its condition but its location and the reuse opportunities that will be created as a result of demolition. Valuable buildings can be removed from the present market but preserved for the future by stabilizing or "mothballing" them. The cost of doing so, as well as ongoing maintenance costs, however, means that stabilization, particularly for the long term, can only be used sparingly.

Table 6: *Considerations for Demolishing or Preserving Vacant Buildings*

Demolish		Preserve
The building is obsolete, by virtue of size, physical character, or poor quality of construction.	*Quality of building*	The building is attractive, of high quality, or of architectural or historic value.
The building has deteriorated to the point that it cannot be restored, or the cost of restoration would be prohibitive in light of the economic value of the property.	*Condition of building*	The building is largely intact and can be restored at a cost that is reasonable in light of the economic value of the property.
The building, by virtue of location and physical character, is not likely to draw the investment needed to bring it back into productive reuse.	*Reuse potential of building*	The building, by virtue of location and physical character, is likely to draw the investment needed to bring it back into productive reuse.
The building is located in an area where the neighborhood fabric has largely been lost through incompatible land uses, abandonment, and demolition.	*Quality of neighborhood fabric*	The building is located in an area that still has a strong neighborhood fabric, and its physical presence contributes to that fabric
Demolition will contribute to the opportunity to carry out a rebuilding or reuse strategy for the area, which may involve either/both rebuilding or alternative "green" nondevelopment. reuses	*Reuse potential of resulting vacant land*	The demolition of the building will result in a potentially unusable vacant lot, rather than an opportunity for meaningful revitalization or green reuse.
The nuisance created by the building and the harm that it is doing to neighbors in its present condition or the surrounding area, in the absence of immediate reuse potential, outweigh the benefits of saving it for possible future reuse.	*Nuisance level of building*	The reuse potential of the building, even if not immediate, outweighs the current harm that the building is doing in its present condition, particularly if enhanced efforts are made to secure or stabilize the property.

Source: Adapted and revised from Mallach (2006)

Reducing surplus land supply is not a strategy in itself. A city may shrink its population or its housing stock, but it cannot shrink its land area. Even in the extremely unlikely event that part of a city's land was annexed to a neighborhood municipality, the land itself would remain.[18] Thus, reducing the surplus land supply is a product of finding new uses for that land, as discussed below (and in more detail in Chapter 6).

Building Housing Demand

As noted earlier, every legacy city has vital neighborhoods, where the neighborhood fabric remains intact, where houses are generally well maintained and usually find buyers. Many, if not most, of these neighborhoods, however, are at risk. Demand may fall short of supply, or it may be adequate to ensure that houses in move-in condition find buyers, but house values may be too low to motivate prospective buyers to purchase houses in need of work, or to prompt builders to construct new houses on vacant lots. Stagnant or declining property values may drive away prospective buyers and discourage existing owners from investing in more than minimal maintenance of their homes. Home owners are being replaced by absentee owners, many of whom may be short-term speculators rather than long-term investors.

Preserving or restoring the vitality of these neighborhoods is critical to the future of older industrial cities. While the specific activities that might be pursued to that end may vary, successful neighborhood revitalization strategies are all based on a single goal—making the neighborhood more appealing to both its present home owners and prospective home buyers, thereby making people more likely to *choose* to buy in that neighborhood.[19] This is discussed in detail in Chapter 5.

When more people choose to live in a neighborhood, its real estate market becomes stronger. Greater real estate market strength, reflected in houses selling faster, commanding higher prices, and appreciating over time, is likely to lead to important changes in how area property owners behave. Both owner-occupants and absentee owners are more likely to upgrade their properties, contractors are more likely to build new houses on vacant lots and rehabilitate vacant houses, and tax delinquencies and foreclosures will decline. Residents who see their neighborhood improving are likely to be more attached to the area. Upwardly mobile residents will be more likely to stay in their present homes or buy new homes in the same neighborhood than to move out. Actively fostering these changes is particularly critical for neighborhoods in older cities in economically weak regions, since in those areas the cost of suburban houses is low and it is relatively easy for moderate-income residents to flee to the suburbs.

How much demand can potentially be attracted to a particular urban neighborhood, and what the characteristics of the households making up that demand may be, will vary from city to city and from neighborhood to neighborhood. It is critical, however, that the universe for building market demand be seen as the entire region, rather than the city alone. If a particular neighborhood begins to draw a larger share of the citywide market, it may flourish, but at the price of drawing demand away from other city neighborhoods, which may result in their destabilization and collapse. Meanwhile, many suburban areas around older industrial cities continue to grow. Between 1990 and 2000, while Detroit was losing nearly 38,000 households, its suburban ring (Macomb and Oakland counties, and the balance of Wayne County) added 130,000 households. Capturing a modest share of that growth could have significantly slowed—if not perhaps eliminated—Detroit's downward population trend during the decade.

The number of different strategies that can be pursued to build housing demand and stabilize urban neighborhoods is considerable, as discussed in detail in chapter 5. Generally speaking, however, they fall into three broad categories which can be described as follows:

- *Increasing the desirability of the neighborhood's housing stock:* making the area's homes more appealing to prospective buyers by providing financial incentives to buy or rehabilitate houses, offering equity-protection insurance, creating new housing that better reflects market demand, and marketing the neighborhood's assets more effectively.
- *Increasing neighborhood stability*: strengthening those features of the neighborhood that are associated with the preservation and potential increase in the value of a property owner's investment (psychological as well as financial), including reducing the number of abandoned houses and foreclosures, reducing crime, and increasing home ownership.
- *Increasing neighborhood amenity value*: strengthening and enhancing those features of the neighborhood that are associated with residents' quality of life, including schools, parks and open space, public transportation, and the overall appearance of the neighborhood, which realtors call "curb appeal."

All or many of these elements need to be integrated into a multifaceted, sustained strategy. Turning around market perceptions is a time-consuming task that may take years; one-shot efforts or short-term initiatives are unlikely to have any meaningful impact.

Targeting Demand

Resources in legacy cities are limited at many levels. As has been discussed, aggregate market demand in most such cities is significantly less than supply. Discretionary public-sector funds that can be used to stimulate demand are in extremely short supply, while many cities cannot afford even to maintain current levels of public investment and service delivery, let alone improve critical services such as schools and public safety.

One of the most difficult issues raised by these conditions is how and to where to direct limited resources. Widespread practices of distributing discretionary resources, in the widely used phrase "like peanut butter," thinly across the entire city, while effective at appeasing diverse political constituencies, lead to little or no lasting change. Despite the political obstacles, a number of cities have, in fact, become more focused in how and where they allocate resources for neighborhood improvement, most notably Richmond, Virginia, where under the rubric of Neighborhoods in Bloom, the city in 1999 directed 80 percent of its discretionary community development funds to six of the city's forty-nine neighborhoods for the ensuing four years, with impressive results.[21] Richmond went through an extensive community consensus-building effort regarding the overall concept, the selection criteria, and the choice of target areas before implementing the program.

While market demand ultimately reflects individual home buyers' decisions, it follows predictable patterns, and it can often be channeled to certain areas directly by offering financial incentives such as tax credits or equity protection insurance, or indirectly by using public or philanthropic funds to create assets like improved schools or restored parks, thereby making those areas more attractive to homebuyers. The need for targeting arises from the likelihood that first, available resources are not adequate to bring about meaningful change at the same time in all of the areas that are at least potential candidates for market demand, and that second, even if they were, aggregate market demand is not likely to be adequate to absorb the supply generated by all of those areas.

While targeting may mean that some areas may thrive and others wither, failure to target may result in more, or all, areas deteriorating through lack of sustainable market demand. This is a particularly difficult issue for local government to tackle, yet failure to do so all but assures larger failure of a legacy city's efforts at transformation and rebuilding.

Finding New Uses for Surplus Land

Reusing those areas within the city that have become progressively less populated, and where vast amounts of surplus land exist, raises other questions. With rare exceptions, lack of demand and the existing oversupply of available land and buildings in still-viable neighborhoods means that this land is not likely to be reused for new buildings, whether residential or non-residential, in the near future, if ever. As a result, cities are faced with a choice. Either this land, the amount of which is steadily growing as buildings are demolished and not replaced, is essentially ignored except for intermittent maintenance and trash removal or new uses are found for the land that do not depend on conventional market demand and do not involve the construction of buildings. These uses are discussed in detail in Chapter 6.

Cities will need to recognize that in many cases, these non-market, non-development uses are likely to be permanent, rather than short-term "holding" uses. Many cities have accepted that there may not be a *short-term* development use for much of their surplus land, and have made land available to neighborhood groups for community gardens on short-term leases in the expectation that this land will be reused sooner or later for development. While this may be true in some areas, it is not true in others. In many areas, lack of demand is not a short-term reality, but a long-term, arguably permanent one.

Nonetheless, it is important to distinguish between areas that, while depopulated today, may have significant assets that make them potentially good candidates for redevelopment in the future and those that lack such assets. Detroit's Delray area, in the city's southwest, while largely depopulated and derelict today, is located between the Detroit River and the relatively healthy southwest Detroit area, with strong locational as well as historical and environmental assets. Should Detroit see its economy and market demand rebound, this area might well offer important future redevelopment opportunities. This may not take place for ten or twenty years, but the opportunities are too valuable not to be preserved. This is not true of other areas in the city of Detroit, where long-term non-market reuse of land is likely to be more appropriate.

The availability of large amounts of surplus land offers the possibility of reimagining the city. As the Cleveland Urban Design Collaborative (CUDC) suggests, it "creates unprecedented opportunities to improve the city's green space network and natural systems. Capitalizing on this moment to set aside land for recreation, agriculture, green infrastructure and other non-traditional land uses will benefit existing residents and help to attract new residents and development." These opportunities are particularly powerful in light of the widespread environmental degradation that was part of both the development of many older industrial cities and their subsequent decline.

While some ideas, such as the expansion of city parks, tend to run afoul of the severe financial constraints facing local governments, other options are available. The CUDC has shown how vacant land in Cleveland can be used to restore the city's ecosystem, improve air and water quality, restore urban soils, create wildlife habitats, and reduce storm water runoff. Philadelphia and other cities are exploring the use of vacant land as a storm water mitigation system, which might obviate the need for hundreds of millions of dollars to deal with the problems of combined storm and sanitary sewer systems, a problem shared by dozens of other older American cities. Another idea being pursued by CUDC as well as others is to "daylight" some of the many buried streams that once ran openly through what is now the city. Opening up a buried stream and creating open space along its banks not only serves valuable hydrologic purposes but creates a recreational amenity that could potentially enhance property values and market demand.

It may be time to begin thinking of urban agriculture as a potentially significant land use and economic activity, rather than as a socially desirable but small-scale and economically inconsequential pursuit. There is a tendency in the media to treat urban agriculture as a human interest story, often involving heartwarming encounters between ex-hippies and photogenic inner-city children, which, however positive in intention, has the effect of trivializing the activity.[22] While the term urban agriculture has often been used to encompass everything from backyard gardening to commercial farming, I use it here to describe something other than community gardening, which has been part of the urban scene since the 1970s and which, because it demands a close spatial relationship between residents of a neighborhood and their gardens, is ironically of little relevance to the question of reusing largely depopulated urban spaces.

Urban agriculture differs from community gardening both in scale and in economic function. It is designed to produce food not for consumption by the gardener and her immediate neighbors, but for larger-scale consumption. At one level, this may mean production of food for a community food bank or soup kitchen or for sale at a local farmers' market; beyond that level, it may involve producing food that can be absorbed by the regional or national food-processing and distribution system. Urban agriculture can potentially become a vehicle for urban transformation. From the standpoint of land use, agriculture offers the possibility of reusing vacant land at various scales, from individual lots to multi-acre tracts, which reflect the actual variety in the size of vacant parcels created through the depopulation of a city's residual space. Since agricultural land is maintained by individual farmers, it avoids the difficult issue of public sector maintenance costs associated with many other green land reuse alternatives.

The benefits of urban agriculture are particularly relevant to inner-city economic conditions. Food insecurity and poor access to healthy food are widespread in urban areas, where low-income urban residents have fewer retail shopping choices, and limited transportation options. Along with addressing food security issues, urban agriculture can create jobs and income streams for inner-city residents, both through farming itself and through the production and distribution of processed food products. Two successful examples are Greensgrow Farm in Philadelphia's Kensington neighborhood and Village Farms in Buffalo.

Bringing agriculture to commercial scale in a shrinking industrial city is fraught with difficulties. Obstacles that have been identified include the lack of farming skills, lack of funds for start-up costs, the fragmentation of land ownership and control, difficulties related to marketing and distribution, crime and vandalism, and the environmental issues associated with the former uses of urban land, as well as the relatively short growing season typical of the climate in most older industrial cities. Commercially viable agriculture requires an infrastructure beyond the fields in which the crops are grown or livestock raised. This infrastructure, which is well established in traditional farming regions, includes schools to train prospective farmers, agricultural extension services to provide assistance with marketing, soil testing, and crop management, food-processing companies, and distribution networks.[23] In Michigan and elsewhere, agricultural extension services are starting to redirect some of their energies toward urban agriculture, a potentially valuable step to enhancing the viability of such strategies for land reuse.

The process of reusing surplus land in shrinking cities will be a slow, gradual, and often difficult one, and is unlikely to save cities much money, particularly in the short run. Significant costs are associated with decommissioning fixed infrastructure, while as Hoornbeck and Schwarz write, "infrastructure operates on a fixed grid and it is difficult to remove components in depopulated areas without impacting the whole system." Only modest savings are likely to be gained by removing streets and street lighting in depopulated areas, while doing so on blocks that still contain a handful of occupied houses raises ethical as well as political issues. Many cities, however, are already quietly neglecting infrastructure maintenance in those areas, while avoiding taking any explicit or official policy stance on the subject.

The issue of the last remaining home owners on a street or block will also continue to be a difficult one. Given the history of urban renewal and the national controversy over eminent domain, any attempt to compel those last home owners, such as the Detroit home owner in the last occupied home on her desolate block who told a reporter, "I refuse to move unless the Lord says so," is doomed to failure. In some cities, this issue will be rendered more sensitive by the painful reality that the remaining home owners in many of these areas are disproportionately African-American and are often old enough to have personal memories of their city's "Negro removal" efforts. While there are many owners who feel trapped in unmarketable houses and lack the money to move, helping them move is likely to be a slow process, hindered by the city's chronic shortage of financial resources.

Ultimately, however, notwithstanding the obstacles, land reconfiguration continues to represent arguably the only viable potential strategy for creating a brighter future for legacy cities. Whether this potential is likely to be realized, however, is far from certain. This is less a technical question than a political or institutional one. To acknowledge shrinkage and its all but inevitable consequences is a political act fraught with risk, while almost any action taken to address it is likely to be difficult, and carry additional risks. Any policy that demands a fundamental change in a community's self-perception, its practice of land use regulation, its use of public funds, and its provision of public services, will be difficult to adopt and, once adopted, to sustain. This leads to the final question to be asked: Do the conditions exist in America's legacy cities under which land reconfiguration can become an effective strategy for rebuilding these cities, or is it destined to remain an aspiration, more discussed than actually pursued?

Notes

1. Since data on non-residential property trends is hard to come by, this chapter will largely deal with residential properties. Anecdotal reports, however, suggest that abandonment of non-residential property, including office space, storefronts, and industrial buildings is, if anything, more extensive than that of residential property.
2. Unfortunately, no reliable data on demolitions as such is available. Although part of the reduction in the inventory may be due to other causes, such as conversion from residential to non-residential use, that part is likely to be very small.
3. This is the sum of properties classified by the U.S. Postal Service as "vacant" and as "no-stat".
4. See, for example, Fabozzi (2005).
5. See Kellog (2010).
6. See Starr (1976). Recent articles that criticize current efforts to recognize and address urban shrinkage by drawing an analogy to urban renewal or the planned shrinkage of the 1970s are fundamentally flawed in that they either fail to recognize or deliberately ignore those differences.
7. This change is well described in Leinberger (2008) and in Breen and Rigby (2004).
8. Deconstruction refers to the selective dismantling or removal of materials from buildings before demolition in order to salvage architecturally significant features as well as potentially useful materials such as oak floors or structural timbers.
9. Data from realtor.com, accessed December 15, 2010. MLS listing prices, indeed, may be skewed upward relative to the actual distribution of houses by value, since listings are likely to be weighted toward those properties with greater prospects of finding buyers, while listing prices themselves are often optimistic assessments of the actual value of the property. Many of these prices, low as they may seem, may actually be little more than wishful thinking.
10. Although rents are not as significant an indicator of market activity as sales prices, they are also quite low in most shrinking cities. With rare exceptions, median rents in these cities are consistently affordable to those earning at or below 50 percent of the HUD-defined Area Median Income.
11. Hyper-low prices create a further problem, in that they motivate unscrupulous speculators (sometimes called "milkers") to buy houses to rent out, while providing little or no maintenance and often paying no property taxes, with the goal of realizing a profit on their initial investment through cash flow alone within two to three years, and then abandoning the property. For further discussion of this and similar investor behaviors, see Mallach (2010).
12. Some of the material in this section appeared previously in different form in Mallach (2011).
13. See Muth (1969) for discussion of the density gradient model.
14. Development of subsidized rental housing projects utilizing the Low Income Housing Tax Credit is something of an exception to this generalization; these projects, reflecting the perverse incentives offered to developers and investors, are often developed in weak market areas in older industrial cities, notwithstanding the fact that existing houses and apartments in decent condition are typically available in large numbers at rents lower than those that will be charged in the subsidized housing. The effect of the addition of these projects to the housing inventory is that demand is cannibalized from

the existing housing stock and the pace of abandonment within that stock is accelerated, at great cost to the public purse and to the taxpayers.

15. A key part of the YNDC strategy for the Idora neighborhood has been their Lots of Green initiative, which was a systematic effort to reutilize every one of the neighborhood's 115 parcels of vacant land in ways that would enhance the neighborhood's vitality. For a report on this project, see: http://www.yndc.org/sites/default/files/Lots%20of%20Green%20Impact%20Statement_small_1.pdf.
16. Twenty percent are vacant, with no apparent use, and 7 percent (or roughly one-quarter of the vacant lots) are being used for some purpose, as evidenced by paving or fencing.
17. Gallagher (2010), pp. 113-117.
18. One could speculate that in some cases, where a distressed older city abuts a healthy suburban municipality, by taking land in the city adjacent to that suburb and adjusting the municipal boundaries to place that land in the suburb's jurisdiction, one could change the market dynamics affecting that land to the extent that it could be reused in ways that would not be possible as long as it remained in the city. This is both speculative and highly unlikely. Moreover, the urban areas with the largest inventories of vacant land are rarely located adjacent to economically stronger suburbs; indeed, typically the city's strongest neighborhoods are located along the city's boundaries.
19. These issues are discussed in more detail in Mallach (2008)
20. The quality of a neighborhood's schools is also a stability value in that—even for households without school-age children—it is often seen as a surrogate for the stability and likelihood of appreciation in house value.
21. The Neighborhoods in Bloom program and its effects are described in Accordino et al. (2005)
22. A recent popular book (Carpenter 2009) reflects this tendency.
23. Detroit, thanks to the still-vital major food-processing and distribution cluster that grew up around its 1890s Eastern Market, has a significant advantage over many other communities, which may have to develop similar networks from a much more limited base. See www.detroiteasternmarket.com.

Bibliography

Accordino, J., G. Galster, and P. Tatian.2005. *The Impacts of Targeted Public and Non-profit Investment on Neighborhood Development*. Richmond, VA: Federal Reserve Bank of Richmond.

Breen, A., and D. Rigby. 2004. *Intown Living*. Washington, D.C.: Island Press.

Carpenter, N. 2009. *Farm City: The Education of an Urban Farmer*. New York: Penguin

Cleveland Urban Design Collaborative. 2008. *Re-Imagining a More Sustainable Cleveland*. Cleveland: Neighborhood Progress, Inc., Cleveland City Planning Commission, Cleveland Urban Design Collaborative, Kent State University.

Fabozzi, F. J. 2005. *The Handbook of Mortgage-Backed Securities*. New York: McGraw-Hill.

Gallagher, J. 2010. *Reimagining Detroit*. Detroit: Wayne State University Press.

Hackney, S. 2009. "Is Right-Sizing the Right Fix?" Detroit Free Press. July 19.

Hoornbeck, J. and T. Schwarz. 2009. *Sustainable Infrastructure in Shrinking Cities: Options for the Future*. Cleveland: Center for Public Administration and Public Policy and the Cleveland Urban Design Collaborative.

Kellog, A. P. 2010. "Detroit Shrinks Itself, Historic Homes and All," *The Wall Street Journal*, May 14.

Leinberger, C. 2008. *The Option of Urbanism: Investing in a New American Dream*. Washington, D.C.: Island Press.

Mallach, A. 2008. *Managing Neighborhood Change: A Framework for Sustainable and Equitable Revitalization*, Montclair, NJ: National Housing Institute.

_______. 2010. *Meeting the Challenge of Distressed Property Investors in America's Neighborhoods*. New York: Local Initiatives Support Corporation.

_______. 2011. "Re-engineering the Urban Landscape: Land Use Reconfiguration and the Morphological Transformation of Shrinking Industrial Cities." *In Engineering Earth: The Impacts of Mega-engineering Projects*, edited by S.S. Brunn, Dordrecht, Netherlands: Springer.

Muth, R. F. 1969. *Cities and Housing: The Spatial Pattern of Urban Residential Land Use* Chicago: University of Chicago Press.

Starr, R. 1976. "Making New York Smaller." *New York Times Magazine*, November 14.

Case Study: Vacancy In Detroit: One Nine-Block Area

Eric Dueweke

The 2009 Detroit Residential Parcel Survey (www.detroitparcelsurvey.org), funded by Living Cities and executed by the Detroit Data Collaborative provided an unprecedented snapshot of vacancy within the city's neighborhoods. But within Detroit's 139 square miles, the best way to comprehend over 90,000 vacant residential parcels is found at a smaller scale—like one nine-block area on its east side. Drexel, Coplin, and Lakeview streets from Mack Avenue north to Canfield can scarcely be called a neighborhood anymore, and while not typical, many similar areas lie scattered across the city.

Solidly built single-family homes constructed mostly in the 1910s and 1920s remained on nearly every one of this area's 312 residential lots until the 1970s. *Figure 1* shows a figure ground diagram of structures from 1949, when Detroit's population was nearly at its zenith. Coplin Street divides census tracts 5123 and 5124, whose combined population in 1950 was 12,497.

By 2010 the population of this area had dropped to 3,158. The 2009 parcel survey revealed that a total of 41 structures remained on the nine blocks, alongside 271 vacant lots—of which 243 were government-owned. Although seven of the 41 houses were vacant, 34 were rated by surveyors as in "good" or "fair" condition, and an analysis of city assessment records shows that as many as 27 of the houses may have been owner-occupied. A figure ground diagram from 2009 is shown in *Figure 2.*

A windshield survey review in February 2011 revealed six additional vacant houses, leaving only 28 occupied homes in the 37-acre area. Government agencies had demolished five houses in this area during the 17-month period since the citywide Parcel Survey. Another six of the 41 properties went to tax foreclosure in 2009 and 2010 alone. The last mortgage loan within the nine blocks was granted in 2005 for $51,000, (the house now stands empty) with the previous most recent mortgages attached to any of the 41 structures recorded in 1999. Thus records

Figure 1.

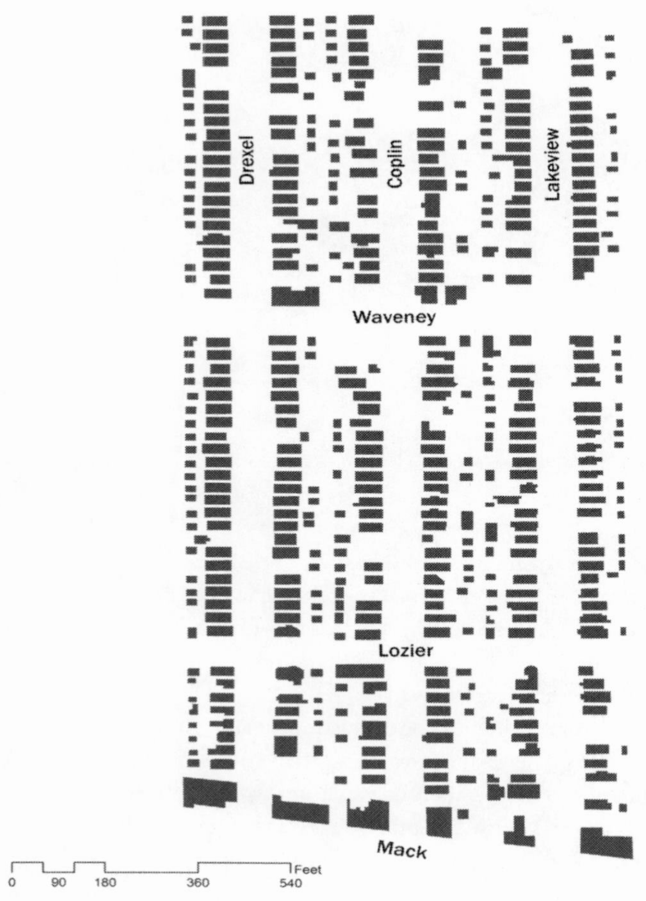

indicate that a majority of remaining homes are mortgage-free and occupied by their owners, several of whom also have taken control of an adjacent vacant lot or two.

Today the City of Detroit continues to provide complete municipal services to residents of these nine blocks. In the summer of 2010, the Department of Public Works constructed new barrier-free curb cuts for the area's barely used sidewalks. Employees of local utility provider DTE Energy privately express concern over maintenance and replacement costs for underground natural gas lines, which have an estimated lifespan of 85 years, in largely empty areas like Drexel/Coplin/Lakeview. Meanwhile, retail and other commercial activity along once bustling Mack Avenue ceased many years ago.

Although some nearby blocks to the north and west saw new construction of subsidized, Low Income Housing Tax Credit rental housing units in 2002, the

Figure 2.

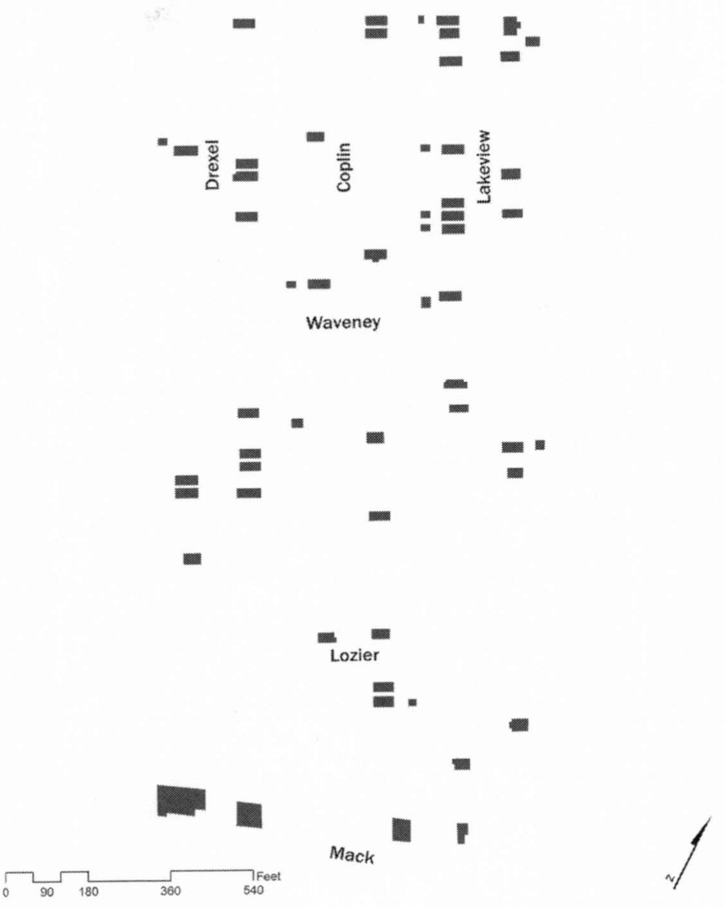

likelihood of any market for near-term development within the nine-block area appears remote. By contrast, two relatively intact neighborhoods exist less than a mile from the area to the east and south. Both MorningSide to the east and Creekside boast strong resident-led neighborhood associations, and both have experienced new residential and commercial developments over the past decade. Yet MorningSide in particular has been hit hard by mortgage foreclosures since 2007 and both neighborhoods host a significant inventory of vacant homes awaiting new residents if they are to maintain stability.

Detroit Mayor Dave Bing launched the Detroit Works Project in 2010 with the long-term goal of aligning city services with land uses. By 2012, Detroiters may witness a strategy to restructure blocks such as those on Drexel, Coplin, and Lakeview streets. Early returns suggest planners are considering a benchmark density of 16 persons per acre; the nine-block area now hovers under three. How the remaining households in this area respond to any plan to further empty their surroundings or reduce their city services should prove instructive for other cities experiencing population decline.

4

Planning in America's Legacy Cities: Toward Better, Smaller Communities after Decline

Hunter Morrison, Northeast Ohio Sustainable Communities Consortium

Margaret Dewar, University of Michigan

Urban planning in the United States focuses almost exclusively on controlling and shaping the effects of growth and is ill-equipped to deal with cities or neighborhoods experiencing sustained disinvestment and depopulation. The American Assembly focused its 110th forum on the challenge of "Defining a Future for America's Cities Experiencing Severe Population Loss." The planning profession's response to the chronic conditions in these cities—which the Assembly defined as "America's Legacy Cities"—is the focus of this chapter. We contend that these historically industrial communities face a set of planning and development challenges resulting both from their development as centers of heavy manufacturing during the late nineteenth and early twentieth centuries and from the widespread downsizing and abandonment of these industrial centers that began in the late 1940s and continues to this day.

Urban planning's perspectives on creating places that improve the quality of life for residents and others has much to contribute to understanding about how to remake these historically industrial communities into better, though smaller, places after they have lost a large share of their peak populations. Urban planning's approaches to involving citizens in making decisions about the future of their cities and neighborhoods can encourage processes that leave residents and civic leaders committed to working toward a better future while realistically accepting that a city will not return to its past. Cities experiencing extensive disinvestment without concerted efforts to influence the direction of change become new kinds of places in any case—but by accident or by surprise—and not in as positive a way as they could. Strategic efforts to control the negative effects of blight on nearby areas, for instance, and to make investments that can reinforce others' commitments to the place hold the promise of purposefully guiding change toward better outcomes. The durability of the built environment and the complexity of legal claims to property mean years of blighting disinvestment pass before neighbors, new owners, and others can reuse structures and vacant land in more positive ways. Planners can take a strong role in shaping and expediting such transformation.

Few U.S. planners choose to work in places where little development is occurring; those who do choose such work find few jobs. By "planners," we mean anyone with or without formal training in urban planning who works on envisioning the future of cities and neighborhoods as places and on implementing those visions. Even formally trained planners have had little exposure to ways that they can apply planning knowledge and techniques to situations where disinvestment, rather than investment, is the principal challenge.

Few publications and little professional training exist to guide those planners as they try to intervene in the process of persistent decline. The challenge for American schools of planning and for the planning profession generally is to develop the ways of thinking and the professional practices that will enable planning practitioners and related design and policy professionals to intervene more effectively in the process of decline taking place in many historically industrial communities. The challenge for individual planners who work in these places is to develop the creative insights, political skills, and professional techniques to work effectively in cities that need to change from centers of past industrial production to cities with more diversified and sustainable local economies. In this chapter, we derive lessons from our experiences as planners in such cities both to contribute to the body of understanding for the profession as a whole and to share several practical insights with planners who choose to practice in these communities.

To date, urban planning as a field has offered little for planners in America's legacy cities.[1] The recent edition of the "Green Book," often called "a handbook of local planning," addresses ways to encourage citizen participation, reuse surplus property, and build on strengths where population has declined, nearly always with the aim of developing again. Several chapters address revitalization of blighted neighborhoods with new development to replace old, abandoned, or obsolete uses but do not consider what to do when such new development is not practically possible.[2] A search of the American Planning Association's Planners' Bookstore in 2010 turned up only two publications that a planner working in an abandoned area of a city with few prospects of new growth would find quite useful.[3] If a planner arrived in a historically industrial community with high levels of abandonment and wanted to gain quick insights into how to plan with decline, rather than against decline, he or she could not readily find useful resources—such as Planning Advisory Service reports (although one on planning in cities after population decline was in process as of mid-2011), webinars, or in-service seminars—directed at meeting that need. And while the American Planning Association's National Planning Conference featured individual sessions on the planning aspects of shrinking cities in recent years, the topic has yet to receive the sustained attention given to managing growth (through applying techniques of Smart Growth and New Urbanism, for instance) or to addressing crises such as that experienced by New Orleans.

The abandonment of America's legacy cities has taken place over decades, not weeks, and severely affects only the Northeast and Great Lakes regions. Perhaps because of this, the fate of these regions' cities, towns, and neighborhoods has aroused little sustained interest in the planning profession. The continued lack of attention to the future of these historically industrial communities is perplexing, however, because many cities in these two regions have experienced the persistent expansion of areas within their boundaries where almost no prospect for development exists—either at present or for years, and perhaps decades, to come. As Robert Beauregard shows, among the nation's fifty largest cities, nine experienced loss of population in every decade between 1950 and 2000—Baltimore, Buffalo, Cincinnati, Cleveland, Detroit, Philadelphia, Pittsburgh, St. Louis, and Washington, D.C. Many other smaller cities, such as Youngstown, have experienced sustained population loss over several decades.[4]

In the Great Lakes states, furthermore, entire metropolitan areas—not just central cities—have experienced little, if any, growth. Development at the edges of these metropolitan areas often comes at the expense of existing development in the core cities and their inner-ring suburbs, leading to a pernicious pattern of no-growth sprawl in outlying rural areas and on prime agricultural land, coupled with abandonment and disinvestment in cities at the center. Thus *the* challenge for planners working in the legacy cities of the Northeast and Great Lakes regions—and New Orleans—is to find ways to manage depopulation and disinvestment in a manner that will achieve goals other than the traditional ones of encouraging or controlling growth.

Some planners and allied professionals have begun to investigate the challenge of depopulation, abandonment, and disinvestment in this country's historically industrial communities. Various universities and policy centers have brought scholars and practitioners together to think through these issues. Several graduate schools in the Great Lakes region now offer courses and design studios that specifically address historically industrial communities. Based on our experiences working in several legacy cities, we suggest redefining the planners' traditional roles to address the characteristics of these cities and the historically industrial communities within them and recommend seven strategic directions that planners can pursue in order to understand and more effectively address the change taking place in these cities and neighborhoods.

Redefining the Planners' Professional Role

As Cassius stated in Shakespeare's *Julius Caesar*, "The fault, dear Brutus, is not in our stars. But in ourselves, that we are underlings." He could as easily have been addressing contemporary planners as he was his co-conspirator when he spoke of taking responsibility for one's status in the civic arena. While the challenges of legacy cities fall well within the purview of urban planning, planners' voices have thus far not stood out in the policy discussion of ways to address disinvestment and property abandonment. A growing number of lawyers, judges, policy specialists, and public officials have elected to fill the gap and have developed ways both to address the challenge and to realize the opportunity vacant property presents to their cities. They have improved administrative approaches to the management of vacant land and structures, gained control of abandoned property through the reform of the legal system, and used code enforcement creatively.[5] They have led the effort to lobby state legislators for the powers necessary to streamline the foreclosure process and address property abandonment at the scale of the problem.

Some planners have collaborated with other professionals to incorporate these strategies and tactics into a broader vision to address what a place can become and to identify the strategic choices that citizens need to make to achieve goals. But too often, the planners' perspective makes little contribution to legal and administrative efforts to champion innovative practices, such as vacant property registration, land banks, or the creation of a dedicated housing court. The work of the planner—in envisioning a better future urban form for a city that is losing population and in showing how various policy approaches can achieve a better future for the place as a whole—remains isolated from work of others addressing the consequences of community disinvestment.

This chapter discusses insights and derives principles from our work in several cities that have lost large shares of their peak populations. Our aim is to contribute to a body of understanding that can support planners' work in such places.[6] One of us (Morrison) was among the planners who led the development of the *Youngstown 2010* plan,[7] following twenty-one years as the director of the City Planning Commission in Cleveland, Ohio. The other (Dewar) has, since 1990, taught courses at the University of Michigan, where graduate urban planning students have developed strategies to strengthen neighborhoods with the help of community partners in Detroit. Over this extended period, she has been involved in numerous discussions about addressing population loss with leaders of community development corporations, their trade associations, leaders of other community-based organizations, and the various collaborations leaders of neighborhood efforts have initiated in that city. Since 2004, she has taught several courses that assigned graduate students the task of working with the Genesee County Land Bank and Flint's neighborhood organizations and develop plans in that legacy city.

We focus this discussion on two cities—Youngstown and Detroit—that, in stark ways, exemplify the challenges and opportunities for historically industrial communities in transition from the "old economy" that fueled them for decades to "new economies," often yet to become apparent. Both Youngstown and Detroit grew to maturity as one-industry towns (Youngstown in steel, Detroit in automobiles) whose fortunes rose and fell with those of the industries they served. Both cities developed their neighborhoods with low-density, detached single-family homes, often owner-occupied. Both have lost three-fifths of their populations from their peak and face the challenge of dealing with widespread abandonment and tax delinquency as a result of the loss of jobs, the flight of middle-class residents to the suburbs, and, more recently, the plague of high-risk mortgage lending. Both have no prospects for a return of the jobs and population that once drove their economies, filled their neighborhoods, and supported their commercial districts and anchor institutions. Both have become poster children of the deindustrialization of North America. Both face the challenge of managing a growing inventory of vacant and often tax-delinquent land and structures. Furthermore, they face the complex problem of the messy and uneven pattern of abandonment. In each city, neighborhoods have experienced different levels of disinvestment and abandonment, so that planners and others responsible for managing the city have difficulty responding to the challenge of abandonment at scale. And, finally, both have leadership working tenaciously to meet these challenges with new language and new strategies and techniques.

Table 1: *Population and Housing Changes in Youngstown and Detroit*

	Census year of peak population	*Peak population in thousands*	*2010 population in thousands*	*Change*
Detroit	1950	1849.6	713.8	-61.4%
Youngstown	1930	170.0	67.0	-60.6%
	Census year of peak housing units	*Peak housing units in thousands*	*2010 housing units in thousands*	*Change*
Detroit	1960	553.2	349.2	-36.9%
Youngstown	1960	51.0	33.1	-35.0%

Sources: U. S. Census Bureau, various years; U. S. Census Bureau, 2010.

Many differences exist, as well; the most obvious is that Detroit has more than ten times the population of Youngstown (see *Table 1*). Youngstown is ahead of Detroit in planning for a smaller city and in implementing a citywide plan so the experiences of each yield lessons in different aspects of planning for a smaller, better city. Youngstown's new plan was completed in 2005; an administration-led process to develop a strategic framework plan has begun in Detroit. In Youngstown, a broadly expressed community narrative and a renewed sense of common mission have emerged, while neither has yet developed in Detroit. In Youngstown, city and university officials have led the planning process. In Detroit, planning for ways to address vacancy without rebuilding has thus far mainly come from community-based organizations, coalitions of community-based developers, and staff in a few city agencies.

Experiences in these two cities and elsewhere show that to have an effective role in planning a city after decline, planners need to see their profession as one that manages change, not just growth, and one that responds to and shapes forces that cause disinvestment and abandonment, not just the forces that fuel new development. Making this conceptual leap is difficult. To work in these places and be effective advocates for their future, individual planners and their local and state professional associations will, of necessity, need to develop the insights, attitudes, and skills to address a range of new issues. The following sections discuss seven lessons for practicing planners. Our discussion emphasizes ways that planning in a city after decline differs from planning in a growing city.

Understand the Depth of the Political Challenge

Planning professionals often avoid the rough-and-tumble of local politics, choosing instead to see elected officials and other civic leaders as policy makers and themselves as professional advisers in a public decision-making framework that, ideally, is rational, transparent, data-driven, and result-oriented. This mindset hampers planners working in cities that are experiencing sustained and often devastating rates of un-employment and population decline. To intervene effectively, the planning practitioner must appreciate the profound difficulty local elected officials and civic leaders have in addressing sustained decline and need to work with them to develop the insights necessary to understand the process of decline, the language they require to engage their constituencies in productive discussions about the challenges the city faces, and the tools that will enable the residents and civic leaders to move forward in creating a city with a better quality of life.

Strong forces interfere with the acceptance of population and employment loss and oppose efforts to plan for a smaller city. At the level of the civic narrative, public acceptance of sustained population decline contradicts the widely-held American belief that population growth equates with "success" and population decline equates with "failure." As nationally syndicated columnist Bob Herbert wrote, accepting population loss communicates a decision "not to rise to the challenges before us" and to watch "greatness …steadily slipping away."[8] American cities—unlike their European counterparts—are relatively young and have known only growth through the nineteenth and much of the twentieth centuries. American cities know no history of urban decline and rebirth as do the many European cities that have experienced the ravages of epidemics and war over centuries. Widespread abandonment of the once-vibrant "old neighborhoods" and once-prosperous downtowns of America's legacy cities has taken place within a single generation as freeway-supported suburbs drew millions of households away from central cities and streetcar suburbs in pursuit of their piece of the American Dream and racially segregated new neighborhoods. The consequences for the people in the neighborhoods left behind have been unprecedented and unnerving.

At the level of local politics, loss of population equates to loss of political power or "clout" and engenders resistance from local political figures who regard that metric as paramount. As a candidate for the mayor of Flint (now the mayor) said during his election campaign in 2009, acceptance of decline "smacks of surrender."[9] Population loss also has profound economic consequences for both city officials and elites, as it typically results in the loss of local wealth. The city's function as a "growth machine" means that both of these groups have much to gain politically and financially from population growth and the increase in the value of land and much to lose from a decline in population and land values.[10] Both of us have attended community meetings where mayors and other elected or appointed officials touted the revival of the city while the audience could readily observe extensive vacant structures and vacant land throughout the area.

Frequently, other constituencies, particularly minority-race groups, oppose any talk of "planned shrinkage." Most of the country's legacy cities had aggressive urban renewal programs that, by the early 1970s, had cleared many well-established African-American neighborhoods without providing better—or even adequate—alternative places to live.[11] Therefore, any hint of further clearance of African-American neighborhoods through planned "decommissioning" raises the specter of more neighborhood destruction and inequitable treatment. Such suggestions have led to strong political resistance.[12]

One insight that the planner can bring to local elected officials and civic leaders is the realization that numerous other cities face similar challenges of disinvestment and decline. All too often, the citizens and leaders of these cities believe that no other similarly affected cities exist with comparable histories and economic structures. They engage in nostalgia, wishful thinking, or heroic gestures and look for the quick fix that will restore their city to its former greatness. Just such a pattern emerged in Youngstown in the years following "Black Monday" (September 19, 1977), when Youngstown Sheet and Tube's Campbell Works abruptly shut down, beginning a four-year period during which Youngstown and the Mahoning Valley lost every major steel mill, ten thousand union jobs, and most of their economic base. In the years following Black Monday, Youngstown leaders attempted, unsuccessfully, to facilitate employee ownership of the mills. When that effort failed, the leadership pursued one "silver bullet" project after another: an Avanti automobile factory, an indoor motor-sports racetrack, a U.S. Department of Defense payroll center, a dirigible assembly plant, an airplane factory, and an air cargo hub at the Youngstown-Warren Regional Airport. Each of these projects was either short-lived or stillborn, and the promise of good jobs to replace those lost when the mills closed went unfulfilled.[13]

While Youngstown initially stood alone, other "steel towns" in Ohio, Pennsylvania, New York, Indiana, and Illinois soon joined it. The auto cities of Michigan and other Great Lakes states likewise experienced major plant closings from the late 1970s on. Other Great Lakes cities have seen their industrial bases erode or disappear. From Akron (rubber), Rochester (Kodak), and Dayton (NCR) to Elkhart (recreational vehicles), legacy cities, large and small, have experienced—or continue to experience—the impact of deindustrialization. Despite the wave of plant closings taking place across the region, Youngstown failed to make common cause with cities like it and, for over twenty years, attempted to go it alone.

While "misery may love company," the need for legacy cities—both in this country and abroad—to acknowledge that they are experiencing similar challenges is more than a simple act of commiseration. It can empower local leaders to think differently about their city's future. Youngstown has experienced just such a transformation in its civic consciousness. The national and international response to Youngstown's precedent-setting planning process opened its citizens' eyes to the fact that other cities were experiencing similar patterns of decline. Youngstown's leadership gained significant insights from Flint, Cleveland, Pittsburgh, Detroit, and other similarly placed cities as citizens began to confront the widespread property abandonment in the city's neighborhoods.

As a result of its engagement with similar cities, Youngstown's leaders no longer promote silver bullet panaceas or portray the city as a helpless victim of forces beyond its control. They now engage with federal and state agencies and with organizations such as the Center for Community Progress (formerly the National Vacant Properties Campaign), Greater Ohio, the Brookings Institution, and the German Marshall Fund to develop new tools locally and lobby for new powers and resources at the county, state, and federal levels. Planners working in historically industrial communities can help their political and civic leadership understand the nature and extent of the challenges facing their cities and develop the political language and policy initiatives to address them. They can also encourage local leaders and organizations to engage with other similarly challenged cities to develop common advocacy strategies directed at securing the powers and resources needed to address these challenges at scale.

Understand the Power of Memory and Civic Identity

In cities that have experienced sustained decline, the planning process should, on the one hand, acknowledge the history and civic identity of the city and its neighborhoods as assets and, on the other hand, enable residents to address openly the wrongs and divisions that are also the legacies of the past. In cities that formerly depended on manufacturing, the deep divisions of race, class, and ethnicity and the profound disruption of urban renewal and interstate highway construction often remain vivid memories.

Historic patterns of division based on race, class, and ethnicity continue to inform contemporary discussions. As these cities developed in the late nineteenth and early twentieth centuries, the owners and managers of large manufacturing corporations used these divisions to slow unionization and control their workers. Neighborhoods were deliberately segregated, reinforcing the divisions that existed within the mills and factories. Later, during the 1960s and 1970s, urban renewal, highway construction, and white flight to the suburbs disrupted these neighborhoods and began the widespread abandonment of once dense working-class neighborhoods. As whites left, the remaining population became increasingly a minority-race one; these residents faced white hostility if they moved to the suburbs, and until the late 1960s they could rarely obtain mortgages. The long-term residents who remained behind saw a dramatic increase in the conversion of single-family houses to rental properties, the arrival of absentee owners and slumlords, high turnover among renters, increasing disinvestment, rising crime, falling property values, and, finally, extensive demolition of vacant structures and the abandonment of entire streets and blocks. In the most disinvested areas, few new homeowners have arrived in recent decades, so discussions about what such areas "should become" often strikes fear in minority and elderly residents who have endured many of the misguided changes that led to their neighborhoods' destruction.

In order to enable citizens of a battered city such as Youngstown to determine what the city can become in the future, the planning process must engage with the past and address deep feelings of injustice, distrust, and loss that these cities' industrial heritage created as by-products. Planners who choose to work in these places often need to act like family therapists or social workers, engaging citizens where they are and helping them move forward together. All too often, deep memories of past injuries impede citizens' ability to envision a promising shared future and take the actions to move toward it. Planners must listen—very intently and very intentionally—as people talk about their history as well as their aspirations. They must learn to appreciate the "family dynamics" of cities and neighborhoods that, in some ways, function as extended families and to encourage those who participate in the planning process to deal honestly and respectfully with one another. Only then can a community come together around a common purpose.

Youngstown's planning team learned that lesson in the course of developing the *Youngstown 2010* plan. Well into the planning process, the team determined that the "usual and customary" citizen participation process was not fully engaging key constituencies, particularly African-Americans. After the final round of community meetings, Community Development Director (and later Mayor) Jay Williams reported to the team that too many citizens had approached him with their concern that the process was not dealing with true issues of importance to them for him to feel comfortable moving forward. The team decided to use an already scheduled public television broadcast on the *Youngstown 2010* planning process to focus on the issue: "Race and Youngstown 2010: Vision or Division?" Citizens of Youngstown were invited to attend and participate in a one-hour live "town hall" broadcast which Williams moderated. He set ground rules of mutual respect and civility and invited attendees to talk openly about their views on race, with the aim of moving the city to a better future. Williams began the session with a video overview of the city's history of race and class conflicts and then opened the floor for discussion.[14] As the hour neared an end, the planning team and the producer agreed that the discussion had not exhausted the topic and decided to reconvene the town hall session in a second broadcast. During that broadcast, the team again decided that the topic needed further airing and, with the audience's concurrence, taped a third hour-long segment.

The team knew that going live to discuss difficult and, at times, inflammatory issues in an open civic forum was risky but essential for the plan itself to have credibility among citizens and gain the full support of the mayor and city council. The sessions were hard-hitting but ultimately therapeutic and cleared the air of the suspicion and distrust that threatened to sink the entire planning process. The strategy of confronting deep-seated injuries and conflicts convinced the public and their political representatives that *Youngstown 2010* was not just another pro forma civic engagement process that pretended to listen to people and then largely ignored what they had to say.

In Detroit, as the open meetings for the development of a strategic framework plan began in fall 2010, planners tried to launch immediately into imagining the city's future despite little preparation, but the baggage of the past interfered. Residents expressed deep distrust of the city officials, who, they said, must have a secret plan, of the foundation leaders who were paying for the planning process for what the residents felt must be suspect reasons, and of other residents who were younger or of a different race.[15] The meetings became settings to air complaints, grievances, and suspicions rather than sessions focused on defining the community's shared vision for its future. The planning process moved into a next stage of meetings in early 2011. This time, the structure of the meetings kept complaint and protest under control. At each meeting, a city official made a PowerPoint presentation that included questions for the audience. Attendees had clickers that allowed them to select an answer to each question from several suggested answers; they could also write comments on pieces of paper. In numerous cases, the answers to these questions had no implications for further development of a plan. City officials answered a number of questions from the audience at the end of the presentation. The process prevented discussion of suspicions and wrongs and allowed no open disagreements or challenges. Although two hundred or so people normally showed up for a meeting, the number dwindled to about half that as the meeting proceeded.

Planners working in legacy cities can also help residents articulate the unique and empowering aspects of their shared history. A city's industrial history is not just a liability like so many contaminated factory sites. The history of a place and its people informs its cultural identity and shapes the shared experiences and values that define "who we are" as a city or a neighborhood.[16] These cities and neighborhoods often constitute communities of memory with a strong sense of group identity that defines a commonly understood "genetic code" of place. While this shared identity can lead to an insularity and parochialism hostile to new ideas and people from outside the area, a planner who understands the value of shared identity as a place-based asset can shape place-specific planning and economic development strategies that build on that shared identity and have a "rightness of fit" that can attract sustained political support.

Just such a collective realignment has taken place in Youngstown. For several decades following Black Monday, the Youngstown business and political communities pursued strategies that bore little relationship to its century-old industrial base: metals and ceramics. Only in the past decade has the city's civic leadership aligned around industries deeply embedded in Youngstown's industrial history. Youngstown State University's College of Science, Technology, Engineering, and Mathematics (STEM) has inaugurated a research-based Ph.D. in Materials Science and Engineering that focuses on the application of advanced "heavy" materials—principally metals and ceramics—to new products, while the region's chamber of commerce and political leadership have focused their efforts on supporting firms that are manufacturing high-quality products from these materials. As a result of this alignment of civic energy around "doing what we know, only better," Youngstown is now home to the world's largest producer of impact-extruded aluminum containers and a major international producer of seamless steel pipe for the natural gas industry, and counts among its most successful local manufacturing firms a company producing lightweight aluminum/ceramic vests for the U.S. Department of Defense and a company providing precision measuring and metals fabricating services to a wide range of industries.

Pursue a Planning Process That Enables Residents to Develop a Shared Vision for a Smaller City or Smaller Sections of a City

The participation and involvement of residents has to extend beyond addressing legacies of distrust and division. In Youngstown, planners led the process that brought widespread acceptance that Youngstown could become a smaller, better, and more sustainable city. A critical factor in the success of the planning process was the decision early in the process to engage residents "early and often" by using many different forums and marketing channels and to advance the planning process at a pace that would enable people to trust that the process—and the plans that resulted from it—truly reflected their aspirations and concerns. The case study following this chapter details this process.

The Youngstown experience showed that this kind of participation differs considerably from the usual public hearings that government planners conduct as required for various purposes. Rather, the goal is to develop a process to elicit real engagement that takes the views of residents seriously in ways that affect the direction of the plan itself as response to residents' input.

The experience of planners working in Youngstown and Detroit suggests several other lessons about public participation, as well. Planners who themselves see possibilities in planning after decline can give residents the facts. They can communicate the scale and extent of the transition taking place in neighborhoods and open a dialogue that enables residents and civic leaders to discuss the reality of becoming a smaller city and the possibility of adjusting their metric of success from size to quality. Planners can use geographic information systems (GIS) and simulation to identify the patterns of decline and growth in their cities and focus limited public dollars on interventions that directly address quality of life by reducing crime and blight, improving mobility and the perception of safety, and identifying economic development projects—such as neighborhood grocery stores—that the smaller market can still support. And they can assume the role of "practical visionary" and help city leaders and residents to imagine an achievable future as a smaller but more sustainable city. Techniques that visualization and representation software make possible can enable planners to show residents and city officials the city's current conditions and help them illustrate what new ideas would mean in neighborhood changes.[17]

By taking these actions, planners gain credibility and work effectively with citizens to envision a realistic future for their neighborhood and their city. In many cases, the public has moved ahead of the planners, politicians, and other civic leaders in accepting the reality of shrinkage and in seeking realistic strategies for addressing the negative impacts of decline. Planners in Detroit encouraged residents to think of vacancy as an opportunity for creating a new kind of place, rather than as a problem.[18] As a result, public meetings held in a very empty area of the city inspired residents to contribute new ideas and insights. They proposed "reinventing" vacant areas rather than pursuing redevelopment plans that likely would not occur.

Engage with Anchor Institutions That Function as Urban Magnets

Hospitals and universities function as some of the most important anchor institutions remaining in legacy cities. Despite their economic importance, city officials and residents often have conflicted relationships with these institutions. While such institutions employ many people and thus have a significant number on their payrolls, they often function as islands of prosperity in high-poverty neighborhoods with which they may have only intermittent and often hostile relationships. These institutions generally have a large physical footprint comprised of an interconnected complex of imposing buildings having little or no relationship to the surrounding neighborhoods. The design of these institutions normally focuses on the often exacting program requirements of the institution's users, with minimal concern for how meeting such requirements will affect adjacent streets, sidewalks, and non-institutional buildings.

Planners working in historically industrial communities typically seek to minimize the negative effects of their anchor institutions on surrounding neighborhoods. They should also ask how best to engage with these institutions in ways that will create place-specific development opportunities in the neighborhoods surrounding them.

To capitalize on the presence of these institutions, planners can see them as magnets as well as anchors, predictably drawing students, employees, visitors, and patients to their city from the surrounding region. Planners should determine how many students daily attend their urban college or university and learn where they live and how they arrive on the campus. They should probe the latent market these students create for housing on or near the campus and the mix of entertainment and retail uses they would support within a convenient walking distance of their classrooms, labs, and housing. Planners should understand the number of new employees the university or hospital hires annually and identify what opportunities exist to house a segment of this market within a convenient walk or short bus ride to the campus or hospital. Of particular interest are faculty members recruited from other cities who enjoy urban living, hospital residents who seek good-quality housing adjacent to the hospital, where they will practice for long hours, and employees looking for affordable workforce housing that will enable them to reduce the cost and inconvenience of the daily commute. Planners should understand the markets these magnet institutions create and work with them to develop the off-campus environments that will attract students, faculty, employees, patients, and visitors and enable them to spend their housing, retail and entertainment dollars in the city.[19]

In short, planners in historically industrial communities have to ferret out latent demand "hidden in plain view." They need to develop land use, urban design and economic development strategies that take full advantage of the opportunities created each day by people coming into their city to work and study.

Youngstown officials pursued just such an approach when they agreed to collaborate with Youngstown State University in the development of a new College of Business Administration. By 2001, university administrators had determined that they needed to replace the College's existing building, a cramped and anonymous classroom/office building constructed in the 1970s and functionally obsolete thirty years later. The college's dean and the university's planning staff began to investigate alternative sites, and city leaders solicited them to leave the confines of the university's central campus and build in downtown Youngstown. The dean rejected the idea of relocating downtown, citing the students' need to attend classes in buildings clustered on the central campus. She did, however, sympathize with city officials' desire to direct some of the energy—and spending power—of university students from the center of campus to the center of downtown, four blocks away. After investigating a number of suitable sites, university administrators and city leaders agreed on a site at the southern edge of the university's footprint, and city officials agreed to construct the site and connect it to downtown and the central campus by developing a streetscape-enhanced roadway between the two and by targeting economic development incentives on properties adjacent to the new road. As a result of this decision, the university developed an iconic, state-of-the-art academic building to meet the needs of the college while linking the campus and the downtown in a direct and highly visible way. Since the commencement of construction, adjacent property owners have invested significantly in their buildings, while the city has seen a welcome influx of students who use the new roadway to frequent downtown establishments.

Manage Neighborhood Change Strategically

As a city becomes smaller, planners must engage specifically in understanding and managing the processes of neighborhood change. Neighborhood planning and community development usually focus on redevelopment, rebuilding, and revitalization. Instead, planners in legacy cities need to figure out approaches other than redevelopment for handling property. At the same time, the combination of stretched city budgets, shrinking Community Development Block Grants, and insufficient staff resources mean that a shrinking city's government often cannot support all the activities needed to manage change in neighborhoods. This resource limitation means that city officials should make difficult decisions about the different kinds of support that varied areas will receive.

Effective management of neighborhood change in the face of decline requires designing and implementing a planning process that neighborhood residents see as fair and equitable. Even in areas where so few people remain that no neighborhood organizations or block clubs exist to speak for residents, planners need to seek residents' views on what trade-offs they would accept, given the city's much smaller population. Residents in denser neighborhoods likewise need the opportunity to deal with the past in the context of envisioning a future for their own areas. Planners need to provide choices for those who have few options and engage in a planning process that involves those people in making the decisions that affect their lives.[20]

In evaluating the future of individual neighborhoods, the planner must acknowledge that some neighborhoods either no longer exist or will not exist. Much of their housing stock is surplus and unsalvageable because demand for many of these properties has disappeared from both the city and the surrounding metropolitan market. Much of this housing is like a dry snake skin; it has done its job and now has no useful future. Many of the most extensively abandoned neighborhoods in Detroit and Youngstown were built rapidly in the early part of the twentieth century to accommodate the enormous numbers of people arriving for work in their booming mills and factories. With a few exceptions, most worker housing built in this era was poorly constructed and is expensive to renovate to meet contemporary standards. Once renovated, such properties do not necessarily sell or rent due to weak demand for housing in these neighborhoods.

In the face of such realities, the planner needs to reimagine and repurpose these neighborhoods and abandon notions of repopulating them for the foreseeable future. Youngstown's plan specifically states, "As a place with fewer people but the same amount of land, Youngstown can afford to be generous with its urban land as it explores new options for the city's neighborhoods and open space systems."[21] Youngstown now allows residents to take over abandoned lots adjacent to their homes.[22] Detroit officials have sold city-owned lots to adjacent owners but have not adopted policies that go as far as Youngtown's. Detroit officials could, for instance, offer long-term leases at little or no rent to residents who care for city-owned land that they have often integrated with other property around their homes.

In heavily abandoned areas, Youngstown officials experimented with a program to encourage residents to relocate to intact streets elsewhere in the city. When residents from these neighborhoods requested repair funding, city planners offered them fifty thousand dollars to buy a new home elsewhere in the city. As of fall 2009, no home owner had accepted the incentive, however, and planners put their efforts into other approaches. In Detroit, Mayor Bing announced in December 2010 that city officials would encourage residents of sparsely settled areas of the city to move to denser areas. While the city's budget deficit motivated the mayor to encourage such moves to try to save money on delivering services in nearly empty areas, no one had apparently analyzed how much money the city would save by reducing services in vacant areas. [23] Mayor Bing's message of wanting to persuade people to move because the city government could not afford to provide services in nearly vacant areas contrasted sharply with the positive message in Youngstown of the prospect of becoming a better, smaller city for all.

With large numbers of vacant lots, city officials in many historically industrial communities are considering uses of vacant land other than for housing and commercial buildings. Planners have a central role in this discussion. They can consider revisions to the city codes and practices that discourage appropriate "non-traditional" urban uses. They should also point out appropriate locations for these new uses, taking account of the activities' location criteria in the context of an overall vision of reinvention of very vacant areas. In Detroit, urban farming has received considerable discussion. Numerous other possible new uses also exist, such as energy generation and deconstruction facilities. In Detroit, years of discussions have been devoted to seeking ways to accommodate community gardening and urban agriculture and to provide assurances about land control. Beginning in 2007, Cleveland adopted new zoning provisions to promote urban agriculture. These zoning-code amendments included the establishment of "urban garden zoning districts," which permit urban gardens and prohibit all other use of a property; reinstated the provisions permitting residents to raise bees, chickens, ducks, rabbits, and larger livestock in urban neighborhoods (and reversed a decision to prohibit these uses made in a code revision a decade earlier); permitted agriculture as a principal use on all vacant residentially zoned lots; and established "urban agricultural overlay districts" to allow larger-scale farming activities in the city.

In the neighborhoods with some blight and some vacant lots, a planner should work with residents on an array of approaches calibrated to address the extent of disinvestment and vacancy in various parts of the neighborhood. Programs to transfer vacant lots to adjacent owners, create community gardens, landscape vacant lots with native plants, and create play lots often strengthen a neighborhood when enough residents remain to care for these. Key in such neighborhoods is to reinforce the residents' commitment to the place and to celebrate their determination to stay so that they continue to maintain their property and remain engaged in neighborhood issues.[24] In Detroit, the Detroit Vacant Property Campaign has made small grants to neighborhood associations to enable neighbors to care for vacant houses and protect houses going through mortgage foreclosure from destruction. In Youngstown, the Raymond John Wean Foundation offers what it calls "Neighborhood Success Grants" of five hundred to five thousand dollars to groups of residents, as well as to community, school, and faith-based organizations to support the development and implementation of creative ideas that can enhance their neighborhoods. Foundations in Cleveland funded community development corporations to implement demonstration projects showing how to reuse vacant land in strategic locations to create new urban landscapes that enhanced neighborhoods (the case study following Chapter 6).

In some of these in-between neighborhoods, building new housing on vacant lots may reinforce confidence in the areas as long as the extent of blight has not reached a tipping point such that interventions will have considerable difficulty stopping decline. One criteria that should be considered when selecting sites is where new housing can inspire other property owners' confidence in a neighborhood. Developers often can acquire vacant land most easily in the most blighted areas, but these often are not the places where new construction should occur. Nonprofit developers, like for-profit ones, need to look for evidence of a demand for housing where they wish to build.

Intact neighborhoods that have not yet experienced much disinvestment and have few, if any, vacant lots nonetheless feel the effect of the continuing loss of their city's population (at the rate of over twenty thousand people each year in Detroit). They suffer from the blighting influence of a few scattered abandoned properties and the wave of mortgage foreclosures that have emptied sound single-family properties and have converted many to investment rental property with absentee landlords. In these areas, planners need to work with residents to enforce relevant city codes, quickly address signs of disinvestment to prevent the incursion of blight, and reinforce residents' confidence that their neighborhoods can remain strong.

All of these types of neighborhoods need quick demolition of dangerous, derelict structures, but few local governments in legacy cities have the resources to remove such buildings quickly throughout the city. Detroit officials have generally prioritized the demolition of structures near schools. Planners can offer ideas about how to carry out demolition more strategically—placing priority on demolitions where much housing remains, for instance, and where residents are working to strengthen a neighborhood. This means that demolitions may rarely occur in the areas of the city that already have substantial amounts of vacant land.

Finally, planners need to address the problems of obsolete neighborhood-oriented commercial corridors. These commercial corridors grew up along the cities' streetcar lines and main arterial roadways and served the older neighborhoods. In the face of population loss and profound changes in consumers' shopping habits, vacant lots and buildings pock many of these once vital strips. The buildings that remain often show signs of disinvestment. While Main Street retail revitalization programs can support a few sections of corridors that still have some intact structures with operating businesses, large sections of these commercial districts no longer meet the needs of contemporary retail businesses and require new purposes. Planners need to work with business associations and with neighbors who live in nearby blocks to speed the process of getting rid of blighted, vacant structures and implementing reuse of vacant land in more attractive, low-maintenance ways. They need to work with business owners to encourage them to locate near nodes of shopping where they will have a larger customer base, although they will pay higher rents.[25]

Identify Legacy Assets and Rediscover the Urban Landscape

To be effective in shrinking legacy cities, the planner must see the city anew, focusing not just on the obvious liabilities left behind as factories closed and neighborhoods collapsed but also on the legacy assets. Identifying these assets requires the planner to understand how the city worked—when it worked—and develop a vision for the future that accounts for and takes advantage of these assets—whether an art museum, a collection of historically significant houses, a nineteenth-century park, or a network of underutilized rail lines and sidings that can support new kinds of uses in vacant industrial sites. Often these assets are "hidden in plain view" from local residents and public officials who continue to mourn the loss of the city's industries and neighborhoods and believe that everything of value disappeared when the factories closed and the jobs disappeared.

Among the most compelling legacy assets of historically industrial communities are the landscapes that remain after decline. Many of these cities grew rapidly, without benefit of a plan or zoning. In the rush to build workforce housing, developers leveled forests, channeled streams into culverts, filled wetlands, and obliterated other natural features. The wide-spread abandonment of mills, factories, and working-class neighborhoods offers these cities an opportunity to restore the natural features and position them as assets for the future.

Understanding the latent power of legacy landscapes requires that the planner look at the land with new eyes. One can try to imagine what the architects and landscape architects who designed these industrial cities during the late nineteenth and early twentieth centuries might have proposed had the urban land now vacant and the watercourse no longer diverted for industrial use been available when they did their work. Youngstown and Detroit are both rediscovering their riverfronts, which mills and factories once lined, and they are exploring the potential of these legacy landscapes. In Youngstown, the Mahoning River functioned for over a century as an open industrial sewer running for thirty miles behind an almost continuous wall of steel mills. With the mills gone, the river has become a prominent feature in the downtown area. City officials are pursuing environmental remediation of the river and the development of a bikeway that would connect the university and downtown to the nearby Mill Creek Park. In Detroit, the Detroit Riverfront Conservancy has transformed derelict, inaccessible riverfront property into the RiverWalk, which now provides public access in a park setting to a stretch of the river near downtown.

Planners can use observation and analysis to propose ways for a city to connect and leverage landscape assets. The *Youngstown 2010* plan did just that, recommending that the city assemble tax-delinquent properties adjacent to several existing parks to expand the green space network, connect the assets with bicycle and pedestrian paths, improve the visibility and accessibility of these resources, and position them to serve as stronger assets for adjacent neighborhoods. Even in Detroit's disinvested neighborhoods, housing around parks often remains in good condition, while many opportunities exist to expand and enhance parks through incorporation of vacant land.[26] The city government, however, faces severe budget constraints and cannot support the maintenance needed to keep parks vital. In the context of a large deficit, the mayor, the city council, and parks officials have considered closing many parks.

Planners can also explore repurposing vacant urban land to restore the city's natural systems. Without the press of population growth, city officials can consider naturalizing abandoned sites with the intent of reducing runoff into aging storm sewer systems.[27] Both the Philadelphia Green and Sustainable Cleveland initiatives explore this topic. In Detroit, plans for sections of the city and for individual neighborhoods pointed to ways to reuse vacant lots for water retention in residential areas with clusters of lots. The Youngstown plan suggests assembling large tracts of abandoned, and often swampy residentially zoned land with hydric soils and repurposing the land as wetlands and wildlife sanctuaries.[28]

Planners can borrow from agricultural practice to introduce the concept of "fallowing" to the discussion about what to do with cleared urban land left after decline. Planners could advocate assembling abandoned sites for an as-yet-to-be-determined use and holding these in a land bank until the sites "ripen" for future reuse. In the interim, these sites can remain as passive landscape elements in a smaller, greener city.[29]

Get Rid of Visible Liabilities

Besides identifying and enhancing the city's assets, planners need to focus resources on minimizing liabilities and their impacts on the city and on neighborhoods. In cities with strong demand for land, a burned-out building or a vacant industrial site quickly gets reused. Typically, only ownership uncertainty or environmental liabilities cause delays. In contrast, cities that have experienced large-scale population and employment loss cannot rely on demand for property to recycle a vacant building or site and return it to productive use. City officials must instead act expeditiously to remove the overhang of surplus housing, commercial buildings, and industrial property that depresses the value of surrounding properties, discourages reinvestment, and can harbor and encourage criminal activities.

Residents and city officials often believe that if only contaminated industrial sites could get cleaned up, new development would occur. However, in legacy cities, such new development does not necessarily follow. In southwest Detroit, an Empowerment Zone program made possible the cleanup of several large contaminated sites where no indication of demand for property existed. The sites remained vacant. The cleanup effort would have done better to focus on cleanup of sites near housing and schools in order to remove a threat to children's health and safety and of sites that many people passed every day, so as to remove an eyesore.[30]

Planners can use available tools such as geographic information systems to assess their city's inventory of blighted and abandoned properties, to analyze patterns of disinvestment, arson, and crime, and to direct limited city resources to removing the most visible and noxious blight. When developing "clean and green" programs, planners can also borrow the site selection techniques that billboard companies routinely apply and target limited resources to the most visible corridors and sites and thus maximize the impact on their city's "curb appeal." These companies select sites based on street visibility and traffic count and value most highly the sites that the largest number of motorists sees. The planner can apply the same approach to the selection of high-visibility sites and corridors for priority blight removal and can encourage greening and maintenance of the cleared sites.

Conclusion

Planners can take a stronger, more effective role in remaking cities after decline if they reframe their work as managing change, not guiding growth and development. They have many opportunities for improving the quality of life in cities after large-scale loss of population and disinvestment in property, but these rarely involve redevelopment. Because of the considerable shift in perspective, planners working in these settings need more resources and opportunities to learn how to manage a city's adjustment after decline. Without these, planners continue to work on development, or they struggle on their own to invent new ways of thinking, when, instead, they could learn from one another. The prospect of reinventing the practice of planning in America's legacy cities and historically industrial communities provides an important challenge for planning professionals and educators for the years to come.

Notes

1. We use the terms "legacy cities" and "historically industrial communities" throughout this chapter. The first term refers to the municipality as a whole, while the second term more broadly refers to cities (usually smaller) that committed their economy almost exclusively to heavy manufacturing and to neighborhoods (usually in larger cities) that grew up close to mills and factories and experienced precipitous population loss after these plants closed. Other terms have emerged to describe cities that have experienced persistent population loss and disinvestment. Residents and leadership criticized the terms shrinking cities and weak market cities for being pejorative and rejected these terms in favor of "cities in transition." We believe that the latter term is anodyne and of little analytic use: Every city everywhere is "in transition" at any given time. (In the words of Bob Dylan, "He not busy being born is busy dying.") Calling the cities confronting the powerful forces of deindustrialization and depopulation "cities in transition" conflates these cities—with their distinct and compelling narratives—with others going through dramatic change of other kinds and fails to give this class of cities a name that is useful when developing the policies and practices that will address the forces they face.

2. Hack, Birch, Sedway, and Silver (2009). See, especially, pp. 71, 88, 146.
3. Mallach (2006); Bonham, Spilka, and Rastorfer (2002). In 2011, the American Planning Association added to this list with a Planning Advisory Service report on urban agriculture (Hodgson, Campbell, and Bailkey [2011]).
4. Beauregard (2009). See also Rieniets (2005), p.24.
5. The sessions of the conferences of the National Vacant Properties Campaign presented these ideas and innovations.
6. Our thinking has benefited from the work of other planners whose publications are helping to create the body of work to turn the planning profession's attention to the issue of planning after decline. For example, see Cleveland Land Lab (2008, 2009); Cleveland Urban Design Collaborative (2006); Mallach (2006); Mallach, Levy, and Shilling (2005); Shilling, Schamess and Logan (2006).
7. City of Youngstown (2005).
8. Herbert (2010).
9. Brooks (2009).
10. Molotch (1976); Logan and Molotch (1987); Elkin (1987).
11. For example, Thomas (1997); Highsmith (2009).
12. Cooper-McCann (2010).
13. Editorial (2011).
14. Western Reserve Public Media (2004).
15. As Bockmeyer (2000) has pointed out, a "culture of distrust" pervades Detroit's politics.
16. Linkon and Russo (2002).
17. For examples of such efforts, see Cleveland Land Lab (2008, 2009); Cleveland Urban Design Collaborative. (2006)
18. For example, Doherty et al. (2008); Bradford, et al. (2007).
19. Rodin (2007).
20. Fainstein (2000); Krumholz, Cogger, and Linner (1975).
21. City of Youngstown (2005), p. 6.
22. Ibid., p. 47.
23. Christie (2008); W. D'Avignon, city of Youngstown planner, communication with University of Michigan urban planning students, October 2009; Gerritt (2010); Aslesen et al. (2010).
24. Morrish and Brown (2000).
25. Adams, et al. (2010).
26. Doherty, et al. (2008).
27. Cleveland Land Lab (2008); Pennsylvania Horticultural Society (2011).
28. For example, Batsakis, et al. (2009); Bralich (2009).
29. See the development of this idea in Nassauer et al. (2008).
30. Casadei et al. (2003).

Bibliography

Adams, L. et al. 2010. *From Vacant to Viable: Strategies for Addressing Commercial Corridors in Detroit.* Ann Arbor: Urban and Regional Planning Program, University of Michigan.

Aslesen, M. et al. 2010. *Model Changeover: Adapting City Services to Detroit's Urban Landscape.* Ann Arbor: Urban and Regional Planning, University of Michigan.

Batsakis, A., et al. 2009. *Filling in the Gaps: A Plan for Vacant Properties in Osborn.* Ann Arbor: Urban and Regional Planning Program, University of Michigan.

Beauregard, R. 2009. "Urban Population Loss in Historical Perspective: United States, 1820-2000." *Environment and Planning* A 41: 514-528.

Bonham, J. B, J. S. Spilka, and D. Rastorfer 2002. *Old Cities/Green Cities: Communities Transform Unmanaged Land.* Planning Advisory Service Report 506/507. Chicago: American Planning Association.

Bockmeyer, J. L. 2000. "A Culture of Distrust: The Impact of Local Political Culture on Participation in the Detroit EZ." *Journal of Urban Affairs* 37, no. 13: 2417-2440.

Bradford, T. et al. 2007. *Towards a Brighter Future: A Plan for Southeast Brightmoor.* Ann Arbor: Urban and Regional Planning Program, University of Michigan, Ann Arbor.

Bralich, J. 2009. "Developing Methods to Establish an Urban Wetland Mitigation Bank on Youngstown's East Side." Youngstown, OH: Center for Urban and Regional Studies, Youngstown State University.

Brooks, A. 2009. "Flint, Mich.: Growing Stronger by Growing Smaller?" National Public Radio, July 13. Retrieved July 13, 2009, from http://www.npr.org/templates/story/story.php?storyId=106492424.

Casadei, A. et al. 2003. *Overcoming the Brownfields Challenge: Steps Towards an Environmental and Economic Rebirth of Southwest Detroit.* Ann Arbor: Urban and Regional Planning Program, University of Michigan..

Christie, L. 2008. "You can't pay them enough to leave." CNNMoney.com, April 24. Retrieved July 10, 2010, from http://money.cnn.com/2008/04/15/real_estate/Youngstown_plan_roadblock/index.htm.

City of Youngstown. 2005. *Youngstown 2010 Citywide Plan.* Youngstown, OH: City of Youngstown.

Cleveland Land Lab. 2008. *Re-Imagining a More Sustainable Cleveland: Citywide Strategies for Reuse of Vacant Land.* Cleveland : Cleveland Urban Design Collaborative, Kent State University.

Cleveland Land Lab. 2009. *Re-Imagining Cleveland: Vacant Land Re-use Pattern Book.* Cleveland : Cleveland Urban Design Collaborative, Kent State University.

Cleveland Urban Design Collaborative. 2006. "Oak Hill Community Design Charrette, Youngstown, Ohio." Kent State University, Cleveland, OH. February.

Cooper-McCann, P. 2010. Rightsizing Detroit: Looking Back, Looking Forward. Senior honor's thesis, College of Literature, Science, and the Arts, University of Michigan, Ann Arbor.

Doherty, K. et al. 2008. Ann Arbor: *A Land Use Plan for Brightmoor.* Urban and Regional Planning Program, University of Michigan.

Editorial. 2011. "Too Early to Speculate on Racetrack." *Warren Tribune,* January 23.

Elkin, S. L. 1987. *City and Regime in the American Republic.* Chicago: University of Chicago Press.

Fainstein, S. S. 2000. "New Directions in Planning Theory." *Urban Affairs Review.* 35,4: 451-478.

Gerritt, J. 2010. "Bing's Drive to Reshape the City is Shaping First Term in Office." *Detroit Free Press*, Dec. 9

Hack, G., E.Birch, , P. Sedway, and M. Silver. 2009. *Local Planning: Contemporary Principles and Practice*. Washington, D.C.: ICMA Press.

Herbert, B. 2010. "When Greatness Slips Away." *New York Times*. June 22.

Highsmith, A. R. 2009. "Demolition Means Progress: Urban Renewal, Local Politics, and State-Sanctioned Ghetto Formation in Flint, Michigan." *Journal of Urban History* 35,3: 348-368.

Hodgson, K., M. C. Campbell, and M.Bailkey, 2011. *Urban Agriculture* Chicago: American Planning Association.

Krumholz, N., J. Cogger, and J. Linner. 1975. "The Cleveland Policy Planning Report." *Journal of the American Institute of Planning* 41: 298-304.

Linkon, S. L., and J. Russo 2002. Steeltown U.S.A.: Work and Memory in Youngstown. Lawrence: University Press of Kansas.

Logan, J. R., and H. L. Molotch. 1987. *Urban Fortunes: The Political Economy of Place*. Berkeley: University of California Press.

Mallach, A. 2006. *Bringing Buildings Back*. Montclair, NJ: National Housing Institute.

Mallach, A., L. M. Levy, and J. Schilling. 2005. *Cleveland at the Crossroads*. Washington, D.C.: National Vacant Properties Campaign.

Molotch, H. 1976. "The City as a Growth Machine: Toward a Political Economy of Place." *American Journal of Sociology* 82,2: 309-332.

Morrish, W. R., and C. R. Brown, 2000. *Planning to Stay*. Minneapolis, MN: Milkweed Editions.

Nassauer, J. I., R. VanWieren, Z. Wang, and D. Kahn. 2008. "Vacant Land as a Natural Asset: Enduring Land Values Created by Care and Ownership." Research report for the Genesee Institute. Retrieved March 2, 2010, from http://www-personal.umich.edu/~nassauer/UrbanDesign/Links/FlintReport_FINAL.pdf. University of Michigan, Ann Arbor. April.

Pennsylvania Horticultural Society. 2011. "Philadelphia Green." Retrieved January 31, 2011, from http://www.pennsylvaniahorticulturalsociety.org/phlgreen/about.html.

Rieniets, T. 2005. "Global Shrinkage." *In Shrinking Cities*, edited by P. Oswalt. Vol. 1, : International Research, pp. 20-34. Ostfildern-Ruit, Germany: Hatje Cantz.

Rodin, J. 2007. *The University and Urban Revival*. Philadelphia: University of Pennsylvania Press.

Schilling, J., L. Schamess, and J. Logan, 2006. *Blueprint Buffalo*. Washington, D.C.: National Vacant Properties Campaign. Retrieved September 21, 2009, from http://www.vacantproperties.org/resources/BUF_Action%20Plan_lo.pdf.

Thomas, J. M. 1997. *Redevelopment and Race: Planning a Finer City in Postwar Detroit*. Baltimore: Johns Hopkins University Press.

U. S. Census Bureau. 2010. 2010 Census, National Summary File of Redistricting Data. Retrieved May 29, 2011, from http://factfinder2.census.gov/.

U. S. Census Bureau. 2010. Census of population and housing, historical decennial censuses. Retrieved July 3, 2010, from http://www.census.gov/prod/www/abs/decennial/.

Western Reserve Public Media. 2004. "Race and Youngstown 2010: Vision or Division?" Northeastern Public Educational Television of Ohio, September 25 and November 30. Retrieved Aug. 13, 2010, from http://westernreservepublicmedia.org/ytow2010.htm.

Case Study: Youngstown 2010: America's First Shrinking Cities Plan

Hunter Morrison, Northeast Ohio Sustainable Communities Consortium

On a snowy December evening in 2002, over fourteen hundred citizens of Youngstown and its surrounding suburbs came together in Stambaugh Auditorium to discuss a vision for their city's future. The setting was apt, Stambaugh Auditorium is a neoclassical performance hall (with acoustics said to rival those of Carnegie Hall) built in 1925 on a site overlooking the Mahoning River. For over one hundred years, the thirty mills that stretched along thirty miles of the river poured out iron and steel, creating the wealth that built both the auditorium and the city which was already known as "Steel Town, USA." In January 1996, nineteen years after the first of these mills was shuttered, Bruce Springsteen played Stambaugh and sang "Youngstown" to a sell-out crowd. Not since that winter night had the people of Youngstown and the Mahoning Valley come together in such numbers to define and celebrate their common identity.

While Springsteen's elegy was about Youngstown's proud past, the topic for that night's discussion was the future of Youngstown. From the *Youngstown 2010* planning team, the audience heard a revolutionary concept: Youngstown should abandon the thought of becoming again the city it once was. Instead, it should accept the reality that it is a smaller city and strive to become a sustainable mid-sized city with a more diverse and balanced economy than it had in the past. Over the next three years, Youngstown engaged in a multi-faceted community planning process that engaged a wide cross section of city and suburban residents in detailed discussions of Youngstown's future. Over five thousand people participated directly in developing the *Youngstown 2010* plan. And on January 27, 2005, thirteen hundred members of the Youngstown community reconvened in Stambaugh Auditorium to discuss the final plan and voice their support.

Youngstown's planning process began in the mid-1990s, when members of the city council decided to update the city's 1951 comprehensive plan and began to sequester the necessary funds. The formal process began in earnest in late 2001, when Youngstown's then mayor, George McKelvey, and Youngstown State University's president, David Sweet, agreed to co-convene a process that would update the city's plan and simultaneously prepare the university's first comprehensive master plan. Mayor McKelvey appointed Community Development Director Jay Williams to lead the city team and President Sweet recruited me to head the university team. The city/university planning team engaged Urban Strategies, a Toronto-based urban design firm, to assist in designing and implementing the planning process. Together, the team and the consultants agreed to pursue a two-part planning process that would enable citizens' issues and insights to emerge and be addressed over an extended period of time. The team decided to divide the work into a "listening and visioning" first phase and a more traditional "comprehensive planning" second phase. The team agreed to define "vision" as "an agreed-upon set of community goals and a description of the changes that would be needed to achieve these goals" and to define plan as "the detailed framework of specific policies and regulations that puts the vision into action."[1]

The team chose to begin the first phase by inviting local leaders to participate in a round of focus groups that would identify the city's strengths, weaknesses, assets, liabilities, aspirations, and fears and help the team frame the broad outlines of a community vision statement. In order to insure that the focus groups represented the full range of community leaders, the team took pains to define leader broadly. The team reached beyond the usual A-list civic leaders to include individuals from unions, churches and other religious organizations, social service organizations, and ethnic associations; student leaders from the university and area high schools—both public and parochial—also participated. The result was a diverse group of over two hundred local leaders who engaged in a dozen workshops about the city's future. The workshops were structured as SWOT analysis (strengths, weaknesses, opportunities, and threats) and each participant was asked for a final thought.[2]

The team and the consultants analyzed the insights from these focus groups and developed a vision statement, which they presented to the public on December 16, 2002. The vision they presented had four "thematic headlines":

- *Accepting That We are A Smaller City* and striving to be a model of a sustainable, mid-sized city;
- *Defining Youngstown's Role in the New Economy* and aligning Youngstown with the realities of the new regional and global economies;
- *Improving Youngstown's Image and Enhancing Quality of Life* by focusing on becoming a healthier and better place to live and work; and

- *Heeding a Call to Action* by adopting an achievable and practical action-oriented plan that will make things happen.[3]

Under each of the headlines the team recommended "Actions" and "Issues for Discussion" for Youngstown citizens to consider and identified a list of topics to address in the subsequent comprehensive planning process. Following the presentation of the vision, Jay Williams led a three-hour open-mike discussion and called for volunteers to help the planning team carry out the more methodical and time-consuming process of developing a new comprehensive plan.

The team then embarked on what became a three-year effort to update the city's existing comprehensive plan, a document first adopted in 1951 and amended in 1974, three years before Black Monday, the day that Youngstown Sheet and Tube's Campbell Works was shuttered and the collapse of the city's economic base began. To sustain the enthusiasm of that December evening, the team established a core of volunteers to conduct neighborhood field studies and convened working groups to deal with specific topics of interest, including the role of the arts in the emerging economy and the future of downtown and the adjacent campus of Youngstown State University. The team carried out formal neighborhood planning sessions and participated in many discussions in church basements, high school and university classrooms, and community group meetings. The team combined this face-to-face communication with quarterly reports to the public, using the facilities of Western Reserve Television, a PBS affiliate allied with the university. The *Youngstown Vindicator* assigned a reporter to cover the *Youngstown 2010* plan and gave the neighborhood meetings and forums consistent and thorough front page coverage. Finally, the team engaged local media and marketing experts to develop and promote the *2010* "brand." The group developed a logo and a strategy that included bumper stickers, billboards, public service announcements, editorial board briefings and the quarterly report to the people on Western Reserve Television. City and university officials agreed to use the *2010* brand to identify major projects then being developed—including a new university recreation center and a new city-owned convocation center—as "Youngstown 2010" projects, thus "doing" while "planning" in accordance with the vision's "Call to Action."

These efforts produced a groundswell of support for a new way forward: "The evolving vision took center stage in the local media and among elected officials as the community became thoroughly engaged in the planning process and excited by the possibilities it held."[4] The depth of support for the new plan was manifested both by the Youngstown City Council's enthusiastic adoption of *Youngstown 2010* as the city's new comprehensive plan in 2005 and by the approval (by 74 percent of Youngstown voters) of a charter amendment requiring that the plan be updated every ten years. Subsequently, Jay Williams ran successfully for mayor of Youngstown. The first African-American to be elected to that office, Williams ran on the promise that he would implement *Youngstown 2010.*

The *Youngstown 2010* plan and process received the Oustanding Community Planning award by the Ohio Planning Conference in 2005. *The New York Times* recognized the plan's idea of "Creative Shrinkage" as one of the "Best Ideas of 2006." Finally, the American Planning Association recognized the team's commitment to extensive and exhaustive public participation with the 2007 National Planning Excellence Award for Public Outreach.

Notes

1. City of Youngstown (2005), ch. 2.
2. Ibid., pp. 17-22.
3. Ibid., p. 18.
4. Ibid., p.17.

Bibliography

City of Youngstown. 2005. *Youngstown 2010 Citywide Plan*. Youngstown, OH: City of Youngstown.

5

Preserving Healthy Neighborhoods: Market-Based Strategies for Housing and Neighborhood Revitalization

David Boehlke, czb, LLC

As happens so often, some of the most creative responses to urban problems are first conceived and tested by local communities and resident groups scattered across America. This has proved particularly true for cities and neighborhoods facing population loss, excess housing, and depressed real estate markets. Instead of trusting in conventional redevelopment tools and policies, these innovators are crafting techniques that treat the loss of resident and investor confidence, which is at the base of distress in low-demand cities.

Locally initiated and having no national sponsors, the innovations are each unique and have different names in the various locations. They use names like Great Homes, Healthy Neighborhoods, Neighborhoods in Bloom, and similar upbeat descriptions of their communities as positive, livable places. But regardless of the labels, similar challenges and shared core values drive these innovations. Learning why these initiatives succeed can give insight into ways to rethink the national conversation about urban policies for many of our cities and suburbs.

In this examination, we will visit small towns that have discovered the value of neighborhood identities and we will learn about older cities that have reconceived vacant lots as community resources. We will examine urban neighborhoods where residents partner with real estate agents to sell houses to strong buyers and we will see places that set higher maintenance standards by offering incentives instead of subsidies. And we will hear repeated messages about the critical role of residents in creating and sustaining market-driven change.

What follows is an analysis of the conditions and assumptions that underpin these innovations and a discussion of how some of these experiments are working even without the resources and support of public policies and conventional funders.

Taking a Fresh Approach

Unwilling to be defeated by the litany of urban problems, local innovators use proactive techniques that vary in their application across the various local markets but have many consistent themes. Examples include the following:

- Housing investments are carefully targeted to aggressively rebuild demand for housing in specific recoverable sites.
- Marketing initiatives focus on the best houses on the best blocks in order to sell to the strongest buyers.
- Neighborhood advantages and assets are given primary attention and the impact of negative conditions, such as troubled rental projects and shabby public spaces, are minimized whenever possible.
- Public programs emphasize the incentives they offer, instead of the subsidies, and they solicit customers based on their capacities, not their limitations.
- Promotional materials avoid affordability jargon and describe neighborhoods as places of choice, where engaged neighbors set high standards of upkeep and community involvement.
- Typical "urban problems" are redefined, such as equity growth being presented as a benefit and not part of a gentrification threat, and crime and drugs being seen as a citywide challenge and not a neighborhood failing.
- Neighborhood and housing improvements are done in ways that build confidence, set higher standards, and contribute to curb appeal regardless of the code compliance outcomes.
- Residents are central to the renewal process and are expected to upgrade their homes, volunteer to improve public spaces, and serve as marketing advocates for the neighborhoods and the houses.
- Neighbors are encouraged to be good neighbors and pay attention to the blocks and to one another and to have fun and enjoy living in a place of choice.

Such positive, demand-based, market-focused actions are common in stable neighborhoods and growing cities where developers, the real estate industry, and confident residents continually promote housing and communities. But for shrinking cities and low-demand neighborhoods, these proactive efforts are nearly revolutionary and run counter to many public policies, which seem to argue that cities with declining populations and neighborhoods are supposed to address their deficiencies and not focus on promoting their assets. Those policies lead to targeting public investment to distressed housing in severely declining areas, serving households with limited incomes. This is the equivalent of rebuilding the auto industry by only marketing poorly-selling models to buyers without the resources to purchase.

Understanding Past Approaches

It is not an overstatement that decades of public policies were structured as if the principles of real estate markets did not apply in low-demand communities. When dealing with excess housing, many public programs primarily offer resources to build more houses or to renovate vacant structures. Beyond needlessly expanding supply, these approaches often magnify local distress.

First, most public funding requires long-term affordability, which usually reinforces concentration of low-income households.

Second, any rehab is done well above the financial ability of nearby households, so the renovations remind everyone that major improvements result only from government subsidies.

Third, these subsidies distort an already at-risk real estate market by offering quality housing at fire-sale prices or by providing mortgage discounts only to low-income buyers.

Fourth, few resources are offered to existing property owners, who usually aren't able to participate in the new standards of investment.

Fifth, few or no resources are available to address the marketing and image issues of the neighborhoods or to rebuild trust among the neighbors.

For many communities, well-intentioned public funding is the final blow in distorting and destabilizing low-demand housing markets. This is clearly seen in cities and neighborhoods where continuing loss of jobs, smaller populations, and reduced buying power have created long-term depressed housing markets. These conditions are well known in the deindustrializing cities of the Midwest and around the Great Lakes. But significantly the pattern is also arising in other older urban and suburban communities that cannot attract enough new residents due to local housing competition as well as in the boom-bust cities, with unstable economies leading to excess housing.

In all cases, the outcome is essentially the same: low demand for housing exacerbates excess supply, which reinforces slow sales, depressed prices, and less qualified buyers. Once the "second choice" neighborhood label is invoked, the pool of home buyers and quality investors shrinks, since these cities usually have other desirable neighborhoods with available housing. As a result, undercapitalized or inexperienced buyers compete with operators of substandard housing to acquire marginal properties. And in many neighborhoods, affordable housing programs further complicate the real estate market by developing even more rental housing or by assisting low-income households into making marginal home purchases. This toxic mix strengthens the perception that the neighborhood is failing. Such a label assures that demand is further reduced and investment falls.

To be fair, these government actions are well intended and merely reinforce disinvestment that is already undermining the communities as a result of deindustrialization, ethnic and racial shifts, out-migration, and other local factors that affect housing markets. Public policies are only one factor in a very complex process. The central dynamic is too many houses with too few buyers with adequate resources to own and maintain properties at a level that retains or attracts other residents. We need public policies that recognize that not all markets across America are the same, but that all markets conform to the same principles of supply and demand.

Starting From a Market Perspective

How these principles function can be better understood if we look at examples of real estate markets in different types of weak market cities.

Low Demand Cities

It is easy to treat all low-demand communities as similar, since they all have too many houses for the population that wishes to live there. But the conditions on the ground are actually highly dissimilar. Gary, Indiana, was conceived and built as a planned community serving the steel industry and its employees. Up until 1970, the scheme seemed to be working, but in reality the decline had already begun. Jobs were fewer, suburbanization was significant, and racial and economic changes were happening across the city. From a high of nearly 180,000 fifty years ago, Gary in the 2010 census had just over 80,000 residents, many of whom are poor and ill prepared to deal with the global economy. Abandoned houses scar almost every neighborhood and housing prices even on the best streets are so low that it is difficult to rationalize any home improvements. Loss of tax revenue results from a cycle of disinvestment that produces more abandoned houses on streets that are not properly paved and allows poorly maintained vacant lots next to the well-cared-for homes of long-time owners.

The conditions that led to this severe downturn were the same that impacted the Michigan cities Saginaw and Flint and the Ohio cities Cleveland and Youngstown. Each has lost about half of its population and substantially lost buying power among the remaining households, but the resulting disinvestment is unfolding in different ways in each place. Saginaw's abandonment is mostly concentrated on one side of town, although prices are depressed across the city. The abandonment pattern leads to whole blocks nearly depopulating, while other areas of the city maintain much of their original character. In Flint, there are thousands of scattered abandoned properties and vacant lots, but the city also has whole neighborhoods with only modest vacancy, usually due to the presence of local institutions and buffers such as parks. Large areas are fully scarred by abandonment, but other areas present themselves as recoverable, although there the finest houses sell for prices so low that low-income residents can buy homes yet are not able to maintain them.

In Ohio, Cleveland has used an extensive array of interventions, but prices are persistently low throughout the city, even in the stable or recovering areas, which are near the lake or are attractive to young professionals. Otherwise, disinvestment is widespread and the city is a jumble of reinvestment project sites next to acres of fallow lots and boarded-up structures. Likewise, Youngstown is becoming a collection of traditional stable neighborhoods, transitioning neighborhoods with open lots spread throughout the blocks, and downsized neighborhoods with few houses and large tracts of unused land.

Although all are excess-housing cities, the above cities are different from Canton, Milwaukee, and Rochester and Jamestown, which are places where population loss has been more modest and where the patterns of disinvestment are different. Both Rochester and Jamestown are dealing with a slow but consistent loss of population that has left behind many desirable areas with a problematic housing stock. In both cities, large houses, especially those converted years ago for multifamily use, are not able to compete in the soft market. These properties are being lost first, but overall prices are so low and demand is so weak, additional properties are becoming vacant and abandoned, a persistent disinvestment that further stymies nearby reinvestment. Canton and Milwaukee also have too many houses, but their particular challenges are intensified because they have racial shifts, which have greatly reduced the pool of renters and buyers in some neighborhoods labeled as "minority only" and have strengthened the competitive advantage of nearby suburbs that are open to the full range of qualified buyers and renters.

Each of these shrinking cities is on a different trajectory and each must create a unique combination of tools to rebuild confidence. The patterns of decline are different, even though they stem from a similar loss of population and the related loss of investor confidence.

Transitioning Cities and Suburbs

When considering low-demand communities, a focus on older industrial cities is too narrow. Some older inner-ring suburbs with housing stock similar to that of the nearby city are facing the same disinvestment patterns as city neighborhoods.

And many mid-century suburbs have lost their competitive advantage. In these suburbs, the 1950s and 1960s ranch houses and Capes often have less than twelve hundred square feet and many offer only two bedrooms and one bathroom. Typically, they were built with minimal insulation, inadequate storage space, and no basement. There is a limited market for such housing even in the best of times, but when the overall market is soft, much better properties are readily available for qualified home buyers, so these houses are sold to marginal buyers who have no other options or to investor owners willing to own buildings that are difficult to manage but can still command good rents. Since sales are depressed, long-term home owners are not able to sell for what they perceive as a reasonable price. This produces neighborhoods with a mix of older owners with little incentive to upgrade their houses, new home buyers without the ability to upgrade the houses, and marginal investors who recognize that equity growth is unlikely and therefore improvements are unwise. This is the same formula for failure that shapes large cities with significant population losses.

Wheat Ridge, Colorado, is a classic suburb with both prewar and postwar housing challenges. It was originally a small city with neighborhoods immediately adjacent to Denver. After World War II, the town became a growing suburb that attracted families to affordable single-family houses that qualified under VA and other federal housing programs. Modest downpayments, easy financing, newer schools, and improving transportation made Wheat Ridge an excellent option. Because there was extensive land, new construction continued into the 1980s, but most older properties from the 1920s through the 1950s are too small and lack the features that can compete for stronger buyers. Today, a large percentage of home owners are seniors or first-time home buyers from Denver's ethnic communities, and many single-family houses are becoming rental properties. Because they were not built to high standards and have high upkeep costs, these houses are poor candidates as rentals and they depress rentals at conventional apartment complexes, which are, therefore, often under-maintained. In many of the neighborhoods, the cycle is only beginning, but the pattern is clearly in place.

Wheat Ridge joins the ranks of hundreds of suburban neighborhoods and cities without marketable products to compete successfully in their regions. While this challenge occurs across the country, it is especially difficult where population is declining or unstable. The demand challenge is increasingly critical where housing was built as part of a boom in advance of expected population growth, such as many cities in Arizona, Nevada, and Florida. The common thread is that there is too little demand for the housing product in some urban areas, whether or not the overall region is stable.

These transforming cities and suburbs are the leading edge of the new low-demand problem. Not burdened with years of failed interventions, they still don't have the right tools to respond to their market problem. Since the central issues are not affordability or supply as addressed by our national public policies, these communities are usually unable to intervene quickly and effectively to deal with the core issues of low demand. Let's look at those issues and see how they shape what must be done.

Defining the Core Issues

Regardless of the type of community, its housing stock, and its reasons for decline, the baseline recognition is that the customers have lost *confidence* that the community can thrive. This loss of confidence can't be resolved by a single action; there isn't a loan product or a code-compliance program or a housing project that will rebuild this confidence. The challenge is complicated and it requires that the community face the impact of *competition* for households, the reality that customers have a wide range of *choice*, that people are seeking stable places with greater continuity *(where markets are predictable or "things just make sense")*, and that local communities have limited capacity with which to respond to a complex set of customer decisions.

In the following examples, each community faced the impacts of strong *competition*, increasing patterns of *choice*, desire for *continuity*, and limited *capacity* to respond. These communities committed to a multi-faceted approach to rebuilding confidence through one or more of four strategies:

- Image-building initiatives, in which the neighborhood presents a positive story about itself to encourage current residents and to attract newcomers
- Marketing and sales programs, in which local leaders identify particular houses and specific market niches for sale and rental of properties
- Standard setting and physical-condition improvements, whereby neighbors and local authorities set standards of property improvements and upkeep that demonstrate that the residents and government value the neighborhood
- Resident involvement, in which the residents support good neighboring behaviors, cooperate on projects, and use positive events to strengthen the social fabric of the blocks and the neighborhood as a whole

When employing these strategies, each community faces unique circumstances, but they all share the same market challenges: too many houses and way too many houses lacking current market features; too few buyers and far too few buyers with the resources to upgrade the houses; and very low prices, which undermine any interest by current owners in upgrading their homes. While each place attempts to influence all four elements of neighborhood health, the approaches and the emphases vary greatly.

Shaping the Community Image

A negative image undermines the ability of any community to reposition itself in a competitive real estate market. Reputation matters, history can shape the future, and positive identity can determine who is attracted to a place. The lack of an image can be equally challenging. This often occurs in places that lack identities connected to a sense of place. In many smaller towns and cities, there are few distinct areas that are thought of as neighborhoods. Local leaders in Geneva, New York recognized that residents did not usually refer to themselves as living in specific neighborhoods. Citizens said they lived in Geneva on a given street. That was the extent of their identification with a place. But these same leaders realized that community problems could not be solved unless residents identified with the community at different levels.

With a population of about thirteen thousand, Geneva leaders realized that the city was not growing and the profile of residents was becoming older and poorer. Housing prices were depressed and the nearby towns had competitive advantages and favorable tax rates. The imbalances could not be solved through government investment alone; resources were too limited to trigger renewal unless residents were directly involved in change. After a one-year participatory process of naming neighborhoods and defining boundaries, there were a dozen identified and named neighborhoods and a defined downtown. This process was managed by the city government's Office of Neighborhood Initiatives and by a group of dedicated volunteers working through the Geneva Neighborhood Resource Center. Today, residents are determining what standards they expect for their blocks and houses. They realize that they must shape the image of their specific neighborhood and that the image must communicate that they value the place, plan to keep it safe and clean, and intend for the real estate market to work for them. The outcome has been an extraordinary involvement by neighbors in creating an awareness of the history of the places, completing neighborhood-wide cleanups, establishing local groups, promoting sales of houses, and encouraging renovations.

Such critical actions by residents in low-demand neighborhoods can happen only if there is identity with place and if the neighbors recognize their role in creating a positive image. Without a sense of place and without an effort to develop and use a positive image, renewal in a low-demand market is impossible, but with a concerted campaign to create an image, it is possible to manage change successfully.

Strengthening the Real Estate Market

Belair-Edison is a collection of neighborhoods in northeast Baltimore. The population exceeds eighteen thousand residents in eight or nine sub-neighborhoods, which have names like Four By Four and Little Flower. There are nearly seven thousand houses of which all but two dozen are row houses. Two bedrooms or three, front porch or not—these are the distinctions among the row after row of brick Belair-Edison houses, most of which were built between 1920 and 1960. The key renewal challenge was how to attract a new group of home buyers. Leaders of Belair-Edison Neighborhoods, Inc., the local nonprofit group, knew that no one action would reposition the neighborhood in the real estate market, but there were changes that could help. The name was promoted in newsletters, by new entry signs to the area, and in press releases. Herring Run Park was cleaned up and replanted and the neighborhood public golf course was promoted. A Main Street project upgraded the commercial strip and, through an outreach program, resident groups focused on self-help block projects and neighborhood beautification. Hundreds of porch lights were installed, there was a dog program called the Bow Wow Pow Wow, and there were neighborhood celebrations, golf outings, and back-to-school events. But even with these and other creative initiatives, the leaders knew that fundamental change would not happen until more and better prepared buyers started investing in Belair-Edison.

This outcome required a series of incentives for buyers: one-on-one counseling, special purchase loans for public employees, and low interest rehab loans for buyers. It also meant tracking sales data to help new buyers make better decisions and working with real estate agents to promote new listings. And there were agent-sponsored open houses for neighbors, so residents could bring their families and friends as part of a Pick Your Neighbor program.

In addition, the organization joined forces with another nonprofit to renovate row houses well above the standard of the neighborhood. This had the dual purpose of showing what could be done with the standard row houses and of attracting new buyers to houses that were move-in ready.

Through these combined efforts and through a dedicated focus on selling to a stronger profile of buyer, Belair-Edison emerged as a neighborhood of choice for households that previously had decided to live elsewhere. Further, this and five other programs proved so successful that now there is a forty-neighborhood program, which has made over $30 million in loans in places that had historically been seen as second choice locations but that today are increasingly extolled as good value for the dollar.

While these multi-faceted efforts were important, Belair-Edison would not have recovered so successfully without a change in the buyers and in the sales prices in the neighborhood. Strengthening the market was the fundamental action that created long-term sustainability.

Improving Physical Conditions

Until recently, the Idora neighborhood in Youngstown, Ohio, faced the disheartening impact of too much empty space. Closed stores, unused rental houses, abandoned buildings, and vacant lots were defining the neighborhood. It was clear that no one was managing this glut of emptiness. This was especially distressing because the past had been so different. For decades, Idora's summers were filled with life and energy. In the years before and after World War II, residents of the city and the whole region knew Idora for the well-loved family amusement grounds called Idora Park. Visitors spent warm evenings traveling to Idora Park through the tree-lined streets filled with the meticulously maintained houses of the neighborhood.

But Idora in recent years was no longer being managed. To respond, concerned residents got involved in the Mahoning Valley Organizing Collaborative. After a year of outreach, it was obvious there was a profound desire to re-envision Idora as a special place. In this transformation, the neighbors joined with the Youngstown Neighborhood Development Corporation to first address the vacant lots and abandoned houses. In less than two years of community work, a new vision is succeeding beyond any expectations.

Instead of vacancy defining Idora, the residents are redefining the neighborhood through initiatives with special emphasis on the Lots of Green program sponsored by YNDC. This program acknowledges that empty space needs to be managed if the neighbors want to control the future of the community. In just over a year, fifty-four abandoned houses were removed and scores of other vacant lots brought into the program. By the end of 2010, 120 lots were improved, and 30 more added in the second year. Each of these lots is seen as an opportunity to upgrade the physical conditions of the blocks, to engage neighbors in managing their neighborhood, and to create a new face for Idora as a place that is greatly valued and loved by its residents.

In many cases, adjacent property owners agreed to be responsible for lots by treating them as side yards. Some of the vacant lots were added to historic Mill Creek Park, which adjoins the neighborhood. Five community gardens were established, along with extensive education programs for children and adults. Replanting projects utilized forty-four additional lots as passive green space, a storm-water demonstration site was developed, and pocket parks were created. To reinforce the changed approach to space, a neighborhood team of young people was contracted to maintain these and other lots. And today momentum is being sustained through a Market Gardener Training initiative, which is educating twenty-five residents in sustainable market gardening.

With abandoned buildings removed and vacant lots back in use, the outcome has been incredible. Emptiness is being managed and Idora is again being thought of as a special place with a unique story, a committed group of neighbors, and excellent housing options. People are discussing its vacant lot programs and its training efforts as examples of what Youngstown needs as part of its recovery. While it does not have the idealized reputation of sixty years ago, Idora has become proof that a neighborhood can successfully remanage its physical environment as part of a larger strategy of community change. A discussion of related efforts by the Idora neighbors is highlighted in the case study at the end of this chapter.

Increasing Resident Involvement

Swillburg is a neighborhood of about nine hundred households located on the east side of Rochester. Anchored by a small park, it is a place of well-maintained houses on quiet streets connecting to a commercial corridor. Only a few years ago, an honest description would not have been so favorable. Then there were too many houses in disrepair, too many yards that were poorly fenced and overgrown, and too many properties not selling to home buyers and not attracting stable renters.

Although it is a city with great assets, Rochester has faced a long decline of population, from a high of 332,000 in 1930 to around 210,000 today. While the decline has slowed to perhaps a thousand persons per year, the impact of a smaller, less well-paid resident workforce depresses housing prices. Moreover, the suburbs are easily reached and offer excellent value in housing.

A creative community-based nonprofit, NeighborWorks Rochester, determined that revitalization required a market-driven approach but that the involvement of residents would be critical. There were many nearby neighborhoods with good images, upkeep, and housing values, so one possible competitive advantage would be engaged residents. To reach these neighbors, the initiative used two effective community-organizing techniques: door-to-door outreach and social events. By knocking on doors, people informed neighbors about activities, programs, and special services. They were told about home-repair loans and cleanup opportunities. Barbecues, picnics, and other social events brought out residents who would normally never have attended neighborhood meetings. This created a broad base of participation as Swillburg improved its home-maintenance standards and increased its marketability. Even the name Swillburg began to be seen as a distinctive and marketable asset.

Four years later, the neighborhood continues to be stable, although the foreclosure crisis has further weakened the Rochester housing market. The program has been so successful that two other neighborhoods, parts of the nineteenth Ward, and The Pocket in North Winton, are both using the same outreach and improvement tactics. Increasingly, residents are taking control of Rochester neighborhoods to build on their assets and reinforce stability.

Geneva, Baltimore, Youngstown, Rochester, and cities like them are taking charge of their futures instead of being captive to the changes happening around them. They have taken to heart the imperatives in preserving healthy neighborhoods. It would, therefore, be helpful if we consider what this term means if we are to create effective public policies.

Committing to a Demand-Driven Healthy Community

In low-demand communities, it is critical to agree on what the word healthy actually means. In some cities, the sale of federally subsidized houses is considered a measure of health. In other places, the fact that only subsidized houses are selling is considered a measure of failure. When neighbors are asked what a healthy neighborhood means to them, the initial answers are remarkably similar across the country: safe, clean, and neighborly. Moreover, when pressed, most residents—especially homeowners—will add that housing values should be stable or rising.

With these observations in mind, the definitions of a healthy neighborhood generally follow two themes: economic soundness and livability. Typical language is "A healthy neighborhood is a place where is makes sense to invest your time, effort, and money and it is a place where the neighbors are willing and able to manage the everyday issues of the neighborhood." Of course, these words carry different meaning in different places, but the central values are consistent. People want to live in communities where they can feel good about the dollars they spend on their mortgages or rents and the time they spend on keeping their homes in good condition. And people want a sense of neighborliness and shared responsibility, which shows that residents value the community and one another.

Across the country, most places are healthy, housing is a good value and is worth maintaining, and community norms are working effectively. But some neighborhoods are beginning to see those conditions fray, and other places have already lost the basic economic and social realities that can support a stable, thriving place.

Defining a Market-Based Neighborhood

The word neighborhood is a tricky one. Similarity of housing types, the existence of boundary streets, the location of parks and schools, and a dozen other markers are used to define neighborhoods. But these definitions are slippery. A boundary street might actually be the spine that runs through a neighborhood and binds it together. A location next to an abandoned school or a notoriously dangerous park might not function well as a neighborhood marker. And if housing similarity defines a place, then huge sections of triple-deckers in Boston or row houses in Baltimore or tract houses in Los Angeles would be all be considered one neighborhood. To recapture health, it is important to define a neighborhood at a scale that can be managed and marketed by neighbors and their allies. Census districts, school boundaries, and planning maps do not define neighborhoods; manageability and marketing potential do.

In healthy communities in both small towns and major urban centers, successful target neighborhoods usually consist of a few hundred houses, perhaps from three hundred to eight hundred units. Since many neighborhoods in large cities are much larger than that, sub-areas within those neighborhoods may have to be targeted. When targeting, smaller is better. It is easier to initiate improvements and to create the relationships needed to sustain long-term change. How to combine various blocks into manageable and marketable units is as much an art as it is a science. It can not be done in the city's Office of Planning; it is achieved through on-site observation of how people live, coupled with ongoing conversations with the neighbors. When this is done, it is relatively easy to trace the history and to catalog the unique assets of a place. This naturally leads to the identity and market questions and to the challenges of upgrading conditions while engaging residents. These characteristics, of course, are the key elements defining a healthy neighborhood.

Developing the Process for Change

Given that our goal is to preserve those neighborhoods with the potential to be healthy places once again, what should happen? When the leaders of a low-demand city determine that they must target specific neighborhoods for market-driven reinvestment, how can the neighborhoods be selected? Is there a statistical formula that weighs such characteristics as vacancy rates, sales prices, percent of home owners, and current and past market performance to predict which neighborhoods will be successful in retaining and attracting stable households? Can a local community estimate in advance how many public dollars will be required? Is there a way to know the extent and nature of conventional and reduced-rate mortgages that will be needed to move a neighborhood to traditional market performance? And how can local leaders identify the various niche markets that will likely need to be attracted to the targeted neighborhoods?

Unfortunately, there are no consistent answers to these questions if we examine neighborhoods that have taken a market-driven approach. There are too many factors that are part of any neighborhood's recovering as a place of choice. Are the typical housing products historic mansions, or worker cottages, or mid-century modern tract homes? Are the blocks relatively intact and uniform, or are there a jumble of different styles of single-family houses and apartment structures? What is the prevailing public conversation about the neighborhood? Is the emphasis on crime and negative behaviors, or is the common story about the continuing neighborliness of the community? And where are the competitor communities and what are their conditions? Responses to such questions only hint at the factors that go into any plan for recovering a community.

While everything can not be known in advance, it is important to learn as much as possible about the character of a place and to begin to match the defining features to likely customers. This means determining where those customers are today and whether they can be attracted to the target blocks. For the strongest potential customers, will this require special financing, or discounted architectural and renovation services, or a marketing campaign, or all of these incentives, or something else altogether? What will encourage customers to choose a specific place among so many options? In some places, rediscovering a long-lost neighborhood history or name can be a key trigger. In other places, the key is the first group of uniquely painted houses or the first appearance of renovation equipment and signs. Or perhaps replacing the worst eyesores with a farmers' market or the restoration of the historic porch on the public library will cause people to notice the neighborhood and include it as a possible choice.

Many different factors contribute to neighborhood desirability, but they all are part of rebuilding confidence in the community. Without addressing the issue of confidence, there can be no sustainable change. This process can be risky. A series of small-scale improvements might convince the current residents that things are improving, but newcomers might not even notice these same changes. A large-scale development project might help potential buyers see dramatic change, but current residents could see the same investment as profoundly destabilizing the economic and social fabric of the neighborhood. A high-quality renovation of the key historic properties might boost the real estate market, but if most structures aren't historic, the recovery could stop after only a few houses. Simply said, the best approaches to neighborhood recovery can not be simply stated.

What can be done? Gather market data in the neighborhood and in its competitors. What do the numbers tell us about the housing products and the competitive communities? Interview those in the last ten households moving in and those in the households moving out. What do they see as desirable and what are the perceived obstacles to recovery? How do different socioeconomic groups express distinct viewpoints? Look at the recovering neighborhoods similar to the target site. What factors support renewed confidence and what conditions seem to be accepted as "normal" for those neighborhoods? Walk every block of the target neighborhood and tally the unique features that will make the place desirable and identify the critical problems that must be minimized before confidence can be reasserted. And, of course, spend time engaging with current residents. Cities with excess housing will not recover because large numbers of residents move in. There just are not enough new people to risk losing any of the stable residents already there. The future of the community will be a partnership of those new and current residents who see the neighborhood as a place they choose to live and not a place where they are stuck.

In almost all cases, an at-risk neighborhood has seen three fundamental changes. The place feels less safe and inviting, it is described as dirty or littered or shabby, and there is an expressed longing for neighborliness. As noted earlier, "safe, clean, and neighborly" is a widely shared mantra that crosses ethnic, racial, economic, and age identities. For current residents, growing equity may be secondary to the more immediate goals of safety, cleanliness, and neighborliness. Of course, a place with those desirable features is a place with increased confidence and place that can likely achieve equity growth.

Faced with this reality, cities must deal with safety, upkeep, and neighborliness as core elements in achieving health and must do this in ways that encourage confidence and don't undermine it. Announcing an anti-drug program reinforces negative images; a community-wide wellness initiative might have as much impact as an anti-drug program but the image is one of proactive change. A crime watch reminds us of a threat, while a good-neighbor block program recalls an idealized earlier time in America. Even a neighborhood cleanup day is best described as a block party that is preceded by a beautification event. Words make a difference when building confidence. The advertising industry knows that we do not want cavities, but they remind us that we really want whiter teeth. A neighborhood becomes a place of choice when we are told it is a special place where people like us are choosing to live and to invest themselves and their resources in their homes and blocks. The message is as important as the reality when it comes to building confidence.

Identifying Obstacles to Market-Based Transformation

If a market-based approach makes so much sense in shrinking cities, why is this not a more common approach? After decades of reduced demand, why do so many community development agencies and nonprofit groups continue to build or renovate housing as a primary tool for improving neighborhoods? Why are so many public investments made in the most distressed sites which have no long-term future?

The answers to these sorts of questions vary significantly in different cities. However, there are some general observations at the core of the strategic reinvestment challenge. These include at least four obstacles to implementing new approaches to neighborhood investment in low-demand cities. Let's consider each one.

Obstacle One: Regulations Are Usually Made For Someone Else's Problem.

Most federal and state neighborhood investment dollars come with significant regulations written into the legislation or crafted by the agencies involved. In the case of federal dollars, there is little attempt to tailor the program to the vastly different housing markets in the United States. Both Minneapolis and Memphis sit on bluffs overlooking the Mississippi River, but their at-risk neighborhood challenges are completely different. A rent of one thousand dollars a month is a great price for a studio apartment in Chicago, but it buys an outstanding house in Saginaw. Even the more market-focused Neighborhood Stabilization Program (NSP) legislation, which was intended to address foreclosure issues, was written to require that 25 percent of all dollars be spent on households at or below 50 percent of median income, whether or not this was the most effective way of reducing the impact of massive foreclosures.

The Home Investment Partnership Program (HOME), HOPE VI, Choice Neighborhoods Initiative, and Neighborhoods of Promise are similar examples of federal dollars that follow Community Development Block Grant-based income criteria at least in part. For cities with excess housing supply, this usually biases the targeting of dollars to places with less chance for recovery. The result is usually locating projects in ways that further concentrate poverty.

Even when local agencies attempt to take market-building actions, obstacles are significant. For example, if federal dollars are used, inflexible rules often disallow partial rehab, so properties must be brought up to a standard that most nearby residents cannot match. The subsidized houses stand out and reinforce the notion that only public dollars are being invested. Even if a local agency tries to just raise curb appeal through neighborhood exterior rehab, there are numerous limitations in the use of federal funds that undermine the intended outcomes.

State government rules should not be overlooked. For example, if the Jamestown, New York leaders wish to demolish a typical large abandoned house, the cost is roughly $16,500. Demolishing the same house two hundred miles away in Canton, Ohio, is much less than $6,500. Both cities act with caution regarding public safety, especially when dealing with asbestos and lead, but the complex rules in the state of New York result in the ten-thousand-dollar difference. The health and safety issues involved in addressing abandoned structures is real in both cities, and both communities are committed to dealing with the problem, but state legislation impacts their relative abilities to deal effectively with dangerous structures.

Of course, regulatory requirements are always open to interpretation by experienced regulators, who comprise the staff of the federal and state agencies that fund community development. They know there are creative ways to use public dollars to reinforce realistic market-based strategies, but how this can be done is usually only explained by agency staff members who are willing to take risks. This is asking a lot of people who are commended for making sure that grantees follow rules exactly. It also assumes that qualified regulators know local housing markets well enough to advise community development staff on how to rebuild housing demand. Recent experience with the NSP projects shows how difficult it is to produce a marketable house in a low-demand environment. The result is usually a compromise: produce few houses and fund them with large subsidies. The premise is that any house can be priced low enough to sell, if the only goal is sale of the property, not the recovery of the neighborhood.

Conclusion: Regulations are too often about housing and not about housing markets.

Obstacle Two: Crafting Projects Is Not the Same as Changing Market Behaviors. Major nationwide for-profit housing development firms make mistakes when forecasting future demand, such as the recent over-building in many states. Indeed, some firms are bankrupt because of an unfounded confidence in the demand for certain types of housing. Markets are not easy to predict, and urban housing demand is no exception.

The staffs of city agencies and community development nonprofits are no more or less skilled than their private industry peers. But city and nonprofit investment is uniquely open to public scrutiny. If a private firm acquires land without an immediate use, it is seen as having foresight. If an agency acquires land and then chooses not to act, it is seen as another inept city project. In the real world, housing development is not easy and public and nonprofit community developers are not experienced in developing housing for a market. Instead, these professionals are well versed in the esoteric world of packaging complex loans with multi-sourced grants for low-income housing. Multi-year complicated projects often focus more attention on the funding sources than on the outcome of the housing. The negotiated product will be layers of loans and grants that have different and sometimes conflicting compliance requirements. Whether the housing still makes sense or the project achieves any neighborhood outcomes can be lost in a decade of packaging of resources.

Yet, city and nonprofit staff members are under enormous pressure to make projects happen. The income of these corporations is often dependent on housing production even if there is little demand for the final product. Moreover, many public officials are elected on promises that given projects will happen. Ribbon cutting is much more dramatic when it takes place at a new housing project than when it occurs at a demolition site. Residents seldom ask for more effective responses to a market problem; they usually just want something fixed. And most national legislation reinforces this notion by biasing grants to favor more housing construction or renovation.

Even if there has been a local decision to be market-focused, there usually is insufficient training of city staff and political leaders in the terminology and goals of housing-market interventions. Few experienced elected officials and staff professionals are adept at understanding soft markets and explaining them to the public in a way that garners support. Repeatedly, seasoned civic leaders explain that the way to "turn around" that notorious neighborhood is to renovate those houses that everyone sees on the main thoroughfares. Soon thereafter, they express surprise that families are not interested in renovated houses on the busiest streets in an already-troubled neighborhood. Of course, families know that sound houses on quiet streets are not selling and they do not want to buy houses at less desirable sites. At some point, the renovated but unused houses become an indictment of the neighborhood and the properties are sold at an even greater loss or are rented with large monthly subsidies. In low-demand cities, there is little margin for such errors. Investment that further undermines a neighborhood must be discouraged no matter how seductive the presentation by the tax credit developer. *Conclusion: Markets need to be built, not more houses.*

Obstacle Three: Commonly Held Ideas Might Not Lead to Commonsense Outcomes. A prevailing common vision reads as follows: If housing is in bad condition, substandard housing should be replaced with quality housing. Once there is quality housing, people will return to the neighborhood and that will support better schools and improved businesses. Outside of a few middle- and upper-income neighborhoods, that scenario has hardly ever worked and certainly has a very poor track record in weak market cities.

Healthy neighborhood approaches argue that if existing housing and neighborhoods in good condition can't be effectively repositioned in the market, there is little likelihood that troubled housing in distressed neighborhoods can spark market demand, regardless of renovation. Confidence just isn't driven by observing public subsidies at work; confidence is built on seeing markets work.

But discussions about buyer or renter confidence can seem trivial when confronted by neighborhood organizers and advocates for the poor who see their task as achieving social justice for ill-served residents of the neighborhood. Certainly the poor are deserving of attention, but it is not always the best idea to serve only that population if the more stable households then choose to leave. This further isolates the poor, even if it is in a new housing project or a renovated rental complex.

Certain discussions get repeated across the country and are now local urban legends. For example, in some cities with massive population loss, neighborhood leaders still worry that new investment leads to gentrification. They point to the two-dozen historic houses on Third Street that were renovated in the 1980s as proof of the growing demand for urban houses. What follows is the fear that funding housing initiatives for those households whose earnings represent over 80 percent of the area median income will encourage those with even higher earnings to move into troubled neighborhoods. This argument is made even when houses in the most prestigious neighborhoods are selling for one year's annual median income. Hidden agendas about race, ethnicity, and low-income residents are ascribed to developers, landlords, and the ever-dreaded young professionals.

Another version of this argument is frankly much more political. It argues that targeting non-poor neighborhoods is not fair and is politically unacceptable. The long-established ward councilperson, the articulate minister, or the esteemed business leader is often the honest, well-intended proponent of this approach. They argue that the subsidy pie is very small and should be expended only where dollars have been spent in the past. These leaders dismiss the idea that elsewhere the same dollars could help many more households of all incomes, build housing equity, and increase the tax base. They see the funds as promised over past years and therefore entitled for future years.

This reasoning prevails because there is seldom the political courage to challenge old practices and to renegotiate past agreements. The words used in discussions about healthy neighborhoods might be useful in the city as it has become, but the words make no sense when referring to the city as it used to be. It takes a sustained and well-orchestrated public information campaign to build the support for a paradigm shift. In cities with the shell shock of population decline every decade, it is difficult to take on past assumptions and to articulate new principles of change. Even if there were political and civic leaders to promote these actions, the concepts regarding healthy neighborhoods have not been documented and explained well enough to empower the leaders to succeed. Where change has happened, there has always been a small number of proponents who worked both openly and quietly to orchestrate the change, and even then, the outcome has often been a cobbled-together compromise.

Conclusion: Changing what we do is hard; changing how we think is harder.

Obstacle Four: Complex Strategies Lack Both a Simple Formula and an Advocate

Perhaps the greatest impediment to using healthy neighborhood approaches in weak market cities is the acknowledged limitations in the model. Frankly, any real estate market intervention will be imperfect. There is an inherent messiness in trying to reposition a neighborhood, marketing mistakes will be common, and community outreach efforts will get rained out. Projects that seemed brilliant in the planning will fail in the execution. Other ideas will blossom because a single person champions the work or because a press article highlights the vision.

Further, a demand-driven approach does not offer a self-sustaining business model. Indeed, if the work made good business sense in the narrow profit and loss sense, conventional developers and real estate professionals would be leading the effort. Rather, housing initiatives in weak markets do not make sense in traditional business terms, but with some strategic targeted dollars and attention to specific details and players, certain submarkets can be stabilized and even grown. Can this produce enough tax revenue to support the actions? Perhaps, but the lack of any ability to show a clear correlation means that public dollars will still need to be spent without proof of a profitable return.

Many of these limitations could be overcome if there were an advocate for healthy neighborhoods, especially for at-risk but recoverable neighborhoods in weak market cities. Regrettably, there is no national intermediary that has the commitment or the capacity to launch such an effort. Most of the national groups are still tracking numbers of units developed or houses repaired or foreclosures avoided. These are all important actions, but they do not attempt to reposition neighborhoods or cities with depressed demand for housing. Barring a sudden change in national housing policy, a major shift by a housing intermediary, or a substantial grant initiative by foundations, there is little likelihood that the healthy neighborhood ideas will evolve as a fully articulated, adequately funded tool for cities in distress.

Conclusion: Markets are messy and no national advocate is willing to get really dirty.

Overcoming Obstacles and Recapturing What Is Valued

Given the structure of funding, regulation, and staff capacity and recognizing the unevenness of community support and the difficulty of the work, it is remarkable that any local efforts at market interventions succeed. Why do communities challenge conventional wisdom and come together to employ more complex tools for neighborhood change? The simplest answer is that these approaches are effective in low-demand situations.

Other neighborhoods in Youngstown want to replicate the Idora experience. NeighborWorks Rochester, which has been involved in the revitalization of Swillburg, is also active in two other parts of the city. Geneva is becoming a model for other small cities and towns seeking to engage their residents. Baltimore is now using healthy neighborhood techniques in dozens of neighborhoods. This is happening because neighbors and neighborhoods are rediscovering their assets and their competitive potential.

Moreover, the principles and strategies of healthy neighborhood interventions are seen as efficient use of resources. The techniques are able to build housing value for households and property owners that have lost equity over years, and the concepts are respectful of residents and, most especially, of lower-income households. Finally, these approaches are able to walk that fine line between our desire to re-create the lost images of past neighborhoods and our practical need to respond to a changing America. Through all of this, the key underpinning value is one of confidence by neighbors in their community and in themselves. It is that confidence that makes a neighborhood healthy.

Case Study: Creating Healthy Neighborhoods In Youngstown

David Boehlke, czb, LLC

Youngstown, Ohio was once a powerhouse of productivity. Hard work in the mills, business innovations, and commercial ingenuity created a city with a rich public life and advantages such as parks, museums, and concert halls. And the financial strength of this leading industrial city supported an impressive downtown. There were elegant houses on beautiful blocks adjacent to desirable middle-class communities and stable ethnic neighborhoods. And this vitality and energy was fueled by smokestack industries that were the envy of the world.

Of course, today the story is very different. Too many major employers have downsized or closed and too many new businesses do not offer jobs of the same quality. Health care and education sectors have grown and some mills have modernized, but the population has continued a fifty-year decline, going from about 170,000 people to a current level just under 67,000. Youngstown is often referenced as a symbol of the deindustrialization of America and is characterized as having abandoned houses, empty lots, and closed factories. But in the last few years, this city has become equally well known for its forthright recognition of its problems and its commitment to becoming a very different place, one that will be smaller, less dense, and thriving.

The test is whether this commitment can be converted into a realistic, achievable plan for reinvention. Can Youngstown orchestrate the strategies to reposition neighborhoods as places where people choose to live? Can it create new standards to manage vacant buildings and lots and to upgrade public spaces? Can it develop marketing programs, promotional strategies, and home ownership incentives to retain and attract the target customers? Can it bring together neighbors as an effective force to improve the neighborhoods?

After only a few years of community work, the answers to these questions are increasingly affirmative. The city is quickly producing practical examples of what the new Youngstown will look like. As a key part of this transformation process, the city government joined with neighborhood residents and partnered with the newly founded Youngstown Neighborhood Development Corporation.

The first major site was the Idora neighborhood. Beyond dealing with the need to manage emptiness, there was a decision to upgrade the neighborhood image, strengthen the real estate market, and engage large numbers of residents in the renewal process. With significant support from the Raymond John Wean Foundation, local leaders embraced the principles necessary to create healthy neighborhoods. They recognized that low demand neighborhoods do not recover because of subsidies or government projects. These leaders resolved to do everything they could to rebuild confidence so that property owners would again be willing to invest not just dollars but also valuable time and effort in owning and managing quality homes. And the leaders resolved to engage as many residents as possible in all aspects of the process so that the renewed confidence could be sustained when direct activities were completed.

Even as parallel initiatives were beginning elsewhere in the city, the Idora results have literally amazed the participants. In addition to the outstanding programs to manage empty space, some of the highlights of eighteen months of work include:

- Addressing the neighborhood image by:
    1. replacing street signs at every corner with new signs that include the neighborhood logo,
    2. re-boarding all marketable vacant houses,
    3. installing neighborhood entry signs,
    4. creating high impact neighborhood murals with residents, and
    5. operating a media and information blitz worthy of any launch of a new product.
- Marketing the neighborhood and the housing by:
    1. rehabbing for sale five houses as examples of "green renovation,"
    2. promoting the sale of currently listed houses, and
    3. encouraging first-time buyers through expanded home buyer education programs,
- Engaging residents by:
    1. facilitating their ability to improve their own homes and yards,
    2. involving residents in the community gardens, the clean-up projects and the murals,
    3. offering extensive training programs on various themes,
    4. working with the neighborhood association to strengthen its role in

the community and expand its membership, and

5. providing a role model to show how to stop bemoaning problems and instead to become proactive about marketing the neighborhood as a great place to live.

These initiatives and dozens of other small actions have combined to literally re-ignite confidence in Idora, a story that is being heard elsewhere in Youngstown. Today Crandall Park North is rebuilding its neighborhood organization and is promoting the community, especially through marketing of specific outstanding properties. Likewise, the Brownlee Woods neighbors have joined with nearby residents to kick off a healthy neighborhoods planning project. And a Lots of Green project, model block efforts, and other activities are just beginning in the ethnically diverse Lincoln Park area. Each place has a different set of challenges and each will benefit form a carefully tailored reinvestment initiative.

The Youngstown city government understands that its role is to make these recoveries possible by using its grants, special lien programs, clean-up assistance and similar tools to support the confidence building efforts of the residents and nonprofits. Local government will no longer attempt to physically rebuild neighborhoods or promote large-scale development projects. It acknowledges that making neighborhoods healthier is the responsibility of the neighbors working with their partners. Further, city leaders also know that this format for community change offers the best potential for effective decision-making in other parts of the community and will use many of the techniques in its re-writing of the zoning regulations for the city.

Today the principles involved in creating healthy neighborhoods are guiding much of the neighborhood renewal in Youngstown, and the results are gratifying. Of course, Youngstown faces years of difficult transformation and it will constantly have to modify its strategies as economic conditions and market forces change. But if it continues to focus on its assets and to build resident confidence, it will successfully transform itself. While Youngstown will not become the place it was in the 1950s, it will again be a place with neighborhoods that people choose to call home.

6

Re-thinking the Places in Between: Stabilization, Regeneration, and Reuse

Terry Schwarz, Kent State University

By definition, shrinking cities have an abundance of vacant property. A smaller population, fewer businesses, and reduced economic activity have far-reaching consequences, since all cities (shrinking and growing) are affected by fundamental laws of supply and demand. Many older cities have built too much and sprawled too much and now they simply have too much—substantially more housing, retail square footage, and office space than are likely to be needed for the foreseeable future. This oversupply of real estate puts downward pressure on real estate values throughout a metropolitan region, with the strongest impacts felt in core cities and inner-ring suburbs.

Numerous strategies for vacant-land management and reuse are being explored in some of the cities most affected by population decline, including Detroit, Cleveland, Youngstown, Pittsburgh, Philadelphia, and Buffalo. Generally categorized as "greening" strategies, these approaches have the potential to stabilize fragile real estate markets, restore urban ecosystems, improve public health and well-being, and foster economic growth.

Managing surplus real estate

The idea of a smaller, greener city provides useful rhetoric for older industrial cities, providing a way to frame the issue of population decline and urban vacancy in positive terms. But smaller and greener is difficult to achieve, especially in the context of declining tax revenues, weak real estate markets, and the profound inertia that can take hold in cities that have been losing population for decades.

Value is derived from scarcity. As such, shrinking cities need to find ways to reduce their surplus of buildings and land in order to stabilize real estate markets. For a city to recover and thrive, this reduction must occur in intentional, strategic, and productive ways. An aggressive example of the real estate–reduction approach is "Wall it up and take a breath," a design concept developed by Peter Arlt and Letzelfreivogel Architekten for the city of Linz, Austria. Linz is an older industrial city, which is in the midst of transforming itself into a cultural center and tourist destination. To reduce the inventory of vacant land and reinforce property values in the city, Arlt proposed the construction of solid masonry walls, nine meters in height, around vacant sites for which there is no anticipated development use. These opaque walls were intended to be built without any fixed date for their removal.[1] The "Wall it up" concept, though it has never been implemented, provides an extreme response to the real estate dynamics in a shrinking city. In growing cities, surplus land is a valuable asset. In shrinking cities, market forces are inverted and surplus land becomes a liability. The out–of–sight, out–of–mind approach represented by "Wall it up" is an extreme measure to reduce supply and stimulate demand.

In American cities, public officials might find an idea like "Wall it up" to be rather preposterous. Yet many cities engage in a similar kind of real estate reduction strategy. Demolition programs in Cleveland, Buffalo, Detroit, and a host of other American cities aim to eliminate blighted and obsolete houses, and reduce the overall housing supply. Municipal demolition programs tend to be extensive in scale. In Cleveland, for example, over one thousand homes are demolished each year. By eliminating excess housing, cities aim to stabilize property values and improve the local real estate market. Some Smart Growth advocates have challenged this strategy, raising concerns that large-scale demolition programs erase urban fabric, reduce density, and limit future opportunities for regeneration.[2] There is a legitimate basis for these concerns. However, given the scale of the vacancy problem, these cities have no real alternative to demolition since there is a vast surplus of housing that is in poor condition and has little or no market value. In some instances, it may be possible to close up or "mothball" vacant buildings to protect them from weather and vandalism, although this would be cost-prohibitive except on a small scale. This process can delay demolition efforts, particularly if there is the potential for a building to be rehabilitated in the future, but vacant buildings cannot survive indefinitely in a boarded up condition. Regular monitoring of mothballed buildings and maintaining minimum interior heat levels are necessary to keep these structures intact. As such, mothballing efforts are generally directed toward architecturally or historically significant buildings, rather than being used on a more widespread basis.

Vacant houses often present a real and immediate threat to public safety. City residents demand demolitions, particularly when vacant houses are structurally unsound, attract illegal drug activity, or have a blighting effect on the appearance of a neighborhood. But large-scale demolition programs raise many difficult questions, such as:

- Do housing demolitions effectively stabilize surrounding property values by eliminating blight, or undermine property values by reducing neighborhood cohesiveness and creating new kinds of blight in the form of unkempt vacant lots?
- Can demolition programs be targeted to protect urban character and preserve historic resources for future use? When hundreds or thousands of houses are demolished in a given year, how can city officials be sure that they are not throwing away the good along with the bad?
- What are the long-term consequences of large-scale demolition programs? Will neighborhoods be irreparably damaged or will they benefit from new development opportunities derived from lot consolidations and targeted infill construction?

These issues are also discussed in Chapter 3 of this book.

Unfortunately, there are no clear answers to these questions. Demolition programs are likely to continue, given the large and growing number of vacant and deteriorated buildings in older industrial cities throughout the Midwest and parts of the Northeast. Taking into account the reality of ongoing demolitions and the vast amount of vacant land that already exists in many cities, strategies for vacant land stabilization and reuse are a critical part of the real estate equation. Instead of "walling it up and taking a breath," shrinking cities can "green it up" and put vacant land to productive use.

The "Reimagining a More Sustainable Cleveland" Approach to Vacant Land Reuse

It is difficult, but essential, for cities to manage vacant land in ways that provide short-term benefits and address long-term goals. One recent effort in this regard is the Re-imagining a More Sustainable Cleveland initiative. In 2010, the City of Cleveland had approximately twenty thousand vacant lots, which amounted to about 3,500 acres in total. The city's strategy is to introduce nontraditional urban land uses that reduce the supply of property and increase real estate values, based on three broad categories:

1. *Holding strategies* are deployed in areas where real estate development is most likely to occur in the near term. The city has mapped core

development areas and identified existing transit-oriented de-velopment nodes that need to be protected and reinforced with infill development as opportunities emerge. Holding strategies are low-cost, low-maintenance greening techniques that create an appearance of stability and stewardship. The goal is to reinforce positive perceptions of a neighborhood and to treat vacant sites as viable opportunities for future development.

2. *Green infrastructure* includes a wide range of vacant land strategies for improving natural systems in the city. A seemingly inevitable consequence of rapid urban growth is the destruction of native landscapes, such as wetlands and waterways, and biological diversity. Today's shrinking cities were the boomtowns of the last century. When development demand in Cleveland was high, the city grew with almost total disregard for underlying natural systems. The inverse is also true: Now that development demand is weak, new opportunities are emerging for ecological reclamation. Surplus real estate can be used to expand and connect parks and green spaces, restore the urban tree canopy, manage storm water, and reclaim badly damaged ecosystems.

   Green infrastructure strategies are intended to be long-term interventions, but the form and function of green infrastructure can be adapted to respond to on-going changes in real estate development demand. For example, a large vacant lot can be landscaped to hold and filter stormwater runoff. If the real estate markets improve and the property one day becomes a desirable development site, the new development project could provide a comparable storm water management function through the use of green roof technology, pervious paving materials for walkways and parking lots, and other best management practices. The most important aspect of vacant land management is the realization that cities constantly grow, shrink, and change. In this context, vacant land is a valuable resource because it allows a city to adapt to changing circumstances in ways that support positive economic and ecological outcomes.

3. *Productive landscapes* are a strategy for extracting an economic return from vacant sites. Vacant land can be used for food production and the generation of alternative energy. From a pragmatic standpoint, scattered sites in an urban setting are not likely to produce large economic returns from agricultural uses, but community gardens and urban farms have an essential role in increasing access to healthy foods for city residents. If development demand increases, acres of land devoted to food production can be reconfigured into a more compact footprint. For example, greenhouses and vertical farming can provide a similar output as a more land-intensive urban farm. As land becomes more valuable, compact agriculture can allow food

production and more traditional urban development to coexist comfortably. Flexibility is the key factor in vacant land reuse. Strategic vacant land management builds resiliency into transitional urban neighborhoods.

Agriculture may eventually become a more economically viable land use in older industrial cities, particularly if farming efforts can be expanded beyond field crops for local consumption. Some examples of how a local food economy can be expanded to create jobs and increase tax revenues include:

- Greenhouse operations to extend the growing season and increase production yields
- Community kitchens and other food processing facilities to add value and profitability to locally grown food products
- Bio-digester facilities that convert food waste and other organic material into renewable fuels and plant-based polymers

Energy production is another possibility for vacant sites. In recent years, it has become apparent that we need to reduce our reliance on fossil fuels. Unfortunately, existing urban infrastructure is not well suited to this task. The electrical grid is not structured to draw energy from a wide range of sources and many alternative energy sources (such as solar power) require significant land area to produce power in sufficient quantities. Low cost vacant land may offer the potential for developing alternative, decentralized energy sources. As federal and state governments invest in projects to expand the proportion of energy demand that is met by renewable sources, cities with an abundance of vacant land may find that they have a comparative advantage in this area.

The Re-imagining a More Sustainable Cleveland approach is essentially a framework for making informed decisions about the disposition of vacant sites. The goal is to manage vacant properties in ways that stabilize current conditions and establish clear patterns for more sustainable urban development in the future.[3]

Three Spatial Models For Shrinking Cities

Strategies for the reuse of vacant land need to be guided by a long-term vision, or at least a reasonable assumption, about what a city is to become. This vision (or assumption) will help to determine how remaining residents, businesses, and institutions can best be supported by city services and infrastructure. In the discourse concerning shrinking cities, there is an ongoing debate as to whether cities should consolidate remaining residents and development activity into compact urban nodes or allow population to disperse in ways that reduce overall urban densities. There are benefits and challenges with both of these approaches. Consolidation and dispersion represent two opposite tendencies, neither of which could ever be fully realized in a shrinking city. In the end, all outcomes will be a hybrid of some sort, and the hybrid model is the third option to consider.

Consolidation: In the consolidation model, a city experiencing population decline would push (or coax) remaining residents together into the most intact and viable parts of a city. Ideally, this would create or preserve dense, walkable neighborhoods. Vacated parts of a city would become parks, forests, or "wilderness" areas, with vibrant interlinked neighborhood nodes set within this system of green space. The appeal of this model is that it enables shrinking cities to retain or re-create a strong sense of urbanity. It also allows for more efficient delivery of city services such as street maintenance, trash pickup, and snow plowing. And it provides a clear–cut approach for managing social infrastructure, since decisions regarding transit, schools, churches, and hospitals could all be made to reinforce clearly established neighborhood nodes.

The consolidation model works well as a design concept, but it may be difficult to implement in the context of a real city. It is rare to find a city with large areas of near total depopulation. Populated and depopulated neighborhoods are often adjacent and interwoven. Patterns of real estate demand frequently shift, making it difficult to determine where to consolidate development and where to decommission neighborhoods and encourage relocation.

The biggest challenge is that even in the most devastated areas of a shrinking city, there may be substantial numbers of existing residents who resist relocation efforts. City residents often have strong ties to their neighborhoods, based on established social networks, memories, and emotional connections that may be invisible to outsiders. Remaining residents often include the most vulnerable members of an urban population—people who are impoverished and entrenched. The needs of these residents must be carefully considered to determine if relocation is truly in their best interests, in order to provide a safer neighborhood, a higher quality of life, and better access to employment opportunities, retail businesses, and transit.

An attempt at the consolidation model began in Detroit in 2010.[4] Detroit may eventually discontinue public services to roughly a third of the city's geographic footprint—this is an idea currently under exploration. Residents in the affected areas would receive incentives to move to one of between seven and nine population centers. The city is exploring the idea of discontinuing services to nearly forty-five square miles of the city.[5] Whether Detroit's consolidation efforts become a model that can be replicated elsewhere remains to be seen. But this is a bold and aggressive attempt to reduce city costs and realign the real estate market.

From a land use perspective, the consolidation model presents further challenges. The underlying idea of consolidation is that vacated parts of a city can be converted to green spaces or revert to a natural state. However, a smaller population may result in lower demand and usage for additional green spaces, and cash-strapped cities may lack the resources to maintain an expanding green space network. Allowing land simply to revert to a natural state is a complicated proposition. Urban land does not automatically return to "wilderness" once people leave and buildings are demolished. Natural ecosystems tend to be highly disturbed by urban development. Changes in hydrology, soil conditions, and microclimates often mean that native species can no longer survive in these altered settings. More likely, vacated areas will be naturalized by invasive species—tough and aggressive plants that thrive in difficult urban conditions. Over time, this de facto vegetation strategy may help to restore soil structure and give way to healthier and more diverse ecosystems. The process is slow and the evolving landscapes may look ragged and weedy for extended periods of time.

Without careful management, vacated areas that are allowed to "return to nature" may trigger negative reactions from neighboring residents and businesses, and have a detrimental effect on surrounding property values. A landscape strategy for managing vacant land in Flint, Michigan and the surrounding county addresses this issue of public perception by proposing a cultivated strip of turf grass at the street edge, with a more natural landscape of indigenous materials beyond. The three-foot wide grass strip can be maintained with a single pass of a lawn mower, keeping the costs of maintenance to a minimum while establishing the appearance of stewardship in transitional neighborhoods.[6]

Dispersion: The dispersion model involves lot consolidations, in which adjacent property owners take ownership of surplus land, increasing lot sizes, and reducing neighborhood density. Small-scale green spaces, community gardens, and other vacant land interventions further reduce the overall density of neighborhoods in response to emerging and evolving patterns of vacancy. The dispersion model is already under way in many older industrial cities, occurring organically as a result of many individual decisions at the neighborhood level. Large-scale demolition programs reinforce the dispersion model, since houses are often demolished based on condition rather than location. It is fairly uncommon for a city to clear an entire block, much less an entire neighborhood, unless a redevelopment project is imminent. More often, demolitions occur in a dispersed fashion, with some concentrations in areas where disinvestment and foreclosures are prevalent.

Since the dispersion model is in effect in many cities (and has been for decades in places like Cleveland and Detroit), opportunities abound for assessing the impacts of changing density patterns on property values, access to services and amenities, and neighborhood character. If the process of dispersion is carefully managed, land–use decision making can occur at the grassroots level through flexible, neighborhood-based strategies. By embracing the dispersion model, cities can avoid the social upheaval and high costs of relocation, as residents are supported in place as a neighborhood evolves.

The downside of the dispersion model is that it can "suburbanize" a city. Neighborhoods that were once dense, walkable, and transit-friendly may become sprawling, incoherent, and inaccessible. Lot consolidations may have long-term impacts, since once a lot is in private hands, infill development is more difficult and density reductions may become permanent. Also, the delivery of citywide services becomes increasingly expensive as fewer residents are dispersed throughout the entire urban footprint, rather than concentrated in core areas. Finally, downsizing of infrastructure networks cannot occur without consolidating residential areas in some way.

Hybrid: A hybrid approach delineates certain areas of a city for consolidation while allowing others to evolve through the process of dispersion. In implementing this approach, a first step would be to identify areas of a city to hold for future development, including both large-scale and infill development. A city can develop its own criteria for selecting and prioritizing development areas. Some criteria may include:

- Condition of existing infrastructure
- Access to freeways and transit
- Current and projected real estate values and development interest/activity
- Land availability, particularly the availability or larger parcels and opportunities to assemble smaller parcels into a larger redevelopment site
- Proximity to anchor institutions and other locational assets
- Current and projected population

In consolidation areas, a city can focus resources and development activity in ways that restore and reinforce density in areas where development is most likely to be sustainable.

Another important step is to identify ecologically sensitive areas for parkland expansion, conservation, and ecosystem restoration. A city can look at its entire inventory of current and soon to be vacant properties and determine which sites should be acquired and protected as part of the public realm. It is important to keep in mind that the most heavily abandoned areas are not necessarily the most logical places for greening strategies. In areas where vacancy levels and abandonment are high and property values are low, a city can assemble large parcels of land—these larger parcels offer the most flexibility and value for a wide range of future uses.

For the land that remains after property has been set aside for public–realm improvements and development interests, a city can facilitate the transfer of land outside of delineated areas to private interests of varying scales, including individual home owners, community development corporations, and neighborhood entrepreneurs.

The main benefit of the hybrid model is that it maintains and reinforces density in areas where new development will be most viable. It offers control of strategic areas and flexibility everywhere else. However, it may be difficult to articulate clear, defensible criteria for developing real estate–holding areas. It may also be expensive to set aside and maintain large areas for green–space expansion, ecosystem restoration, and other improvements to the public realm. Furthermore, some degree of suburbanization is likely to occur in areas outside of real estate holding and green space expansion areas. And inequities are inherent in this type of dual strategy, because the choices a city makes will have measurable impacts on property values.

Designing For the Places In Between

In 1991, the Department of Landscape Architecture and Regional Planning at the University of Pennsylvania produced a vacant land resource book as part of the West Philadelphia Landscape Plan. This pioneering effort, led by landscape architect Anne Whiston Spirn, established a useful typology for urban vacancy, combined design concepts, and potential uses for each type of vacant site. Vacant land types included isolated vacant sites, corner lots, connector lots, dispersed vacancy, and multiple contiguous blocks of vacant sites. Design ideas were introduced for infill construction, private gardens, play lots, outdoor markets, meadows, orchards, pocket parks, and other uses.[7]

In 2008, the Cleveland Urban Design Collaborative and Neighborhood Progress, Inc. produced a vacant land pattern book to serve as a guide for pilot projects throughout the city of Cleveland. The pattern book included design concepts for gardens, small-scale farms, parks, parking lots, geothermal wells, infill development, native–planting schemes, and other interventions, along with cost estimates for implementing these concepts.

Parcel-based design ideas for vacant land are most effective when they can be aligned with a citywide vision. The reuse of vacant land is an ongoing process, evolving over the course of many years and involving thousands of decisions, large and small, throughout a city. In Cleveland, the guiding vision was derived from the twin objectives of restoring urban watersheds and eradicating hunger in city neighborhoods and throughout the region.

Watershed Restoration

Like many cities in the Great Lakes region, Cleveland has an abundance of water and an intricate pattern of natural hydrology that extends from the suburbs into the city. But most of the city's water is hidden. Streams and creeks were contained in culverts many years ago when the city's rapid growth required the erasure of indigenous waterways. But now, as the city's vacancy grows, there is an unprecedented opportunity to restore a more natural pattern of hydrology through the assembly of vacant sites in alignment with buried waterways. A public policy could be established to declare vacant land on top of or within the vicinity of a buried culvert as off-limits to development.

From an ecosystems perspective, it was never a good idea to build on top of water. As a city's portfolio of vacant land continues to grow, sites that coincide with buried waterways can be set aside, assembling a green network one parcel at a time. It is important to note that daylighting streams (or restoring them to a natural condition) is a vastly expensive proposition. As such, it is unlikely that all of Cleveland's culverted waterways will ever be restored to a wholly natural condition. However, there are numerous examples where stream daylighting strategies are being deployed. For example, Cincinnati's Lick Run is currently being restored as a naturally flowing above ground waterway. This will help convey storm–water runoff to Mill Creek, and reduce combined sewer overflows (CSOs). Combined sewer overflows are a problem in older industrial cities throughout the Midwest and Northeast. In these cities, sanitary sewers and storm sewers often run through the same trench. In heavy rains, untreated sewage and storm water mix and are subsequently discharged into rivers, streams, and lakes. This is a major source of water pollution, and cities that have CSOs are obligated by the Federal Clean Water Act to correct the problem. But the solutions are very expensive, requiring major infrastructure investments, at a time when many of the cities impacted by this issue are experiencing declining tax revenues and fewer residents to share the economic burden. The Lick Run project is being funded as part of Cincinnati's long term control plan for addressing CSOs. The stream restoration will reduce CSO volumes and it is also intended to provide an urban amenity to attract residents and investment back to the city.

Not all stream daylighting projects are intended to address CSO issues. Kalamazoo, Michigan's eighteen million dollar effort to daylight Arcadia Creek was part of a flood prevention and downtown redevelopment plan. The creek area is now a festival site, hosting events that generate twelve million dollars in annual revenues. Annual property tax revenues near the restored creek have risen from \$60,000 to \$400,000.[8]

Even when stream daylighting is cost-prohibitive, it is still potentially useful to assemble vacant properties along the actual (or approximate) paths of buried creeks and streams, re-establishing native landscapes on these properties to restore surface hydrology. The culverts would remain intact, for now. But the intermittent strands of vegetation that emerge through vacant land assembly would direct rainwater along more natural paths along the surface of the ground, allowing for infiltration into the soil, rather than runoff into the storm sewer system. These would not be manicured green spaces or engineered storm water features. Instead, an approximation of Cleveland's pre-settlement landscape could be restored in the form of slightly wild and beautiful greenways, which could evolve into high functioning natural landscapes. There are several benefits to doing this:

- By preserving the land above culverted streams, the possibilities remain open for future daylighting projects, because culverts will fail eventually and new resources may become available for future stream restoration.
- In Cleveland, the paths of buried waterways intersect with parks, schools, and many other amenities. Plus, they all lead to the Cuyahoga River and Lake Erie. Natural greenways above culverted streams would allow for new bike and pedestrian connections, resulting in a more coherent and accessible green space network for the city.
- Natural greenways would increase biodiversity and wildlife habitat in urban neighborhoods.
- Perhaps most important, it would be transformative, from an urban design standpoint, to have these strands of wilderness meandering through city neighborhoods. They could be the green stitches that hold together an increasingly fragmented and fragile city.

Older industrial cities face enormous costs when addressing aging sewer infrastructure. In Cleveland, the CSO problem will cost the region more than three billion dollars to correct. A systemic approach to using vacant land for stormwater management will establish a green infrastructure network for the city, aligning vacant land reuse strategies with the substantial technical and financial resources of the regional sewer district.

Hungerproof City

Shrinking cities often have concentrations of impoverished residents, many of whom experience chronic hunger. Vacant land is a resource that can be used to generate calories. Cleveland's vision is to create a hungerproof city, in which the regulations regarding the use of vacant land and flexible land open up new opportunities for getting vegetables and protein to the people who need them most.

Zoning laws that accommodate urban agriculture, farm animals, and the sale of locally-produced food products can help support the needs of residents and enable micro-scale entrepreneurs to develop economically viable models of local food production. A new agrarian model for declining cities is beginning to emerge—one that puts vacant land to productive use and accommodates all kinds of people, along with their chickens, goats, and bees. Cleveland adopted two zoning ordinances intended to promote agriculture and address chronic hunger. The first ordinance (adopted in 2009) allows farm animals to live in urban neighborhoods, provided they are courteous to their human neighbors. The ordinance allows residents to keep chickens, ducks, rabbits, and bees but not roosters, geese, or turkeys. A typical residential lot can have up to six small animals and two beehives. The second ordinance (adopted in 2010) permits urban agriculture as the principal use of a vacant residential lot. Previously, agriculture was allowed only as an accessory use. This ordinance also allows farm stands as a conditional use on residential lots when the produce is grown on site. In adopting these zoning ordinances, Cleveland gave greater legitimacy to the burgeoning urban agriculture movement, which has helped to foster greater self-sufficiency among city dwellers.

A hungerproof city accommodates a variety of agricultural operations, including small gardens, large farms, greenhouses, and agriculture incubators, brought together in attractive multitasking farmscapes. Over time, the patterns of agricultural production can be integrated into urban neighborhoods to feed the hungry and create compelling places that people will want to live near and visit.

Large-Scale Land Reclamation

Maintaining growing inventories of vacant land is a major expense for many older industrial cities. For example, the city of Cleveland spends $3.3 million per year to mow and maintain vacant lots across the city. The number of lots grows each year, even as the city's capacity to maintain them dwindles.

New methods are needed to shift vacant land practices from stabilization to reclamation. This will reduce the high cost of vacant land maintenance and maximize the potential benefits for city residents and urban ecosystems. The main objectives of vacant land management programs are typically to improve the aesthetics of vacant sites and to enhance adjacent property values. But vacant land management can also provide other valuable benefits, such as a reduction in maintenance costs, an improvement in ecological functions, and reduced public exposure to soil-based lead and other contaminants.

In many cities, a postdemolition strategy consists of sowing grass seed on vacant sites. Aside from the cost of ongoing maintenance, vacant sites present ecological challenges. Turf grass planted on vacant sites offers relatively limited benefits in terms of ecosystem performance. Based on soil tests performed by the U.S. EPA on vacant sites in Cleveland, the storm water infiltration on a typical vacant site is roughly equivalent to that of a paved parking lot. Most likely, this is because urban soils tend to be compacted and this compaction is further increased by the heavy equipment used for building demolition. Also, turf grass has a shallow root system and does little to reduce soil compaction and allow for the infiltration of storm water.

Vacant sites can offer more opportunities for storm water collection and infiltration if a wider range of vegetation is planted on vacant land. At the scale of a city, increased storm water infiltration helps to improve water quality and reduce flooding. Turf grass offers little benefit in terms of wildlife habitat and biodiversity. A wider range of plant materials on vacant sites could enhance urban ecosystems by creating habitat for birds, butterflies, pollinators, and other wildlife. A more diverse landscape would also begin to restore fertility to degraded urban soils so that the city's tree canopy could be gradually expanded. Increased soil fertility also ensures more complete ground cover on vacant sites, which would, in turn, reduce human exposure to soil-based contaminants such as lead and other heavy metals that are prevalent in many older neighborhoods.

An optimal mix of plant materials needs to be identified that will provide habitat, increase biodiversity, reduce soil compaction, increase storm water infiltration, reduce the city's maintenance costs, and provide full soil coverage on vacant sites. These plants (or seed mixtures) must also be low in cost, easy to establish, and have a high survival rate in challenging urban conditions. Furthermore, the plants must form a landscape that is aesthetically and culturally acceptable in city and suburban neighborhoods. Large-scale vacant land stabilization can be achieved through several interrelated alternatives. Cities can adopt new protocols for the planting and maintenance of vacant sites and implement these practices on properties after building demolitions have taken place.

As discussed previously, indigenous plant communities do not automatically become reestablished when a neighborhood's population declines and formerly developed properties are abandoned. If a city seeks to restore some aspects of its presettlement landscape and support a mature urban forest, soil ecosystems must first be restored by introducing smaller scale vegetation on urban lots. Grasses, ground covers, prairie plants, and perennials add organic material to existing soils and reduce soil compaction. Over time, vacant sites may begin to support larger scale plants, shrubs, and trees, leading to the return of something that begins to resemble a native ecosystem.

Vacant land reclamation efforts require a sound scientific basis in order to be effective. In Cleveland, the Northeast Ohio Ecosystem Consortium (NEOECO) was established with the support of the National Science Foundation's Urban Long–Term Research Area Exploratory grant program (ULTRA-Ex). NEOECO is a group of environmental and social scientists, natural resource management professionals, urban planners, and landscape designers who provide scientific and technical guidance for the ecologically-motivated redevelopment of vacant land, as a mechanism for creating social and ecological stability within distressed urban neighborhoods.

NEOECO's work includes:

- Development of a rapid assessment tool based on expert scientific knowledge that will allow communities to evaluate vacant properties for reuse for ecosystem services (for example, storm water mitigation, urban agriculture, soil/water purification, biodiversity, etc.)
- Characterizations of existing ecosystem services provided by vacant and

re-purposed lands (for example, community gardens, and the economic and social value of these lands to local communities)

- Long-term studies comparing changes in ecological, hydrologic, and social variables in response to redevelopment for ecosystem services

This evolving research is based on conditions in Cleveland but will have applications for land assessment and management for older industrial cities throughout the Great Lakes region, and possibly beyond.

Transitional Urban Landscapes: In a depopulating city, surprising land use juxtapositions become increasingly common. Low density and high density neighborhoods may exist side by side. Agricultural uses may spring up in and around the urban core. Prairies, meadows, and orchards may emerge as a growing presence in the urban landscape. Unpredictability can be disconcerting and disorienting, but it can also be part of the authentic charm of an older industrial city. Urban design efforts should focus careful attention on the seams between incongruous land uses and deploy landscape strategies that cultivate public acceptance of more natural vegetation in urban settings.

Infrastructure Issues

Older industrial cities are often faced with the dual challenges of an aging infrastructure and dwindling municipal revenues. It can be a struggle to maintain an infrastructure network that was designed to accommodate the needs of a much larger population, and cities are learning how to do more with less. Many cities have been forced to cut back on street and sidewalk maintenance, often without a formal plan or public input. Some cities, most notably Detroit and Youngstown (OH) have explored ways to scale back infrastructure networks in response to population decline. Physical infrastructure (transportation, water/sewer, energy) is difficult to reconfigure; social infrastructure (schools, hospitals, transit) offers greater flexibility and adaptability to demographic changes.

Cities may attempt to reconfigure or downsize infrastructure in an effort to reduce costs. Smaller infrastructure networks require fewer public service employees to maintain and can result in lower maintenance costs. But there are also several compelling reasons for cities not to downsize existing infrastructure, including:

- *Capital costs:* There is an immediate, tangible capital cost to removing surplus infrastructure. Roads, bridges, and sewers cannot just be abandoned, as this can create public hazards. The immediate capital costs of removing infrastructure must be weighed against a possible maintenance savings sometime in the future. In other words, it will be necessary to spend significant public dollars today for a possible incremental benefit in the future. Public works officials may be hesitant to bank on this strategy, particularly since research and established best practices are sparse in the area of decommissioning infrastructure.

- *Network capacity*: Infrastructure operates on a fixed grid. It is difficult to remove components in vacated areas without impacting the whole system. Water, sewers, roads, and power lines often need to extend through depopulated neighborhoods in order to get to areas of the city and region where concentrations of people continue to live and work.
- *Uncertainty*: Patterns of growth and shrinkage are difficult to predict. As such, it might be better to incur the costs of maintaining an entire infrastructure network at some minimal level rather than to remove infrastructure that may need to be reinstated at some point in the future. There is little evidence that maintenance cost savings from downsizing infrastructure would outweigh the opportunity costs of removing something that might prove useful in the future.
- *Redundancy*: When cities are dealing with aging infrastructure, redundancy is useful. Bridges fail, water and sewer lines break, and pumping stations need to come offline for maintenance. Redundant aspects of an infrastructure network provide a back-up that enables a city to provide continuous service in the event of emergencies and infrastructure failure.
- *Competitive advantage*: Surplus capacity—particularly in water, energy, and transportation infrastructure—is a competitive advantage that can be used to attract businesses and economic development to a city and surrounding region. Eliminating surplus infrastructure in response to current budgetary challenges could prove counterproductive over the long term.

Rather than eliminating infrastructure, shrinking cities might focus instead on optimizing the use and functions of existing infrastructure in ways that reduce current costs while preserving opportunities for future growth and development. Asset management strategies, better coordination across infrastructures, and the use of smart technologies can help to optimize infrastructure investments in shrinking cities.

- *Asset management*: It is common practice for cities to inventory their assets and make assessments of the condition of each asset. This helps to establish priorities for infrastructure acquisition, maintenance, repair, and renewal. Shrinking cities can particularly benefit from efforts to improve and optimize data collection and analysis regarding infrastructure assets. Good data enables cities to set clear and defensible priorities for spending limited resources. Because shrinking cities tend to face acute resource constraints, improvements in these analytical processes for infrastructure decisions may be of particular value.

- *Coordinating across infrastructures*: There has been very little research into the ways in which changing practices in one infrastructure sector may yield costs savings or efficiency improvements in other sectors. For example, while the cost savings from decommissioning roads may be minimal, it is possible that removing large quantities of pavement in depopulated areas could yield hydrological benefits, which, in turn, reduce storm water management costs. Similarly, improvements to public transportation infrastructure may yield substantial reductions in overall energy use and demand. While there is no hard data to confirm that substantial savings can be achieved through any of these kinds of cross sector changes, it would seem appropriate to investigate these relationships further as a potential approach to infrastructure changes in response to population decline.
- *Smart Technologies*: Technological advances may enable cities to manage infrastructure more efficiently and effectively. In the energy sector, advanced metering methods may enable both decentralized energy production utilizing geographically dispersed parcels of vacant land and access to information that would enable residents and businesses to understand how their behaviors influence the amount and cost of electricity they use. In the transportation sector, new technologies may enable both faster and more efficient reports about congestion and traffic patterns that can yield more efficient time management for travelers, reduced costs, and environmental benefits. In the water and wastewater sectors, new technologies may allow for better and less costly leak detection processes for water systems, as well as automated systems for predicting failures in levees and for monitoring water quality. These technological advances will benefit all cities but may be of particular value in older industrial cities, where the process of providing equitable and cost effective infrastructure investments is more difficult.

More research is needed in the area of sustainable infrastructure for shrinking cities. Until the short and long-term benefits of downsizing infrastructure can be determined and quantified, cities should proceed with caution before making major reductions to existing networks.[9]

Conclusion: Managing Decline For Sustainable Re-Growth

In the United States, population is projected to grow from about 308 million people in 2010 to between 419 and 439 million people in 2050. This rapid growth is expected to occur through a roughly even split between new immigrants and increases in the natural birth rate.[10] Shrinking cities in the United States exist in the context of national growth. This is markedly different from the situation in Europe and Japan, where shrinking cities exist in shrinking countries.

National population growth in the United States may present some opportunities for older industrial cities. Looking at the ten major cities that have lost the most population between 1950 and 2000 (Detroit, Chicago, Philadelphia, St. Louis, Cleveland, Pittsburgh, Baltimore, Buffalo, Boston, and Washington, D.C.) one can see that the total population loss among these cities is about 4.5 million people. This loss, while obviously significant for the cities involved, is relatively small when viewed against the net national population growth of 129 million people expected by 2050.[11]

A national smart growth policy could help to direct at least a small percentage of the anticipated population growth at the national level toward the repopulation of older industrial cities. In the same period between 2010 and 2050, the United States needs to reduce its carbon emissions significantly—perhaps by as much as 80 percent—to avoid irreversible environmental damage as a result of climate change.[12] Reclaiming older industrial cities and the embodied energy they represent can be a critical component of a national strategy for reducing carbon emissions.

There are tremendous uncertainties as to the future of older industrial cities. It is difficult to tell whether population decline will continue unabated in some cities, or whether populations will stabilize and turn toward eventual regrowth. It seems unlikely that cities experiencing substantial and ongoing population loss will ever regain their peak populations. But opportunities may emerge for gradual repopulation and the long term stabilization of urban real estate markets. In positioning older industrial cities for the future, the emphasis needs to be on managing current conditions of decline while simultaneously laying the groundwork for sustainable redevelopment over the next forty years and beyond.

How we deal with "the spaces in between" will have a major impact on the ability of older industrial cities to recover and thrive in the new century. Strategic land use decision-making, an emphasis on the restoration of urban ecosystems, and close attention to the design of interrelated urban systems will guide these cities on a path toward recovery.

Notes

1. Oswalt (2006).
2. Gratz (2010).
3. Cleveland Land Lab (2008).
4. Detroit Works Project (2010).
5. Wattrick (2010).
6. Nassauer and VanWiereny (2008).
7. Sprin, A.W., et. al. (1991).
8. Hamilton County Planning and Development (2011).
9. Hoornbeek and Schwarz (2009).
10. Alperovitz (2009).
11. U.S. Census (2000).
12. Alperovitz and Williamson (2010).

Bibliography

Alperovitz, G., and T. Williamson, 2009. *Climate Change, Community Stability, and the Next 150 Million Americans.* College Park: Democracy Collaborative, University of Maryland.

Cleveland Land Lab, 2008.

Colgan, I., "Case Studies in University Led Neighborhood Revitalization." Available at http://www.development-concepts.com/blog/2010/06/case-studies-in-university-led-neighborhood-revitalization/.

Gratz, R., "Saving Shrinking Cities." Huffington Post. Available at http://www.huffingtonpost.com/roberta-brandes-gratz/saving-shrinking-cities_b_670389.html.

Hamilton County Planning and Development. 2011 "Community Revitalization Resulting from Stormwater Management Strategies: Case Studies." Hamilton County Planning and Development.

Hoornbeek, J. and Schwarz, T., 2009. *Sustainable Infrastructure in Shrinking Cities—Options for the Future.* Cleaveland: Center for Public Administration and Public Policy and the Cleveland Urban Design Collaborative, Kent State University.

Oswalt,Phillip, ed. 2006. *Shrinking Cities. Vol. 2, Interventions.* Berlin: Hatje Cantz.

Nassauer, J., I., and VanWieren, R. 2008. *Vacant Property Now & Tomorrow: Building enduring values with natural assets.* Ann Arbor: Genesee County Land Bank Authority and Michigan Sea Grant.

Re-imagining a More Sustainable Cleveland 2008. Cleveland: Neighborhood Progress, Inc., and Cleveland Urban Design Collaborative, Kent State University.

Sprin, A.W., et al. 1991. *Vacant Land: A Resource for Reshaping Urban Neighborhoods. Philadelphia Landscape Plan.* Department of Landscape Architecture and Regional Planning, University of Pennsylvania.

Wattrick, J., "Downsizing Detroit: Mayor Dave Bing says city will incentivize residents to move into 7 to 9 core areas," *MLive.com.* December 09, 2010.

Case Study: Re-Imagining Cleveland: Pilot Land Reuse Projects

Bobbi Reichtell, Neighborhood Progress, Inc.

What does a city built for 900,000 residents do when it has less than half of that population, has 3,300 acres of vacant land, and wants to create a healthier, greener, and more economically vibrant city? Key partners from multiple sectors are responding to the foreclosure and vacancy issues in Cleveland, Ohio, through visionary data-driven planning, policy, and system changes, land-reuse demonstration projects, and critical collaborations across organizational boundaries in the Re-Imagining Cleveland initiative.

With over two decades of sustained investment by local and national funders and a history of collaboration among nonprofits, city government, and the private sector, Cleveland has built a significant community development record that has been recognized nationally. Shifting to respond to the impact of national housing and economic market forces, along with regional demographic shifts in population, that same nonprofit, government, and university collaboration is being used to create a visionary plan to help the city use vacant land to remake itself. The long-term goal is to build a community stewardship movement in Cleveland by providing ideas and resources to residents to repurpose vacant land, putting the most current and expansive data available in the hands of community development corporations, and working across sectors on policy and system changes that address foreclosures and vacancy.

As the city of Cleveland increased the number of demolitions of blighted and foreclosed homes, there was a dramatic increase in vacant land. Current estimates of vacant lots are approximately twenty thousand (7 percent of the city's land mass), with the city adding approximately fifteen hundred per year through its increased demolition effort fueled by stimulus funding. The resulting vacant land can either become a deficit to neighborhoods or be developed as an asset for the remaining residents.

The purpose of the Re-Imagining Cleveland initiative is to create new urban landscapes that better serve communities. These landscapes are envisioned to be made up of sustainable, distinctive neighborhoods with more efficient and valuable housing surrounded by repurposed land providing community benefit. Whether this land is used as green spaces, community gardens, urban farms, or creative storm water-management systems, its future is being determined and shaped by community residents and nonprofit community development corporations (CDCs) in partnership with Cleveland city government.

The Re-Imagining Cleveland initiative began with a partnership between Neighborhood Progress, Inc (NPI), a local community development funding intermediary, the city of Cleveland's Planning Department, and Kent State University's Urban Design Center (KSU UDC) on a vacant land study. The initiative brought together over thirty local government and non-profit agencies with expertise in land use, environmental planning, storm water management, parks, agriculture, brownfields, and economic development to develop proactive strategies to right-size Cleveland and manage vacant land. Through this study, the City's Planning Department developed a land use decision matrix for evaluating appropriate reuses of vacant land in light of economic variables, sustainability goals, and local quality-of-life factors. An Idea Book for Vacant Land Strategies was developed by NPI and KSU UDC, which provides designs, budgets, resources, and guidance to the public as a tool in building a community-land stewardship movement in Cleveland.

Based on this work, a small pilot initiative was privately funded and organized by NPI and carried out in six city neighborhoods. About $50,000 of foundation funds were provided to community development corporations which in turn, worked with neighborhood groups and individuals to develop twenty small-scale vacant lot projects in strategic locations. Recognizing the enthusiastic reception by residents and CDCs, who at last had access to resources and strategies to address neighborhood vacant land issues, NPI and the city agreed to expand the pilot program citywide. Cleveland's Community Development Department provided $500,000 of NSP funding from the Department of Housing and Urban Development, and NPI raised foundation funds and in-kind services. Currently, over fifty demonstration projects are being implemented around the city. The primary land reutilization strategies fall into the following categories:

- Greening, small parks, and walking paths
- Urban agriculture—community gardens, urban farms, vineyards, and orchards
- Side-yard expansions and lot splits between neighbors
- Storm water management—rain gardens and bioswales
- Off-street parking with pervious paving

- Remediation of polluted sites through bio- and phyto-remediation techniques.

The program has enabled a range of people, from seasoned community leaders to first-time project entrepreneurs, to engage in remaking their streets, if not their whole neighborhoods. There are people like forty-year-old Curtis Banks, who was inspired to follow in his father's footsteps and creating a new community garden in the Hough neighborhood, previously known for its riots in the 1960s. He says, "When I was a little kid, there was a house torn down next to us. My father, being just one generation removed from sharecropping, loved to play in the dirt. He would plant gardens every year and supplement feeding the family with what he grew in that garden. He often grew more than we could consume, so he would give stuff away to people who were in need. So it became part of me to want to carry on that tradition of gardening."

A few streets away, Mansfield Frazier, a locally-renowned civic activist and writer in his sixties, is becoming an entrepreneur with the development of the Château Hough vineyard. With program funding, he has planted hundreds of grapevines on a prominent vacant corner that is flanked by vacant buildings on either side. He will expand to many more lots over the next few years and plans to open a winery—a stone's throw from the nationally acclaimed Cleveland Clinic.

And there is Todd Alexander, who along with two friends, is creating east side and west side urban farms in the Central and Ohio City neighborhoods. They are putting their entrepreneurial spirits and recent college degrees in sustainability into action and helping to address "food deserts," areas where fresh fruits and vegetables are limited. They are part of a new breed of twentysomethings who are putting Cleveland on the national "local food map" and creating new career paths in urban agriculture. (Cleveland is ranked second nationally in local food by SustainLane.)

To enable this work, the Cleveland Community Development Department Land Bank is working hard to surmount regulatory issues with HUD in order to be able to respond to the increased volume of vacant land and the public's interest in it. The city's Land Bank program, the holding agent for eight thousand of the city's twenty thousand vacant lots, has crafted policy and administrative changes to streamline vacant lot disposition. The city's Water Department is crafting new policies and fee structures for water usage to accommodate community and entrepreneurial vacant land reuse projects. The City Planning Commission and the Cleveland City Council have adopted zoning changes and legislation that protect gardens and farms through garden-district zoning and allow for easier use of land for agricultural purposes, including keeping small livestock and bees. To foster local food entrepreneurs, the Cleveland Economic Development Department offers a small grant and low-interest loan program for market gardens and urban farms for start-up business costs.

Where is all of this headed in the short and long term? A vacant land council is being organized to coordinate the myriad vacant land initiatives being carried out by public agencies and private nonprofits. An evaluation is underway to compare Cleveland's program with those of Flint, Indianapolis, Pittsburgh, Philadelphia, and Baltimore. Planners are studying how to move this work to scale. Aligning public resources, community energy, and technical knowledge on the most challenging issues is beginning to create powerful changes that will serve the city well for decades.

7

Human Capital And Legacy Cities

Robert Giloth, The Annie E. Casey Foundation

Jillien Meier, Maryland Hunger Solutions

This chapter addresses the question of whether shrinking United States cities, or legacy cities, face unique human capital challenges—beyond the extreme loss of jobs and population over many decades—compared to other cities and the national experience.[1] Is poverty more severe in these cities, limiting their ability to build human capital and take advantage of new business and job opportunities? Is there a greater mismatch in legacy cities between the skills needed by employers and the skills of the workforce? Similarly, do these cities face larger problems with "spatial mismatches," in which people who need jobs don't live near the places that have jobs? Is the civic capacity needed to fashion innovative partnerships and services severely compromised?

A relevant and related question is whether, and to what degree, legacy cities should even focus on human capital strategies for children, young people, and adults, given their overarching challenges of jump-starting economic development, amassing vacant land for new uses, and right-sizing government service delivery. After all, workforce investments in the context of high unemployment are frequently more about rearranging the queue, not accessing net new opportunities.[1] Isn't economic development the paramount objective? Yet equity and fairness are also important goals, especially because benefits from new development do not automatically flow to low-income residents, and they sometimes produce negative impacts. These are the kind of questions we hope to explore in order to provide useful advice for public, private, and civic leaders and policymakers concerned with the future of shrinking cities.

In the end, we argue that shrinking cities should:

- Develop two-generation human capital plans, focused both on parents and children, that carefully balance current and future needs and economic and human development
- Take advantage of economic and workforce assets like anchor institutions, existing businesses, sector or industry strengths, as well as local assets
- Develop a pipeline of effective programmatic investments in skill acquisition and work experience
- Create regional workforce partnerships for strategy development, coordination, implementation, and accountability
- Support physical and economic revitalization approaches that contain a human capital component
- Embrace a policy agenda that addresses the unique human-capital challenges of shrinking cities.

This chapter explores the human-capital challenges facing legacy cities and the nation, examines labor-market data for a sample of shrinking cities, considers alternative strategic frameworks for guiding human-capital investments in these places, provides estimates of the investment required, identifies promising practices for a human-capital agenda in shrinking cities, and concludes with recommendations for program and policy consideration.

The Human Capital Challenge

Most U.S. cities and metro areas face serious human capital challenges, given that many low-income residents have neither the skills nor the education needed for jobs that can sustain a family. Many of these residents live in neighborhoods disconnected physically and socially from job centers. Some face significant barriers to economic success, such as criminal records, limited English skills, and physical and mental health problems. The challenges are likely to grow more pronounced in the coming decades, given the enhanced skill requirements of new job creation, global competition for workers and companies and the impending retirement of skilled baby boomers.[2] While the economy is projected to produce large numbers of lower-skilled, entry-level jobs in retail, service, and health care, many of the best opportunities will be in so-called middle-skill jobs that require workers to have some college education and will become available in such sectors as health, manufacturing and construction.[3] Georgetown University's Center on Education and the Workforce projects the availability of eighteen million jobs by 2018 that will require a postsecondary level of education.[4] Meeting this demand for jobs and skills in a timely and sustainable way will stretch local capacity for many reasons, not the least of which is that 88 million adults in the United States have at least one educational barrier: no high school diploma, no college degree, or limited English skills.[5] This isn't just a question of improving children's educational prospects. A two-generation approach to developing human capital is needed because more than half of those who will comprise the 2030 workforce are already working.[6]

Future skill requirements underscore the importance of meeting a set of workforce and education challenges touching on both children and parents:

- Ensuring that adults have adequate work experience and increasing labor force participation
- Improving school readiness and third grade reading achievement
- Increasing high school completion and postsecondary educational attainment
- Closing literacy and numeracy skill gaps
- Improving basic and technical skills of existing workers
- Giving workers the skills and credentials required by new and modernizing businesses

In most cities, not just those that are shrinking, these challenges are magnified by mismatches between where workers live and where jobs and businesses are located; a systemic disconnection between economic, workforce, and education investments; the fragmentation of workforce/education institutions and systems across regions; and the inadequacy and/or poor targeting of public and private resources aimed to enhance human capital.[7]

Policy and programmatic answers that address these challenges are becoming better defined and more widely adopted, although it will be a challenge to increase the size and reach of the most promising efforts. There is also a broader recognition of the need to improve the skills of workers and job seekers to benefit both those workers and the employers. Human capital challenges and investments, for example, have moved from low on the list of priorities for the business community to the top of their concerns about successful economic development.[8] Business and economic developers talk about the "talent gap" as a fundamental driver of wealth creation, yet the United States lags behind in educational achievement, especially in the disciplines of science and math, when compared to other advanced economies and our primary competitors.[9]

The United States needs to build highly effective education pipelines that take children from early childhood to postsecondary achievement; provide opportunities for adults to learn new skills and adapt for career advancement; promote employer-recognized training and education credentials, as well as industry-focused training; and develop new, affordable financing mechanisms for skill attainment. In addition, there should be a greater role and set of incentives for businesses to define skill requirements, provide on-the-job supports for career advancement, and target investments in human-capital training.[10] These approaches remain difficult to achieve on a large scale because of resource constraints, institutional fragmentation, bureaucratic funding "silos," improper or nonexistent incentives, lack of employer buy-in, skill gaps, weak skill-acquisition norms, and a lack of overall national leadership on human-capital development. Moreover, current economic conditions make entering or reentering the labor market more challenging for young workers, as well as those with fewer skills and more workforce barriers. These problems are exacerbated in shrinking cities and other depressed regional labor markets.

Many planning documents for legacy, or shrinking, cities simply extrapolate from the list of national human-capital priorities and promising practices to the policy, rather than develop customized interventions. Many of the human-capital investments being made throughout the country are appropriate for shrinking cities, as well. Our belief, however, is that these cities also need to think carefully about the unique challenges they face before rushing to adopt what everyone else is trying. Without taking this step, they run the risk of missing the factors essential for constructing and implementing viable human capital agendas that complement overall economic-revitalization strategies. Shrinking cities risk severe investment mismatches that they can ill afford.

Do legacy cities have any advantages for reinvigorating their human capital investments? Many shrinking cities have universities, health-care institutions, and philanthropic legacies that provide important resources and leadership.[11] Frequently, these cities also have a legacy of manufacturing strength that, while battered by change, endures in the form of supply chains, industry knowledge, institutions, and human capital. Finally, the emergency situation facing these cities may, if addressed productively, enable shrinking cities to more easily reinvent institutional arrangements and systems that are now impeding progress. A good example of such a comprehensive vision is contained in the American City Agenda for Cleveland.[12]

A Closer Look At Legacy Cities

Shrinking or legacy cities are places that have lost substantial population and employment over multiple decades.[13] They are a subset of the one hundred or more distressed industrial cities of various sizes across America. In the process of decline, these cities have lost many of the resources needed for economic revitalization and may, therefore, have lost some measure of the institutional capacity necessary for sustained innovation. For these cities, the "old way" of doing business is no longer tenable, but dramatic change is difficult, as institutions naturally protect what has come before. An overarching question for all of these cities is whether the population decline has actually ended.

Many legacy cities are concentrated in the Rust Belt and Great Lakes region, but the list also includes places like Richmond (CA) and New Orleans. On average, these cities have lost a third of their employment/population base and several, such as St. Louis and Youngstown, lost more than 50 percent of their population by 2000 from their peak size around 1950. Many of these cities have lost an additional 10 percent of their population in the past decade.[14]

In general, legacy cities are contained within regions that have declined or are experiencing slow growth, what are sometimes called "weak market" regions.[15] And many shrinking cities are part of substate or multistate regions that are experiencing decline, such as the Midwestern Rust Belt. What this means is that shrinking cities cannot simply rely upon creating better connections to the economic vitality of their regions, although such opportunities certainly exist. Yet, one must keep in mind that shrinking cities are not all the same in terms of the degree of loss, the mix of remaining economic activities and populations, and their legacies of philanthropic and civic resources produced by the corporate leaders of the past economy.

Tables 1, 2, and *3* summarize a range of demographic and employment statistics for a sample of shrinking cities: Cleveland, Detroit, Pittsburgh, Buffalo, Rochester, and New Orleans, along with national data, to put the employment conditions of these shrinking cities into perspective. Key statistics include employment loss, unemployment, employment participation rates, median age of the workforce, rate and concentration of poverty, high school graduation, college attainment, migration rates, and suburban or city job comparisons.

Table 1: *Demographics in Shrinking Cities*

City	*Population*	*Population Change (1990-2009)*	*Median Age*	*Poverty*	*MSA Poverty**	*Immigration*
Buffalo	270,240	-17.6	34.8	28.6	13.6	6.1
Cleveland	431,369	-14.6	35.9	30.2	13.6	4.9
Detroit	910,921	-11.3	33.7	33.2	14.2	6.5
New Orleans	354,850	-28.5	36.7	23.4	15.9	5.1
Pittsburgh	311,647	-15.7	35.5	21.7	11.8	7
Rochester	207,294	-10.5	31.9	29.1	12.3	7.7
United States	307,006,550	23.4	36.5	13.5	N/A	12.4

*Kneebone and Berube, 2008.
Source: U.S. Census Bureau, 2009 data
(http://factfinder.census.gov/home/saff/main.html?_lang=en).

Table 2: *Educational Attainment in Shrinking Cities*

City	*No Diploma*	*High School Diploma*	*Some College*	*Associate's Degree*	*College Graduate*	*Graduate Degree*
Buffalo	13.3	31.4	19.9	7.9	12	9.3
Cleveland	18.4	35.7	20.3	5.8	8.5	5.2
Detroit	16.9	34.4	23.6	6.1	7.5	4.7
New Orleans	12.1	28	20.7	3.5	17	12.3
Pittsburgh	9	31.4	15.9	7.3	17.3	15.9
Rochester	14	27.6	17.6	8.9	14.4	10.2
United States	9.1	29.3	20.3	7.4	17.4	10.1

Source: U.S. Census Bureau, 2009 data (http://factfinder.census.gov/home/saff/main.html?_lang=en).

Table 3: *Employment Data in Shrinking Cities*

City	*2009 Unemployment Rate*	*MSA Unemployment Rate*	*2009 Employment Rate**	*MSA Employment*
Buffalo	12.1	7.2	52.2	58.2
Cleveland	16.6	8.8	50.2	59.5
Detroit	22.1	11.5	42.9	56.4
New Orleans	12.5	8.2	53.6	57.6
Pittsburgh	8.1	6.3	55.7	57.8
Rochester	10.7	6.6	53.6	59.5
United States	7.2	N/A	59.9	N/A

*Refers to civilian labor force currently employed.

Source: U.S. Census Bureau, 2009 data (http://factfinder.census.gov/home/saff/main.html?_lang=en).

Overall, legacy cities have lost proportionately more employment than the nation as a whole, have higher unemployment and poverty rates, lower employment participation, a lower number of high school graduates, a lower proportion of college graduates, fewer in-migrants, and more pronounced spatial mismatches. The comparative age profile for these cities shows that they are roughly similar to other cities, but have slightly more people over the age of sixty-five.

But shrinking cities are not all the same. Detroit stands out with more pronounced labor-market challenges across a number of variables, especially for labor-force participation, unemployment, college attainment, and poverty. New Orleans, even before the dramatic changes resulting from Katrina's aftermath, had higher rates of labor-force participation, college attainment, and immigration, and somewhat lower rates of poverty, although still higher than national rates. Likewise, Pittsburgh's poverty rate is higher than the national average but lower than that of many other legacy cities; its employment participation approaches the national average, as do its rates of college and graduate school attainment.

The tables show that shrinking cities are more racially segregated than other areas and they capture the geographic mismatch between where jobs are and where workers live. As shown in *Table 4,* the sample cities have Dissimilarity Indexes above the national weighted average of .64, a measure of racial segregation, with Detroit, Cleveland, and Buffalo experiencing significantly higher levels of racial segregation. Detroit, Cleveland, and Rochester also have higher rates of concentrated working poverty (ZIP codes in which more than 40 percent of taxpayers claimed the Earned Income Tax Credit) compared to other cities in their regions, as shown in *Table 1*.[16]

The Metro Dissimilarity Index in *Table 4* measures the racial segregation of a region. The Employment Mismatch Index in *Table 4* measures the separation of the African-American population from jobs.[17] All of the six sample cities have higher measures than the national average, with Detroit's being the highest.

Table 4: *Dissimilarity Index and Job Sprawl in Shrinking Cities*

City	*2000 Metro DI**	*Employment MI ***	*Job Sprawl***
Buffalo	0.766	66.2	68.4
Cleveland	0.768	62.0	75.4
Detroit	0.846	71.4	92.4
New Orleans	0.671	64.2	55.6
Pittsburgh	0.66	59.2	36.6
Rochester	0.671	64.2	55.6
Average of the 6 cities		64.7	N/A
Average of all urban regions with more than 500,000 people	0.64	56.5	71.1

*U.S. Census Bureau Tables, 2000

** Michael Stoll, Brookings, February 2005.

Finally, Detroit, Cleveland, and Buffalo have significantly more job sprawl than the other three sample cities and are above the national average for metropolitan areas with more than 500,000 people. Of these three metropolitan areas, Detroit has by far the highest employment concentration outside a ten-mile ring surrounding central business districts.[18]

These data show that customized planning is needed to meet the special characteristics of each shrinking city. Yet there is an unmistakable pattern: These cities have higher unemployment and poverty, lower employment participation, and more people without a high school diploma. It is also clear that there is a racial divide that must be addressed.

Legacy cities face additional challenges beyond the sheer numbers of jobs needed, such as mismatches between available jobs and workers' skills. Workers may lack the skills or job readiness they need, be unavailable to fill industry needs, or be in the wrong place to move into available jobs. There may be a deep gap between workers' skills and the jobs that are available, creating a question of how much remediation is possible in the short run to meet economic development needs. These mismatches lead to jobs going unfilled, people placed in jobs for which they are not fully qualified, or firms deciding not to create jobs in certain locations.

Institutional Capacity For Change

Additional issues related to governance and regionalism need to be addressed if human-capital investments are to be successful in shrinking cities and regions.[19] While shrinking cities may not be worse off than other cities in terms of these factors, weak civic infrastructure will have disproportionate negative effects on the capacity of these places to change course. In fact, conditions such as extreme decentralization and job sprawl are related to governmental fragmentation in shrinking cities and their metro areas in such places as Detroit.[20]

The overall concept of "civic infrastructure" developed by the National Civic League refers to the vision, leadership, relationships, organizations, and networks that can be drawn upon to address vital community issues.[21] Some shrinking cities, such as Cleveland, are recognized as having a strong civic infrastructure.[22]

Several institutional factors have to be grappled with if human capital investments are to be successful and achieve a large scale within regions. These include:

- Diminished bonding and social capital undermines the ability of people to find jobs and the social supports needed to keep jobs, essential parts of labor market functioning
- Fragmentation of government, private sector, and civic organizations translates into a lack of leadership and resources to develop new kinds of effective partnerships[23]
- High civic transaction costs are required for building partnerships and carrying out institutional redesigns in areas with fewer resources and more complex needs, with some needs perceived as more important than human capital, at least in the short run[24]

Future research needs to explore the role of these factors in labor market functioning and in impeding the development of effective responses to economic and demographic change. Our hypothesis for this chapter is that these factors do play an important role in shaping human capital responses for shrinking cities.

Strategic Human Capital Options and Their Implications

There is a common tendency to search for and then replicate social programs that address specific needs in the labor market, whether for employers in an industry sector such as health care or for specific populations like the formerly incarcerated or mothers on welfare. This is not a bad thing in general, although it can add to the overall fragmentation of effort. But shrinking cities need to be more strategic because they have fewer resources and a greater need to link workforce development efforts with economic development. Without this concerted action, further population and job losses are possible. As we have just observed, shrinking cities are not all the same.

Two contrasting strategic frameworks showcase seemingly opposing approaches to human capital priorities and planning. A third, mixed approach offers a practical compromise. Strategic thinking of this kind will go a long way to ensuring the development of focused strategies and a better sense of the risk and opportunities.

Build Economic Development Strategies Based on the Existing and Likely Supply of Human Capital

The mantra for this approach is "Grow your own." People have left shrinking cities and new migrants are unlikely to come back in the short term in any great numbers. The people who remain are likely to stay because of preferences or economic ties such as jobs or housing that cannot be sold, or because they are unable to move anywhere else. In other words, the current population is the human-capital base upon which to build the economic future of the city. Improving the quality of this human capital will, we would expect, meet the needs of employers and, if successful, produce overall increases in regional income.

What are the implications of this approach? Two are obvious. First, cities should go after jobs and businesses that align well with the skills and work experiences of the existing population. Second, cities should go full out to develop the skills of the existing population—retirees, older workers, young workers, youth, and children. That means focusing both on people in jobs and those who are unemployed. Philadelphia estimates that raising the skills of its residents to comparable state levels would result in an 11 percent increase in income, or $1.8 billion.[25]

One downside of this focus on the existing population means a city may forgo jobs and businesses that require higher skill requirements. Given current skill levels, a city may be able to attract only service or retail businesses requiring low-skilled workers, but even attracting and keeping those businesses may be challenging because of declines in overall consumer income. And developing sufficient skills is a long and uncertain process that may take a decade or more, especially in the context of addressing long-term poverty issues that require more than workforce investments.

Focus Human Capital Investments on Current and Future Economic Development Needs and Opportunities

This approach suggests that human-capital strategies should be firmly rooted in the current economic base of a community and the likely economic development opportunities of the future. A community should develop skills among its job-ready workforce and attract the people it needs to fulfill these opportunities rather than focusing primarily on enhancing the skills of existing residents. Increasing jobs and economic development is the priority.

What this means is that human-capital strategies need to be focused on all jobs and occupations with the most relevance to present and future economic development. Cities should ask how they can retain high-level and middle-skill jobs—how they can attract new workers to fill these jobs who are likely to stay in the community—what place-based developments and urban amenities would make a community more attractive to higher-skilled workers and their families; and, finally how they can attract new residents to fill human-capital needs and start new businesses?

A downside of this approach is that it is simply not feasible from either an economic development or political point of view. That is, new people with high skill levels will not beat a path to shrinking cities in the short run. And neglecting or writing off the current population, especially communities of color, may backfire politically, reinforce community stress and dysfunction, and consequently undermine the overall ability of a city to market itself to the rest of the world.

Take a Mixed Approach to Developing Existing Human Capital and Attracting New Human Capital for Economic Development

A mixed approach may, in fact, be the most prudent course because of the inherent uncertainties in the other two approaches. Increasing the capabilities of low-skilled populations is difficult, but so is predicting the likely success of economic-development investments in places that human capital has abandoned. A mixed approach acknowledges a necessary humility in the face of the daunting challenges of revitalizing shrinking cities.

First and foremost, a human-capital strategy should focus on the current needs and opportunities of existing firms and institutions. That means doing everything possible to help fill jobs, no matter where candidates come from. It also means supporting the career development of existing workers who have demonstrated a commitment to the community. A second strategy is to focus on adults who are working on skill development, particularly those who have done some college work and who are involved in training programs. Creating "bridge" programs for those with good basic skills is a good step.[26] Finally, building a prekindergarten-to-college pipeline is essential—with a focus on all young people having access to strong early education, being able to read well by the third grade, graduating from high school, and making a successful transition into postsecondary education.

Attracting and retaining talent is also a part of a mixed strategy, but it should be pursued with care and focus. Some relocating businesses may bring their own workforces. That's a good thing if workers move to town and firms committed to local hiring in the future. Similar strategies may build on the unique geographic, cultural, or institutional resources, such as universities, hospitals, and other anchors.

The downside of the mixed approach is that it can lead to a city or region doing too many things at once and losing focus. This challenge is especially relevant for shrinking cities because their resources are more limited. Reflecting on what's working and not working may be the only way to invest appropriately and make midcourse corrections.

Human Capital Dilemmas

The data on legacy or shrinking cities and the contrasting strategic frameworks for human capital investment underscore a set of dilemmas that need to be acknowledged. These are relevant for all cities, but they play a disproportionate role in shrinking cities, some mattering more than others, depending upon local conditions and human-capital priorities.

Dual-Customer Workforce Development

A dual-customer approach has become the recognized paradigm for effective workforce investment.[27] In the past, workforce efforts largely emphasized the development of skills and readiness of workers or job seekers in relative isolation. This approach proved ineffective in many respects because it did not fully take into account what employers needed to reduce turnover and increase productivity. Today's workforce-investment strategies pay greater attention to both business and worker customers, recognizing that responding to employers' definitions of readiness and skills is essential. Yet the closer attention we pay to satisfying the employer, the more workforce development has to serve workers who are more job-ready and skilled, potentially leading to "creaming," which means less attention goes to those job seekers with greater needs.

Customization

It's important to recognize that workforce and education investments need to be customized to meet the needs of different populations. A common mistake is to adopt highly visible "silver bullet" programs that promise to solve the workforce problem. Behind the rhetoric of these programs, however, are major challenges related to readiness requirements like literacy and numeracy, a major drop-off between the number of those who apply and who actually enroll, and an additional drop-off in the number of those who complete training, enter the workforce, and retain jobs for the long term. To be sure, different population groups require different approaches to achieve the necessary mix of job readiness, basic skills, and technical skills.

Poverty

Addressing poverty is not accomplished solely through workforce development and education, but economic well-being is certainly a major component of that effort. And concentrated poverty produces additional effects on limiting opportunities and labor-market connections.[28] A matrix of factors contributes to poverty and perpetuates its effects on children, families and communities. Poverty and race are inextricably linked. Concerted, targeted efforts are needed in all places to reduce poverty and the related problems of community safety and deterioration.[29]

Spatial Mismatches

Spatial mismatches between the location of people and jobs are a common problem facing metropolitan regions.[30] Business preferences and incentives, infrastructure investments in transportation and housing, and racial segregation have shaped this separation. Many strategies have been attempted to overcome the mismatch: housing mobility, improving access to cars and public transit, business incentives, and new public planning and investment protocols. While there has been lots of experimentation, these geographic mismatches remain. All the interventions are either expensive or run up against deeply entrenched interests and preferences. In the long run, we need to change the geographic configuration of people and business in regions. In the short run, shrinking cities have to assess the relative importance of spatial mismatches and what tactical interventions are feasible.

Migration

Migration is a natural contributor to healthy labor markets. People come, people go, and people stay put. In legacy cities, a lot of people have left, a lot of people are staying, but not a lot of new people are coming. In the long run, this balance needs to be restored. One way to facilitate this is by adopting a broader regional approach to workforce development. Then there are specific strategies to attract migrants, a potentially dangerous, updated version of "smokestack chasing," now focused on the "creative class," footloose artists and new immigrants to the United States. Given the overall projected growth rate of the population, might shrinking cities offer new opportunities? Perhaps, but chasing immigrants might lead to ignoring better human-capital bets closer to home.

Building Economic Development and Workforce Development

Building a link between economic development and workforce development is now seen as a reasonable goal for most cities and states.[31] Workforce issues have moved up the priority list for the business and economic development community, and all cities need a workforce with adequate and growing skills to be successful in the new economy. Yet workforce- and economic-development approaches are quite different and are not easily aligned.[32] Economic development often focuses on short-run transactions or long-term infrastructure, while workforce and education focus on long-term skills acquisition and reforming systems. Mismatches between the two approaches are inevitable, particularly in key aspects such as timing, location, and the quality of jobs being created. At the same time, many see missed opportunities for tighter links between the two. They advocate for community-benefit agreements to ensure that jobs created by new infrastructure investments go to local residents.[33] Several points of intersection are promising. Sector- or industry-based strategies that identify sectors that will grow over the long term offer an opportunity to plan short- and long-term approaches for education and economic development, fostering business engagement in the process.[34] Market development for new industries, such as clean energy, offers real opportunities for linking economic and workforce development.

Changing Human Capital Systems

Changing human capital systems must complement and support promising practices and pilot programs.[35] And it is the only way to reach a major scale over the long term. These systems include those created through the Workforce Investment Act (WIA) and the Temporary Assistance for Needy Families (TANF) program, early childhood programs, adult education, K-12 education, and community colleges. Too often, human capital plans reflect a narrow interpretation of what is possible given legislative mandates. The focus should be on developing overarching system-change plans that are anchored in local assets, acknowledging the importance of these public resources and how they can contribute and identifying new ways to align these systems to achieve overall human capital priorities. Additional resources will be needed to make progress on bold human capital agendas. A good place to start is to create regional systems or coalitions of agencies that pursue a similar set of human capital priorities.

Civic Capacity

Civic capacity is the ability of local leaders to produce social coalitions that can pursue long-term improvements in education and workforce development.[36] This is a challenge in the human-capital arena for several reasons. First, we have already called attention to institutional fragmentation, along with the challenges of defining problems, solutions, results, and measures of progress.[37] Second, human-capital institutions are frequently governed by what have been named "employment regimes," inward-looking institutions more concerned about self-preservation than in creating "performance regimes" concerned with system changes and bold aspirations.[38] It is paramount that shrinking cities overcome these disincentives and obstacles to human-capital development. The "call to action" for shrinking cities may help local leaders come together, but progress on human capital has to be seen as a critical, long-term component of city and regional revitalization. Civic leadership has to promote community priority-setting and accountability for a set of important human-capital outcomes.

There is no one solution to any of these dilemmas that works for all shrinking cities. In fact, these dilemmas may look quite different in different contexts. But human-capital investment plans will certainly need to grapple with these dilemmas if cities are going to make sustainable improvements. A first step is to take an honest and thorough look at the functioning of local labor markets. A second step is to become active in a learning network of shrinking cities and study human-capital innovations around the country. A third step is to organize civic coalitions to get behind a human-capital agenda and set of results.

Closing Human Capital Gaps

Before we offer a sample of potential human capital investments for shrinking cities, we need to ask a basic question: What level of ambition, scale, and investment in human capital should shrinking cities embrace? We've seen that human-capital gaps in shrinking cities are quite dramatic. What should be the target for change?

We calculated a series of "closing the gap" estimates that project how much change would be required for shrinking cities to have similar human-capital rates for important indicators compared to their metropolitan areas or their states, such as employment or poverty. Comparison to metro areas is especially relevant because most of the metropolitan areas of shrinking cities have experienced only slow or modest growth.

Table 5: *Closing the Gap in Shrinking Cities*

	Buffalo	*Cleveland* *	*Detroit* *	*New Orleans*	*Pittsburgh*	*Rochester*
High School Graduation						
# of New H.S. Graduates Required[1]	849	N/A	N/A	6,754	12,705	1,312
% Population Change Required [2]	0.50%	N/A	N/A	3.10%	6.09%	1.00%
5-Year Average [3]	170	N/A	N/A	1,351	2,541	262
* *The percentage of high school graduates in the city is higher than in the MSA*						
The Employment Gap						
# of New Permanent Workers Required [1]	12,883	31,855	93,070	10,541	5,462	9,595
% Population Change Required [2]	6.00%	9.32%	13.50%	3.96%	2.05%	5.92%
5-Year Average [3]	2,577	6,371	18,614	2,108	1,092	1,919
The Community College Gap						
# of New Associates Degree Holders Required [1]	4,938	3,434	8,189	2,969	2,940	2,893
% Population Change Required [2]	2.84%	1.21%	1.44%	1.36%	1.40%	2.25%
5-Year Average [3]	988	687	1,638	594	588	579
Reducing Poverty						
# of Persons Lifted Out of Poverty Required [1]	41,000	72,875	174,065	24,650	30,998	34,944
% Population Change Required [2]	-15%	-16.60%	-19%	-7.50%	-9.90%	-16.80%
5-Year Average [3]	8,200	14,575	34,813	4,930	6,200	6,989

Notes:

1. The number of people needed to equalize the city rate for the indicator with that of the MSA ("The Gap")
2. The Gap that needs to be closed stated as a percentage
3. The annual change required if The Gap is to be closed over a five-year period

Table 5 provides closing-the-gap estimates for employment rates, high school diplomas, community college degrees, and poverty rates, and comparing them to data for metropolitan areas. These are not small gaps, even when spread over five years. For example, in Detroit, 93,000 more people need to be employed, more than 18,000 a year for each of five years. Another recent estimate showed that Detroit would need to add 75,000 jobs, when compared to the national average.[39]

The gap in community college degrees demonstrates the major skill gap that has to be tackled for the new economy. Yet these cities and their surrounding regions (defined as the metropolitan statistical area, or MSA) are roughly comparable on a number of educational attainment measures. Finally, the poverty gap is substantial for all the cities when compared to their MSAs.

We would have to detail costs, availability of resources, and likelihood of success for each of these closing-the-gap estimates to understand their full implications. And there are multiple approaches to reaching these goals, including economic development, employment, and training and mobility strategies. In the workforce world, most cities have few resources devoted to skill training compared to the overall need—hundreds of individual training accounts rather than thousands. A similar gap exists for adult education and graduation rates for community colleges. On the other hand, increasing the number of working poor adults with children who file for the Earned Income Tax Credit is a relatively low-cost effort, brings in new regional income and is a proven approach to poverty alleviation.

Table 6: *4th Grade Reading Proficiency in Shrinking Cities*

	Buffalo	*Cleveland*	*Detroit*	*Pittsburgh*	*Rochester*
4th Grade Reading Proficiency					
Total Students, PreK-12	34,225	49,952	94,907	27,945	32,711
Total 4th Grade Students	2,447	3,537	6,915	1,983	2,365
# of Newly Proficient 4th Graders [1]	539	991	900	900	473
% Population Change Required [2]	22%	28%	13%	16%	20%
5-Year Average [3]	108	198	180	64	95

Notes:

1. The number of children needed to equalize the city rate for the indicator with that of the state
2. "The Gap" that needs to be closed as a percentage
3. The annual change required if the Gap is to be closed over a five-year period

Data sources: New America Foundation, Federal Education Budget Project (http://febp.newamerica.net/k12/la),

U.S. Department of Education, National Center for Education Statistics (http://nces.ed.gov/ccd)

Table 6 provides closing-the-gap estimates for third-grade reading achievement by comparing results for children in shrinking cities to children statewide on state tests for fourth graders. Third-grade reading achievement is a good benchmark for school progress and is a predictor of future human-capital achievement.[40] As can be seen, a significant achievement gap exists between shrinking cities and their states. Cleveland, for example, would need to have 991 more children, 28 percent of all fourth graders, improve their reading abilities to have the same rate of proficiency as does the state. Unless addressed, similar gaps will occur in each subsequent year, leading to even more underachievement. Boosting third grade reading begins before or at birth, involves parenting and quality early-childhood care, school readiness, transitioning to quality schools, and attention to the barriers that get in the way of regular attendance. It essentially involves building a "conveyor belt," in the words of Geoffrey Canada of the Harlem Children's Zone. Doing this at scale will require major system change and the reallocation of resources, as well as new resources.

Shrinking cities will need to set bold but achievable targets for human-capital investment. We have already identified the problem of working on too many fronts in the context of diminished opportunity, resources, and civic capacity. Cities will have to make careful choices about where to start and how to build out their interventions over time.

Examples of Human Capital Investment for Legacy Cities

A lot of promising examples exist to guide human-capital investments in shrinking cities, many of them homegrown in these cities or in other cities experiencing significant transitions. Not all the evidence is in about the overall effectiveness of these approaches, but we believe it is useful to offer a sense of the range of investment opportunities. We are not encouraging cities to dabble in a little bit of everything in order to further program proliferation, but we do believe that making a handful of solid investments that build on promising models is the way to go. We underscore the importance and interconnections among five strategies:

- Human Capital and Education Pipelines
- Human Capital and Hard-to-Employ Workers
- Human Capital and Economic Development
- Attracting and Connecting People and Jobs
- Human Capital Matching, Planning, and Investing

Human Capital and Education Pipelines

A key strategy is to build two-generation pipelines from early childhood to post-secondary college attainment. This approach could start with strengthening a cluster of schools or as individual programmatic interventions that then can be linked together, such as improving graduation rates from community college. It is the continuum and the management of transitions, persistence, and graduation that will make the difference.

Talent Dividend. The Talent Dividend initiative is a regional effort to better prepare students for college and promote postsecondary educational attainment for all ages. The effort, part of a national one by CEOs for Cities, focuses on increasing college-readiness, college graduation rates, therate of transfers from community colleges, and the degree completion rate for older adults.[41]

The Northeast Ohio Council on Higher Education coordinates the Talent Dividend program in Ohio with a steering committee of economic development organizations, businesses, and civic organizations. The program offers a continuum of supports, from dual learning opportunities for high school students taking college courses to increased social supports, college application preparation for families and increased supports for teachers.[42]

The Strive Partnership. The Strive Partnership of Cincinnati operates as a pre-kindergarten to college pipeline, ensuring that children are ready for school, supported throughout their academic careers, and prepared for careers upon college graduation. The partnership is a coalition of early-childhood advocates, district superintendents, college and university presidents, community funders, business leaders, and service providers, all with a commitment to coordinated advocacy, aligning funding to meet shared goals, and data-driven decisions.

The Strive Partnership uses data to track its progress in addressing seven key areas to maximize students' academic success: kindergarten readiness, fourth grade reading proficiency, eighth grade math proficiency, high school graduation and ACT scores, postsecondary enrollment, and postsecondary completion. Strive partners report increased student achievement across three public school districts, including high school graduation rates, fourth-grade reading and math scores, and the number of preschool children prepared for kindergarten.[43]

Strive is being replicated around the country and inspiring quite a bit of attention because of its results to date and because of its methodology for achieving "collective impact."[44] In Cincinnati, they are also attempting to apply this methodology to the fragmented, multisectoral workforce systems.

Austin Polytechnic Academy. This college- and career-prep high school focuses on skill development and credential acquisition as part of a larger sector-based development strategy in Chicago. In an effort to support workforce development, the Chicago Renaissance Manufacturing Council identified manufacturing as an industry poised for growth and is striving to strengthen the city's manufacturing base and address important human-capital needs identified by businesses.

The program delineates skill-building and job-training strategies by grade level. Freshman and sophomores at the academy are introduced to the technologies used in manufacturing and engineering professions and learn basic skills required for career development. Juniors and seniors shadow workers at local firms and learn about the manufacturing business and various career paths. Students have the opportunity to earn nationally recognized credentials in metalworking, and they gain vital career experience through summer jobs and internships with the academy's partner companies. Students in the program have the opportunity to acquire industry-specific skills through a Manufacturing Technology Center, which features the same computerized, high-tech equipment used by modern manufacturers. The program's students continue to succeed in gaining National Institute for Metalworking Skills credentials, with 100 percent of students having passed their certification exam in 2010.[45]

Kalamazoo Promise. Kalamazoo Promise is another example of an education pipeline developed to revitalize a city and encourage economic development through postsecondary educational attainment opportunities. Kalamazoo Promise provides full scholarships to any public college in Michigan for all graduates who received their elementary and secondary schooling in the Kalamazoo Public Schools.[46] To date, the initiative has paid $21.3 million in tuition and fees.

Results are mixed for the program, according to an evaluation conducted by Western Michigan University. Enrollment in the Kalamazoo Public Schools has increased by 12 percent, and with 2,336 graduates eligible for the scholarship program, 82 percent have received funding and continued on to college. Retention is the biggest hurdle for the initiative, as about a third of the scholarship recipients were not in school for the winter 2010 semester.[47]

Graduate! Philadelphia. This joint initiative of the Philadelphia Workforce Investment Board and the United Way of Southeastern Pennsylvania promotes learning opportunities for low-income working adults with some college experience by encouraging reenrollment, degree completion, and additional credentialing. The program partners with businesses, government agencies, postsecondary institutions, and service providers.

Philadelphia ranks 92nd among the one hundred largest U.S. cities in terms of college attainment among members of the workforce. At the same time, eighty thousand Philadelphians between the ages of twenty-five and forty-five have more than one year of college credit but no degree. In coordination with program advisers, Graduate! Philadelphia offers workshops for perspective students to help them assess goals, document previous credits, identify appropriate college programs, and apply for financial aid. The program also offers free academic counseling. As of January 2010, Graduate! Philadelphia had helped 470 adults re-enroll in college and had worked with 1,500 adults to help prepare them to enroll.[48]

Human Capital and Hard-to-Employ Workers

While skill development and postsecondary certification are central to income growth and career development, many people have a difficult time attaching to work in the first place. Employment data in shrinking cities confirm that this is a common challenge, which is frequently related to literacy and other barriers to work. A number of worthy approaches are tackling this challenge.

Towards Employment. This Cleveland program offers a dual approach to supporting hard-to-employ workers. By focusing on both job seekers and employers as customers, Towards Employment addresses the human-capital and workforce-development needs in Cleveland. Workshops provide training on resumes, applications, mock interviews, soft skills, and connections to credentialing programs. Career consultants facilitate career adaption and help job seekers re-connect with the job market.

Towards Employment partners with employers to bolster their existing workforce and provide on-the-job support through the Reach Project for those experiencing barriers that threaten continued employment. This program aims to provide on-the-job supports for career advancement and continued skill-building opportunities, while helping employers reduce employee turnover. Towards Employment helps workers obtain reliable transportation, child care, and necessary tools and uniforms. The legal staff resolves criminal warrants, child-support cases and credit issues and works to prevent evictions and foreclosures.[49] In a 2009 study of the Reach Project, two years after the start of the program, 67 percent of program participants obtained wage increases and 95 percent of participants who sought promotions received them.

Deconstruction. Transitional jobs supported by physical redevelopment are one way to create first steps for people re-entering the workforce. Deconstruction initiatives eliminate the blight of vacant properties, create jobs, and save money on building demolition. Frequently, these programs target the hard-to-employ workers and provide entry-level construction work as shrinking cities undertake physical improvements and come to grips with population losses through right-sizing efforts. It will be important to link these starter jobs with career development in construction over time.[50]

Deconstruction involves dismantling buildings and salvaging material for reuse and recycling, reducing the disposal of material in landfills and providing low-cost materials for renovations. The average cost of demolition per house is six thousand dollars, which includes three thousand dollars in dumping fees. The average cost of deconstruction is twelve thousand dollars per house, but 80 percent of the materials in a home can be reused, recycled, or sold.[51]

The city of Saginaw, north of Detroit, partnered with Habitat for Humanity to create a deconstruction business to deconstruct homes, using a combination of state and city funds. In 2007 the city had at least one thousand abandoned houses. The city is working to hire and train workers identified through the city's homeless shelters and the state's prisoner-reentry initiative.[52]

Deconstruction jobs will not necessarily turn into a self-supporting business or industry, given the weak demand for housing in shrinking cities. They do, however, represent a way to create jobs as the physical environment of these cities is reconfigured.

Alternative Staffing Organizations. These organizations provide a sheltered way for workers and employers to get to know one another. This is especially important for workers who are new or returning to the labor force and are addressing employment barriers. The staffing organization takes the risk and agrees to address workplace problems. Alternative-staffing initiatives play a vital workforce development role in areas where many job seekers have skill gaps and low levels of educational attainment.

The Gulf Coast Alternative Staffing Initiative combines the business model of a staffing firm with the social mission of workforce development. The initiative develops employment connections by matching the current needs and existing opportunities of business with area job seekers. It promotes and expands employment opportunities for individuals with barriers to employment by providing job-training opportunities and workforce-readiness support. What sets the initiative apart from most workforce-development programs is the variety of fee-based services it provides for employers, including job placement, applicant screening, and orientation and training for selected applicants.

Gulf Coast Alternative Staffing is a start-up, making it difficult to assess results. Emerge Staffing of Minneapolis, a more mature alternative-staffing organization, gives a sense of the potential of this kind of intervention. It serves mostly people with multiple barriers to employment, including many who have a criminal record, no high school diploma, or are homeless. Data shows that Emerge's clients are more likely to be placed in jobs with higher hourly wages and more days of work, with a third of all placements leading to permanent jobs.[53]

Human Capital and Economic Development

Linking economic development and the development of human capital can be difficult. A good way to do it is to build connections through investments related to place-based assets like anchor institutions, large and growing industry sectors, or physical redevelopment projects. There are likely to be public policy levers connected to these kinds of projects that can help forge workforce- and economic-development alignment. We cite a few examples here.

Evergreen Cooperative. Evergreen Cooperative of Cleveland combines job creation and wealth building by leveraging the economic strength of the city's anchor institutions. Evergreen is a partnership between neighborhood residents and key anchor institutions: the Cleveland Foundation, the city of Cleveland, Case Western Reserve University, the Cleveland Clinic, and University Hospitals. Evergreen starts employee-owned businesses, with three businesses launched as of early 2011: Evergreen Cooperative Laundry, Ohio Cooperative Solar, and Green City Growers Cooperative.

Three of the city's biggest anchors—the Cleveland Clinic, University Hospitals and Case Western Reserve University—annually procure more than three billion dollars in goods and services. The focus of the cooperative is to partner with these anchor institutions to identify local purchasing opportunities that could catalyze a network of local businesses that hire their workforces directly from the neighborhoods.[54]

The Cleveland Foundation estimates that the project will eventually result in ten new business start-ups, the creation of five hundred jobs in five years, thirty million dollars in additional loans and tax credits and asset accumulation of up to $65,000 per employee.[55]

Evergreen Cooperative Laundry, which was launched in July 2009, has secured $5.8 million in public-private financing and expects to clean more than ten million pounds of bed linens annually and create fifty new jobs in the community.

Ohio Cooperative Solar performs large-scale installations of solar panels on the roofs of the city's biggest nonprofit and public institutions, including the Cleveland Clinic. This cooperative also will perform weatherization services for households in Cleveland. It will eventually employ about fifty workers.

Green City Growers Cooperative will be a year-round, large-scale food production hydroponic greenhouse on fourteen acres in the heart of Cleveland, with five acres under glass. It will produce several million heads of lettuce per year, along with herbs and other crops. The greenhouse will employ fifty local residents.

BioTechnical Institute of Maryland, Inc. The BioTechnical Institute of Maryland, Inc., located in Baltimore, is capitalizing on the strength of a major anchor institution, Johns Hopkins Hospital and University, and the development of an emerging bioscience industry that demands skilled laboratory assistants, an employment opportunity within reach of many neighborhood residents.

Founded in 1998, the institute partners with public and private social services agencies, workforce-training providers, and schools. Recognizing an opportunity between the unfulfilled workforce needs of Johns Hopkins and the needs of the local unemployed and underemployed workers in low-wage jobs, the program seeks to fill the workforce and human-capital needs in East Baltimore. The initiative provides free training to qualified adult high school graduates who are unemployed or underemployed to help them become entry-level lab technicians. It is a good example of a sector-based workforce partnership (or intermediary) that knits together the partners and resources for career advancement.[56]

In 2006, the organization created BioStart, a twelve-week pre-training "bridge program" to help students build their math and reading skills while learning jobs skills. Upon completion, students begin a nine-week laboratory assistance program and students earn one hundred internship hours, which often lead to permanent jobs.

The program reports that its graduates have achieved an 80 percent job-retention rate, with 75 percent of graduates placed in jobs within three months of program completion and earning an increase of $6,600 in their first year after graduating.

Attracting and Connecting People and Jobs

The geographic separation of people and jobs is a particular challenge for shrinking cities and their residents in both metropolitan areas and multistate regions. A related challenge exists in terms of attracting new talent and helping existing residents move to job-rich regions. There are no simple ways to overcome these spatial mismatches and restore the balance of in- and out-migration. Yet, it must be a priority. A few examples of how this may happen are shown here.

Vehicles for Change. Vehicles for Change is a low-income car-ownership program that helps adults overcome transportation barriers to employment. The program operates in Maryland and the District of Columbia and works with social service agencies to identify and screen customers who meet income and employment requirements. Customers buy cars for seven hundred dollars with a loan from the program. Since the program began in 1999, it has matched customers with three thousand cars.

The University of Virginia evaluated the impact of Vehicles for Change as part of a study to address major barriers to employment for Virginia's TANF population. The authors recommended expanding the program as a TANF-funded program in Virginia as a low-cost way to strengthen workforce connections for the hard-to-employ workers. Seventy-three percent of its customers reported obtaining better jobs or promotions resulting in an average salary increase of $4,500.[57]

Attracting Immigrants. As shrinking cities experience increasing levels of out-migration, many have turned toward attracting immigrants as a means of counterbalancing population decline and jump starting economic development and business creation. Cities are employing a variety of strategies to attract immigrants, such as building welcome centers, connecting prospective immigrants with ethnic enclaves, and providing multilingual city web sites and employees. Unfortunately, few comprehensive strategies have gotten off the ground.

Global Detroit is a part of the larger economic-development effort under the New Economy Initiative in Detroit. The leaders of Global Detroit are working to increase immigration and the ethnic diversity of Detroit to better position the city to take advantage of economic-development opportunities.[58]

A study by Global Detroit found that immigrants in southeast Michigan are more likely to possess a college degree than the nonimmigrant population (37 percent compared to 23.7 percent) and are more likely to obtain degrees in science, technology, engineering, and mathematics.[59] In Michigan, immigrants were nearly three times as likely as native-born residents to start a business between 1996 and 2007, and 35 percent of the international patent applications in 2006 had an immigrant as a key inventor.[60]

In an effort to increase immigration to Detroit, the initiative is developing a range of services and incentives to attract immigrants, including creating a welcome center, streamlining the visa process, and developing an attraction and retention program for Michigan colleges.

In Pittsburgh, the philanthropic community is taking a lead role in exploring and encouraging the connection between immigration and economic development. The Heinz Endowments awarded nonprofit organizations $800,000 in May 2010 to attract immigrants to the city, to encourage foreign students to remain in the area upon degree completion, and to teach the community about international diversity. Through these investments and city-led efforts to attract immigrants with jobs, affordable housing, and ethnic enclaves, Pittsburgh hopes to achieve the success of larger metropolitan areas and the economic growth that accompanies increased immigration.[61]

Finally, planning for an international welcome center in Cleveland began in 2010 after a report on the contributions of immigrants to the regional economy and civic life. The report identified promising components for the welcome center from around the country.[62]

Human Capital Matching, Planning, and Investing

Organizing the workforce and education systems on a regional basis is important in developing coordinated strategies, aligning human-capital investments, engaging with employers, linking economic and workforce development, and advocating for appropriate local, state, and federal investments. Many programs around the country that provide examples of how to craft regional coalitions and link workforce and economic development, including the Department of Labor's Workforce Innovations in Regional Economic Development (WIRED) initiative and the new federal Sustainable Communities program.

Cleveland's Workforce Investment Board. Cleveland's Workforce Investment Board pivoted in 2008 from facilitating employment connections to a greater emphasis on serving employers. The board focuses on matching and placing job seekers with potential employers, retaining successful job placements, and improving business productivity and competitiveness through existing worker skill development. This change followed a thorough review that showed that in previous years the agency has spent 80 percent of its budget on job seekers and 10 percent on employers. This resulted in a large network of training providers and social service agencies with a cadre of job seekers who completed job-training programs, only to remain unemployed.

Along with a new emphasis on working with business, the agency is expanding its scope to increase access to state and federal funds for job training. It will also advocate for broader workforce issues, including support for postsecondary education, addressing workers' transportation barriers, attracting business, and building partnerships with philanthropic institutions.

In six months of operation in this new role, the Workforce Investment Board has facilitated forty-two hundred interviews for job seekers and placed fourteen hundred job seekers, as compared to fifteen hundred placed in all of 2009. The agency has made connections to three thousand employers.[63]

East Baltimore's Economic Inclusion Policies. Baltimore provides a prime example of a local development initiative supporting physical revitalization projects with a strong human-capital component. The East Baltimore Revitalization Initiative, launched in 2001, is working to transform a distressed neighborhood, relocate several hundred households, and develop eighty-eight acres for life sciences and biotechnology research facilities, retail development, recreational space, and mixed-income housing.[64]

In 2002, East Baltimore Development, Inc., the nonprofit entity leading the project, developed an economic-inclusion policy to provide residents with job opportunities and local, minority-, and women-owned businesses an opportunity to contract for some of the work. The policy requires that contractors first offer hiring opportunities to East Baltimore residents, with an emphasis on job seekers displaced by the EBDI project. Under the policy, contractors must use local residents for 15 percent of commercial construction hours and 20 percent of residential construction hours.[65]

In 2007, EBDI expanded the program to create a dual-purpose workforce development pipeline that provides support to both job seekers and employers.[66] Working with the Mayor's Office of Economic Development, the first pathway connects job seekers with training, career counseling, and case management. The second pathway assists employers in meeting local hiring requirements, identifying job-training needs, enrolling job seekers in customized training programs, and offering job-placement services.

Since the workforce development pipeline was initiated, 632 residents have registered and 234 residents have been placed in jobs, with an 84 percent retention rate.[67] As of October 2010, the East Baltimore project has employed 1,715 workers, with 39 percent hired from Baltimore, including 15 percent from East Baltimore.[68]

A similar policy has been adopted in Camden, New Jersey, which demonstrates how smaller, shrinking cities can adopt economic inclusion policies as part of human capital development. In the city's 2002 Master Plan, a human-capital policy was outlined, containing a "Camden First" hiring requirement on all publicly funded projects. All city loan and contract documents include incentives and requirements to recruit from a qualified pool of city residents. This public contract requirement extends to municipal contractors by requiring them first to do business with neighborhood-based firms that can provide products and services relevant to a project activity.[69]

The New Economy Initiative. The New Economy Initiative (NEI) for Southeast Michigan, launched in 2008, is a unique philanthropic initiative aimed at revitalizing the regional economy. Ten national and local foundations have committed $100 million to this eight-year initiative to spur metro Detroit's innovation-based economy.

NEI's workforce investments support sector- or industry-based training by capitalizing on Detroit's extensive philanthropic assets and the basic skills and technical skills of the existing workforce. The initiative builds on Detroit's overall workforce focus in four sectors: advanced manufacturing, alternative energy, defense and homeland security, and transportation distribution and logistics. A sector-focused approach in health care is under development.

The initiative focuses on improving regional coordination and effectiveness of the workforce system by strengthening the links between workforce development, education, and economic development and through collaborative strategies that respond to the increasingly complex needs of both workers and employers. NEI recently awarded three million dollars in grant funding to support the Business Accelerator Network—a region-wide collaborative effort comprised of Ann Arbor SPARK, Automation Alley, Macomb-OU INCubator, and TechTown—to further focus on attracting and retaining businesses in the region. This new regional network will share best practices, sponsor events focused on addressing issues and goals that impact southeast Michigan, support business plan development, and leverage funding to grow business in the region. NEI will focus on leveraging the significant success of these organizations and bringing their work to scale. These four business accelerators have invested in 339 start-up companies, creating more than one thousand new jobs for the region.[70]

NEO@Work. NEO@Work is a talent-development initiative started in 2003 by the Fund for Our Economic Future, to align the economic-development efforts of a sixteen-county region in Northeast Ohio. The Fund is a partnership of private, public, civic, and philanthropic leaders and invests in business creation, business attraction, and workforce development.

NEO@Work has three components. The first is a network of innovators in the workforce and education arena with new ways of developing talent and skills for the twenty-first century. The second component is a complementary seed financing fund that supports, replicates, and expands promising talent innovations with capital and technical and management assistance. The third component is a public policy and public will agenda that seeks to build civic and policy support for enhancing northeast Ohio's talent and skill development.

NEO@Work plans to invest and leverage $4.5 million in philanthropic resources in at least twelve initiatives over its first three years that will result in raising the skills of ten thousand people and assembling a network of talent innovators.[71] NEO@Work received federal Social Innovation Fund resources for these promising efforts.

Scaling Human Capital Investments

Small, effective programs are insufficient to close the dramatic human-capital gap faced by many shrinking cities. In fact, program proliferation may itself contribute to the diffusion of civic energy and impact, a particular problem in a time of diminishing resources. Yet there is no single investment that will solve the human-capital problem for shrinking cities. More financial resources are part of the answer, but we focus here on several other key approaches to scale.

A first approach is for communities to be as clear as possible about the highest-priority results they want to achieve and where they believe the big payoffs will be both for the short and long term, whether its high school graduation and transition to postsecondary, attracting new workers or increasing the skills of the existing workforce.

A second approach is then to build better systems, not more programs. Shrinking cities have to make sure that existing resources are deployed in the most effective manner. Inside-outside coalitions of stakeholders dedicated to achieving specific results is a promising approach to achieving "collective impact," in which the contributions of many are knitted together and made accountable for specific results. This approach requires ongoing performance management.

A third approach is to integrate human-capital investments by industry. For example, if health care is a major local industry, a city might want to have a health-care track in schools, programs to increase incumbent workers' skills and career opportunities, community college industry-wide training for in-demand positions, certification programs for immigrant health-care workers, and employment linkage with health-care purchasing.

A final approach is to work with the best, most effective programs to scale up and build on their success. Scale will have to be defined carefully for each of the efforts. Investments will have to pay attention to organizational infrastructure and capacity at the same time that programs are expanded.

Thinking about scale can be paralyzing in this environment. The big challenge for every community is to align its public, private, and philanthropic resources to support common results and the most effective interventions to achieve these results.

Human Capital Policy Supports For Legacy Cities

Improving workforce skills and attracting new skilled workers will require that shrinking cities do more than operate good programs and redirect existing resources. These cities will also need a robust policy agenda that supports human-capital development and makes it a part of overall economic revitalization. Fleshing out a policy agenda of this kind is beyond the scope of this chapter, but we have identified key components:

- Create incentives and bonuses for P to 16 educational institutions to innovate, to create better student transitions, persistence, and competencies, and ultimately to produce more graduates.
- Create pools of public, private, and philanthropic resources to underwrite child savings accounts, college tuition, and vocation-retraining funds for low-income residents.
- Align and focus infrastructure investments to create anchors for economic and human-capital development.
- Ensure that all major public investments are linked to economic-inclusion policies that guarantee jobs for residents, invest in career pathways, and support local business development.
- Set poverty-reduction targets for shrinking cities and create opportunities to integrate existing resources into poverty-reduction interventions.
- Create incentives for regional coordination, planning, and implementation of joint workforce and economic-development efforts.
- Support strong sector-based economic- and workforce-development investments and partnerships that build on the competitive strengths of shrinking cities.
- Craft more attractive business incentives for upgrading the skills of existing workers and supporting the skill development of new workers.
- Create a new generation of enterprise zones for shrinking cities that supports the development of new industries and markets and the human-capital needed for them.
- Develop a package of mobility incentives that assist low-income, low-skilled residents of shrinking cities to relocate to more job-rich regions.

Conclusion and Challenges Ahead

Our answer to the primary question posed by this chapter is that shrinking cities indeed face some distinctive human-capital challenges. At the top of the list is the overall loss of jobs and population. But the demographics, skills, and geographic dispersion of people and jobs complicate human-capital development. And many shrinking cities have also experienced a decline in the civic and institutional bonds and capacities that support the innovative responses that are needed for these cities to adapt to changed economic circumstances.

This chapter has sought to clarify the human-capital challenges faced by shrinking cities and to identify effective responses and investments. Acknowledging likely employment mismatches, capacity requirements, and strategic and policy tradeoffs has underscored the need for shrinking cities to avoid becoming captive to fashionable program ideas or just continuing to embrace the old way of doing business. Shrinking cities face great pressure to work on many fronts at once, but at the same time they have less room to get things wrong. Most important, shrinking cities need a cadre of business and community leaders that will fight for the right kinds of human-capital investments for both the short and long term.

Notes

1. Gordon and Turok (2005).
2. National Center on Education and the Economy (2008).
3. Holzer and Lerman (2007).
4. Carnevale (2010).
5. National Commission on Adult Literacy (2008).
6. National Skills Coalition (2009).
7. Giloth, ed. (2004).
8. Eisen, Jasinowski, and Kleinert (2005).
9. Kempner (2008).
10. Siegel and Seidman (2009).
11. Vey (2007).
12. Living Cities (2010).
13. Mallach (2010).
14. Mallach and Brachman (2010).
15. Vey (2007).
16. Kneebone and Berube (2008).
17. The Employment Mismatch Index compares the proportion of African Americans to the number of jobs in an area's ZIP codes and calculates how many people would have to move in order for consistent balance to be achieved across the region.
18. Glaeser, Kahn, and Chu (2001).
19. Mallach and Brachman (2010); Stone, et al, (2001).
20. Glaeser, Kahn, and Chu (2001).
21. Parr (1993).
22. Giloth and Dewitt (1995).
23. Mallach and Brachman (2001).
24. Stone, et al (2001).

25. Philadelphia Workforce Investment Board (2007).
26. Alssid, Goldberg, and Klerk (2010).
27. Giloth (2004)
28. Wilson (1996).
29. Lind (2011)
30. Stoll (2005)
31. McGahey and Vey, eds (2008); Seigel and Seidman (2009)
32. Kleiman, et al (2009).
33. Altstadt (2010).
34. Giloth (2004).
35. Herbert (2010).
36. Stone, et al (2001).
37. Giloth (2004).
38. Stone, et al (2001).
39. American Institute of Architects Sustainable Design Assessment Team (2008).
40. Annie E. Casey Foundation (2010).
41. Cortright (2008).
42. Northeast Ohio Council on Higher Education (2010).
43. Strive Partnership (2011).
44. Kania and Kramer (2011).
45. Austin Polytechnical Academy (2010).
46. Miron and Cullen (2008).
47. Mack (2010).
48. Loschiavo (2010).
49. Towards Employment, "Great Needs, Greater Responses. Annual report" (Cleveland: Towards Employment, December 2009).
50. Altstadt (2010).
51. Miller (2010).
52. Suniga (2009).
53. Spaulding, Freely and Maguire (2009).
54. Cimperman (2009)
55. Dubb (2010).
56. Giloth (2004).
57. Asbury, Ganpath, and Hull (2009).
58. Tobocman (2011).
59. Tobocman (2010).
60. Tobocman (2011).
61. Andrews (2003).
62. Gaylord (2010).
63. Benders (2010).
64. East Baltimore Development, Inc. (2011).
65. East Baltimore Development, Inc. (2011).
66. Washington (2010).

67. Washington (2010).
68. East Baltimore Development, Inc. (2010).
69. Planning Board for the City of Camden (2002).
70. Tobocman (2010).
71. Fund for Our Economic Future (2010).

Bibliography

"A Promising Future: Will an Imaginative New Approach to Economic Development Work? February 2008. *The Economist*. Accessed August 1, 2011. http://www.economist.com/node/10650702?story_id=10650702.

Alssid, J., Goldberg. M. and Klerk, S. 2010. "Building a Higher Skilled Workforce: Results and Implications from the BridgeConnect National Survey." Workforce Strategy Center and The Joyce Foundation.

Altstadt, D. 2010. "Building Opportunity." Washington, D.C.: Working Poor Families Project.

American Institute of Architects Sustainable Design Assessment Team. 2008. "Leaner, Greener Detroit." New York: American Institute of Architects.

Andrews, L. 2003. "Destination Pittsburgh?" Pittsburgh: Carnegie Mellon University, Center for Economic Development.

Annie E. Casey Foundation. Undated. "FES Baltimore City Sheet: Casey in Baltimore: Creating Successful Futures for Children and Families." Baltimore: Annie E. Casey Foundation.

Annie E. Casey Foundation. 2010. "Early Warning! Why Reading by the End of Third Grade Matters." Baltimore: Annie E. Casey Foundation.

___________. 2010. "The East Baltimore Revitalization Initiative: A Case Study in Responsible Redevelopment." Baltimore: Annie E. Casey Foundation.

Asbury, K., Ganpath, D. and Hull, S. 2009. "TANF: Increasing the Workforce Participation Rate." Charlottesville : University of Virginia Batten School of Leadership and Public Policy.

Austin Polytechnical Academy. 2010. "Austin Polytechnical Academy Brochure." Chicago: Austin Polytechnical Academy.

Benders, L. 2010. "Workforce Development v. 2.0. Cleveland/Cuyahoga County Workforce Investment Board, Employment Connection." Cleveland: Workforce Investment Board.

Carnevale, A. P., Smith, N. and Strohl, J. 2010. "Help Wanted: Projections of Jobs and Education Requirements Through 2018." Washington, D.C.: Georgetown University Center on Education and the Workforce.

Cimperman, J. December 2009 – January 2010. "Evergreen Cooperatives Leading the Way Toward a Sustainable Cleveland." *Eco Watch Journal*.

Cleveland Foundation. 2009. "The Greater University Circle Initiative." Cleveland: Cleveland Foundation.

Cortright, J. 2008. "City Dividends: How Cities Gain by Making Small Improvements in Metropolitan Performance." Chicago: CEOs for Cities.

Dubb, S. 2010. "Green Business, Worker Co-ops, Anchor Institutions & Social Enterprise: The Cleveland Experience." PowerPoint presented at the Social Enterprise Alliance, San Francisco, CA.

East Baltimore Development, Inc. July 2011. "EBDI Economic Opportunity Plan & Procurement Policy." Baltimore: East Baltimore Development Inc. Accessed August 1, 2011. http://www.ebdi.org/uploads/pdfs/EBDIEconomicOpportunityPlanandProcurementPolicy-RevisedJuly2011.pdf.

East Baltimore Development, Inc. October 2010. "Economic Inclusion: Third Party Monitoring & Compliance Verification Report." Baltimore: East Baltimore Development Inc.

Eisen, P., Jasinowski, J. and Kleinert, R. 2005. "2005 Skills Gap Report – A Survey of the American Manufacturing Workforce." Washington D.C.: National Association of Manufacturers, Deloitte.

Fund for Our Economic Future. 2010. "NEO (NorthEastOhio)@Work: Innovative Talent Development for a Thriving Regional Economy." Cleveland: Fund for Our Economic Future.

Gaylord, B. 2010. "Cleveland Needs More Immigrants: Why and How to Welcome More Foreign Born Residents." Cleveland: Jewish Community Federation of Cleveland.

Giloth, R., ed. 2004. *Workforce Development Politics: Civic Capacity and Performance.* Philadelphia: Temple University Press.

———. 2004. *Workforce Intermediaries for the Twenty-First Century.* Philadelphia: Temple University Press.

Giloth, R. and Dewitt, J. 1995. "Mobilizing Civic Infrastructure: Foundation-Supported Job Generation." *National Civic Review* Summer/Autumn (Fall): 196-209.

Glaeser, E. L., Kahn, M. and Chu, C. 2001. "Job Sprawl: Employment Location in U.S. Metropolitan Areas." Washington, D.C.: Brookings Institution Center on Urban and Metropolitan Studies.

Gordon, I. and Ivan T. 2005. "How Urban Labour Markets Matter." In *Changing Cities: Rethinking Urban Competitiveness, Cohesion, and Governance*, edited by Nick Buck, Ian Gordon, Alan Harding, and Ivan Turok. Basingstoke, England: Palgrave Macmillan.

"Graduate! Program Growing," January 12, 2010. Philadelphia: *Metro*.

Hebert, S. 2010. "Changing Systems Is Like Moving a Mountain." Baltimore: Annie E. Casey Foundation.

Herman, R. T. and Smith, R. L. 2009. *Immigrant Inc.: Why Immigrant Entrepreneurs Are Driving the New Economy (and how they will save the American worker).* Hoboken, NJ: John Wiley and Sons, Inc.

Holzer, H. and Lerman, R.I.. 2007. "America's Forgotten Middle-Skill Jobs." Washington, D.C.: Workforce Alliance.

Kania, J. and Kramer, M. Winter 2011. "Collective Impact." *The Stanford Social Innovation Review.* Accessed August 1, 2011. http://www.ssireview.org/articles/entry/collective_impact/.

Kempner, R. T. 2008. "The Talent Imperative for Older Industrial Areas." *In Retooling for Growth,* edited by Richard M. McGahey and Jennifer S. Vey. Washington D.C.: The Brookings Institution.

Kleiman, N., Oppenheim, E. and Vogel, C. with Weisberg, L. 2009. "A Tale of Two Systems: Linking Economic Development and Workforce Development." New York: Seedco Policy Center.

Kneebone, E. and Berube, A.. 2008. "Reversal of Fortune: A New Look at Concentrated Poverty in the 2000s." Washington, D.C.: Brookings Institution Metropolitan Policy Program.

Lind, D. January 24, 2011 "The Bright Side of Blight." *New York Times*. Accessed August 1, 2011. http://www.nytimes.com/2011/01/25/opinion/25lind.html

Living Cities. October, 2010. "An American City Agenda in Ohio" accessed Aug.5, 2011 at www.livingcities.org

Loschiavo, B. February 1, 2010. "Graduate! program gets more sites." *Philadelphia Business Journal.* Accessed August 1, 2011. http://www.bizjournals.com/philadelphia/stories/2010/02/01/focus3.html

Mack, J. November 7, 2010. "The Kalamazoo Promise turns 5: Program sends hundreds to college, reshapes KPS, but 'still a work in progress.'" *Kalamazoo Gazette*. Accessed August 1, 2011. http://www.mlive.com/news/kalamazoo/index.ssf/2010/11/the_kalamazoo_promise_turns_5.html

Mallach, A. May 2010. "Facing the Urban Challenge: The Federal Government and America's Older Distressed Cities." Washington, D.C.: Brookings Institution Metropolitan Policy Program.

Mallach, A. and Brachman, L.. 2010. "Shaping Federal Policies Toward Cities in Transition: A Policy Brief." Columbus, Ohio: Greater Ohio Policy Center.

McGahey, R. M. and Vey, J. S., eds. 2008. *Retooling for Growth: Building a 21st Century Economy in America's Older Industrial Cities.* Washington D.C.: The Brookings Institution.

McKinsey Global Institute. 2010. "Changing the Fortunes of America's Workforce: A Human Capital Challenge." San Francisco: McKinsey Global Institute.

Miller, T. April 22-23, 2010. "Case Study of A Successful Urban Deconstruction Program – Saginaw County Land Bank." Presented at the Midwest Urban Deconstruction Forum, Chicago, Illinois.

Miron, G. and Cullen., A. 2008. "Trends and Patterns in Student Enrollment for Kalamazoo Public Schools." Kalamazoo, MI: Western Michigan University College of Education.

Moore, S. September 30, 2009. "Vehicles for Change Month—Promotion to Help Clear Neighborhoods of Unwanted Vehicles." *Inside Charm City.* Accessed August 1, 2011. http://insidecharmcity.com/2009/09/30/vehicles-for-change-month-promotion-to-help-clear-neighborhoods-of-unwanted-vehicles/.

National Center on Education and the Economy. 2008. *Tough Choices or Tough Times.* San Francisco: Jossey-Bass.

Parr, J., 1993. "Civic infrastructure: A New Approach to Improving Community Life." *National Civic Review.*

Philadelphia Workforce Investment Board. 2007. "A Tale of Two Cities." Philadelphia: Philadelphia Workforce Investment Board.

Planning Board of the City of Camden. 2002. "FutureCAMDEN: Master Plan Summary Report." Camden, NJ: Planning Board of the City of Camden.

National Commission on Adult Literacy. 2008. "Reach Higher, America: Overcoming Crisis in the U.S. Workforce." Washington, D.C.: National Commission on Adult Literacy.

National Skills Coalition. 2009. "Toward Ensuring America's Workers and Industries the Skills to Compete." Washington, D.C.: National Skills Coalition.

Schmitt, E. May 30, 2001. "To Fill Gaps, Cities Seek Wave of Immigrants." *New York Times*,

Northeast Ohio Council on Higher Education. *The Northeast Ohio Talent Dividend: Progress by Degrees*. December 2010. Cleveland: Accessed August 5, 2011. http://noche.org/talentdividend Siegel, B. and Seidman, K.. 2009. "The Economic Development and Workforce Development Systems: A Briefing Paper." New York: Surdna Foundation.

Spaulding, S., Freely, J. and Maguire, S. 2009. "A Foot in the Door: Using Alternative Staffing Organizations to Open Up Opportunities for Disadvantaged Workers." Philadelphia: Public/Private Ventures.

Stoll, M. A. 2005. "Job Sprawl and Spatial Mismatch between Blacks and Jobs." Washington, D.C.: Brookings Institution Metropolitan Policy Program.

Stone, C. N., Henig, J.R., Jones, B.D. and Pierannunzi, C. 2001. *Building Civic Capacity: The Politics of Reforming Urban Schools*. Lawrence, KS: University Press of Kansas.

Strive Partnership. "Striving Together Report Card." Accessed August 1, 2011. http://www.strivetogether.org/education-results-resource/striving-together-report-card/

Suniga, J. March 9, 2009. "Deconstruction project will save Saginaw money." *NBC 25 Mid-Michigan*,

Tobocman, S. December 2010. "Global Detroit: Final Report." Southeast Michigan: New Economy Initiative.

———. February 8, 2011. "Immigration is key to building a 'Global Detroit.'" *Model D Media*, Accessed August 1, 2011. http://www.modeldmedia.com/features/tobocman060610.aspx

Towards Employment. 2009. "Annual Report: Great Needs, Greater Responses." Cleveland: Towards Employment.

U.S. Census Bureau. 2005. "General Demographic Characteristics: 2005," American Community Survey. Washington, D.C.: U.S. Census Bureau.

______. 2009. "General Demographic Characteristics: 2009," American Community Survey. Washington, D.C.: U.S. Census Bureau.

Vey, J. 2007. "Restoring Prosperity: The State Role in Revitalizing America's Older Industrial Cities." Washington, D.C.: Brookings Institution Metropolitan Policy Program.

Washington, C. October 2010. *Workforce Development & Economic Inclusion Update*. Baltimore: East Baltimore Development Initiative.

Wilson, W. J. 1996. *When Work Disappears: The World of New Urban Poor*. Chicago: University of Chicago Press.

8

Addressing the Racial, Ethnic, and Class Implications of Legacy Cities

June Manning Thomas, University of Michigan

Why address racial, ethnic, and class-related issues in a book about developing strategies for America's cities experiencing extreme population loss, "legacy cities?" After all, these topics are related to broad social trends that could be extremely difficult to change using strategies of any kind. The decentralized landscape in U. S. metropolitan areas developed long before the present period, building upon trends that started in the early twentieth century but gained full force with the post-World War II buildup of suburbia. This decentralization began as a racially and in some cases ethnically exclusionary movement and always contained elements of class exclusiveness as well, a process that continued unabated for decades and continues still. The worst of at least racial and ethnic exclusion is supposedly over, but spatial mobility and access for low-income people remain serious problems. Since this book focuses largely on proactive strategies, one might well ask, Is a discussion of race, ethnicity, and class superfluous?

It is not. We argue that the topics of race, ethnicity, and socio-economic status are at the very heart of the dilemma facing cities experiencing major population loss in the U.S., even though present conditions are rooted far in the past and not easily changed, and that trying to resolve at least some aspects of that dilemma is a pivotal task. In spite of the best hopes of social reformers, civil rights legislation and the gradual lessening of social prejudice have not eliminated disparity and unequal access to opportunity by race and ethnicity, and even less so for low-income people of color. The disparity is both a cause and a result of cities distressed by population shrinkage. As a cause: Dating from just after World

War II, suburbanization—all but closed to minority-race families and supported in several specific ways by federal and state policies—contributed to the white working-class and middle-class flight that first led to the pattern of population decentralization, which eventually yielded cities shrinking in terms of both population and jobs, a basic pattern in many U. S. metropolitan areas. As a result, many central cities remain severely imbalanced with regard to race, ethnicity, and income level, in comparison with their metropolitan areas. Many such cities contain a disproportionate share of low-income people, particularly of those belonging to a minority race. These cities struggle to maintain fiscal health and firms that contribute to a strong economic base, and yet they face high municipal service costs, affecting their ability to retain and serve existing residents and firms as well as to attract new ones.

Rather than ignore such conditions, it is important to discuss them, for two main reasons. The first reason is social justice. It is essential to retain a focus on social justice as we help develop next steps for cities that have experienced persistent population decline. Social justice is not an easy concept to define, but one approach would be to avoid various forms of oppression of certain categories of people, which is the way Iris Marion Young and David Harvey approach the topic.[1] The need to avoid oppression suggests that people should not be deprived of their rights as citizens, or marginalized, or made to bear the burden of social change without just compensation or full redress of the true impact of such change on their lives.

This definition of social justice—avoidance of various forms of oppression—gains substance and historical context when we consider that the urban renewal era, formally ended in 1974 but continued in informal ways after that,[2] offers specific examples of social injustice, and lives on in the memories of many central-city residents and their descendants.

Aided by federal funding, cities targeted certain neighborhoods for demolition in preparation for redevelopment, and many of these neighborhoods were inhabited by racial and ethnic minorities of low income. Often these were the residential areas with the oldest and most dilapidated housing stock, an oft-cited justification for clearance, but in addition many areas selected were strategically located for other purposes, such as situating higher-income housing near central business districts or providing land for institutions such as hospitals and universities. The trauma of those days—characterized by forced condemnations; relocation practices with insufficient provision for adequate replacement housing; decades of fallow land and stalled projects even after speedy relocation and clearance; shattered neighborhood networks and social support systems—lingers in the form of distasteful memories of official oppression in the name of "progress." Such experiences would suggest that, today, plans to reorder the central-city landscape in order to accommodate reduced population size—for example, by reducing city services or discouraging new construction in certain areas of the city—would, of necessity, need to avoid such injustice.

Another approach to defining social justice would be to aim for more equal, or less skewed, outcomes for city residents by striving to make sure that all people live in safe and properly serviced neighborhoods, a situation that is not the reality for many, and is disproportionately unlikely for low-income racial minorities. The concept of social justice also has a "process" dimension, which refers to the rights people have to participate in decision-making that affects their lives, through such means as engaging in meaningful and inclusionary dialogue about alternative futures. This aspect of social justice would call for full consultation concerning any major land use or municipal service changes that cities are planning to undertake in the future, changes that could very well affect people's lives and livelihoods.

Because of the need for social justice, then, we should aim for social outcomes that do not oppress people or leave them deprived of homes, jobs, access to food, and other basic necessities of life, whether because of their race or ethnicity or income level, and for a decision-making process that is inclusionary. How this translates into actual practice is not always clear, particularly since the current political system fragments arenas of responsibility. Contemporary central-city leaders, for example, must observe the principles of social justice as they wrestle with dilemmas related to population decline, yet they may have woefully inadequate resources to ensure more equitable outcomes, one aspect of social justice. Furthermore, they could legitimately argue that it is unjust for a region to place the entire responsibility for the area's neediest residents upon their municipalities, particularly since racially-selective exodus played a major historical role in creating current central-city circumstances. This suggests that the scale of responsibility is metropolitan, rather than municipal.

In addition to general principles of social justice, a second reason that it is important to look at race, ethnicity, and class disparity when discussing the topic of legacy cities is to inform possible proactive strategies. Racial, ethnic, and class demographics heavily affect present and future conditions of America's most distressed cities. Understanding this concept is necessary in order to move forward with clear-headed information and solutions. For example, city leaders may know that the proportion of their residents who represent racial minorities is growing compared to the proportion of whites. Yet they may not understand subtle changes in such trends that may help them develop responsive action. An example of such a trend is the growing Hispanic population in many cities; another example would be a decline in measurable levels of highly concentrated poverty that some observers noted after the 2000 census. Watching immigration or poverty trends could be an essential part of city leaders' strategy to build on potential assets.

Because of the need for both social justice and clear-headed solutions that fit the context, we undertake two tasks in this chapter. The first is to summarize a few conditions relating to race, ethnicity, and poverty that affect cities experiencing large-scale population loss. In doing this we will build upon the work of Robert Beauregard, who has authored the first chapter in this book. The second is to discuss some possible corrective strategies that seem reasonable in the face of existing conditions. The strategies we are presenting are neither original nor exhaustive, but they could nonetheless help us explore the implications of changing patterns of settlement. Existing conditions of social differentiation continue to threaten many efforts that all levels of government undertake to help legacy cities enhance their futures. At the same time, current trends suggest possible positive outcomes that need to be recognized and understood.

In this chapter, we are using the U. S. Census Bureau's definition of the term race, even though this is a social construction that has very little reality in biology. In the United States, we quite commonly refer to black (or African-American), Asian, and white as separate races, along with several others, but in fact these categories are not always mutually exclusive and people who self-identify as "mixed" in race are growing in number. The U.S. Census Bureau has wrestled for some time with this issue of racial categories and has changed definitions several times over the last few decades. Currently, a person officially classified as "white only" could come from German, Italian, Lebanese, or Saudi Arabian roots. By ethnicity, we are referring to a sense of shared history, culture, and identity that is often associated with nationality but that can be quite varied even within one country. We are treating the term Hispanic as an ethnic term in this chapter, and we will look occasionally at poverty rates, easily measured and described, as one indicator of socio-economic status.

Conditions

Diversity by race and ethnicity appears to be a permanent condition of many of the cities that are surviving and thriving in the new global economy. This does not mean that diversity is an essential characteristic: Largely homogeneous populations in Japan, for example, have fared quite well in raising up Tokyo as a global power, as have the multiethnic but single-race Chinese in several key cities. But in comparison with these places, the United States is a multiracial and multiethnic nation built upon a fabric of comparatively recent diversity rather than on many centuries of relative homogeneity. Polyglot peoples are a fact of life in cities such as New York, San Francisco, and Chicago, cities that demonstrate that the new post-industrial economy did not kill very large central cities but, rather, often made them more important. The presence of citizens of international origin is a part of the strength of these key American cities, as these people help provide diverse economic ventures as well as workers of many skill levels.

Consider, for example, the case of New York City. Although this city variously lost and gained population over the last few decades, it remains a major population center, with over eight million people, and it has become a center for the global economy as well as host for people from all over the world. In 2000, 36 percent of the city's population was foreign-born. Of those, 19 percent came from Europe, 3 percent from Africa, 24 percent from Asia, and 29.8 percent from the Caribbean, with 22.8 percent from Central or South America. New York City has its share of poverty, with 15 percent of families estimated as falling below the poverty level during the period 2005-2009, but this is lower than in many other older cities, and the city on the whole has a considerable amount of critical mass, resources, and vitality. In recent years, buoyed by economic prosperity, New York City has systematically addressed such challenges as providing housing for its middle- and low-income population. In this case, the extraordinary diversity of the population appears to be an important part of this city's identity in a global era.

New York City is a special case, a prototype for the new urban-form "global city," and such cities have major stores of resilience. Chicago, as another example, is not technically a global city on the order of New York. It is located in the same Midwest region as several major cities losing population, and it has experienced its own share of population and industrial decline. Yet 21.7 percent of its residents were foreign-born in 2000, half of these from Central America, and increases in in-migration from the previous decade had been enough to overcome population loss as both whites and blacks fell in numbers. The city's population expanded by 112,000 during the 1990s, but the white population dropped by 48,000 during that decade, and the black population fell by 23,000. In contrast, the Hispanic population rose by 128,789 during the 1980s and by 207,792 during the 1990s.[3] Clearly, without this level of Hispanic influx, largely channeled into ethnic enclaves populated by specific Hispanic nationalities, the city would undoubtedly have shrunk in size yet again during the 1990s. Even so, the city's overall population fell between 2000 and 2010, dropping 6.9 percent, largely on the basis of fewer blacks and a lower influx of Hispanics. Chicago gained only 25,218 Hispanics and 21,190 Asians from 2000 to 2010, and the white population declined by a mere 2,480 people, but blacks, although still one-third of the city's people, dropped in numbers by 177,401 during that decade.

Although Chicago experienced a recent decade of population growth in the 1990s, it then, in large part because of black exodus, declined in numbers during the early 2000s. In many large cities, especially in the U. S. Midwest and Northeast, population has declined continuously and without remittance over several decades. Some of the reasons for this are economic, such as decline in the industrial sector and a shift of economic activity to other regions. But another set of reasons is social: Problems related to the racial segregation and isolation of low-income people have lingered and led to even more fragmentation within metropolitan areas.

Segregation

Many cities facing precipitous population decline struggle with a lack of resources and a disproportionate share of low-income citizens, many of them of minority-race status. Unusually high proportions of racial minorities, in a context of metropolitan racial segregation and concentrated poverty, can make it difficult for older core central cities to survive in contemporary times. This is true not because certain racial minorities are always poor but because they are disproportionately so, and because the racial profile of existing neighborhoods still apparently affects housing choices.

Years of surveys have revealed that all racial minorities do not face the same level of segregation or residential prejudice; African-Americans experience higher levels than other groups. Since in many metropolitan areas blacks as well as lower-income people are concentrated within central cities, even during an era that has seen the increased suburbanization of blacks and other racial and ethnic minorities, central cities may bear the burden of the negative effects of this historic pattern of separation. They may encounter drastically falling tax revenues and increased costs for municipal services but have access to few resources to support them because so many people and businesses have fled or refused to move into the central city. Furthermore, once city services fall, crime rates increase, or schools decline, moving out of a distressed central city or inner-ring suburb or refusing to move in becomes a rational act. As suburban options have opened up for black middle-class families, many have moved out of central cities, leaving behind increasing proportions of lower-income blacks who are not as mobile.

Among the authors who have documented the negative effects of racial segregation and concentrated poverty are William Julius Wilson, who has written several books, including *The Truly Disadvantaged: The Inner City, the Underclass and Public Policy,* and Douglas Massey and Nancy Denton, authors of *American Apartheid: Segregation and Making of the Underclass.* These authors have helped us visualize the effects of racial and income segregation. Wilson explained the implications for children and young adults raised in areas of central cities where they had little access to positive role models, in the form of professional-class people of their own race or other races; little ability to attend schools that enabled them to gain necessary education and market skills; and, once graduated, little or no access to jobs or other legitimate means of earning a livelihood. Massey and Denton measured segregation and explained its effects, pointing out that a number of forms of such segregation exist. According to the index of dissimilarity, one such measure, racial separation between blacks and whites within certain key metropolitan areas remained high in 2000. The areas with highest segregation between blacks and whites included metropolitan Detroit, which contains a distressed central city within its midst, but also places such as Chicago and New York City, which have not suffered nearly as much population and economic decline in their central cities. Therefore, racial segregation within the metropolitan area is not necessarily associated with high population loss or with poor economic performance of the region or its central city, if that central city is strong enough to weather whatever negative effects might arise.

Metropolitan racial segregation nevertheless continues to be a part of the problem facing distressed central cities; racial division fueled much of the decentralizing flight of first whites and then other races, and some cities thus abandoned have not survived intact. Although demographers have measured a slight lessening of racial segregation within metropolitan areas, such segregation has continued at a high level even in suburban areas. In 2009, Massey and his colleagues noted that racial segregation is declining but still very high; income segregation between the poor and the rich, also as measured by the dissimilarity index, is not quite as high but is growing.[4] In addition, racial preferences continue to influence residential patterns, particularly for whites, a proportion of whom still hesitate to live in neighborhoods with predominately black residents.[5] This pattern of avoidance has enormous implications for heavily black central cities, which may need to attract middle-class and professional residents of many races, including whites, in order to protect or enhance their tax bases.

The Brookings Institution's 2010 report, *The State of Metropolitan America*, noted major shifts in demographic characteristics of major metropolitan areas and their central cities. They confirmed that the metropolitan African-American population was suburbanizing rapidly in the United States, as were other racial and ethnic groups. They noted that metropolitan areas varied in their ability to adjust to new economic realities; they organized metropolitan areas into several categories and found two sets that are characterized by particularly low growth. The older "industrial core" metropolitan areas, located in the Midwest but also found in the Northeast and Southeast, have less population diversity and lower educational levels compared to other kinds of regions, as well as slow growth. The "skilled anchor" metropolitan areas, also slow-growers with less diversity but with higher educational levels, in-migration, and amenities, were located largely in the Midwest and Northeast. Several metropolitan areas within these two categories contain cities that have lost large proportions of their populations, but those in "industrial core" metropolitan areas face particular challenges.

Race, Ethnicity, and Poverty

In a 2009 article, author Robert Beauregard noted that among the top fifty central cities in size for the year 2000, several had lost population in both the 1980s and the 1990s. He called these the "persistent twelve," listed in *Table 1*. Population loss for each of these selected central cities during the 1990s ranged from a low 2.5 percent for New Orleans to a high 12.2 percent for St. Louis during that same decade. The last column in *Table 1* shows that all cities continued to lose population from 2000 to 2010 except Washington, D.C., and Philadelphia. New Orleans is, of course, an outlier, because of Hurricane Katrina and related flooding of the city's levee system in 2005, but it experienced population decline even before then. *Table 1* shows that the percentage of foreign-born population in eleven of these twelve cities is low compared to the national average of 12.4 percent but that generally the central cities in "skilled anchor" metropolitan areas have larger percentages of foreign-born people than cities in "industrial core" areas.

Table 1: *Population in "Persistent Twelve"* Cities, 1990- 2010, Organized by Metropolitan Area Status and Percent Foreign-Born*

Central City	*Population 2010*	*% Foreign-Born 2005-2009*	*% Change in Total Population 1990-2000*	*% Change in Total Population 2000-2010*
In "Skilled anchor" metro areas:				
Philadelphia, PA	1,526,006	11.0	-4.3	0.6
Milwaukee, WI	594,833	9.5	-5.0	-0.4
Pittsburgh, PA	305,704	7.0	-9.5	-8.4
St. Louis, MO	319,274	6.3	-12.2	-8.3
Baltimore, MD	620,961	6.2	-11.5	-4.6
Cincinnati, OH	296,943	4.1	-9.0	-10.4
Average Rate		7.35	-8.6	-5.3
In "Industrial core" metro areas:				
Detroit, MI	713,777	6.5	-7.5	-25.0
Buffalo, NY	261,310	6.1	-10.8	-10.7
New Orleans, LA	343,829	5.1	-2.5	-29.1
Toledo, OH	287,208	3.3	-5.8	-8.4
Average Rate		5.18	-6.4	-18.6**
Other				
Washington, D.C.	601,723	12.5	-5.7	5.2

Source: Calculated from U. S. Census Bureau data. Estimates from 2005 to 2009 are from the American Community Survey, based on the average of estimates for indicated years.

* The "persistent twelve" are those U. S. central cities among the top fifty in size for 2000 that lost population in both 1980-1990 and 1990-2000. For discussion, see Robert Beauregard, "Urban Population Loss in Historical Perspective: United States, 1820-2000," *Environment and Planning A* 41 (2009): 514-529. The three categories of metropolitan areas come from the Brookings Institution (2010).

**This average is 15.3 percent excluding New Orleans, an outlier because of flooding and its aftermath.

In addition, population loss from 2000 to 2010 was less in the six "skilled anchor" central cities, with an average 5.3 percent decline, than in the five industrial core cities, which averaged an 18.6 percent decline, or 15.3 percent excluding New Orleans. Thus the "industrial core" central cities suffered greater population decline as well as lesser levels of immigration compared to cities in "skilled anchor" metropolitan areas.

Each of the twelve central cities has relatively high family poverty rates compared to the U.S. average of 9.9 percent, according to 2005-2009 census estimates. Of the cities listed, the average family poverty rate estimated for the cities located in "skilled anchor" areas was 18.6 percent, which is high, but not as high as the average poverty rate for "industrial core" cities, which was 23 percent. Particularly stressed in terms of estimated poverty levels were the industrial cities of Detroit (28.3 percent), Cleveland (25.4 percent), and Buffalo (24.9 percent).

The number of households lost is perhaps more crucial for distressed cities than population decline, since decline in numbers of individuals could simply be due to the aging out of families' children, late marriages, or other demographic considerations, whereas loss of households means loss of occupied housing units, with all that implies in terms of housing vacancy and decline in the residential housing market. Also important is how many households a central city has lost since its peak year (for households, often different from the peak year for people). The twelve cities varied greatly in terms of their household loss, with Detroit and St. Louis losing the most between their peak household years and 2010, 48 percent and 45 percent, respectively. *Table 2* groups the twelve cities by higher or lower household loss between their peak household years and 2010,[6] a categorization that reveals changes in occupied housing-unit demand, a particular problem for cities experiencing abandonment because of falling demand for a previous number of housing units. Cities that experienced especially high loss of households include Detroit, New Orleans, Cleveland, St. Louis, Buffalo, and Pittsburgh.

Table 2 provides "white only" population figures, divided into two categories: those cities that experienced relatively high loss in number of households between their peak population years and 2008, and those that experienced gains or less household loss over that time period. We're using "white only" because it is increasingly complex to measure racial categories, particularly with various racial mixtures; tracking the presence of people who self-identify as "white only" reveals the presence in a city of majority-race people, who have historically had the greatest flexibility in housing choices.

In *Table 2* we see the expected: Whites were indeed a decided minority in many cities that we are examining, particularly Detroit, Baltimore, New Orleans, Cleveland, and Washington, D.C. The difference between high household-loss cities and low household-loss cities in terms of proportions of whites, however, is not dramatically different. What is decidedly different is that those cities that lost a higher number of households over several decades also lost a larger percentage of their white population from 2000 to 2010. The percent change in white population during the 1990s varied widely, with high losses of whites in the less stressed cities as well as the more stressed, in terms of household loss. On the other hand, the biggest losses from 2000 to 2010 appear to be in the cities that lost more households in the long term; those six experienced declines in their white populations that averaged 20 percent, compared to only 5.1 percent declines in the cities with less household loss over time, or with gains. That the cities with higher household loss experienced population drops among resident whites more dramatically than the other cities suggests a possible continued link between total population decline and white decline.

Table 2: *"White Only"*Population Change in Twelve Cities, 1990- 2010, Classified by Household Change from Peak Population Year to 2010 and Percent White 2*

City and Household Loss or Gain (in %)	*"Whites only" as % Population 2010*	*% Change in White Population 1990-2000*	*% Change in White Population 2000- 2010*
Higher long-term loss			
Detroit	10.6	-47.6	-35.0
New Orleans	33.0	-21.7	-23.1
Cleveland	37.3	-20.7	-25.5
St. Louis	43.9	-24.5	-8.1
Buffalo	50.4	-25.0	-17.3
Pittsburgh	66.0	-15.2	-10.8
Average	40.2	-27.8	-20.0**
Lower long-term loss, or gain			
Baltimore	29.6	-28.4	-10.8
Washington, D. C.	38.5	-2.0	31.4
Philadelphia	41.0	-19.5	-8.3
Milwaukee	44.8	-25.0	-10.7
Cincinnati, OH	49.3	-20.3	-16.6
Toledo	64.8	-14.0	-15.5
Average	44.7	-18.2	-5.1

Source: Calculated from U. S. Census Bureau data, with proportion of household loss since peak household years calculated by the author (see note 6 for specifics).

*"White only" respondents indicated that they were "white" as defined by the census, without racial mixture. "Whites" includes many specific ethnic or nationality groups.

**This number is -19% without New Orleans.

We see the unexpected, as well, in *Table 2*: Whether because numbers had fallen so low that they could only rebound (a phenomenon called "regression to the mean"), or because of some other trends, conditions were apparently very different from 2000 to 2010 than during the previous decade. Although white population numbers continued to decline, the rate of loss was lower in several of the first set of cities, including Detroit, St. Louis, Buffalo, and Pittsburgh. In the second category of cities, the number of whites leaped upward in Washington, D.C., growing by 31.4 percent between 2000 and 2010, with the level of white population decline less compared to the 1990s in Baltimore, Philadelphia, Milwaukee, and Cincinnati. Why was the level of white presence in those nine cities dropping less rapidly than in the previous decade? We need to know more about these specific cities' circumstances. One possible explanation is that a subpopulation of whites was moving into these cities at the same time that others were leaving. In a number of these cities, new and rehabilitated housing developments specifically aimed toward professional workers would have played a part in stoking this phenomenon. Another possible explanation is that a remaining core of whites stayed because they were comfortable with their central-city surroundings.

Changes in the presence of Hispanics, the nation's fastest-growing minority, are also instructive, as *Table 3* shows for twelve cities. Although a small portion of the total population, the Hispanic population has shown dramatic increases over two decades in all of the cities we are discussing. This growth appears to be faltering only in Detroit: The number of Detroit's Hispanics increased during the 1990s by 65.7 percent, but only by 3.2 percent in the 2000s, during the decade of a dramatic population slide for that city. Nevertheless, Detroit continued to benefit in numbers from the 1990s boost in Hispanic population and in other ways from the vibrancy of the city's southwest area, which houses much of its Hispanic community, complete with Latino-owned businesses, restaurants, and churches influenced by Hispanic culture.

Buffalo, Cleveland, Milwaukee, Philadelphia, and Washington, D.C., all contained at least 9 percent Hispanics in 2010, again with strong growth rates in this population segment, for an increase of 43.8 percent in Milwaukee and 45.5 percent in Philadelphia during the 2000s. Particularly noteworthy is the apparent trend for cities that lost lower proportions of households over several decades to average higher rates of increase in Hispanic population, an average 61 percent increase in the 2000s, than cities that lost high proportions of households, an average of 23 percent over the same decade. This association suggests that Hispanics may be key population boosters for these central cities. The question then becomes whether these trends will continue, and whether the cities more stressed from household loss than others can further elevate their numbers of Hispanic people.

Table 3: *Hispanic/Latino Change in Twelve Cities, 1990- 2010, Classified by Household Loss from Peak Population Year to 2010 and Percent Hispanic*

City	*Hispanics/ Latinos of Any Race 2010*	*Hispanics/ Latinos of Any Race as % of Population 2010*	*% Change in Hispanic/ Latino Population 1990-2000*	*% change in Hispanic/ Latino Population 2000- 2010*
High long-term household loss				
Buffalo, NY	27,519	10.5	36.9	24.7
Cleveland, OH	39,534	10.0	49.7	13.8
Detroit, MI	48,679	6.8	65.7	13.8
New Orleans,LA	18,951	5.5	-14.0	24.7
St. Louis, MO	11,130	3.5	37.0	3.2
Pittsburgh, PA	6,964	2.3	27.6	58.5
Average		5.3	33.8	23.1
Less long-term household loss, or gain				
Milwaukee, WI	103,007	17.3	81.8	43.8
Philadelphia, PA	187,611	12.3	44.5	45.5
Washington, D.C	54,749	9.1	37.4	21.8
Toledo, OH	21,231	7.4	29.8	23.9
Baltimore, MD	25,960	4.2	45.5	134.7
Cincinnati, OH	8,308	2.8	77.3	96.4
Average		8.9	52.7	61.0

Source: Calculated from U. S. Census Bureau data; see Table 2 for explanation of household-loss categories.

Strategies

Conditions facing the cities we have been discussing are challenging. Although racial segregation has abated in U. S. metropolitan areas, income segregation has increased. Unwillingness on the part of many whites to live in predominately black neighborhoods has continued as a problem. Twelve central cities that we examined experienced population loss from 1980 to 2000, with only two cities, Philadelphia and Washington, D.C., experiencing population gains from 2000 to 2010. The twelve tended to have fairly high poverty rates, low proportions of foreign-born populations, and declining proportions of white populations (except for the nation's capital). At the same time, white population loss slowed in most of these cities during the 2000s compared to the 1990s, and all twelve received an influx of Hispanics during the 2000s.

These findings lay the groundwork for suggesting possible strategies to help address conditions of racial, ethnic, and class disparity in the context of social justice. To do so would require a leap of faith, due to the long-term intractability of the problems at hand and the barriers set in place by time, culture, and the very structure of the metropolitan political system. Nevertheless, a few strategies do exist that might help mitigate current circumstances in relation to these topics. We'll offer brief comments on a few: increasing diversity of the population, attending to economic development, building bridges within the city and the region, and pursuing a social-justice agenda.

Increasing Population Diversity

One need for cities experiencing severe population loss is a more stable and diversified population. One of the major difficulties has been that metropolitan areas where central cities have lost large numbers of people and households have seen too much regional fragmentation, especially with regard to race and poverty status. At the same time, cities that have been able to attract foreign-born residents have enhanced their labor pool as well as their economic prospects. One potential strategy is to encourage foreign-born populations to move to central cities; another is to attract diverse populations, including Hispanics and whites.

Immigration. Encouraging immigrant communities could be one of the best ways to enhance the population diversity shrinking cities need, as well as to increase numbers of people and families. To encourage immigrant communities is no small undertaking, of course, since typically immigrants seek places of opportunity and may avoid places that they perceive as under-resourced. Furthermore, national policy strongly influences the number of immigrants allowed into the country. In many places given up for lost, however, immigrants have managed to settle and to form ethnic enclaves that have created vibrant communities where none existed before. Immigrants appear to provide several major benefits through such actions. One is that immigrants are often associated with economic innovation; another is that ethnic enclaves can encourage economic growth in many forms, including tourism. Foreign-born populations can also help rejuvenate communities and neighborhoods that are no longer attractive to native-born Americans.

One of the most famous urban theorists to argue that immigrants are important to local economies is Richard Florida, who made this point in several books about creative-class cities. He calculated a melting pot index, composed largely of the percentage of foreign-born population in the metropolitan area, which he found to be highly correlated with high-technology economic activity as he measured this. While other scholars have contested some of his findings, strong support exists at least for his claims about the importance of foreign-born populations. Long before his studies other scholars had found a link between immigration and economic performance. Some researchers have documented the global influence of immigration not just in the United States but in other countries as well, while others have offered in-depth case studies, as has Anna Lee Saxenian, who explored the influence of highly skilled immigrants in elevating California's Silicon Valley. But one of the earliest researchers on this topic was George Borjas, who suggested that even low-skilled immigrants brought benefits to metropolitan areas and to the national economy, due to a complex set of reasons, which included increased efficiency and expansion of local markets.[7]

One of the ways these benefits can be realized is through the establishment of residential and commercial ethnic enclaves, which themselves can become engines of growth. Ethnic enclaves, in contrast to ethnic or racial ghettos, are usually voluntary and purposeful, established to provide mutual support. At their best, such enclaves can provide culturally familiar niche neighborhoods for new immigrants, thereby allowing them to survive in spite of limited proficiency in English or low per capita income. Some research has suggested that such enclaves generate an unusually high self-employment rate compared to native-born areas, and that they may lead to other economic benefits, as well. In addition, they may spur tourism simply by offering a context in which people seek to gain exposure to a foreign culture, as has happened in numerous Chinatowns and Mexican neighborhoods throughout the country. Add to this the fact that such enclaves often lead to rejuvenation of the housing stock in previously abandoned neighborhoods, and a picture of an elegant form of reuse emerges.

Individual localities have a limited ability to change national immigration laws or to entice national or ethnic groups who have no reason to move to their areas. However, a number of people have begun to consider ways in which to make given localities and states immigrant-friendly. The Global Detroit project, spearheaded by former state representative Steve Tobocman, is an excellent example, and the project's online report identifies a number of such strategies that can help make immigrant groups and foreign corporations feel welcome and be inclined to attract like-minded people from abroad. Some necessary steps may include reaching out to existing foreign-born communities and making sure they understand how valued they are in a particular urban area. Other more proactive steps include developing a retention program for foreign university students, or attracting global firms or foreign investors, and some of these efforts require largely initiative and vision rather than vast sums of money.

The same points that apply to foreign-born populations also apply to native-born Hispanics, as well as Asians, and other racial and ethnic groups. In some cases, it may be possible to support enclaves that are made up not just of foreign-born racial and ethnic minorities but also of the progeny of such immigrant communities, as has happened for example in Chinese communities in Chicago.

However, children and grandchildren of foreign-born immigrants are less prone to stay in ethnic enclaves, and they may instead move outward, aiming for the same suburban, noncentral city lifestyles as do families of domestic background. Thus it is important not to rely on the attraction of immigrants as a singular strategy.

Incentives for Diverse Populations. Another form of diversification could come by way of attracting a greater variety of people, not necessarily from immigrant roots, to move into central cities or convincing those already there not to leave them. A great part of the shrinkage in the central cities we examined happened because of the falling proportions of white residents. We mentioned that some researchers have found fairly strong evidence that a proportion of white house-buyers shy away from neighborhoods that contain black families, even if the relative percentage is small; this phenomenon increases the higher the percentage of black families in a particular neighborhood. This means that when a neighborhood or city becomes predominantly black, it becomes increasingly difficult to attract whites and, in addition, other groups, such as Hispanics and Asians; this is the case, at least, in cities studied thus far. However, this same research also suggests that blacks shy away from predominantly black neighborhoods, preferring racially integrated neighborhoods.[8] This sets up an imbalance that leads to integration eventually turning into segregation yet again, since whites would refuse to move in after a certain point of racial mixture, and blacks would try to move out to avoid strict racial segregation. This is a situation that for predominately black neighborhoods increases the likelihood of housing abandonment as the housing market fails to operate properly and potential buyers dry up. This was true long before the housing crisis, which created such a high foreclosure rate in many neighborhoods that no one would willingly choose to live there.

Policymakers will have to be aware of these population dynamics in order to craft effective strategies to counter them. One such strategy could be to create incentive programs for populations of diverse races and ethnicities, including whites. As just one example, an incentive program organized by three key Detroit institutions—Wayne State University, the Detroit Medical Center, and Henry Ford Hospital—will pay employees to buy housing units or rent within a certain area of central Detroit. While the effects of the strategy have yet to be seen, it is a promising venture, modeled in great part upon a similar program under way for some years in Philadelphia, where the University of Pennsylvania and allied institutions have attracted new residents to specific neighborhoods.[9] Because the employee base of these institutions is much more racially diverse than the city's population, with a much larger proportion of whites, we can anticipate that many people taking part in this program will be white. This should help to make the area around these institutions a much more racially diverse area, and much more comfortable for whites. Of course, at the same time it will be important to offer a level of service that will not drive these residents back out again. Here, critical mass would be important, with city government making sure that at least the services and activities around the protected areas are such as to encourage commitment. One possible difficulty here is that other areas may resent what they see as an unfair advantage for protected areas, and so city government would need to approach any such strategy very carefully.

Although we don't know exactly which whites, Asians, blacks, and others would be most inclined to move back into central cities that have lost large proportions of their populations, professionals working with key institutions and people who do not have school-age children would be prime candidates for such migration. Families with children are possible as well, but the choices are more complex; many school systems in distressed central cities are struggling—and thus are less desirable for middle-income families—because of the very problems we described related to loss of revenue, racial isolation, and income segregation. Thinking through ways to attract younger adults to live in central cities would be important, especially since evidence suggests that racial prejudice among younger adults is not as entrenched as prejudice among older adults. A strategy to attract young adults could include a number of creative solutions, such as professional clubs, festivals, and artistic events.

Proactive Economic Development. Another necessary action would be to undertake proactive economic development. This is of course easier said than done, and the argument could be made that such cities have been trying to do this for many years. They could be working very hard at a few key economic development projects but be in need of a broader vision to consider other possibilities. The pro-immigration effort we cited above, Global Detroit, created an economic development study that suggested ways to diversify the metropolitan economy through closer ties to international corporations and other business opportunities. This approach would become a forthright attempt to tap into the global economy by attracting diverse people with the skills needed for such an economy. But all this would require an orchestrated strategy, including creating effective ways to nurture small businesses and support entrepreneurs.

What has passed for economic development in many legacy cities has really been an attempt to hold on to, or to woo through tax incentives and other similar means, the old industrial sector, which has, however, changed in profound ways. It is becoming increasingly apparent that such an approach to economic development will no longer work. Also falling out of favor is the idea that casinos, sports stadia, or other such high-profile projects can boost the local economy enough to offset profound and long-term losses in commerce and industry, an approach that also has proved to be insufficient. Instead, it will be necessary to look to new economic ventures, and to train a workforce that is capable of participating in something other than the failing industrial sector, once a haven for those with only a high school diploma, which no longer suffices, as discussed in Chapter 7. A part of such a strategy would require revamping educational systems that have in some cases reached the point of collapse. This leads us to our next two categories of strategy making: building bridges and social justice.

Building Bridges

Another key set of strategies will involve trying to build bridges among people strongly fragmented by politics, economics, and place. This is a huge topic, one that would actually require a separate chapter, because one of the obvious places to start would be to look at bridging barriers within the metropolitan area between citizens of various municipalities. Rather than tackle that giant a topic, here we will just mention a few ways to develop smaller-scale efforts that do not require reforming government relations within metropolitan areas.

Building bridges across racial, ethnic, and class barriers can take place at a number of levels. These could range from the institutional down to the individual. In terms of the institutional, it would be helpful if civic leaders and prominent organizations took public stances on the importance of overcoming racial and ethnic prejudice and poverty, as well as their effects. Although it is not clear that such visible stances make a difference in terms of impact, they help provide an environment that does not tolerate continued prejudice and denigration of people because of their income levels or skin color. Some organizations have become dedicated to overcoming such barriers through such consortia as faith-based organizations or civil rights groups.

Then in addition to the proper tone of rhetoric, we need action. This could involve, for example, foundations getting together and creating consortia dedicated to helping to resolve critical issues of differentiation and isolation. Key foundations have undertaken such efforts throughout the country, as have intermediaries, but some of them will need to change their agendas from trying to push one path to reform, such as building new housing or offering interracial social events, to promoting another, which might imply working for housing set-asides and inclusionary zoning. That would be a strategy for giving poor people access to suburban communities, but we will need new strategies in order to help get suburban people moving into central cities. A good start would be to look at new ways to envision community development in central-city neighborhoods, particularly in the wake of the 2007 housing crisis, which has made construction of new housing, the favored activity of many sponsors of community development, moot, since foreclosed houses exist in great abundance. And while we are on the topic of moving, it is noteworthy that some businesses and corporations have made conscious decisions to move from suburban campuses into central cities, because of the advantages of economic agglomeration or clustering, and encouraging such efforts would be good in terms of social justice as well as for economic reasons.

At the individual level, we still need educational programs to help people understand the continuing effects of prejudice. Many people believe that the battles concerning this topic are over, when they are not. As long as society remains as fragmented as it is, and as long as the unwanted are isolated in neglected central cities, we have a problem. It will be necessary to continue to seek ways to overcome this historic inertia in relation to racial and income-based disparity. One simple strategy that some institutions have used is to organize their workers to participate in direct-assistance programs such as tutoring in local public schools. The Detroit public school system has organized thousands of enthusiastic volunteers of all races and from many localities to assist the public school teachers in enhancing reading skills for their youngest pupils. This kind of one-on-one interaction is an excellent example of action at the individual level. Another strategy is for corporations to adopt certain elementary school classes, offering personal mentoring, or to create internship programs for inner-city youth.

A Social Justice Agenda

Several of the above points, of course, relate very well to what we have called "a social justice agenda." Such an agenda involves not only steps such as the few we have indicated but also the continual improvement of intact and salvageable central-city neighborhoods so that they are able to survive. The needs are so great that almost anyplace a group or organization can be started, whether in employment or business development or youth training, will be helpful. But all of these initiatives would take money in order to have a serious impact, and part of the problem is that central city governments do not have the resources to provide the services that citizens deserve, or the schools, or the access to secure housing and available food sources or the means to offer effective public safety, in part because many of these things should not be solely dependent upon the public sector. And so for a central-city government experiencing major fiscal problems in addition to a loss of people and commerce, what is its social justice agenda? It is not as if such a government is purposefully oppressing a part of its population. It is very likely itself a victim of historical forces within the metropolitan area, which left it holding the bag for several more well-to-do municipalities, many of which managed to organize themselves so as to protect their citizens from exposure to the unwanted.

The typical stressed central city is so limited in resources that it needs the best workers, the smartest bureaucrats, and the most experienced council members and mayor to make even a dent in the problems it must solve. This particularly has meaning in Detroit, where the city learned, to its sorrow, that one incompetent or corrupt city government administration can do a world of harm, not only in terms of the city's reputation, which has a major impact upon potential residents and businesses, but also with regard to the life chances of the citizens living within its borders and dependent upon the proper working of that city's government. In this case, social justice would demand not necessarily equalized outcomes for all municipal services, although that would be a wonderful goal to aim toward.

Neither does it imply simply a just process, although assuredly any decisions that are made, particularly about land use or neighborhood reconfiguration, should involve the best principles of consultation and participation. What social justice does demand, at the least, is principled, purposeful, honest government, and leaders who will do their best to improve the city under even the most trying of circumstances. This should be expected no matter what conditions are to be addressed.

Another obvious need in this situation is for the political leaders, staff, citizens, and businesses of more well-to-do municipalities to set aside the tendency to demonize and isolate the central city with a high minority-race population—opposing regional transportation or taxation systems, for example—and to support any opportunity for cooperation and support. This would be in the name of social justice but also in recognition of the integrated fabric of metropolitan areas, since a collapsed urban core affects the areas around it in many ways. Yet, unfortunately, almost everything about the way U. S. local governments have been set up within metropolitan areas appears to counter any cooperative, altruistic, or unifying tendencies that might be needed.

Notes

1. Harvey (2002); Young (1990).
2. Although the Community Development Block Grant (CDBG), established in 1974, formally ended new allocations for "urban renewal" initiated under the Housing Acts of 1949 and 1954, redevelopment projects in process continued for many years thereafter. CDBG moneys funded many of those. Also noteworthy is the massive highway construction of the same period, 1950s–1970s, which many people confused with urban renewal because it sometimes had the same effect on minority neighborhoods. The worse ills of relocation funded with federal dollars were abated with reforms mandated in the Uniform Act of 1970 and subsequent iterations. See http://www.hud.gov/offices/cpd/affordablehousing/training/web/relocation/overview.cfm
3. Lewis et al. (2002).
4. See Massey, Bothwell, and Domina (2009).
5. Charles (2003).
6. Levels for cities with high household loss are Detroit (-48 percent) from 1960 peak to 2010, St. Louis (-45 percent) from 1950, Cleveland (-38 percent) from 1960, Buffalo (-33 percent) from 1960, New Orleans (-31 percent) from 1990, and Pittsburgh (-29 percent) from 1950. Cities with lower household loss or gain are Cincinnati (-18 percent) from 1960, Baltimore (-14 percent) from 1970, Toledo (-10 percent) from 1980, Philadelphia (-7 percent) from 1970, Milwaukee (-5 percent) from 1980, and Washington D.C. (+2 percent) gain from former peak in 1970 to 2010.
7. Florida (2004); Saxenian (2002);Borjas (1995).
8. Charles (2003).
9. See Spangler (2011).

Bibliography

Beauregard, R. 2009. "Urban Population Loss in Historical Perspective: United States, 1820-2000." *Environment and Planning A* 41: 514–529.

Borjas, G. 1995. "The Economic Benefits of Immigration." *Journal of Economic Development Perspectives* 9:3–22.

Charles, C. 2003. "The Dynamics of Racial Residential Segregation." *Annual Review of Sociology* 29: 167–207.

Clark, W. and S. Blue. 2004. "Race, Class, and Segregation Patterns in Immigrant, Gateway Cities." *Urban Affairs Review* 39:667–688.

Farley, R., S. Danziger, and H. Holzer. 2000. *Detroit Divided.* New York: Russell Sage Foundation.

Florida, R. 2004. *The Rise of the Creative Class.* New York: Perseus Books.

Harvey, D. 2002. "Social Justice, Postmodernism, and the City." In *Readings in Urban Theory.* 2d ed, edited by S. Fainstein and S. Campbell, pp. Malden, MA: Blackwell.

Lewis, J., M. Maly, P. Kleppner, and R. Tobias. 2002. "Race and Residence in the Chicago Metropolitan Area 1980 to 2000." Chicago: Institute for Metropolitan Affairs, Roosevelt University, and Office for Social Policy Research, Northern Illinois University.

Massey, D., J. Rothwell, and T. Domina. 2009. "The Changing Bases of Segregation in the United States." *The Annals of the American Academy of Political and Social Science* 626: 74–90.

Saxenian, A. 2002. "Silicon Valley's New Immigrant High-Growth entrepreneurs." *Economic Development Quarterly* 16: 20–31.

Spangler, T. 2011. "Philadelphia Story: Detroit's Midtown Is Studying Success for Its Rebirth." *Detroit Free Press*, February 17.

Young, I. M. 1990. *Justice and the Politics of Difference.* Princeton: Princeton University Press.

9

Reforming Local Practice in Governance, Fiscal Policy, and Land Reclamation

Paul C. Brophy, Brophy & Reilly LLC

Alan Mallach, Center for Community Progress

In December 2010, the mayors of Los Angeles, Chicago, and Philadelphia, three of America's greatest cities, participated in a discussion at a Brookings Global Summit on Cities. Despite their generally buoyant dispositions, it was a grim discussion, filled with their frustrations about making their cities' financial ends meet. They described city governments with too little revenue to meet current and long-term obligations. Their challenge, they reported, was compounded by the reality that they saw little or no help in sight from either state governments or the federal government, all of which were facing budget constraints of their own.

These three men—Antonio Villaraigosa, Richard Daley, and Michael Nutter—were capable mayors who had been coping in a professional way with their budget realities. Yet they appeared frustrated, angry, and discouraged about the prospects of their cities for finding bright new futures and competing well globally, the theme of the Brookings convening.[1]

These three cities, for all their problems, are healthy compared to America's legacy cities, which have experienced significant and sustained population loss. For the mayor or city manager of a legacy city, the budget challenges are even more difficult. In these kinds of cities:

- *The tax base has eroded.* For example, in constant dollars, Saginaw, Michigan, had gross municipal revenues of $72 million in 1978. In 2008, its revenues were $31.6 million, a 56 percent drop.

- *Cuts have been made to city services and continue to be made.* Flint, Michigan, has cut the number of sworn police officers from over three hundred in 2001 to barely one hundred in 2010.
- *Dealing with scarcity has become the dominant political reality in these cities.* Members of city councils clamor to hold as much of a shrinking pie as possible for their districts or constituents.
- *Intergovernmental solutions appear increasingly remote,* as suburbanites, unaware of the interdependencies between them and the region's central city, show little interest in engaging with its needs.

Yet a strategy of constant retrenchment, while perhaps leading to short-term balanced budgets, can be fatal to the city's aspirations for change, and its ability to offer current and future residents a decent quality of life and to reverse its decline in population and jobs. Faced with laying off police officers or housing inspectors, or with laying off city planners, few cities choose the former, yet the latter may be as important to the city's long-term prospects.

What are city government leaders to do? As the earlier chapters in this book have indicated, there are many challenges to intervening in legacy cities. This chapter suggests some of the ways local practice can be reformed to adjust to the radically changed circumstances and to set a course adapting the city to its new reality. In the first section, we look at local governance—the institutions and capacities that cities need to build in order to address their immediate issues and long-term goals. The second section focuses on ways in which local governments can tackle the fiscal crises that threaten to undo the efforts they have been making. The final section looks at the challenges cities face in addressing the issue of land reclamation, a central—arguably *the* central—issue facing the nation's legacy cities.

Throughout the United States, cities are trying to reform their local practices to help cope with their immediate financial crises. The even bigger challenge is for them to be able to manage the short-term challenges while also creating opportunity for change over the longer term and, in so doing, rebuild their fundamentally broken economies and reconnect the central city to the broader regional economy.

Reforming Local Governance

Legacy cities raise complex questions of how government should be reorganized and reformed, as well as how broader governance approaches, such as community engagement public-private partnerships, can be pursued to address these cities' challenges. This section will also look at the issues of capacity in local government, and the emerging efforts to rethink the governance relationship between cities and their regions.

New Partnerships

Virtually every successful twentieth century American city has succeeded economically and built a stronger civic foundation because of some form of partnership between local government and nongovernmental civic leadership. Businesses, nonprofits, organized labor, and government achieved consensus on major issues and brought public and private will and capital together to achieve major improvements. One classic example of this kind of partnership was in Pittsburgh, where after World War II the Democrats in city government joined with the Republican business establishment through a CEO-driven organization, the Allegheny Conference on Community Development, to clean the city's air and bring vibrancy to downtown. This partnership lasted almost uninterrupted for over fifty years.

The Allegheny Conference is only one of the many government-business relationships that evolved in America's cities to create a form of city and regional governance that worked to keep cities strong following World War II. These include Civic Progress in St. Louis, Cleveland Tomorrow, and the Vault in Boston. As corporate America has changed, however, and greater citizen involvement in key decisions has been sought, the traditional business-government duopoly, a top-down partnership, has had to make room for broader engagement of a larger number of increasingly informed and involved residents and interests.

Xavier de Souza Briggs has written that this evolution can best be thought of as the development of "civic capacity," a term that can be described as the extent to which the sectors in a community are capable of collective action on public problems, and capable of choosing to move to solve their problems. Some places have made this transition well and are developing this civic capacity, but in many legacy cities, this tradition of civic-governmental partnerships has weakened and even collapsed. The typical large American corporation has moved from one deeply concerned with its local settings to one focused on national and international concerns, so that what happens in its key locations is far less important to the corporate leadership than it once was. Many large corporations have left legacy cities, either for their suburbs or for other parts of the world, or have been bought by firms headquartered elsewhere. Many cities, particularly smaller cities, no longer have a locally based business leadership ready or willing to engage in addressing the city's issues. As a result, in many legacy cities, previous governance partnerships—be they General Motors and mayors in Flint or the elite CEO structure of the Allegheny Conference in Pittsburgh—have atrophied.[2]

As the dominance of these largely two-pronged partnerships has ended, new, more multi-dimensional forms of governance are being sought in many cities, engaging business, neighborhood organizations, churches, interest groups, anchor institutions, and others to shape their city in respective cities for the short and long term. This can be a healthy development for cities, increasing the number of stakeholders and building more democratic partnerships. Putting such broader partnerships together, particularly in legacy cities, however, is deeply challenging for the following reasons:

- Legacy cities often have fewer resources to support a civic structure. While there are important exceptions, especially where there are strong private foundations present, many cities simply lack the private wealth to support sustained civic engagement.
- The politics of scarcity often means that one-time coalitions may have broken down as interests fight for a piece of a shrinking pie.
- Accumulated anger, disillusionment, and even a form of collective depression among city residents, after decades of municipal decline, often combined with governmental incompetence and corruption, real or perceived, make it difficult to focus on a future for a city, as the belief that the best days of the city are in the past is widespread.
- Local government itself is often a less capable partner in a local governance situation, for many reasons, including recurrent budget crises and the broader issues of capacity discussed below.

Yet despite all their challenges, many of the people who have remained in these cities share an underlying love of their communities—a love that can be tapped for the good of the whole if their anger, disappointment, and disillusionment can be overcome.

New governance structures need to be created and fostered that combine a more effective, capable city government with new stakeholder groups. These new approaches should include the business community but need to go beyond the traditional government-business relationships in order to tap the energy of residents who love the city and their organizations to help them work through the tough issues and position their city to thrive again in a new form. These new structures need to focus on building economic opportunity for the people living in the city, and rebuilding the city's economy—business by business, job by job—with entrepreneurial spirit and determination.

New partnerships and alliances are already beginning to form in many of these cities—relationships that are tapping the energy of new players.

In Philadelphia, PennPraxis (the clinical arm of the University of Pennsylvania's City Planning School) has teamed up with the William Penn Foundation, WHYY, and the *Daily News* to organize vibrant new coalitions to work on very important civic issues, including the future wellbeing of the Delaware River waterfront and the city's large park system. Residents are kept informed about city issues through the well-designed website PlanPhilly.com. The approach taken by PennPraxis and the William Penn Foundation is a good example of the importance of partnerships that succeed at bringing in new partners and that tap new energy in tackling a city's long-standing challenges. Through their efforts, the Delaware waterfront is now seen by many more people as a strong regional asset that needs to be protected from the politics of bad real estate dealmaking.

In St. Louis, a strong coalition of business, institutional, and other interests united to transform the 1,296-acre Forest Park into one of the region's major physical assets. The site of the World's Fair in 1904, Forest Park attracts more than twelve million visitors annually. Even though St. Louis has a smaller population than Washington, D.C., and far fewer tourists, the Trust for Public Lands found that Forest Park had more visitors in 2008 than the Mall in Washington, D.C.

These new arrangements, and many similar ones, utilize new communications methods and social media to further their organizing efforts, and are supported by a broad base of informed residents, business owners, and interest groups whose voices are heard, and which are able to achieve consensus on important future organizational directions and priorities. The creation of such broad-based partnerships is clearly important, and may even be seen as a necessary condition, for a legacy city to be able to address the challenges it faces. To build such partnerships, however, city governments may have to change the way in which they relate to nonprofit, civic, and neighborhood organizations as well as to individual residents. Rather than attempt to maintain a top-down approach, as has often been the case in the past, city governments must be able to forge such true partnerships.

Perhaps not a formal partnership, but equally important, is the relationship of city government and its residents. Successful governance demands that residents be engaged in the process of city improvement, particularly in the course of making tough decisions about resources and land utilization that are part of a legacy city's reality. Whether in the course of carrying out Richmond's Neighborhoods in Bloom program, or the process of framing the Youngstown 2010 plan, effective, systematic citizen engagement is a condition of success for any such initiative.

Building Capacity

City governments still play the central role in the rebuilding process, as reflected by the dominant role played by Mayor Menino in Boston or Mayor Daley in Chicago. It is hard to dispute that without their leadership over the past decades, neither city would be as strong and vital, for all its remaining problems, as it is today. Similarly, the absence of effective mayoral leadership over long periods has undoubtedly added to some other cities' problems today. The ability of the city to deliver cost-effective and high quality public services, and to engage with developers, lenders, and nonprofits in the process of rebuilding are equally important. One might say that a successful city needs three forms of capacity:

- Leadership: the ability of the senior elected and appointed officials to provide effective, visible direction for the city, setting a clear agenda and ensuring that all partners move forward together

- Managerial: the ability of the city to deliver effective services and to provide clear, transparent governance
- Technical: the ability of the city to plan effectively for the future, to frame effective strategies for change, and to leverage public and private resources for housing and economic development

Many legacy cities, particularly the smaller ones, are at a serious disadvantage in this arena. The combination of middle-class flight and the anger and discouragement of those left behind has led to a dynamic where the pool of highly capable and politically engaged citizens, particularly those willing to run for public office, has markedly shrunk. Some of those running for office appear more interested in the trappings of office than in the substance, while minuscule voter turnouts in local elections—often less than 20 percent of eligible voters—exemplify disillusionment with the political process.

Problems of managerial and technical capacity are multifaceted. Cities in fiscal crisis simply lack the resources to hire highly qualified personnel in enough numbers to carry out all of the tasks that need to be performed. When confronting the need to lay off municipal personnel—a common problem today—the positions of planners and others who do not provide direct services are often seen as less important than those of police or fire personnel, on whom the city's safety depends. Many legacy cities have inadequate capacity in these areas, reflecting many different factors, including long-term fiscal constraints; lack of understanding of the city's personnel needs and willingness to appoint unqualified or poorly qualified individuals to key positions; low salary scales incapable of attracting first-rate professional or managerial staff; and corporate cultures and management systems that fail to support or reward excellence, or even competence. Many cities, moreover, lack key support systems for strong management and technical performance, such as a data system capable of tracking local conditions, municipal and other activities, and outcomes.

These problems will be difficult to solve, particularly in light of the long-term nature of legacy cities' fiscal crises, which will make significant new hiring by these cities unlikely in the foreseeable future. This is an area where the private sector and higher levels of government can play a critical role:

- State governments and local universities can develop training and mentoring programs to build the capacity of local employees, a pool that includes many individuals with energy, intelligence, and a commitment to their city.
- Cities can partner with nonprofit and private entities to leverage government resources. The city of Cleveland has entered into a formal partnership with many of its CDCs, under which CDC staff perform many code enforcement functions, leveraging the city's staff capacity.

- States and the federal government can "embed" trained personnel in local governments. Under the state of Michigan's NSP2 plan, a consultant hired by the state is recruiting a cadre of people with skills in planning, housing rehab and related areas who will be placed with city governments and county land banks throughout that state.

Stronger leadership, however, must come from within city government. Efforts need to be pursued both to build the pool of present and future leaders and to provide the necessary support to those elected to office so they understand the challenges they face and the opportunities that may be available and thus can make informed, responsible decisions.

Building Regional Cooperation

A further challenge to governance in legacy cities is the extent to which the potential solutions to their problems require a metropolitan area-wide approach. The typical metropolitan area in America's Northeast or Midwest is made up of dozens, even hundreds of separate counties, cities, towns, and villages, each with its own government, taxing, and land use authority. Few of these regions have any bodies—other than the transportation planning agencies mandated by federal law, known as metropolitan planning organizations, or MPOs—capable of bringing about intermunicipal cooperation or regional planning. While some MPOs have played a strong role in bringing communities together, most have tended to define their responsibilities narrowly in the framework of federal law.

The problem is compounded by the accumulated distrust and poor communication between many central cities and their suburban neighbors. The record of central city-suburban cooperation and creativity is mixed. Competition for resources and businesses have tended to make inter-municipal dynamics appear to be a zero-sum game, where one municipality could win only at the expense of the other. Suburbs have seen little advantage in cooperating with the central city, while cities have tended to turn inward, seeing little potential in better relationships with people whom they often see as adversaries rather than potential partners.

A pioneering effort was made by former mayor Richard M. Daley of Chicago. In 1997, he invited mayors from nine suburban municipal associations to unite in a common cause of pushing beyond the boundaries of local interests in order to serve the greater interests of the region. The Metropolitan Mayors Caucus, which grew out of that discussion, is today an active collaboration between Chicago and the suburban associations, serving as a force for thinking, change, and advocacy on behalf of a region containing eight million people in 273 municipalities.

On an equally large scale, Team NEO has been established to lead economic development efforts in a sixteen-county region in Northeastern Ohio, including the cities of Cleveland, Akron, Canton, and Youngstown. Many valuable efforts, however, are more modest than the Chicago Metropolitan Mayors Caucus or Team NEO. In St. Louis, Mayor Slay has reached out to St. Louis County to explore the possibility of the county providing services within the city, while in New Jersey, with the encouragement of state government, cities like Camden are exploring the regionalization of policing functions between the city and adjacent suburban municipalities.

The central point is that neither legacy cities nor many of their suburban neighbors can afford to continue to operate as self-contained entities, whether with respect to economic development, planning, or public service delivery. Successful economic development is a function of regional success, while mounting fiscal constraints make it increasingly difficult for current fragmented models of service delivery to meet the needs of citizens and businesses. Building regional forums for coordinating transportation planning and economic development, creating vehicles for sharing and consolidating services (and even municipalities), and developing models for breaking down the urban-suburban barriers that have impeded effective cooperation are all critical steps in the revival of legacy cities.

Reforming Local Fiscal Policies

America's legacy cities are in a state of severe fiscal crisis. Facing growing deficits, they are cutting back on services, laying off hundreds of municipal employees, canceling capital projects, and cutting back on repairs and maintenance of their cities' facilities and infrastructure. While every recession creates fiscal difficulties for local governments, this one has hit older, poorer cities with particular intensity. In cities like Flint, Cleveland, or Gary, which are losing significant numbers of both people and jobs, the current financial crisis is merely the latest and most severe blow in a long-running pattern of increasing fiscal instability and stress, to the point where their very survival as government entities is at risk.

Examples abound. Michigan cities are doubly hit hard by the state's persistent economic problems. Drastic budget cuts are being made in virtually every city. Lansing, the state capital, cut over a hundred positions in local government, including dozens in police and fire departments in May 2011. Over the past ten years, Flint has cut the number of its police officers from 336 to 103, or nearly 70 percent, and the number of firefighters has decreased from 252 to 118, or over 50 percent. These are among the smallest complements of public safety personnel relative to population for any city in the United States. Saginaw's municipal workforce went from 761 in the 1980s to 465 by 2008, while between 2001 and 2010 Dayton, Ohio, cut over eight hundred jobs, or nearly 30 percent of its total workforce. Meanwhile, a large and growing part of these cities' revenue is going to cover health benefit and pension costs. 40 percent of the 2010 Flint, Michigan, budget went for benefits and pension costs, while in Camden, New Jersey, the share of the city's budget allocated to those costs increased from 16 percent in 2003 to 29 percent in 2009.

In order to continue to provide essential police, fire, and sanitation services, cities have cut other services—such as parks, recreation or city planning—to the bone. As a result, the ability of these cities to deliver public services of adequate quality, to maintain the city's infrastructure and physical plant, and to offer its citizens a decent quality of life has become questionable. If people are not safe and do not feel safe, and if parents do not feel a city can provide their children with a quality education, those who can are likely to leave that locality. Yet, the realities of these cities is that cuts are being made in these areas simply because there is not enough revenue to sustain a minimally adequate level of services in these areas.

The problem is heightened by budget shortfalls in state government and by the growing pressure in Washington, D.C. to cut federal discretionary expenditures. The prospect of significant help for strapped older cities from states and the federal government is remote.

These conditions, which are not a short-term reaction to the recent fiscal crisis and recession, but reflect long-term structural imbalances affecting legacy cities, have begun to raise questions about these cities' very viability. Alarm bells have been sounded that those imbalances could lead to growing numbers of municipal bankruptcies. While the specter of massive municipal bond defaults raised by some is likely to be illusory, the possibility that many older cities may be incapable of paying their bills, or meeting their growing obligations with respect to retiree pension and health benefit costs, is a real one.

If this crisis is to be averted and America's legacy cities are to be put on a path where restored prosperity is a realistic prospect rather than an illusion, creative ways of thinking about and addressing the fiscal crisis must be found. Regional solutions and state intervention are two approaches that need to be explored, yet even more far-reaching strategies may be needed to address this crisis.

Thinking Regionally

A central—although not the only—cause of legacy cities' fiscal imbalance is the extent to which a limited and shrinking local tax base is called upon to support a wide variety of services and facilities, many of which are regional in nature. One method to mitigate local financial stress, therefore, may be to spread the costs borne by local governments for services and assets that are largely regional in nature across the larger region, so that the costs of these regional assets are not borne entirely by the central city, or to redistribute regional revenues to better reflect the regional cost distribution.

In the Pittsburgh area, Allegheny County enacted a 1 percent sales and use tax in 1994. Half of the proceeds of this tax go to the Allegheny Regional Asset

District (RAD), which distributes these funds to support and finance regional assets in the areas of libraries, parks and recreation, cultural, sports, and civic facilities and programs. Half of the remaining funds are allocated to municipal governments, based on a formula weighted to help distressed communities. These proceeds are used to assist in shifting the tax burden away from property taxes and to support municipal functions such as roads and police protection. In 2011, RAD allocated $81.1 million, of which 32 percent went to support libraries, 31 percent to parks, trails, and other green spaces, 18 percent to the stadiums and arena, 8 percent to regional facilities (zoo, aviary, Phipps Conservatory), and 10 percent to arts and cultural organizations.[3]

A more ambitious effort at revenue sharing was mounted in the Twin Cities region of Minnesota, where, under a program established in 1975, 40 percent of the tax revenues from new non-residential development throughout the region goes into a regional tax-sharing pool, which is redistributed to municipalities within the region on the basis of need. By 2010, over one-third of all of the commercial and industrial rateables in the region were contributing to the pool, which has been credited with significantly reducing revenue disparities throughout the metropolitan area.

These approaches can help ameliorate fiscal conditions in legacy cities. Even so, the Twin Cities and Allegheny County initiatives are two of only a handful of such programs around the country, although in a number of cases this issue has been addressed through regional consolidation, or unigov, as in Indianapolis, Nashville, and Louisville.

In 2000, Ned Hill and Jeremy Nowak proposed a more radical approach, calling for a partnership between the federal government and distressed local governments. They suggested a program under which local governments would lower taxes and fees for a ten-year period, with the revenue losses made up for by the federal government, in exchange for significant reforms in public administration. By lowering taxes and fees, these jurisdictions would become more attractive places for businesses and reduce the cost of home ownership and rental operation, helping them compete more successfully for residents and business investment. A radical approach like this may be needed in legacy cities if they are going to prevent local short-term decisions such as those taking place today that have serious negative effects on the business climate and quality of life in these cities, making them even less able to compete globally or in their regional markets.[4]

The Role of State Intervention

Municipalities are creatures of state governments, and states have been dealing with municipal fiscal issues for a long time. Many states enacted laws during the Depression to address the epidemic of municipal bond defaults that were then taking place. These laws were often designed, however, less to put distressed municipalities back on their feet than to ensure that bondholders received their money. Today, many states have mechanisms through which they can intervene if a city or county reaches a point of fiscal stress that jeopardizes its ability to meet its financial obligations or provide adequate public services.

These mechanisms take many forms, and they are sometimes referred to generically as "financial control boards." In recent years, control boards have been established by state governments for many cities, including Pittsburgh, Buffalo, and Springfield, Massachusetts. Under a 1990 statute, the state of Michigan has appointed emergency financial managers to take control of a number of cities, including, at different times, Flint, Ecorse, and Pontiac. Although New Jersey has a Depression-era state law that empowers the state's local finance board to take control of a municipality's finances, it enacted a special law in 2002 to make possible a more comprehensive state takeover of the city of Camden, which remained under state control until 2010.

These statutes (with the partial exception of New Jersey's legislation) are predicated on a central assumption—namely, that municipal fiscal problems can not only be solved through short-term solutions but also through "accounting" solutions, such as improving fiscal management, eliminating waste, and finding greater economies and efficiencies in the conduct of municipal operations. There is no question that fiscal management can be improved in most cities, and there is little doubt that waste and inefficiency are sadly present in many distressed older cities. That is not in dispute.

The problem is that mismanagement, waste, and inefficiency are at most the visible and lesser portion of the cities' fiscal iceberg. While a financial control board can make short-term changes that may give the city—particularly if the economy is improving—a short-term boost through more efficient tax collection, the elimination of a handful of unneeded positions, or the restructuring of services for greater efficiency, the long-term, chronic problems at the root of the fiscal crisis remain unchanged. Short-term improvements quickly reach a plateau, while the actions of the control board or emergency manager fail to address the long-term decline taking place.

The activities of control boards can potentially make matters worse. To the extent that their efforts at short-term fiscal stabilization involve increasing already high local taxes, reducing already limited public services, or cutting back already inadequate investment in municipal infrastructure and capital stock, it can exacerbate the existing cycle of decline by further undermining the quality of life offered its residents, or rendering the city even less attractive for investment by individuals, families, or businesses. *Short-term "solutions" may end up making a city's long-term prospects even more problematic.* Long-term structural problems demand long-term structural solutions. In Camden, although the clear intent of the law was to create sustainable revitalization of the city as well as to straighten out the city's financial problems (and which provided a special appropriation of $175 million to that end), poor execution and leadership resulted in a situation where the city was no better off—and arguably worse—when the state relinquished its authority than when it initially took control.

This is not always the case. State intervention was clearly beneficial both in Chelsea and Springfield, Massachusetts, where the level of mismanagement prior to intervention was particularly egregious, and, notably, where the state control board and managers were focused not only on short-term fixes but also on laying the groundwork for long-term viability.

Taking the Fiscal Crisis Seriously

Given this reality, what are the implications for federal, state, and local policy-makers? Most important, it means that we need a fundamentally new approach to addressing fiscal stress in older cities, not only one that focuses on short-term cash flow and budgetary requirements but one that is designed *from the beginning* to foster long-term change in these cities' fiscal reality in order to end the vicious cycle of decline in which so many of them are caught. This means taking short-term actions that do not impair a city's long-term viability, while laying the groundwork for long-term strategies to build the local economy, reuse vacant and underutilized land, and stabilize or grow the local population. It also means looking at long-term strategies that have rarely been considered, including recognizing the regional nature of so many of the issues facing older municipalities, and moving across municipal boundaries to find solutions. We suggest that this approach needs to contain both short-term and long-term strategies.

Improving the Short-Term Picture

The need for long-term strategies does not negate the importance of focusing on short-term change. In addition to improving fiscal management and efficient delivery of services, cities should explore other strategies to increase revenues and better manage costs. In so doing, they must recognize that any such steps are only stop gaps, employed to better set the stage for long-term change. In addition to seeking ways to increase revenues without creating negative consequences—a difficult proposition—cities need to rethink how they deliver public services. Privatization has long been used as a strategy by local government; while it is clear that it is not a panacea, properly designed and carried out, it can result in significant savings. In severe cases, restructuring of public employee wage and benefit programs may have to be considered. Devolution of municipal services to special service districts can work in some areas, while partnerships with community-based organizations (CBOs) is an area that has been less explored. Cleveland has entered into a compact with a number of its neighborhood-based community development corporations, under which they supplement the city's code enforcement efforts.

Taking control of the city's land inventory, as discussed further in the next section of this chapter, is a critical part of both the short-term and long-term strategy for any legacy city seeking to both stabilize its fiscal situation and begin the process of regeneration.

One of the knottiest issues facing older cities is the cost of municipal payrolls, and even more so, the costs of pensions and health care benefits to municipal retirees, which continue to mount even as the individuals receiving them are no longer providing services to the community. It is a difficult issue because there is a good deal of unfairness about requiring present or former municipal workers to pay for conditions they did not cause and cannot control; moreover, it is important to understand that *whatever steps are taken to reduce payroll and pension costs, they do not solve the long-term structural problem.* At the same time, the shortfall in many cities is so great, and the likelihood of additional state aid so remote, that in some cases there may be no alternative.

The issue of pension costs is likely to become more severe in the future, because—although cities may currently be meeting their obligations—a large number of municipal pension funds are severely underfunded. The Pennsylvania Public Employee Retirement Commission (PERC) found that twenty-seven municipalities have pension plans funded at less than 50 percent of liabilities. While this is a small percentage of that state's municipalities, included in the group are the state's three largest cities Philadelphia, Pittsburgh and Scranton—which alone account for 45 percent of all local government employees in the state.

Cities cannot solve this problem on their own. Cities like Dayton or Flint simply will not be able to find the money internally to both meet current obligations and fully fund their future ones. One way or another, the states or the federal government will have to take a substantial part of the responsibility for finding a solution; what is critical is that it be a genuine solution, one that does not impose future crippling obligations on the same municipalities that government is seeking to help.

Tackling Long-Term, Chronic Fiscal Stress

The *only* way to eliminate chronic fiscal stress and structural deficits in older, distressed cities is to place these cities solidly on the road back to being socially, economically, and physically healthy communities, with the density of population and agglomeration of activities to play a central role in their regions' economies. If that is to happen, many changes have to take place at many levels. Cities must be able to define and articulate their vision for their future as stronger, healthier—although in many cases smaller—cities. They must also rethink their "business model," how they pay for and deliver public services, while partnering with business, academia, and nonprofit organizations to frame credible strategies for land reutilization and economic growth. State governments need to restructure how they create programs and allocate resources for cities, in order to level the playing field between cities and their suburban and rural neighbors and focus resources on supporting systemic change in cities rather than propping up the status quo.

Where a city has lost a large part of their historic population and job base, the process of transition to a healthier city also involves reimagining the city as a smaller city, based on its current—and realistic future—population and economic base, not the population and industry it had in 1960, or even 1920. That is likely to involve rethinking not only the use of surplus land and buildings but also the pattern of service delivery and the configuration of the municipal infrastructure, as in Saginaw, Michigan, which has designated a one-half square mile area on the city's east side as a Green Zone, which will be gradually returned to nature.

Finally, state and local government need to grapple with the underlying reality that a central reason for the fiscal crisis of older cities is the massive imbalance in public resources and service demands within the cities compared to their suburban surroundings. As vast proportions of each city's wealth, whether jobs, businesses, or middle-class and wealthy residents, have moved to the suburbs, the cities have had to deal with a shrinking resource base and an increasingly resource-dependent population within inflexible municipal boundaries. Suburban Haddonfield, New Jersey, only a few miles from urban Camden, has ten times the per capita property tax base of its urban neighbor.

Some cities, such as a Philadelphia or Chicago, may be large enough and may retain enough economic resources to rebuild from within; that is not an option, however, for most smaller legacy cities, which lack the internal resources to go it alone. Unless fundamental changes take place to the way in which regional resources are allocated and service delivery boundaries defined, the vision of a stronger, healthier Flint, Youngstown, or Rochester may remain unreachable. This, too, poses a challenge for state governments, which set the ground rules for how those resources are allocated and the boundaries defined.

As in other areas, state government plays a critical role. While it is unrealistic to expect significant growth in state aid for older cities in the near term, state governments continue to provide a variety of resources to local governments in general state aid or revenue sharing, but through funds dedicated to economic development, workforce development, brownfields cleanup, and much more. Each state should examine all of the resources that it *does* make available to local governments in order to determine how they can be structured to maximally encourage and support transformative change at the local level, rather than maintaining the status quo. States must also determine how they can support and actively motivate the creation of regional vehicles for provision of services and redistribution of public revenues.

Reforming Local Land Reclamation

Legacy cities typically contain something widely viewed as a liability, but which is actually a potentially valuable long-term asset—its inventory of vacant land and buildings. This asset is growing in many of these cities.

If vacant land and buildings are to become a real asset, cities must take a radically different view of vacant property. Cities should use their legal powers and resources to gain control over the vacant land inventory to control its immediate and interim uses and to develop the ability to identify and move strategically toward properties' most effective long-term reuse. As a first step, however, cities must build the machinery they need to gain legal control of the land. Land speculation is the enemy of the long-term good of a city in its efforts to stabilize and rebuild its distressed real estate markets.

This is not merely a technical or managerial step on the part of many cities; on the contrary, it may often involve a fundamental change in the attitude of local government in two critical ways. First, city leadership needs to understand the potential of vacant and underutilized property and see it as the asset it can become; and second, they need to accept responsibility for the future of those land parcels and buildings, rather than avoid that responsibility or treat it as no more than an annoying nuisance.

In moving toward a new way of addressing land reclamation, each city must first reconsider its basic approach to its property inventory and then build both the legal and managerial systems it needs to take control over its future. Central to those systems is a clearly defined vehicle through which the city can exert control over its land.

Develop a Citywide Approach to Land Reform

The principles for citywide land reform were outlined in a 2002 report by Paul Brophy and Jennifer Vey from the Brookings Institution. That report laid out ten steps for urban land reform, some of which are particularly relevant for legacy cities. These include the following:

- *Know Your Territory.* Cities need to establish versatile, readily updated information systems that inventory property owned by the jurisdiction and other governmental bodies, and that track properties that are becoming available for public ownership through tax foreclosure or through the foreclosure on other public liens. This inventory should also include properties that have been foreclosed by financial institutions. This knowledge base is fundamental to a city's ability to plan a future for its vacant land and neighborhoods.

- *Develop a Citywide Approach to Redevelopment and Reuse.* Chapter 3 describes the planning issues faced by shrinking cities and explores how planners should address them. A strategy to reuse vacant land, similar in scale to that being developed by Mayor David Bing and his staff in Detroit, is a central element of any overall planning strategy. A key issue for legacy cities is the need to make tough choices about where to invest scarce public resources, and to concentrate on neighborhoods that have sufficient market strength to hold their populations and businesses and build on that strength to enhance adjacent areas over time. This is in stark contrast to long-established and widely followed approaches that funnel the lion's share of resources into improving a city's weakest areas. As described in chapter 3, in legacy cities (as well as in many others), targeting scarce resources to the weakest market areas is not an effective neighborhood improvement strategy, In these cities, typified by weak housing markets and declining populations, the smartest redevelopment and reuse strategy is to hold population and to begin to regrow the population of the city by strengthening areas that already hold appeal for identifiable market segments, while encouraging people who are "stranded" in distressed areas to move to the stronger areas. Those areas that are emptying out may best be designated for nonresidential land uses, and even for land uses that are quite novel for American cities—urban farming, city forests, and recreational spaces that could be created along "daylighted," or reopened, buried streams. These approaches are now being tested in many legacy cities. Some of Cleveland's initiatives are described in the case study after chapter 6.

- *Implement Neighborhood Plans in Partnership with Community Stakeholders.* Any strategy for transforming a distressed city that has lost a large part of its population, and that is dotted with heavily abandoned and disinvested neighborhoods needs the active support and engagement of community stakeholders. Fostering effective citizen involvement in the planning process is especially challenging in settings where the overall health of the city may require targeted investment in a few selected areas and the gradual emptying out of other areas. Involving residents and businesses in such settings is particularly difficult.

The approach must not only be citywide; it must be strategic, and integrated with other activities of government, as well as with those nongovernmental stakeholders, such as community development corporations, which can contribute significantly to the results.

Assemble the Tools to Address Land and Property Issues

Mounting a successful strategic effort at land reclamation requires leadership and capacity, as with other critical aspects of governance, but it requires something more—putting the legal tools in place to address these issues. The work that the Genesee County and other Michigan land banks are doing to get control of vacant properties in that state's cities would not have been possible without the 1999 reform of state property tax foreclosure law, which ensured that county land banks, and not speculators, could get control of properties that went into property tax foreclosure. Similarly, strong vacant property receivership laws in Massachusetts and in the city of Baltimore have enabled local officials and nonprofit organizations to motivate the owners of vacant properties to put them back into productive use, or risk losing them as a result of a court order appointing a receiver to take control of the property.

Municipalities need strong tools to encourage the owners of problem properties to maintain them or restore them to use; and, where owners fail to maintain their properties, they need to have a means to take control of those properties. A strong vacant property receivership law, under which the city or a qualified nonprofit organization can petition the court to appoint a receiver of a neglected vacant property is an example of the former, while a strong tax foreclosure law is an example of the latter.

The number of separate legal tools that ideally should be in place is considerable, reflecting the reality that there are many different types of problem properties and many different circumstances that lead a property to be vacant or poorly maintained. A number of states, for example, allow municipalities to use what is known as "spot blight" taking, under which a city or county can use eminent domain to take a vacant property that is blighting its surroundings and recover it to a responsible owner, without having to go through the extensive and expensive process of creating a redevelopment or urban renewal area. Some cities including Pittsburgh, Philadelphia, and Newark have used this power creatively to gain control of problem properties.

In contrast to "spot blight" taking, which can only be pursued by a municipality where it is explicitly permitted by state law, many municipalities have enacted vacant property registration ordinances using the local police power, or—where available—the city's home rule power under its state laws. These ordinances provide an effective means for the city to police its vacant properties, to cover some of the city's costs through a registration fee, and to ensure that owners secure them properly and carry adequate insurance coverage. Under Wilmington, Delaware's innovative ordinance, the annual fee rises steeply with every year that the property remains vacant, a strong incentive for owners to put their properties back to use. Although no state law explicitly authorized that ordinance, the Delaware Supreme Court found that it was legally enacted, as it fell within the city's power to take action to protect its citizens' health, safety, and welfare.

These are examples of the sorts of tools that may be needed for a city to mount an effective citywide attack on vacant and problem properties. In some cases, the appropriate legal tools can be created through a local ordinance or through local implementation of a state law. In other cases, new state laws may need to be written, or existing laws amended. Local officials must pay close attention to what happens in their state capital, both advocating for better legal tools and opposing steps that would reduce their ability to address these issues. Early in 2011, for example, advocates were able to derail an effort in the Georgia legislature to enact a bill that would have all but eliminated the ability of that state's cities and counties to enact workable vacant property registration ordinances.

In the final analysis, however, the legal tools are only as good as the will and capacity of the city to implement and enforce them. The 1999 Michigan property tax foreclosure reform would have meant little in Genesee County without the leadership of county treasurer, Dan Kildee, and others to use the new law as a springboard for a countywide land bank. Similarly, a vacant property registration ordinance is of little value unless the city makes a concerted effort to get owners to register, and fines those who do not.

This is a function of both will and capacity. Even with the will, the city needs to put in place the personnel with the skills and technology support to carry out these tasks. In a time of severe fiscal constraints, this is not easy. Still, it is feasible. Cities have found that technology can dramatically improve efficiency in code enforcement. Some cities have developed partnerships to leverage limited city resources; the city of Cleveland has created the Cleveland Code Enforcement Partnership, a formal agreement between the city and nineteen of the city's CDCs, under which they follow up on properties referred to the city's Department of Buildings, work with property owners to initiate repairs, and track changes in ownership, foreclosure proceedings, and vacancy. Finally, cities need formal vehicles to take control of land, maintain it, and plan for its reuse.

Create Vehicles to Take Control of Land

After World War II, American cities created redevelopment authorities to revitalize their downtowns and distressed neighborhoods. These agencies worked in partnership with the federal and state governments to assemble and clear land, upgrade infrastructure, and sell land for new development. They had the power to buy, own, and sell land, finance development, and use eminent domain where needed to assemble sites. A few of these agencies, such as Pittsburgh's Urban Redevelopment Authority, which continues to be the "go to" place in city government for land acquisition and disposition, still exist. Most, however, have faded in their role and often gone out of existence with the demise of urban renewal as a public strategy.

While the historical track record of redevelopment authorities is mixed, they highlight the importance of having effective vehicles to address urban land issues. Today's equivalents in some respects are the land bank agencies that have been created in many cities[5] and that play a critical role in acquiring and holding vacant and underutilized properties for future use. Successful land banks take control of tax delinquent and other neglected properties and have the specialized skills needed to be responsible custodians of vacant land and buildings and to strategically deploy land (through sale or lease) for new uses that support city and regional plans and are compatible with the city's evolving future direction. Land banks in Genesee County (Flint), Michigan, and Cuyahoga County (Cleveland), Ohio, have become a major force in addressing the problems of blighted properties and land reclamation in those communities.

This approach is in direct opposition to the so-called privatization of city assets—the sale of tax liens and the sale of property at very low prices. Such a technique may produce short-term income but seriously limits or even eliminates the ability of local government to gain control of its land inventory, control the future use of land, and bring future land uses and development to scale. It fails to recognize that vacant properties can be an opportunity as well as a burden.

Following the lead of cities and counties in Michigan and Ohio, cities around the nation are examining their legal powers and administrative machinery to create vehicles to take control of land and maintain it for however long it takes until appropriate private reuse opportunities emerge, whether that reuse is for redevelopment or for a use, such as a public forest or urban agriculture, that seems alien to our historical idea of urban land uses. Such a vehicle can take many different forms. Under the Michigan and Ohio laws, the land banking entity is a public authority at the county level, a public body dedicated to carry out this specific responsibility. In other states, land banking may be done within the structure of general government—such as Trenton's Division of Real Estate in the city's Department of Housing and Economic Development—or through a contract between the city and a qualified nonprofit entity. What is important is that land banking —holding and maintaining land—be seen as an explicit responsibility of government, and that it be viewed as a long-term responsibility, reflecting the long period of change and transformation that will be needed to restore vitality to America's legacy cities.

Conclusion

Reforming local practice in America's legacy cities requires both dramatic change to existing practice and the ability to build on the city's existing strengths.

Governance changes must go beyond city government to bring in stakeholders from every segment of the economy and the civic space. Local leaders, public or private, must be able to tap into and ignite the energy latent in these communities to create opportunity, so that they can work their way back to prosperity and health. Public and social media can be very effective in engaging stakeholders in the twenty-first century, and they need to be used more extensively.

Local government itself needs to be transformed to tackle the challenges. Governmental silos need to be broken down in order to address complex issues that cut across traditional departmental boundaries and to mount multifaceted place-based initiatives. Addressing these complex issues, however, will require far more capacity, both managerial and technical, than many cities today can command.

Tackling the fiscal dilemma, particularly in a time when states are experiencing budget deficits and the federal government is politically and financially constrained in its ability to act as a partner, is particularly difficult. Short-term solutions that raise taxes and fees or cut services and infrastructure investments are part of a vicious cycle that may further exacerbate the negative investment climate in a city and work against any future return to prosperity.

The accumulation of vacant land and buildings in legacy cities is a short-term burden, and an important asset. Cities need to rethink their approach to their land inventory and to adopt the legal tools and build the mechanisms they need to hold land for uses that can respond to market forces and ultimately serve as the means to bring about stronger and healthier cities.

Notes

1. The discussion can be viewed at http://www.time.com/time/video/player/0,32068,740668828001_2041178,00.html
2. Briggs (2008), pp. 143-183, presents a thorough description of Pittsburgh's progress toward modernizing its civic-governance structures.
3. See http://www.radworkshere.org/.
4. Recently, the Obama administration has launched a pilot program under which it will work with a small group of legacy cities to test the potential of a more effective partnership between the federal executive branch and those cities. The program, called Strong Cities, Strong Communities (SC2) is aimed at breaking through the departmental silos at the federal level to learn how the federal government can become a more effective partner with legacy cities to improve capacity locally, to bring flexibility to the execution of federal programs, and to adapt initiatives for greater success. While the goals of the program are admirable, it is hard to see how it will have a major effect without additional targeted funding to these cities.
5. See Alexander (2011) for an extensive discussion of this subject.

Bibliography

Alexander, F. 2011. *Land Banks and Land Banking.* Washington, D.C.: Center for Community Progress.

Brophy, P. C. and J. S. Vey, 2002. "Seizing City Assets: Ten Steps to Urban Land Reform." Washington, DC: Brookings Institution, Center on Urban and Metropolitan Policy, and CEOs for Cities.

De Souza Briggs, X. 2008. *Democracy as Problem Solving: Civic Capacity in Communities Across the Globe*, Cambridge: MIT Press.

Hill, E. W. and J. Nowak. 2000. "Nothing Left to Lose: Only Radical Strategies Can Help America's Most Distressed Cities." *Brookings Review* 18, (no.3): X-X. February.

Lubove, R. 1996. *Twentieth-Century Pittsburgh: Government, Business and Environmental Change*, Pittsburgh: University of Pittsburgh Press.

MacDonald, C. 2011. "Private Landowners Complicate Reshaping of Detroit." Detroit News, February 3.

Thompson, K. 2011. "With Detroit in Dire Straits, Mayor Invites Big Thinking." Washington Post, February 8.

Trust for Public Land. 2010. 2010 City Park Facts. Washington, D.C.: Trust for Public Land.

10

New State And Federal Policy Agendas: Realizing The Potential Of America's Legacy Cities And Their Regions

Lavea Brachman, Greater Ohio Policy Center

Introduction

During the past few years, increasing attention has been paid to those American cities that, despite the urban revival of the 1990s and 2000s, have continued to lose population and jobs, in many cases shrinking to two-thirds or less of their peak population. These cities are becoming increasingly impoverished while losing ground in the competitive global marketplace.

Yet these legacy cities and their metropolitan areas remain crucial to the future American economy, in that they contain a significant share of the nation's assets on which to build its future prosperity. However, it is unrealistic to expect that market forces will, on their own, provide the impetus for the revival of these cities. This is particularly true at a time when the American economy as a whole is likely to follow at best a slow, gradual path of recovery for the next few years. These cities often find themselves caught in a Catch 22 situation, in that limited resources dictate that any meaningful change in their condition will require resources and practices beyond those that they and their metro regions alone can provide. Many state and federal policies, moreover, have contributed to their decline—intentionally or not—and must be replaced or reformed to regenerate healthy cities and regions.

This chapter[1] argues that current policies, particularly at the state level, are blocking these places' revival, and that a significant reframing of policy and new approaches to investment are needed. A growing chorus of practitioners and academics has pointed to the need to reexamine state policies and the need for state policy innovation,[2] in order to unleash legacy cities' competitive potential and position these cities for a role in the next economy.

This chapter takes a critical look at the current policy framework by identifying these cities' key characteristics and the challenges they pose to help define the necessary policy reforms.[3] These reforms are grounded in five principles or building blocks for change: (1) make strategic investments; (2) build capacity to institutionalize reforms that foster long-term change; (3) enhance the power of these cities and their regions through governance reform; (4) leverage their unique assets and innovative potential; and (5) reshape disinvested areas with alternative uses. Later, this chapter fleshes out these principles with examples of key state and federal policies, showing how they can align for maximum impact. These principles are grounded in two underlying propositions: first, that state policy is central to the recovery of these cities; and, second, that federal policy should be aligned with state policy to nudge state governments toward policies more supportive of their older cities and to support strategies for change developed by local officials, organizations, and citizens.

Much of the condition of legacy cities and their metros is attributable to a series of market failures over many decades. They are no longer competitive in their traditional economic roles but have not yet found new roles to substitute for the old ones. Ultimately, only the private market can provide a strong economy or housing demand. However, government can foster the strategies and initiatives that enable those markets to work better and empower their residents to better compete in those markets, laying the groundwork for economic revitalization and physical transformation.

While the majority of the reforms discussed here are place-based reforms that focus on advancing these cities' physical transformations and reshaping their built environment, these reforms are necessarily linked to a broader set of reforms stimulating economic revival—that including policies to encourage business creation, workforce retraining and innovation—to allow these places to compete in a global economy, as well as fiscal reform to enable these cities to sustainably provide the public services and infrastructure their citizens and businesses need. While there is no single silver bullet that alone will make the difference, the principles and reforms outlined here should be a significant start.

The Features of Legacy Cities Define Needed Policy Reforms

Common Characteristics

Reforms must be responsive both to the demographic and socioeconomic realities of these places and to their market potential; they must be capable of being tailored to these cities' shared characteristics while retaining sufficient flexibility to avoid a "one size fits all" approach.

Legacy cities are a particular class of American city—older, predominately industrial cities that did not share in the urban revival of the 1990s and 2000s and have continued to decline, losing population and jobs. These cities, which are disproportionately but not exclusively located in the Northeast and Midwest, include many major cities, including icons of American history like Pittsburgh, Detroit, and Cleveland, and a host of medium-sized ones, such as Flint, Gary, and Youngstown. While the policies discussed in this chapter are primarily meant to apply to cities of populations over fifty thousand,[4] many smaller cities, such as Chester, (PA) East St. Louis (IL) and tiny East Liverpool (OH) (once a center of the American ceramics industry), share many features with their larger counterparts. The needs of these smaller cities will also have to be addressed, but in other ways, perhaps through regional strategies at the state level.

These legacy cities have much more than population decline and loss of manufacturing jobs in common. As they have lost their employment base, they have experienced increasingly concentrated poverty and become steadily poorer. Their workforce is less educated and is more likely to be unemployed than elsewhere, while their remaining middle-class residents continue to flee to the suburbs. In a phenomenon sometimes called "sprawl without growth," new developments proliferate at the exurban fringe of their metropolitan areas, while the core continues to hollow out. Many of the counties surrounding these cities are seeing population loss as well, although usually lagging behind that of their central cities.[5] A shrinking population means weak housing demand; rents and house prices are low and vacancy rates are high. As property values decline and the population becomes poorer, municipal revenues shrink and the cities' ability to provide services and maintain their infrastructure deteriorates. More and more houses, storefronts, and factories are abandoned by their owners, while vacant lots proliferate and entire blocks become vacant. These common features need to inform and shape the policies described later in this chapter.

These cities also share powerful assets for future revitalization: important universities and medical research centers, such as Carnegie Mellon University in Pittsburgh or the Cleveland Clinic, while fifty-five Fortune 500 companies are headquartered in these cities, as well as many others in their suburbs. Riverfronts and lakefronts, magnificent park systems such as Philadelphia's Fairmount Park or Forest Park in St. Louis, and a wealth of historic neighborhoods all represent quality-of-life assets. Yet all of these assets, which are important not only to the cities but to their metros and the entire nation, are being undermined by sustained decline—in many instances fostered by state policies that affect the state's older cities adversely and unequally.

Federal and state policies need to be tailored not only to account for the significant differences between legacy cities but also the difference between these cities and those that are growing and attracting private investment—older cities like Boston and San Francisco as well as Sun Belt cities like Phoenix and Houston—reflecting the fundamental difference between the temporary setbacks in the wake of the Great Recession and the systemic, sustained decline of the legacy cities.

Differences

Despite similarities, major variations exist in the economic condition and fiscal capacity of these cities, as well as their unique assets and opportunities. So while the common picture of decline and poverty is shared by all cities in transition, great variation exists among these places both in terms of degree of decline and evidence of revival. Although Pittsburgh has lost over half its peak population, it has begun to spawn a new high-tech economy, building on its educational and medical centers, as described in Sabina Deitrick's case study, "Pittsburgh Goes High Tech." On indicators such as its unemployment rate or percentage of residents with college diplomas, Pittsburgh is not far from national averages. Refugees from the automobile industry are creating new green industries in Detroit, while the Washington Avenue corridor in St. Louis and Cleveland's Warehouse District are becoming vibrant downtown neighborhoods.

One size policy does *not* fit all. Federal resources must be directed to these cities, but with the flexibility to respond to their wide variation in assets and weaknesses. States, which will play the pivotal role in these cities' resurgence, need to incentivize growth, target resources, and support strategic investments based on local decisions and priorities. In framing sound federal and state policies, it is important to recognize these variations, and to be able to design approaches and target resources in ways that build on the assets that exist, while being realistic about the constraints.

The Policy Challenge

Although population and job loss have been realities in legacy cities and their regions since the 1960s or earlier, it is only recently that many of these places have begun to recognize their condition and grapple with those realities. This long-term pattern of denial not only reflects the political obstacles facing those seeking to tackle this issue but also the extent to which growth and success are all but synonymous in American society, and the absence of a model that could accommodate both shrinkage and success as anything other than contradictions. Nevertheless, localities are moving forward with innovative practices, making well-developed, tailored state and federal public policies needed even more to support these nascent local efforts.

Youngstown, Ohio's 2010 plan, described in Hunter Morrison's case study, "Youngstown 2010: America's First Shrinking Cities Plan," and the *Re-Imagining a Sustainable Cleveland* initiative, described in the case study by Bobbi Reichtell, are two examples of the pioneering work taking place. In 2010, following Dave Bing's election as mayor, Detroit embarked on the Detroit Works Project, a comprehensive effort to plan around what is coming to be known as the "shrinking city paradigm," addressing not only land use and environmental policies but also schools, workforce, and economic development issues, in order to build a comprehensive strategy for the city's future. These three cities are not alone. Many other cities, including Dayton, Rochester, and Flint, are looking closely at themselves and coming up with creative strategies to reconfigure land areas, engage anchor institutions, revitalize neighborhoods, and rebuild local economies undermined by recession and deindustrialization. Among many examples, we can cite Rebuilding Together Dayton, a strategy to stabilize neighborhoods and prevent further abandonment; and the Evergreen Cooperative in Cleveland, which is leveraging the demand for supplies and products from that city's anchor institutions to create employee-controlled green business ventures.

These are but a few of the initiatives that recognize the unique opportunities and assets that legacy cities offer. Such strategies, however, are still relatively uncommon. With additional state and federal support—not necessarily financial—far more innovative local practices are likely to emerge.

Local Constraints and Policy Implications

While these cities and their leaders have begun to plan for a different future, the scope of the obstacles facing them has vast implications for state and federal policies. These obstacles include limited financial resources, weak regulatory and institutional tools, and inadequate capacity.

Financial Resources

Change is expensive. Investments must be made that may not pay off for years or decades. At the same time, local governments today, faced with declining revenues, find it difficult to finance even the basic public services that their citizens and businesses need. Local governments, CDC partners, and other local participants will need additional financial resources if they are to be able to implement ambitious, difficult transformational plans. In distressed cities and their metros, where markets are weak and private investment is limited or all but nonexistent, additional public sector resources are essential to jump start the market and reverse the downward economic spiral, yet it is unclear where these revenues will come from.

Regulatory and Institutional Tools

While many legal changes have taken place in the past decade, including abandoned property law reform in Indiana, New Jersey, and Pennsylvania changes to tax-foreclosure laws in Ohio, Michigan, and Georgia and land bank legislation in

Ohio and Michigan, many cities still lack the regulatory and legal tools they need to enable them to control their environment and foster a healthier future. These may include the ability to enforce strong planning and land use controls and gain control over problem properties in a timely fashion, as well as the regulatory flexibility to allow them to implement programs and offer targeted incentives efficiently and effectively. Regional cooperation within metros is hindered not only by the history of municipal fragmentation but also in some states, by the absence of institutional vehicles such as regional planning agencies or councils of government through which cooperation could be fostered.

Capacity

Without the capacity to plan and implement effective strategies and make sound data-based decisions, even the strongest legal and institutional tools may fail. Legacy cities, particularly small ones, have far too few effective leaders and capable, well-trained managers and professional staffs to address their challenges. They will need help to foster stronger leaders, build the capacity of existing personnel, and recruit and train new people with the skills and commitment the cities need, along with technical assistance for specialized tasks that may be beyond local capacity.

A growing number of local leaders understand the relationship between long-term, large-scale population loss and the challenges facing their cities, and are ready to confront those challenges. The role of state and federal government to address local constraints so cities can build on their strengths is critical. While ultimately it will be the cities' residents who will rebuild their communities, they cannot do it alone. State and federal governments have a stake in the future of legacy cities and should provide them with the tools and support to change legal framework and build a better future. At the same time, local participants must do their part not only by developing their resources and capacity but by finding the will to use those resources for change.

Structural Weaknesses in Policy Making[6]

The weaknesses in the policy-making structure at both the state and federal levels are deep-seated and long-standing; however, the time has never been more right to adopt new ways of doing business. Both state and federal policy making have been beset with at least three major structural problems: the absence of coherent and comprehensive strategies, lack of coordination among different federal and state agencies, and failure to maintain a sustained commitment to these cities. While the political will to address urban regeneration has fluctuated over the years along with the level of resources devoted to those efforts, the reasons for the lack of impact from federal and state initiatives go beyond those issues.

Absence of a Coherent Strategy

Both state and federal programs have typically been reactions to problems, targeted at symptoms rather than at the root causes of urban decline or neighborhood deterioration. Moreover, since the 1949 Housing Act, urban revitalization and subsidized low-income housing production have been conflated in federal policy, to the disadvantage of both. While providing lower-income housing is an important federal responsibility, it is a very different goal from that of rebuilding the social and economic vitality of cities, which is undermined by the concentration of poverty in those cities, and will ultimately come from the ability of the public and private sectors to create a healthy housing market for people at all income levels.

Similarly, few of the activities pursued by state governments, or by legacy cities themselves, over the past decades have been grounded in a strategic framework designed to build a stronger future city. States and cities have scattered billions in investments not only in new housing but in new schools and public facilities, without weaving them into larger strategies or targeting them to areas with strong assets for future revitalization.

None of these investments has taken into account the implications of sustained population loss—that is the number of housing units, schools, storefronts, and, indeed, the amount of land needed by these cities' shrinking populations was far smaller than what was needed in 1920 or 1950. Not only have policies that scattered resources thinly across an entire city or region had little impact but they have foreclosed opportunities to preserve areas that could still be productive and vital.

Lack of Coordination

Perhaps less visible, but equally significant, is the lack of coordination among the many federal and state agencies and programs whose activities affect the future of older cities, such as departments of economic development, environment, transportation, jobs, and family services. The problems of coordination are conceptual, structural, and mechanical. Coordination of multiple programs across different agencies is difficult even when they agree that they have a common goal and mission; many programs, however, that may have a direct and potentially powerful effect on the future of urban areas and metro regions are not viewed by their managers as "urban programs." Lack of coordination at the state level, where many of the federal policies are executed, exacerbates these problems.

Failure to Sustain Commitment

Administrations and legislatures come and go, and short attention spans are typical of many governmental systems. However, some state and federal programs appear to be frozen in time, going on year after year with little or no change, while others are short-lived and die before they have been implemented sufficiently to make a difference. Comparing those programs that survive for decades with those that come and go raises a troubling issue. The programs that survive year in and year out tend to be the broadest and least targeted ones.[7] Tightly focused or narrowly targeted programs have smaller constituencies and are far more susceptible to being cut in times of financial constraint or political change. Such programs, however, are often more effective within their particular compass than loosely defined, thinly spread programs like CDBG, which has gradually devolved into a form of benign patronage largely devoid of strategic purpose. If targeted programs are to be truly effective, however, they must be sustained. The process of restoring cities in transition to vitality will be a protracted one, which will require sustained support rather than one-shot infusions of money. Cities must be able to depend upon a long-term public commitment if they are to carry out the kind of strategic planning needed to ground successful transformative efforts. The ability to sustain commitment to such programs, once enacted, however, may be a more difficult political challenge than the ability to initiate such programs. Policy makers should look to a set of "principles of change," such as those articulated here, as a roadmap to help put policies into a more objective, analytical framework.

Maximizing Prosperity in Legacy Cities: The Central Role of State Policy[8]

Despite—or because of—the structural weaknesses in their policy making, states already play a central role in shaping legacy cities' predicaments. As a correlative, state policy reforms must maximize the potential for them to succeed and help set them on a path toward recovery. Using Ohio as an example,[9] this section addresses why these cities are critical to their states and why states should play strong, creative roles in addressing their future.

First, state governments need to address the future of their cities, because the cities' health is critical to the state's future growth. Ohio's economy, for instance, is driven by its major metros, each made up of a large central city and its surrounding suburban communities, and the exurban villages and rural areas that are home to people who commute to work in urban settings. Ohio's seven largest metro areas are home to 71 percent of its population, 76 percent of its jobs, and 80 percent of the state's gross domestic product.

While the core cities make up only part of that base, metropolitan prosperity closely tracks the health of the central city. A 2007 Brookings Institution study reviewed changes in metropolitan area employment, wages, and gross metropolitan product from 1990 to 2000 and found that central city weakness and metropolitan area weakness went hand in hand. Of sixty-four weak central cities in the study, forty-six were in weak metros; and only three were in strong metros. Not surprisingly, city strength and metropolitan strength also correlate: of fifty-seven strong cities, forty-two were in strong metros and only two were in weak metros.[10]

Studies have also found a correlation between central city strength and broader metropolitan prosperity, including a close relationship between city and suburban job growth.[11] Three different studies have shown that central city decline and wide gaps between the economic health of cities and suburbs are linked to slow income growth in metro areas.[12]

Second, a legacy of these cities' collective history is that they contain the lion's share of the institutions—particularly universities and medical centers—likely to play an important role in future economic growth. Indeed, state and local ability to capitalize on urban assets may be the single most important factor determining whether many places will revive. Legacy cities' major anchor institutions are economic engines; their financial, intellectual, and creative resources are likely to drive these cities' and regions' future economies.

These cities house major state and private universities as well as important medical care, education, and research facilities. Other institutions, such as churches, museums and arts centers, libraries and the like, also play a role, on a more modest but still significant scale.[13] The Cleveland Clinic has spun off twenty-four companies over the course of the last ten years and has partnered with neighboring anchor institutions to form BioEnterprise, a business-formation initiative aimed at strengthening Cleveland's bioscience sector. Similarly, the University of Cincinnati Medical Center accounts for more than fifty thousand jobs and generates approximately four billion dollars in economic activity in its region every year.[14] Cleveland alone still contains the headquarters of eleven of the nation's Fortune 500 companies.

Anchor institutions make outsized contributions to these cities' economies, but they also generate quality of life and neighborhood development, because they understand that these cities must be attractive and compelling places to live and do business in order to attract the most talented professors, physicians, and entrepreneurs. In contrast to past eras, when economic development in these older industrial cities was driven by extractive resources or natural harbors, today the quality of life that cities offer their present and prospective residents has become a critical factor in defining the economic development potential of the city and the region.[15]

Third, states are *already* deeply involved in the future of older cities. Through investments in state universities and medical centers, states will inevitably have a critical impact on the future of the cities where those facilities are located. States' decisions can determine whether and how those institutions will contribute to revitalization and economic growth in the cities or whether they will sit on the sidelines. Most states also pump billions of dollars each year into legacy cities through school aid, municipal aid, public assistance, and workforce development funds, much of it dictated by the poverty of these cities and their residents. These are investments, and states need to maximize their return. At present, however, state investments in cities are scatter-shot and often at cross-purposes. For instance, Ohio has invested $27 million of state brownfields funds in twenty-two Cleveland-area sites as well as $12.8 million in Cleveland-area institutions through a state program geared toward fostering innovative research with commercialization potential (Third Frontier); at the same time, by failing to support key inner-city transportation and infrastructure repairs, the state undermines its overall investment strategy.[16] A more targeted investment strategy would reap far greater results

Fourth, states have historically tilted the playing field against central cities, so it is not unreasonable to ask the state to restore the balance. Cities are creatures of the state. State laws, regulations, and policies establish the ground rules for what cities can and cannot do and set the stage for how and where development occurs. State tax laws determine whether cities and townships compete or collaborate. Many states have put in place tax policies, resource allocation decisions, business-location incentives, and other policies that have stacked the deck against central cities, investing resources in ways that have weakened the cities' ability to compete and compounded their problems, including:

- Perpetuating fragmented local governance, encouraging suburbs to compete with cities for businesses and economic development rather than cooperate for the greatest overall benefit to the region
- Creating fiscal systems that are often weighted against cities and older suburbs
- Distributing gasoline tax revenues in ways that shortchange cities, directing funding to highway construction and reducing funding for transit options
- Allocating low income housing tax credits in ways that reinforce concentrated poverty
- Creating cumbersome state tax foreclosure laws that foster speculation and hinder redevelopment and the productive re-use of existing sites
- Maintaining economic development funding programs that incentivize greenfield development over reuse of urban sites[17]

A 2007 Brookings report commented, "Unfortunately, over the past half century state policies and practices have generally not been favorable to urban areas. At best, these communities have been treated with benign neglect, with state programs and investments focused predominately on managing urban decline, as opposed to stimulating economic recovery. At worst, state policies and investments have actually worked against cities, facilitating the migration of people and jobs (and the tax base they provide) to the metropolitan fringe, while reinforcing the deterioration of the core."[18]

While states have made some investments in smart, focused metropolitan transportation projects, such as the $20 million in Ohio recovery funds allocated to the "Opportunity Corridor" in Cleveland, and $25 million for a streets project near Nationwide Children's Hospital in Columbus—linking transportation funds to an anchor institution—the systematic slighting of Ohio's cities is evidenced recently by the distribution of stimulus funds provided by the American Recovery and Reinvestment Act "like peanut butter" to almost every one of the state's eighty-eight counties rather than targeting resources to the metropolitan economic engines. While these practices do not absolve city governments and institutions from their share of responsibility for their current condition, the fact remains that they are operating on a playing field tilted against them by the state.

Fifth, local government fragmentation puts cities at a disadvantage, causing systemic fiscal imbalances that promote decentralization and sprawl. States can provide the leadership, incentives, and policy changes to undo this fragmentation. Research shows that more fragmented regions tend to have greater inequities in local tax bases: The Cleveland area is high in both fiscal inequality as well as governmental fragmentation.[19] Disparities are made worse by the fact that residents of incorporated Ohio cities pay a disproportionate share of the cost of the services county governments provide to suburban and rural townships. A 2002 study of Lucas County, home of Toledo, found that residents of incorporated areas paid up to fourteen million dollars per year to subsidize services to unincorporated townships.[20] Thus, with high service demands but lower tax bases, Ohio cities must constantly struggle to provide good schools, adequate infrastructure, and quality services without overburdening their taxpayers, putting them at a competitive disadvantage with outer jurisdictions in attracting and retaining residents and businesses.

Yet, the cities and their metros are interdependent, and their futures are closely linked. The state needs to step in to level the playing field between cities and townships and foster inter-municipal and regional cooperation to benefit both cities and their surrounding metro areas.

Sixth, cities simply lack the resources to solve their problems. Their loss of population and jobs has rendered them disproportionately poor, starved of the fiscal resources they need to provide decent public services, let alone invest for future growth. *In theory, population loss in itself should not mean impoverishment, but the particular dynamics of population loss in older industrial cities mean that it all but inevitably does.* As manufacturing jobs have left, people with limited formal education have found it increasingly difficult to find work that pays a living wage, while young people and those with competitive skills and education increasingly have left the cities, moving to areas offering greater opportunities on the coasts or in the Sun Belt. This has led to a vicious cycle. As cities lose population, the people who remain behind are poorer, less likely to be part of the workforce, and more dependent on services provided by municipal and county government. Additionally, the proliferation of vacant properties increases themunicipal cost burden for police, fire, and other services. Boarding up and maintaining properties in just three neighborhoods cost Cleveland more than $35 million in lost taxes and extra services in 2006. Dayton lost or spent twelve million dollars in dealing with vacancy and abandonment.[21]

Paradoxically, it is expensive to be a poor, distressed city. As the real estate market becomes steadily weaker, cities must provide ever-larger subsidies, through direct financial support or tax concessions, to attract development that they hope will reverse the tide. At the same time, the income and property tax bases available to finance services or offer incentives are steadily diminishing, and the ability of the city to provide even a minimum threshold level of services is impaired. Even though states are also in difficult fiscal situations, they have more resources on hand than their distressed cities, while many constructive changes can be implemented at little or no additional cost.

Finally, as states cast off the shackles of old policies that are holding our cities back and generate policies that leverage local innovation, they can also be proactive with the federal government. As we have discussed, the most carefully considered federal policies can be neutralized or undone by state policies that conflict with the federal policy goals. The prolonged crisis in which these cities find themselves demands that federal and state actions leverage one another, acting symbiotically to ensure the maximum "bang for the buck."

Similarly, states must position themselves to be genuine partners to the federal government, not merely more lobbying entities, by building local capacity to utilize federal programs and resources effectively, developing their own models for change, and encouraging innovative local practices. States should work to shape the federal government's approach on priorities that matter to them, such as redefining the meaning of a sustainable community, getting funds earmarked for land banks, and emphasizing the need for multijurisdictional land use and transportation planning. Programs in each of these categories are discussed in greater detail below. States should take advantage of the Obama administration's proactive approach to governing and compete aggressively for available federal funds. States' efforts to leverage federal action cannot be mere rhetoric. To make their actions meaningful, local, regional, and state leaders should join forces to forge a united front and articulate a clear vision for federal action in these areas.

Reframing and Aligning Federal Policies Toward Legacy Cities

While the federal government plays a more limited regulatory and institutional role than state government, federal financial resources can have a strong influence over the ways in which states exercise their regulatory and institutional powers and direct their discretionary resources, and over the ways in which local governments pursue regeneration activities. Thus, even where the federal government may not have direct responsibility, regulatory authority, or enforcement power, it can play an important role in fostering the tools that are needed to build stronger cities.

These cities need to be the focus of distinct federal strategies addressing their particular circumstances, rather than generic approaches grounded in a generalized notion of urban revitalization. This is not to suggest that no federal resources should be directed to the more successful cities, such as Boston or Chicago, which have their share of challenges and severely distressed neighborhoods. Strategies for change in strong market cities, however, are fundamentally different from those that best fit legacy cities. Federal policies and programs should reflect those differences, although targeting legacy cities raises political issues. Politicians and others in those cities may see themselves as being placed in a policy "ghetto" defined by their distress. At the same time, these cities are far less than a majority of the nation's population or metropolitan areas, although historically they constitute the country's economic backbone and source of innovation, and retain significant assets for the future.

The centrality of state policy in shaping the future of these cities makes it even more important that federal policies maximize constructive state action, leveraging reforms in areas from fiscal policy to governance, from workforce and infrastructure to regional development and land reuse. Federal policy can directly or indirectly influence state policies in several different ways:

- Neutralize or overcome entrenched traditions that have become cultural impediments to change, such as resistance to operating cross-jurisdictionally, deep-seated belief in local control, and long-standing practices of allocating public funds without regard to need or merit
- Mitigate these entrenched attitudes and practices by encouraging the targeting of resources, rewarding innovative governance and service delivery, and promoting cross-jurisdictional planning
- Incentivize creative state programming, such as state cross-agency legacy cities initiatives
- Create competitive advantages for cities and metros that will level the playing field by leveraging local and regional assets.
- Prioritize neighborhood stabilization in market-ready areas

In this age of a more activist federal policy stance toward urban and metropolitan areas, unless new federal policies simultaneously affect cities and their metropolitan areas, they will be far less effective in changing economic conditions and building stronger legacy cities. While this chapter focuses on recommendations for new federal programs that specifically target these cities, new programs of broader applicability as well as existing programs can be explicitly recrafted to further change in legacy cities as well.

Principles for Federal and State Policy Reform

Jump-starting the process by which legacy cities forge new economies and new physical configurations demands both new policies and better alignment of federal policies, state policies, and local practices. While perfect alignment is impossible to achieve, even incremental changes will not happen by accident, but must be pursued systematically and intentionally. State and federal policy should be crafted so that they can respond flexibly to local conditions and engender sustainable growth practices.

Five Principles for Change

Toward that end, federal, state, and local policy and practices should advance five principles that are crucial building blocks for change:

Make strategic investments

Investments need to be strategic, targeted, and prioritized. Those investments that are not targeted, given the limited resources available, may seem to benefit everyone, but in reality, they benefit no one, because they are too scattered and too limited to catalyze change or foster sustainable communities. Public-sector decisions should be market- as well as need-driven to attract private-sector investment and lead to sustainable economic growth, thus ultimately generating a greater return both financially and qualitatively for the state, its localities, and their residents. This is critical in light of today's scarce resources and budget constraints.

Build capacity to institutionalize reforms

Urban leaders need to develop new ways of thinking about land use, and apply new tools to make informed decisions about resources. This is highly demanding, in cities that have often lost much of their civic and political capacity. Cities will need to cultivate and support strong leaders, capable managers, and savvy practitioners to successfully utilize complex tools to develop sustainable growth strategies.

Advance governance reform to empower these cities and their regions

Most legacy cities are so interwoven with their surrounding cities, villages, and townships that their municipal boundaries seem little more than an historical artifact. The same economic problems confronting central cities are spilling over to many suburbs, particularly in the inner ring closest to the city. Adoption of governance reform and other new collaborative measures formally recognizes the shared challenges and possibilities facing jurisdictions, acknowledges that these jurisdictions cannot succeed alone, and encourages regions to jointly develop effective policies and programs.

Leverage the cities' unique assets and innovation capacity
Reflecting their historic roles, legacy cities often contain major educational and health care institutions—known as "anchor institutions"—as well as industry clusters, philanthropic institutions based on bygone industrialists' generosity, and natural amenities such as waterfronts. Many of these assets have national or international significance. Their presence in these cities allows them to make contributions that can disproportionately benefit the entire city and region.

Reshape disinvested areas for alternative uses
Long-term land reconfiguration requires the ability and will to distinguish those parts of the city where market strength can be built from areas that may offer in the future other economic development opportunities, and, finally, from areas that have no realistic development potential in the foreseeable future. This last category may be a relatively small area in some cities but may represent one-third or more of the total land area of others. Maximizing control of disinvested areas allow a city to plan alternative land uses that are consistent with the city's plan and the community's interests.

Policy Recommendations

Examples of state and federal policy recommendations[22] organized around these principles are offered below.

Make Strategic Investments to Bolster Stable Areas

Many of the strongest neighborhoods in legacy cities are under threat. These areas urgently need help to reverse the destabilization caused by declining property values, foreclosures, deteriorating public infrastructure, and threats to the neighborhood's quality of life. Targeting the vacant boarded-up properties in such neighborhoods for rehabilitation and reuse is critical to any stabilization effort, since their presence can have a particularly destabilizing effect on adjacent properties, and on the neighborhood as a whole.

As areas are stabilized, and as a city's larger reconfiguration strategy advances, long-term strategies designed to further strengthen each neighborhood cluster become more critical. These can include transit improvements, developing infill housing to increase densities within some neighborhoods in order to make transit more feasible, and reinforcing neighborhood commercial nodes and employment centers. Federal and state governments should support these locally-driven activities, complementing strategic efforts already underway based on plans to distinguish areas with strong market potential from areas to be greened or held for future development.

Channel State and Federal Resources to Support Locally-targeted Neighborhood Initiatives

States should establish targeted neighborhood revitalization strategies to direct their investments in housing, school construction, transportation, and other areas to locally- designated market-viable neighborhoods in order to advance local revitalization strategies. Similarly, most federal and state neighborhood revitalization programs should be targeted at viable but threatened neighborhoods rather than at the most deeply disinvested areas. Funding should be directed to viable neighborhood clusters, tailoring them to each city's distinctive local characteristics, while helping them build their capacity to lead local initiatives focusing on rehabilitation and reuse of existing structures. Programs should provide technical assistance to support local efforts to implement their revitalization strategies, making sure investments are made in strategic ways that will strengthen the vitality and market strength of those areas and offer viable alternatives to continued car-dependent development at the metropolitan perimeter.

Federal policy initiatives can influence state and local strategies by redirecting resources to preserving viable neighborhoods, such as upgrading private rental housing in stable neighborhoods, including restructuring the Low Income Housing Tax Credit to focus on upgrading existing housing rather than creating new units in areas of rental-housing surplus.

While categorizing areas as worthy or unworthy of particular investments is fraught with political dangers, states need to show leadership and make hard decisions, targeting resources on the basis of rigorous analysis of market and other conditions and prioritizing place-based redevelopment strategies that build on institutional and locational assets, in tandem with local targeting of neighborhood investments.

Adopt Clear Federal Definitions and Standards for Sustainability in Cities Losing Population

In a context where "growing smaller but stronger" is the ultimate goal of legacy cities,[23] sustainability of their economies and physical environments takes on a different meaning than it does in other places that are balancing continued population growth with dwindling natural resources. A revised definition of sustainability, rooted in the reality and the challenges of these cities, should be embedded in every relevant federal program and should explicitly create opportunities for strategic investments in these cities that make the natural environment, including open space, air, and water quality, central to their regeneration.[24]

Execute Cross-Agency Programs to Model Emerging Federal Cross-Agency Programs.

New federal-level cross-agency collaboration between EPA, DOT, and HUD can set a standard for similar efforts at the state level to further cost savings, more rational decision making, and increased programmatic efficiency. Federal policies can encourage such efforts by funneling part of the funding designated for oversight of new federal programs like the Sustainable Communities grant or our proposed "Race to the Top" Urban Policy Initiative through state agencies, requiring cross-agency collaboration as a condition of using funds. States should instigate "bottom-up" programs to reinforce cross-agency approaches such as Pennsylvania's Community Action Teams (CATs), under which state government offers one-stop support for catalytic revitalization projects identified by local public- and private-sector leaders. These cross-agency programs can lead or support local investment strategies.

Prioritize Federal Transportation Funds to Link Land Use and Transportation, "Fix It First" Activities, and Transit Funding

Reauthorization of the federal transportation bill provides an opportunity to benefit legacy cities by amending the federally mandated transportation planning process to reward multijurisdictional plans linking land use and transportation and set aside funds for "fix it first" infrastructure improvement projects or transit projects likely to generate significant economic development benefits. Federal transportation policy should require states to work in partnership with local leaders who would identify local priorities and provide technical assistance to help cities and metros identify

areas targeted for investment. Investments that connect vital neighborhoods with transportation programs through aligned federal and state policies will have greater impact, as well as encourage regional collaboration.

Build Capacity to Institutionalize Reform and Ensure Long-Term Change

Lack of capacity encompasses a variety of problems, ranging from weak leadership to lack of technical capacity—both in terms of the number of people and their skills—difficulty framing strategies and taking effective action, and lack of solid information for decision-making.

Modernize State Statutes to Offer More Flexible Planning and Zoning Tools at Both Local and Multijurisdictional Levels

Many states have antiquated planning and zoning laws out of sync with changing demands of city and regional planning. Land use regulation needs to be more closely linked to comprehensive planning, and inter-municipal and regional co-operation and coordination in planning and land use needs to be encouraged to establish comprehensive planning and zoning policies that successfully stimulate and guide growth. States should create task forces to review and reframe their land use policies and rules, particularly as they affect older cities and their metros.

Examples of state and federal policy recommendations organized around these principles are offered below.

Inaugurate a "Race to the Top" Urban Initiative

Modeled on the "race to the top" education initiative, where the Obama administration used federal power to "incite reform," as the *New York Times* columnist David Brooks observed, "without dictating it from the top," this initiative could also offer a "contest" to encourage state policy reforms tied to specific local results, such as building regional economic development strategies based on collaboration with anchor institutions. This approach can be catalytic, allowing states to make fundamental, transformative changes that have been blocked by embedded cultural barriers and preservation of the status quo. By tying funding to results and new ways of doing business, states would be encouraged to direct resources to build local capacity, a step that not only maximizes federal funding but reduces the need for ongoing costly state involvement in local planning and projects. Using federal funding as a lever to overcome state resistance to change and collaboration would be money well spent.

Create State-Level Data Clearinghouses

States should ensure that local governments and their partners have access to the best realistically available data for planning and decision making, including up-to-date economic and housing-market data at the neighborhood or census-tract level, and for tracking the number and location of vacant properties or mapping properties in foreclosure. In partnership with county and local governments and universities, states should create central data clearinghouses to ensure that state resources are spent wisely and effectively and that municipalities have the tools they need for planning.[26] Case Western Reserve University's Northeast Ohio Community and Neighborhood Data for Organizing (NEO-CANDO) data system, which has been recognized as a national model, has helped Cleveland conduct targeted foreclosure outreach and improve planning and targeting of community development resources. With state assistance, other cities could replicate Cleveland's system, tailored to local needs and conditions.[27] As legacy cities develop comprehensive planning strategies, they will need guideposts to help them strategically allocate resources and investments. Sound data-driven decisions can enable leaders to leverage local assets and bolster vital neighborhoods.

Create a Federal Program to Build Local Capacity
Federal planning funds for programs like the HUD Sustainable Communities initiative and others should be used to build local leadership, technical, and managerial capacity. The best-laid plans are wasted if leadership and capacity do not exist to implement them. The federal government can lead in designing programs to address these concerns, including more traditional training and technical assistance activities, as well as initiatives to engage new graduates to work in legacy cities or to "embed" experienced professional staff in those cities for fixed periods.

Advance Governance Reform to Link Cities and Their Regions.

A particular feature of legacy cities' metros is that the cities are more dependent on their regions for achieving prosperity, and the communities that make up the regions are themselves more interdependent, since they share a smaller growth pie. A proactive federal role could help states and regions find the political will to build regional collaborations, which may eventually lead to activities such as regional land use planning and regional economic development plans. This is a particularly important principle in which to get federal, state, local alignment right, since state policies that continue to offer perverse incentives for competition and fragmentation could significantly distort the effects of any federal policy that might try to encourage regional collaboration.

Prioritize State Funding to Jurisdictions Adopting Comprehensive Plans and Strategies Reflecting the Realities of Population Loss and the Need for Land Reconfiguration
Some places, although not all, are eager to adopt new approaches to economic development and land use. By linking state resources to such local strategies, states can incentivize collaboration between older cities and neighboring jurisdictions that share the same problem of too much land for too few people, or encourage strategic redevelopment approaches that stress outcomes linked to larger community and economic development planning, rather than simply put state money into discrete, unrelated transactions.

Enact State Incentives for Shared Services, Inter-municipal and Regional Planning, Joint Taxation Districts, and Where Appropriate, Local Government Consolidation
Regional fragmentation and the division of authority between municipal and county government mean that successful strategies to create stronger cities are likely to require inter-municipal cooperation, such as joint planning and program implementation by adjacent cities, villages, and townships, and city-county cooperation in areas such as land banking. The state should encourage municipalities and counties to share services, coordinate planning and land use activities, or

merge, by making it simpler and less costly to initiate such efforts, and by providing financial incentives, such as enhanced school-facility funding, for communities that undertake serious intergovernmental reforms and engage in meaningful intermunicipal and regional strategic planning.

Reward Collaboration Between Municipalities and Metropolitan Planning Organizations (MPOs) with Federal Incentives

Encouraging collaboration between municipalities and MPOs is a logical federal role—either through direct grants to localities or by tying conditions to state funding, such as the incentives in a "race to the top" initiative or as part of the HUD Sustainable Communities initiative already under way. Federal mechanisms to reward regional collaboration, as well as state policies to encourage coordinated planning, shared services, and mergers, not only unite jurisdictions to confront shared challenges but also augment local and regional capacity, providing forums for civic leaders to exchange ideas, expand dialogues, learn new skills, and collaborate in designing new practices. As metro-level decision making becomes a shared process, municipalities and townships are more likely to make sustainable growth decisions that benefit the entire region, instead of privileging some jurisdictions at the expense of others.

Leverage the Cities' Unique Assets and Innovative Capacity

State and federal policies should leverage these cities' remarkable assets, including anchor institutions such as medical centers and universities; riverbanks and lakefronts, the water resources that once drove industrial location; unique and irreplaceable historic buildings, old-fashioned main streets, and downtowns; and cultural icons such as galleries, concert halls, and museums.

Create State Anchor Institution Transformation Zone Programs

States should use economic development resources to create a network of *anchor institution transformation zones* to incentivize development around urban universities and medical centers. These zones, which would be fewer in number and more systematically targeted than enterprise zones in states like Ohio, would be designated areas surrounding universities and hospitals located in older cities' core areas. The state would offer other incentives for residential and commercial development, while state institutions would be required to target their own investments to maximize economic growth and neighborhood revitalization in their surroundings. These zones should be available to both public and private institutions. Implemented in conjunction with public-sector business-cluster policies (discussed below), they can become drivers of local economic development.[28]

Make Support of Local Business Clusters a Central Theme of Federal Policy. Many legacy cities have identified industry clusters (such as polymers in Akron or biomedical specialties in Cleveland) that build on their pasts, while some states have introduced the concept of cluster growth and development. The federal budget should include planning grants to identify local clusters, providing funds to support a federal clusters research and data-gathering center.[29] States should maximize federal assistance by strengthening workforce intermediaries, for example, to help workers and employers reinforce local business clusters.

Encourage and Support Local Efforts to Utilize Urban Waterfronts as Significant Economic and Quality of Life Assets
States should help localities repurpose their waterfronts as economic and quality-of-life assets with projects that maximize waterfront access. States could reallocate infrastructure funds to remove existing infrastructure blocking the city from the water, or could redirect downtown revitalization funds. In Milwaukee, a freeway, which for years was an ugly barrier between the city and the Milwaukee River, was razed to make way for a now-thriving commercial and residential area. The state made demolition possible by removing the freeway's designation as a "transportation corridor" and contributing funds.[30] Cities like Milwaukee have seen significant growth in commercial development, property values, and tax revenues by turning their water bodies into assets. Fostering such changes may also require additional infrastructure investment, or different ways of integrating developments into a single investment strategy. This strategy leverages local assets and also targets resources strategically.

Legacy cities are already well positioned to develop local business clusters, particularly around universities and medical centers. These institutions are often the cities' largest employers, and they continue in many cases to grow and generate the activity that can attract additional housing development, businesses, jobs, and amenities to an area. To develop robust policies that leverage the unique assets of legacy cities, the cities will have to prioritize and target their investments. Strategic investment in areas surrounding anchor institutions, industry clusters, and natural amenities like waterfronts maximizes the value of investments by building on the city's concentration of assets. Strategies that link different building blocks become powerful instruments of change.

Reshape Disinvested Areas

Urban reconfiguration also takes place through reshaping areas where market demand no longer exists into green areas integrated into the city's fabric, from community gardens and miniparks to urban farms or ecosystem restoration projects. State and federal neighborhood revitalization programs, actualized through strategic investments, work in tandem with programs that reshape disinvested areas for alternative uses. Capacity-building tools, such as comprehensive planning, modernized zoning and planning statutes, and regional collaboration, are crucial to effectively coordinate the complementary processes of strategic investment in vital neighborhoods and creative reuse of disinvested areas.

Enact Statewide Land Bank Legislation and Provide Federal Funds for Their Support

Michigan and Ohio already have strong legislation enabling counties to create viable land banks, while Pennsylvania and New York are actively pursuing similar legislation. Land bank policies at the federal and state levels should complement and reinforce each other. Existing land banks in Michigan's Genesee County and Ohio's Cuyahoga County have demonstrated that well-run land bank entities provide benefits to the city and county far greater than the laissez-faire practice of allowing land and buildings to be held indefinitely by speculators. Where land bank statutes already exist, states should help metropolitan counties create land banks and build their capacity to exercise public control over their land. Where they do not, states should pass legislation that gives counties the ability to acquire, hold, and dispose of properties. Land banks are powerful and multifaceted tools that can target resources strategically to vital areas and encourage planning for alternative uses in disinvested areas, as well cross-jurisdictional collaborative planning. While these land banks are organized to be self-financing in the long run, a modest federal funding stream would provide critically needed capital early in their formation and provide some impetus for passage of land bank statutes in states that have not yet done so. Federal funding would allow new land banks to lay the groundwork for redevelopment, particularly in neighborhoods where vacant properties are concentrated and can be aggregated. Federal funding could also help them undertake the demolition as well as the site preparation needed to make possible green land uses such as urban agriculture. This would help avoid the transactional, "single parcel" approach that has dominated redevelopment in legacy cities in transition, and pave the way for future private-sector activity.

Encourage Collaboration at State and Local Levels to Foster Innovative Planning and Implementation Strategies for Land Reconfiguration

Federal competitive grant programs should be targeted in whole or in part to communities with substantial population losses and large inventories of vacant properties. Through legislation and/or departmental action, the federal government should support the development of strategic regeneration plans and demonstration projects for vacant property renewal in these cities in order to facilitate targeting and leveraging of governmental and nonprofit resources in distressed communities.[31] Federal funding for land banks should be part of a larger effort to encourage meaningful local planning and be linked with other proposed initiatives, such as neighborhood revitalization funding, to target viable neighborhoods, so that local efforts result in coherent rebuilding strategies rather than in piecemeal efforts.[32]

Create an Urban Agriculture and Greening Extension Program Within State University Extension Services

States can promote conversion of vacant and abandoned properties to open and green space by developing an urban extension program to provide municipalities, community groups, urban farmers, and environmental planners with technical support for greening activities such as urban agriculture, storm water management,and ecosystem restoration.[33] While urban agriculture could potentially exist at a scale sufficient to become an economic development as well as food security resource in these places, commercial-scale agriculture is unlikely to be achieved without a support infrastructure linked to processing and distribution networks and without information provided by extension services to urban farmers on soil conditions, crop alternatives, and market opportunities, as well as creative ways to address both the challenges and opportunities unique to agriculture in an urban setting. The state can also provide local governments with information on revising their land use regulations to permit urban agriculture, and help school districts develop agricultural education programs and use locally grown produce to feed their pupils. While some urban agriculture will take place on large vacant properties, looking much like conventional farms except for their urban setting, other models of urban agriculture should also be explored, such as farming that can utilize vacant industrial structures, and aggregated microfarming, where a single operating and distribution network creates economies of scale in farming numerous small, separate properties—a model pioneered in San Francisco and Portland, Oregon.

Conclusion

An ambitious policy agenda has been outlined in this chapter. To accomplish even a fraction of the recommendations laid out here would be great progress. At the same time, the future of these legacy cities still hangs in the balance. While impressive local innovations are emerging, there is little hope for a comprehensive, sustained recovery without state policy reforms and parallel federal policy interventions. This chapter is a call to action to build state and local networks to advocate for these policy reforms and create the policy climate that will enable legacy cities to participate in the global economy.

Notes

1. This chapter draws on prepared under the auspices of a grant from the Rockefeller Foundation to the Greater Ohio Policy Center in 2009–2010. See Mallach and Brachman (2010).
2. See also Katz, Bradley, and Liu (2010).
3. The author of this chapter owes a debt of gratitude to Brookings Senior Fellow, Alan Mallach, with whom she coauthored two papers that form a partial basis for this chapter and whose deep understanding of these issues and great insights helped shape this author's thoughts on this topic. The author also thanks Alison Goebel for her editing assistance and advice.
4. This universe of cities includes at least sixty American cities with a population over fifty thousand in 2000, that have lost over 20 percent of their peak population.
5. Mallach and Brachman (2010a), p.11.
6. This section derives in part from Mallach and Brachman (2010).
7. CDBG, for example, which has survived largely unchanged since 1974, is distributed by formula to 1,177 separate towns, cities, and counties and can be used for almost any purpose plausibly related to benefiting low-income households or reducing slums and blight. While meeting that modest standard, therefore, it can be used for any activity that reflects local political wishes. As a result, it has built a strong national constituency, rather than one concentrated in a single region or type of community.
8. See chapter 4.
9. Due to the unusual number of cities and metropolitan areas in Ohio, this section uses Ohio and its cities, in particular, as prominent examples to illustrate the importance of state policy, but the points can be generalized to include other similarly situated states.
10. Vey (2007), p. 17-19.
11. Hill Brennan (2005), p.4
12. This relationship has been identified in a variety of separate studies; see Vey (2007), p.80.
13. A 2000 study of the economic impact of the Cleveland Museum of Art found that it generated directly and indirectly 656 jobs in the Cleveland region, as well as $20.1 million in annual personal income and $5.2 million in annual state and local government revenues. See Robey and Kleinholtz (2000).
14. Tripp Umbach Consultants (2002).
15. Berube (2007), p.45.
16. Brookings Institution and Greater Ohio (2007), p.17.
17. In Ohio, a minimum acreage requirement in the original design of the state's Job Ready Sites program, designed to develop sites for new businesses, and the scattershot nature of the state's urban enterprise zone program are examples.
18. Brookings Institution Metropolitan Policy Program (2007), p.6.
19. Orfield, Luce, and Ameregis (2008).
20. Hinton and Beazley (2005), p. 5. Available at http://uac.utoledo.edu/Publications/public-service-delivery-fiscal-impact.pdf
21. ReBuild Ohio and Community Research Partners (2008).
22. Greater Ohio & Brookings Institution (2010); Mallach and Brachman (2010a)
23. Mallach and Brachman (2010a)

24. During the 111th Congress, several proposals redefined the meaning of sustainability, while at least one bill addressed the needs of cities in transition by providing funds to cities and their metropolitan areas experiencing large-scale property vacancy and abandonment.
25. Brooks (2010).
26. The office of former Ohio Secretary of State Jennifer Brunner instituted a new website, http://www.sos.state.oh.us/SOS/betterLives.aspx, that tracks some statewide economic data and trends useful to local and regional planning efforts, although it appears not to be particularly place-based or localized except in a few instances, such as the foreclosure and green space data, which are by county.
27. Using a wide range of data sources and data sets, including foreclosure filings, recorded sheriff's deeds, scheduled sheriff sales, water shutoffs, code-enforcement reports, and building data, NEO CANDO's neighborhood data system provides an "early warning system" for at-risk vacant and abandoned properties on a parcel-by-parcel basis for a seventeen-county region. See http://neocando.case.edu.
28. Ohio has over sixty-nine private, four-year colleges; thirteen public universities, with twenty-four branch and regional campuses; and fifteen community colleges and eight technical colleges scattered throughout the state. Many are located in shrinking cities, including Cleveland, Cincinnati, Dayton, and Springfield, to name a few.
29. Introduction of the Strengthening Employment Clusters to Organize Regional Success(SECTORS) Act by Ohio senator Sherrod Brown in 2009 recognized the importance of the labor force, or supply side, of cluster development and offered federal grant support for aggregating worker-training needs by industry and developing post-secondary curricula that match industry demand.
30. New Urban News (2004)
31. A similar recommendation appears in Vey and Austin (2010).
32. In addition to creating new programs, federal policy makers should reexamine and revise current federal programs, such as the Low Income Housing Tax Credit (LIHTC) and CDBG. Current statutory provisions or guidelines may undercut their intended results by, for example, encouraging construction of additional low-income housing in already-saturated weak markets or increasing concentrations of poverty.
33. A model of state support for development of local food systems can be found in the Illinois Food, Farms, and Jobs Act of 2007, which established the Illinois Local and Organic Food and Farm Task Force to study and recommend strategies that the state could take in the development of local food systems. It included identifying land preservation and acquisition opportunities for local and organic agriculture in rural, suburban, and urban areas and explored financial incentives, technical support, and training necessary to help farmers to transition to local, organic, and specialty crop production, and other strategies.

Bibliography

Freeway Razing Sets Stage for $250 Million in Development. 2004. *New Urban News.*

Berube, A. 2007. *MetroNation.* Washington, DC: Brookings Institution.

Brooks, D. 2010. "Race to Sanity." *New York Times.*

Greater Ohio Policy Center, Brookings Institution. 2010. *Restoring Prosperity: Transforming Ohio's Communities for the Next Economy.* Columbus: Greater Ohio Policy Center.

Hill, E. W., & Brennan, J. 2005. "America's Central Cities: The Location of Work." *Journal of the American Planning Association*, 71-74.

Hinton, H., & Beazley, M. 2002. *Analysis of the Fiscal Impact of Public Service Delivery Practices in Lucas County, Ohio.* Toledo: Univerity of Toledo Urban Affairs Center.

Katz, B., Bradley, J., & Liu, A. 2010. *Delivering the Next Economy: The States Step Up.* Washington, DC: Brookings Institution.

Mallach, A., & Brachman, L. (2010a). *Ohio Cities at at Turning Point: Finding a Way Forward.* Washington, DC: Brookings Institution.

———. 2010. *Shaping Federal Policies Toward Cities in Transition: A Policy Brief.* Columbus: Greater Ohio Policy Center.

Orfield, M., Luce, T., & Ameregis. 2008. *Northeast Ohio Metropatterns.* Ameregis.

ReBuild Ohio, Community Research Partners. (2008). *$60 Million and Counting: The Cost of Vacant and Abandoned Properties to Eight Ohio Cities.* Columbus: ReBuild Ohio.

Robey, J. E., & Kleinholtz, J. (2000). *Economic Impact of the Cleveland Museum of Art: A Tourism Perspective.* Cleveland: Economic Research Department, Greater Cleveland Growth Association.

Tripp Umbach Consultants. (2002). *University of Cincinnati Medical Center Economic Impact.* Cincinnati: University of Cincinnati.

Vey, J. 2007. *Restoring Prosperity, The State Role in Revitalizing America's Older Industrial Cities.* Washington, DC: Brookings Institution.

Vey, J., & Austin, J. 2010. *The Next Economy: Rebuilding Auto Communities and Older Industrial Metros in the Great Lakes Region.* Washington, DC: Brookings Institution.

Case Study: Building a Coalition to Pass a State Land Bank Statute

Lavea Brachman, Greater Ohio Policy Center

In February 2010, the Greater Ohio Policy Center—a statewide nonprofit think tank, advocacy, and stakeholder involvement group—issued a pathbreaking report, *Restoring Prosperity to Ohio: Transforming Ohio's Communities for the Next Economy*, in partnership with a national think tank, the Brookings Institution Metropolitan Policy Program, that laid out a comprehensive blueprint for state policy reform and made thirty-nine recommendations aimed at transforming Ohio's metropolitan areas to better compete in the next economy. Within two months of the report's release, Ohio's General Assembly (GA) passed one of the report's cornerstone policy recommendations, providing for countywide land banks in counties with a population of sixty thousand or more—essentially covering all sixteen major metropolitan areas in the state. Cuyahoga County (Cleveland) already had a land bank, since the GA passed the bill in April 2010, three counties have set up land banks—Lucas (Toledo), Montgomery (Dayton) and Mahoning (Youngstown) Counties—while at least two more are seriously investigating it, including Franklin (Columbus) and Hamilton (Cincinnati). *What is the importance of the land bank? How did the Greater Ohio Policy Center, which was instrumental in getting the land bank legislation passed, accomplish this task? And what are lessons for future state-level policy making?*

What is the Land Bank's Critical Role and How Is It Formed?

A land bank is a critical tool in a state like Ohio, where the vast majority of the cities are experiencing significant population loss and associated high property vacancy and abandonment rates—as high as 20 to 30 percent in some neighborhoods. A land bank provides counties with the ability to acquire vacant and abandoned properties—primarily but not exclusively through tax foreclosure—and hold and dispose of the properties in ways that strategically promote development and are responsive to market activities. A land bank has the additional value of acting as a repository for properties unattractive to developers. The land bank has the power to hold and efficiently manage and maintain properties pending reclamation, rehabilitation, and reutilization, thus reducing the chance of properties languishing and further blighting their neighborhoods. Additionally, a land bank can also undertake countywide land use planning to maximize single-vacant-property reuse and area- and neighborhood-wide redevelopment potential. In Ohio, land banks are a separate nonprofit governed by a board comprised of statutorily identified local representatives, but Ohio's county treasurers play a uniformly critical role, because they hold the power to foreclose on properties.

How Was Passage of the Land Bank Statute Accomplished?

Strong Local Partnerships. A nonprofit advocacy organization, The Greater Ohio Policy Center, established a land bank advisory group early on that developed into a strong network of partnerships with key local leaders around the state and deployed that network strategically, particularly county treasurers in the key urban counties, to advance the land bank cause. Ohio has traditionally been a fragmented state, with eight major cities and metropolitan areas that—while in decline for almost three decades (according to traditional measures of economic vitality and growth)—still retain unique cultural and economic identities as well as a cadre of separate business and civic community leaders. So successfully passing legislation requires support from multiple metropolitan areas in order to demonstrate its relevance across regions and the political spectrum. Local advocates from the land bank advisory group came to Columbus, the state capital, to testify multiple times before different GA committees about the importance of this tool to revitalizing their cities. Some of the strongest supporters in Greater Ohio's network were county treasurers, who tapped their state representatives. These "inside game" players advocated for the bill through channels the nonprofit could not itself access and galvanized local support that the representatives needed.

Narrowly Scoped Statutory Jurisdiction. Responding to concerns about potentially unknown financial and staff burdens that could arise from implementation of this new tool as well as to a perception that this tool was primarily targeted at the urban areas, application of the statute's scope was narrowed. Surprisingly, despite Ohio's multiple metro regions and urban cores, the GA's leadership positions are traditionally dominated by legislators with rural roots, due to the proliferation of small-unit governments, called "townships." Therefore, while a county's decision to to operate a land bank under the statute is completely permissive—and thus it would have made the most sense to advocate for passage of a land bank statute applicable to all Ohio's eighty-eight counties—emerging objections from the "rural" legislators (or the nonurban area representatives representing counties outside the immediate metros) caused advocates to construct the legislation to apply only to counties with certain threshold population levels, thereby hoping to ensure passage.[1] In doing so, advocates sacrificed some quality for expediency, at least for the time being; however, on the positive side, this left the door open later to make statutory modifications that would enlarge the land bank's scope in several ways.

Existing Land Bank Models. The neighboring state of Michigan had passed a land bank statute in 2003 that provided a compelling model for Ohio, because of Michigan's proximity as well as its similarities (despite an intense sports rivalry!) in governance structure, population demographics, and political composition to Ohio. National experts could be brought in who talked about the success of the land bank in Michigan and other places and its relevance for Ohio's cities. Also, Cuyahoga County (Cleveland) had managed to get its own land bank statute passed the previous year, which paved the way and piloted the concept for the rest of the state, although due to the fact that it was not fully functioning yet and to Cuyahoga's dominant urban politics and culture, its fledgling land bank was not viewed universally in Ohio as the best statewide model. Nevertheless, these models collectively set clear examples the financial requirements of land banks, the savings generated by land banking, what responsibilities land banks do and do not undertake, and how land banking can stabilize distressed neighborhoods.

Acting as an Effective Intermediary Between Local Interests and State Policy Makers and with National Experts. Related to the use of models, Greater Ohio was able to play a unique role as an effective intermediary, due to its connections both within and outside Ohio. As a nonprofit, it not only used its own advocacy and education capability but also served as an interface between local interests and state policy makers as well as with national experts and those from other states who could make the case for the land bank, based on real experience and expertise.

Limited Opposition from the Usual Suspects. A strong banking lobby, for instance, in Ohio often defeats legislation that is perceived as posing government interference in the housing or financial markets. However, the banking and related interests were distracted by other bills being proposed that were more "activist" from their perspective (e.g., a moratorium on foreclosures, requiring bank ownership of foreclosed properties, etc.) and were potentially more targeted at stable neighborhoods.

Mechanisms Maximize Local Control. Finally, the Ohio land bank statute is notable for its ability to be tailored to each local jurisdiction—an extremely important element in a state whose constitution contains a strong "home rule" provision and where there is a deep-seated tradition and culture of local control and small-box active local government. The land bank board's composition allows for local discretion over how many comprise the board and also its exact composition (from a designated array of choices, including private sector appointees, and municipal and township representatives).

What Are the Lessons For Future State-Level Policy Making?

In many ways, a fortuitous set of circumstances came together to spark passage of the land bank statute—including existing models, a strong statewide network, willing sponsors, and a respected advocacy group with strong bipartisan ties to coordinate the field support and advocacy. However, the process of passing this statute also exemplifies how a legislative process should ideally work.In this instance, advocates were willing to compromise and recraft language in the midst of the process and sacrifice less important elements—such as the composition of the board and the number of counties included—for the greater good of the larger land bank concept. The true heroes of the process were the local leaders and local elected officials who saw the urgent need for a new tool to address the exploding problem of vacant and abandoned properties and pressed for state policy changes to make way for their need to innovate for the benefit of their communities.

Notes

1 Rural representatives' constituent counties apparently were concerned about being pressured to form a land bank for which they lacked capacity and potentially sufficient properties to make it financially feasible.

11

Learning from Abroad: Lessons from European Shrinking Cities

Jörg Plöger, Research Institute for Regional and Urban Development (ILS)

The phenomenon of shrinkage is often—although not always or entirely—linked to the process of economic restructuring. The decline of certain cities' industrial base has been the main cause for many of the subsequent urban problems such as rising unemployment, welfare dependency, population decline and out-migration, physical decay of the urban environment or housing vacancies. The aim of this chapter is to present insights about the impact of deindustrialization on older industrial cities, particularly highlighting some of the approaches and strategies that have been used in different European cities to overcome the problems associated with urban decline and "shrinkage." This chapter draws on research about so-called weak market cities. In a more general, wider definition, weak market cities are understood as older industrial cities that have experienced or are experiencing decline due to economic restructuring.[1]

The main research questions are these: Is there a common trajectory of growth, crisis, decline, and—possibly—recovery and regrowth for industrial cities? Can we identify a recovery, and if so, what were the contributing factors? How successful have the applied measures been, and are signs of recovery validated by ground-level evidence? Is the resurgence strong enough to face further urban challenges such as the recent economic and financial crisis?

The assumption is that although most of the urban development process is likely to be driven by exogenous factors—which the cities can not influence and have to react to—the actions taken by cities themselves do have a local impact.

If a city is thus responding to the urban crisis with dedicated, well-prepared, and innovative actions then it is likely to outperform those peers that are confronting similar problems.

The selection of case studies therefore includes cities in an intermediate phase of recovery. They have neither reached advanced stages of recovery, unlike some larger old industrial cities (for example, Barcelona, Milan, or Manchester), nor are they still in full decline as are several smaller, often mono-industrial cities located in Europe's "rust belts" (for example, those in the Ruhr area in Germany or in northern England). The sample thus includes cities in Western Europe that are showing some fragile signs of recovery yet are still struggling with many problems. The following cities were chosen: Sheffield (England), Belfast (Northern Ireland), Leipzig and Bremen (Germany), Bilbao (Spain), Turin (Italy) and Saint-Etienne (France), all of which are emblematic industrial cities for their countries. With the exception of Saint Etienne, they are also centers of regional importance in their respective national settings.

Interestingly, all these cities produced urban strategies during their recovery trajectory, which served as guidelines for future actions. The main policy objectives, however, varied between cities. Although a wide range of themes were identified, a focus on specific issues can be identified in each case. These issues may include prioritizing the attraction of companies and inward investment, focusing on retaining and attracting high-skilled groups, reacting to shrinkage and its associated problems, or improving community and social cohesion. Some of the actions to support these strategies are discussed below, such as new modes of governance, including partnership-based approaches, large-scale projects, neighborhood renewal, or confronting the skills mismatch.

The Rise and Fall of Industrial Cities

Industrialization and Urban Development

Industrialization had a profound impact on rapidly transforming societies and fueled urbanization across Europe. Regional differences, however, can be distinguished. First, the timing of industrialization varied between countries. The industrial revolution started almost simultaneously in English cities such as Manchester and Birmingham. Following Britain, the wave of industrialization spread to the Continent as well as to North America.

Second, industrialization sometimes occurred disconnected from previous urban development, thus bypassing the historic roles of particular cities such as being a convenient marketplace, a safe bastion or a religious or political center.[2] It involved cities with important functions such as London, Cologne or Amsterdam as well as places that were previously merely villages or small towns. The latter is true for some of the cities that emerged in the Ruhr area in Western Germany, where the location of mines and industries since the 19th century transformed a mostly rural hinterland without significant towns into a major industrial agglomeration.

In contrast with the later urban development in the United States,[3] the European cities selected here were founded in medieval times and had already acquired specific functions —especially trade and administration—before being transformed by industrialization. Bremen had evolved as a major port associated with the prosperous Hanseatic League. Its role as a transport and trading hub gave it relative political autonomy, which is reflected in its status today as a city-state. Further south, Bilbao fulfilled similar functions as a port and trading center. Belfast, also a port city, became the administrative center for the British colonization of the Ulster region in Ireland from the seventeenth century onward. Benefiting from its location, Turin developed into a gateway city on important transportation routes. In the sixteenth century it also became the capital of the Duchy of Savoy, and in the nineteenth century it become the first Italian national capital after the unification of Italy. Likewise, Leipzig benefited from its location on transportation routes in Central Europe and emerged as a major trading center in the late middle ages. In Saint-Etienne, proto-industrial activities pre-dated the city's emergence as a major industrial center in the nineteenth century.

The rise of industrial cities was linked to their location. The first industries were located in close proximity to natural resources such as coal or iron ore. The connection to transportation infrastructure in order to be able to move raw materials or processed products was another important factor, explaining urban growth adjacent to important waterways, roads, and particularly railway lines.

Figure 1: *Long-Term Population Change, 1800–2005*

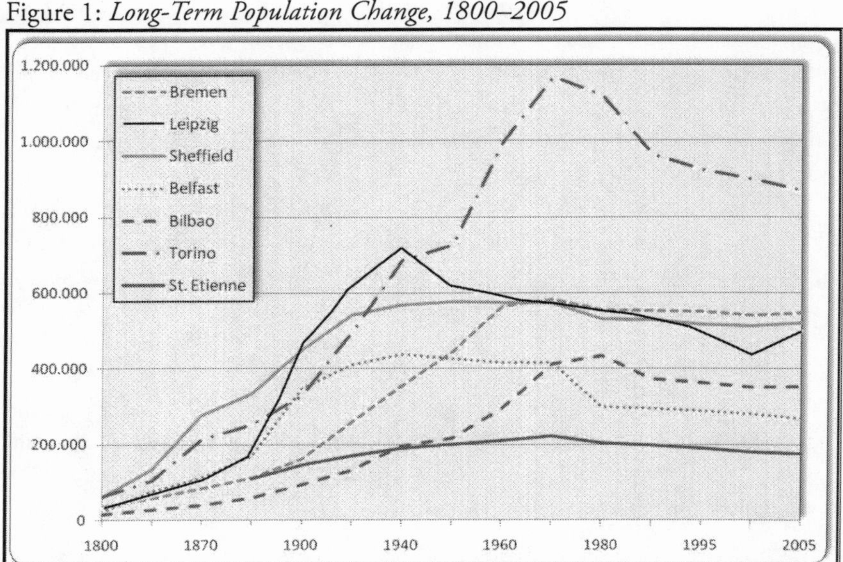

Source: Official statistics from national, regional, and city offices[4]

In some of these cities, proto-industrial activities had already emerged in the eighteenth century, including coal mining and steel production in Sheffield, textile manufacturing in Belfast, or shipbuilding in Bremen. In the nineteenth century these cities quickly evolved into industrial giants, building on their strategic and productive advantages .[5] Their enormous urban growth was fueled by a constant inflow of workers from other regions. As shown in Figure 1, in most cases, the sharpest rise in population occurred in the period between the final quarter of the nineteenth century and the outbreak of World War I in 1914. Industrialization then saw the emergence of large industrial companies, such as Harland & Wolff in Belfast, at one point the world's largest shipbuilding company; major steel producers in Sheffield or arms manufacturers in Saint-Etienne. In addition to these heavy industries, further technological progress spurred the rise of newer industries. Examples include aircraft production in Bremen, chemical industries in Leipzig, engineering in Belfast, and automobile production inTurin.

Economic Restructuring

The collapse of some of the key industries in these cities cannot be viewed in isolation from global processes of economic restructuring. Although some industries such as mining and steel production were already facing problems, economic growth of the post-war period and the rise of further—more elaborate—industries did not initially offer grounds for major concern. A key turning point was reached when the industrialized countries entered economic recession in the early 1970s, symbolized by the oil crisis in 1973. It became clear that the global economy was undergoing a profound transformation. The Fordist mode of mass production was more and more being replaced by a post-Fordist mode of flexible production.[6] In an increasingly connected world, companies were constantly forced to adapt to shifts in the global marketplace. Facilitated by decreasing transportation costs (for example, through the containerization of sea transport) and the rise of new communication technologies, new, globally linked production systems and commodity chains emerged.

This led to an increasing global division of labor.[7] To reduce production costs and to react to growing international competition, companies started outsourcing production to countries offering lower production and workforce costs. At the beginning, this included mainly low-skilled, low-tech parts of the production process, but later—with the development of a skills base in industrializing countries—more complex elements.

These processes often resulted in the collapse of certain industrial sectors and a dramatic reduction in the workforce employed in manufacturing in older industrial cities. In most such cities, moves toward a service economy have not yet compensated for those job losses.[8]

Urban Decline

The impact of economic restructuring on older industrial cities was substantial, although it varied from city to city. As a rule, cities dependent on old heavy industries such as mining (for example, Sheffield, Saint-Etienne, and Leipzig), steel (for example, Bilbao and Sheffield), or shipbuilding (for example, Bremen, Bilbao, and Belfast) suffered most. Another factor was the varying degrees of government intervention and subsidies across countries to alleviate the problems associated with industrial decline. Other factors included the degree of modernization or the level of diversification of the industrial structure. Mono-industrial, or "one-company," cities lost their economic rationale when their major employer collapsed. Cities that were once a driving force behind the economic growth of their respective countries became liabilities heavily dependent on transfer funds.[9]

Table 1 indicates the massive loss of industrial employment from the early 1970s to the early 2000s. In this period, cities lost between 35 percent (Turin) and 76 percent (Belfast) of all industrial jobs. Leipzig experienced an even more dramatic decline (87 percent) in a very short period after the transition from a socialist to a market-based economic system after 1990.

Table 1: *Loss of Manufacturing Jobs, 1970–2005*

City	*Year*	*No.*	*Year*	*No.*	*Loss No.*	*Loss %*
Bremen	1970	122,730	2003	67,966	55,000	45
Leipzig	1989	101,095	2004	13,648	87,447	87
Belfast	1973	67,000	2001	15,828	51,172	76
Sheffield	1971	117,100	2004	30,810	86,290	74
Bilbao	1970	124,539	2001	68,066	56,473	45
Turin	1971	492,791	2005	322,000	170,791	35
Saint-Etienne	1977	69,727	2001	41,104	28,623	41

Source: Official statistics from national, regional, and city offices. Data either for city (Bremen, Leipzig, Belfast, Sheffield) or metropolitan/provincial level (Bilbao, Turin, Saint- Etienne); numbers in italics have been rounded off.

The economic restructuring is clearly illustrated by the change in the proportion of the workforce employed in manufacturing between 1970 and 2005 (*Figure 2*). Sheffield suffered the most dramatic decline, with a drop from 55 to 13 percent. In all cities other than Turin less than 20 percent of the workforce is now employed in manufacturing. In comparison, the share of manufacturing employment in some U.S. older industrial cities, such as Pittsburgh, Baltimore, and Philadelphia was already lower in 1970 and continued to decrease to levels below 10 percent until 2005.

Across Europe, fear of closures and job losses resulted in labor struggles that were sometimes fierce. Sheffield played a major role during the national miners' strike in the UK in the early 1980s. In Bilbao and Bremen, dockers and other workers went on lengthy strikes. In Belfast, the loss of industrial employment exacerbated already hostile relationships between the Protestant and Catholic communities.

Figure 2: *Proportion of Workforce in Manufacturing Employment, 1970-2005 (in %)*

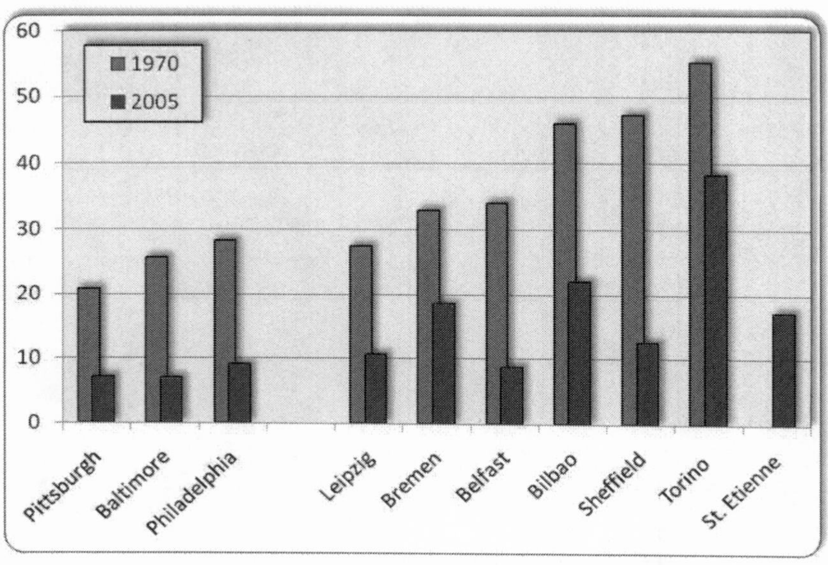

Source: Official statistics from national, regional, and city offices. The statistics for Leipzig are from 1990 to 2005 only.

A direct consequence of job loss was the rise of social problems, such as unemployment and welfare dependency. In most of our cities unemployment peaked in the mid-to late-1980s. *Figure 3* shows the steep increase in unemployment rates between 1970 and 1990. Industrial decline particularly affected the low-skilled workforce. Workers in this group were generally the first to lose their jobs when companies started reducing the workforce or moving parts of production to lower-cost locations. They also have encountered the biggest difficulties in reentering the labor market, making them prone to long-term unemployment and de facto exclusion from secure employment.

These social grievances translated into increasing sociospatial inequalities. Traditional working-class neighborhoods, which also received the main inflow of labor immigrants, were hit hardest by job losses. These areas showed increasing indices of deprivation due to the spatial concentration of multiple social problems. The variation between neighborhood unemployment rates within cities suggests increasing spatial polarization. As *Figure 4* shows, this variation reached up to 20 percent as in the case of Saint- Etienne.

Figure 3: *Unemployment rates for selected cities, 1970-1990 (in %)*

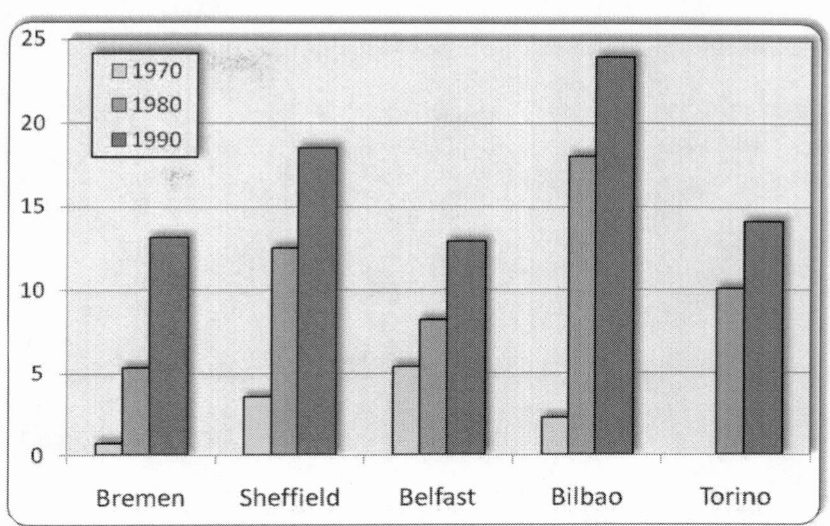

Sources: official statistics from national, regional and city offices

Notes: Leipzig and Saint Etienne not included due to lack of data before 1990; comparing statistical data across European countries is often problematic due to variations in measurement and data availability.

Figure 4: *Variation in Unemployment Rates Between Neighborhoods, 2001 (in %)*

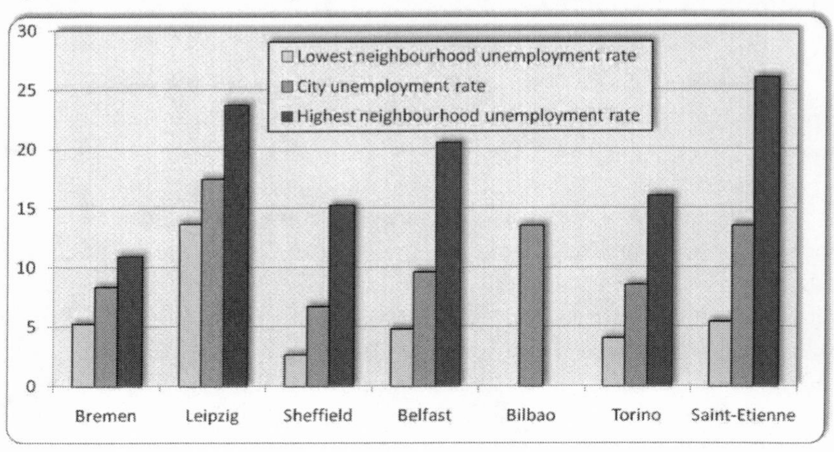

Source: Urban Audit (2003). Bilbao is not included in Urban Audit.

With the economic boom of the postwar period and the rise of white-collar employment, industry was in demand of workers, which set in motion manifold migratory processes from less developed regions or countries. Yet, with ongoing deindustrialization, industrial cities experienced a population decline (*Figure 5*). UK cities such as Sheffield and Belfast already started losing population in the 1950s, mostly due to suburbanization—similar to developments in the United States. The remaining cities experienced population decline from the 1970s onward.[10] Unlike the unemployment rates, which usually peaked during the 1980s, most cities reached their lowest population only in the late 1990s or later—or have even continued to decline, like Belfast. Still, population decline was even more severe in older industrial cities in the United States.

Figure 5: *Population Decline, 1970–2005 (in %)*

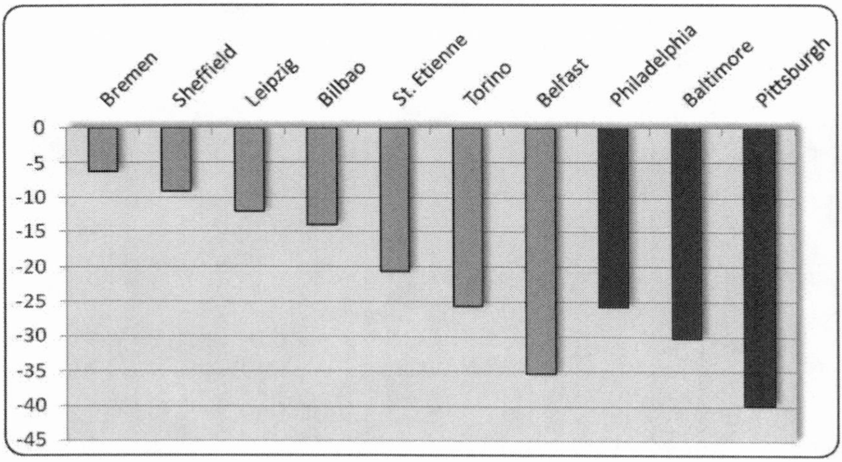

Bremen Sheffield Leipzig Bilbao St. Etienne Torino Belfast Philadelphia Baltimore Pittsburgh

0 -5 -10 -15 -20 -25 -30 -35 -40 -45

Source: Official statistics from national, regional, and city offices.

Population decline was caused by (a) a negative natural population balance due to an aging population and (b) by increasing out-migration; the latter being related to two main processes. On the one hand, younger, more mobile, and better-qualified persons moved toward employment opportunities in more economically dynamic regions. On the other, middle-class families fleeing pollution, urban decay, and social problems relocated to new suburban developments. While the suburban share of the regional population is still lower than in U.S. cities, where suburbanization started earlier, it has increased in all European cities since 1970. Suburban growth was particularly strong in Belfast, Bilbao, and Leipzig (*Figure 6*). The problems associated with suburbanization are manifold.

In countries like Germany, where taxation is based on the place of residence, not the workplace, cities surrounded by wealthier suburban municipalities such as Bremen are deprived of taxes, while still having to finance costly infrastructure and central functions—for example, universities, hospitals, cultural institutions.[11] Furthermore, suburban sprawl causes an unsustainable urban landscape due to land consumption, increasing car dependency, rising social inequalities in the city/

Figure 6 : *Proportion of Metropolitan Population in Suburbs, 1970–2005 (in %)*

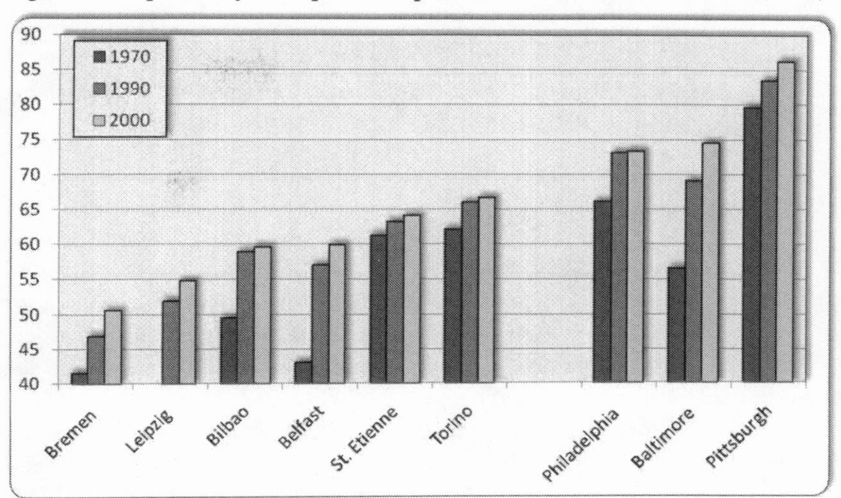

Source: Official statistics from national, regional, and city offices. Leipzig data available only from 1990; Turin data for 1995 instead of 2000; Sheffield not included.

region, and costly infra-structures to maintain in the future. In East Germany, cities had practically no suburban hinterland until 1990, due to strict regulations on settlement patterns. Following reunification, the mostly-rural municipalities surrounding Leipzig were transformed by new residential and commercial developments in a rapid process of "Wild East suburbanization" [12] driven by investors taking advantage of a "control gap" while East German local authorities were adapting to West German planning and land-use systems. Suburbanization was also fueled by the availability of federal subsidies for home ownership and the decay of the inner-city housing stock.

In addition to the above-mentioned problems, the cities were confronted with further challenges associated with urban decline and shrinkage, such as:

- **Physical decay** of the cities, with an increasing number of derelict buildings and vacant brown-fields due to abandonment and lack of investment creating a negative image.
- **Housing market crisis** due to increasing vacancies and a lack of investment in the existing stock. In Leipzig, the majority of the housing stock was dilapidated after decades of under investment. More than sixty thousand units, 20 percent of the entire stock, had fallen vacant prior to the year 2000.
- **Lack of modern amenities** for the middle classes, such as specific housing types or cultural and leisure facilities.
- **Environmental problems** contributed to the low quality of life. In

Leipzig, air, water, and soil were seriously polluted due to chemical industries, coal-fired power plants, and open-cast lignite mining.

- **Budgetary crisis** due to insufficient funding, inability to maintain infrastructure and services for a declining population, decreasing tax base, and rising public debt.

Urban Recovery

In their search for a way out of their crisis, the cities applied a wide range of strategies and measures. This section of the chapter analyzes the attempts used to confront the many challenges. It will present some findings about the particular approaches by focusing on the topics of strategy development, new agencies, large-scale projects, neighborhood renewal, and skills development.

Before these topics are discussed, information about the individual recovery trajectories will be provided. In order to understand the sequence of events and actions throughout the process, we considered the period from the early 1970s until the present.[13] The following questions will be addressed: How was recovery initiated? Was there an identifiable turning point? Who were the main participants? Did leadership play a role? Which focus for future development was identified?

The Recovery Trajectory

In order to analyze the recovery trajectory, we investigated whether a turnaround point or phase could be identified for each of the cities. A turnaround indicates that the low point of decline has been reached and that signs of urban recovery can be observed.[14] Turning points do not suggest, however, that all problems associated with the urban crisis are resolved or that all measurable indicators report a positive trend. Rather, they constitute symbolic moments that may reflect real or perceived recovery. Different factors can explain the turnaround, such as new landmark buildings representing physical renewal, a shift toward optimism for the future by the population, new political leadership, or a more dynamic labor market. In short, they reflect a general feeling by decision makers and citizens that "the worst is over."

We were able to identify turning points or, in some cases, turning phases in most of the cities, with the possible exception of Saint-Etienne and, perhaps, Belfast, which still showed significant problems and a more fragile urban recovery. The timing of the turning points varied. In Bilbao and Turin, local decision makers and urban experts placed them in the first half of the 1990s. In Sheffield, Leipzig, and Bremen, they were identified for the second half of the 1990s, sometimes extending into the early 2000s. As the timelines for Bilbao and Leipzig demonstrate (*Figures 7* and *8*), the individual recovery trajectory can be framed as a constellation of specific events, political shifts, involvement by particular participants, and physical landmarks, among other factors. All trajectories shared common characteristics, yet also varied in other aspects.

Figure 7: *Timeline of Important Events, Bilbao*

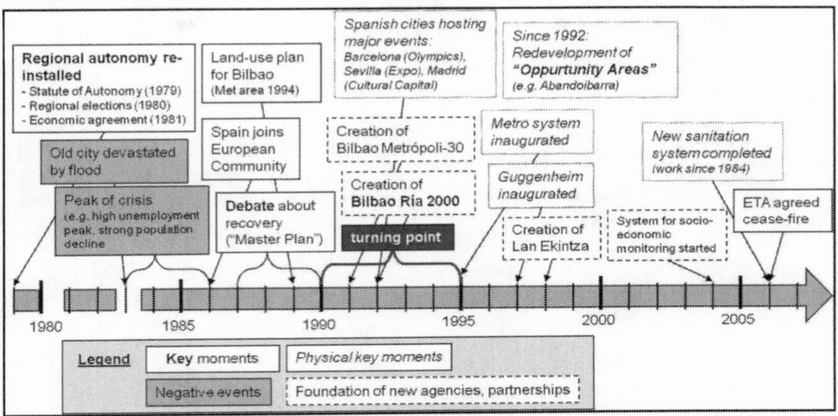

Figure 8: *Timeline of Important Events, Leipzig*

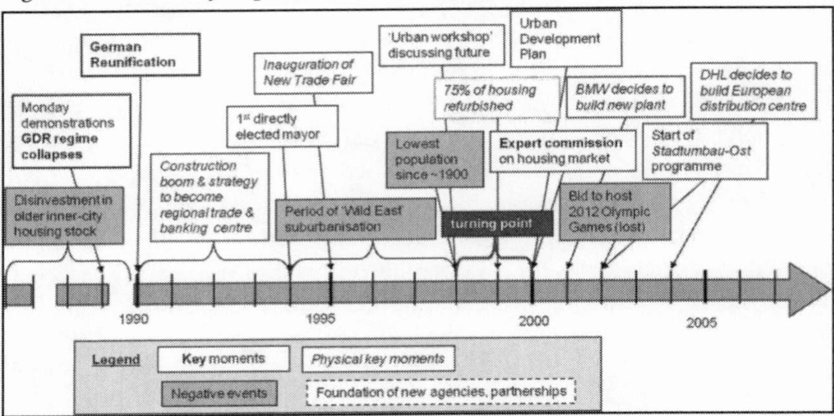

We can distinguish between endogenous and exogenous factors throughout the process. A starting point was the eventual recognition from within the city leadership that economic restructuring was unavoidable and that responding to the crisis was urgent. In order to be successful, new approaches had to be carried out by a coalition of participants. This involved a difficult process of negotiation, consensus-building, and multi-sectoral collaboration.

Strong leadership was important to guide the process. In cases like Leipzig, a new political leadership had emerged with the political transformation after the

German reunification. This was accompanied by an urban civil society, which had been suppressed under socialist rule but had ree-merged with the demonstrations against the GDR regime. In combination with the general optimism of the post-unification period, this created the momentum for change. In Sheffield, a partnership-based approach to urban policymaking with a new chief executive replaced former "old industrial" power constellations. Support for interventions came from new funding streams to core cities by the newly elected Labour government.[15] In Turin, a major change came with the first directly elected mayor in 1993 and the increasing involvement of local bank foundations in regeneration issues.

During the regeneration discourse, city leaders attempted to convince the urban public of the need for readjustment. The change of the mindset from the former industrial self-conception—which was disappearing more quickly in reality than in the minds of the people—toward a new post-industrial identity was a difficult task. In order to succeed, city leaders had to propose a new vision for the future. Every city emphasized different objectives. In the case of Bremen, for instance, city leaders started shaping the transition from "port city"—based on harbor-related activities and shipbuilding—to "city of science"—based on high-tech sectors and research and development.[16]

Apart from framing local conditions, these approaches need to be seen in combination with further exogenous factors. Major political events allowed for change in some cases, including the impact of German reunification on the development in Leipzig or of the peace process in Northern Ireland on the development in Belfast, both during the 1990s.

Several of the case study cities benefited from the devolution of power to regional and local governments throughout the last decades. After Spain returned to democracy in the 1970s, the regions were reinstated as important levels of government. The Basque Country was particularly successful in negotiating a substantial degree of autonomy from central government. In combination with a reemerging strong Basque leadership, autonomy was instrumental to the recovery process of Bilbao, the region's major city. Elsewhere, local political leadership was strengthened in the 1990s by implementing the direct election of mayors, as in Turin, Saint-Etienne, and Leipzig.

Throughout Europe—and in contrast with the situation in the United States—recovery actions were supported by the availability of funding programs from different tiers of government that were designed to help cities and regions experiencing structural change. EU structural funds for regional cohesion granted substantial resources to less competitive regions, including old industrial ones. Since 1994, the Urban program of the EU addressed the issue of urban polarization and supported measures in disadvantaged urban neighborhoods. On the national level, programs such as Soziale Stadt (Socially-Integrative City), implemented by the federal and state governments in Germany in 1999, offered funding for integrative renewal approaches in deprived neighborhoods. In many cases, city governments also designed their own programs in order to confront specific problems when external funding was regarded as insufficient or inappropriate.

Strategic Orientations

All of the cities in the sample developed urban strategies in order to overcome their crises, and these strategies varied in their actual implementation. While cities like Leipzig used them to inform local planning and policymaking, cities like Belfast considered them advisory documents not necessarily connected with actual implementation. The overall strategy was sometimes shaped by a forward-looking vision about how a city tried to reinvent itself in order to be "equipped for the future" (for example, Bremen). In other places, such as Leipzig, it was more closely related to the actual problems and focused on ways to deal with them. The different approaches are discussed below.

In the late 1980s, all layers of government in the city of Bilbao started working toward a strategic plan. The main objectives were to reverse the image of a declining, polluted city with concentrated social problems and to become an attractive location for investors and tourists alike. A project-oriented approach was chosen to deal with urban decline, with a new agency, Bilbao Ría 2000, created to implement the strategies (see below).For Leipzig, we can identify two main types of action: The first focused on economic development. This can be explained by the collapse of the economic base. An investor-friendly strategy was designed, with the aim of attracting new companies and becoming more competitive. It succeeded in attracting two car manufacturing plants, those of BMW and Porsche. With large-scale investments in the airport and in highways, the city also attracted several logistics companies, including online retailer Amazon and freight company DHL. The second type of action was designed to deal with what can be labeled as "shrinking city problems," such as population decline, weak housing markets with high vacancy rates, and physical decay of many buildings after decades of disinvestment, and costly, oversized infrastructure. A major objective was to increase the appeal of the city as a residential location in order to attract and retain inhabitants. Due to the magnitude of these problems, Leipzig was forced to engage in new areas of policy development, and the city hosted several roundtables and workshops in the late 1990s in order to discuss approaches for the future. The strategic focus on urban renewal was supported by many different, often innovative approaches and instruments, some of which are discussed below. In 2001, Leipzig's experiences formed the basis of the major federal urban renewal program confronting the problems of shrinking cities, known as Stadtumbau.

The thematic focus of these cities' strategies was informed by (a) other approaches that were tried elsewhere, (b) local innovative ideas, and (c) building on functions perceived as strengths. Bilbao and Bremen illustrate how some of the local thinking and ideas were influenced by developments elsewhere. In Bilbao, decision makers learned from key regeneration programs in other Spanish cities since the late 1980s, particularly those associated with three major events during the "Spanish year" of 1992, when Barcelona hosted the Summer Olympics, Seville hosted the World Expo, and Madrid became the European Capital of Culture. Apart from that, local planners and decision makers gathered ideas about how to regenerate the riverfront by visiting early waterfront redevelopments in Baltimore and Glasgow.

In Bremen, the recognition of the need for ongoing economic restructuring during the 1980s was combined with the belief that future economic success depended on high-technology and knowledge-based innovation sectors. The growth of Silicon Valley and its link to higher-education institutions gave rise to ideas for strengthening the technology and natural sciences profile of the University of Bremen and linking it with new high-tech sectors.[17] The creation of a technology-based business park on land surrounding the university physically reflects this approach (Photo 1). The Economic Policy Action Program initiated in the mid-1980s and the Special Investment Program throughout the 1990s provided significant support for these objectives. The latter was made possible through substantial financial aid (2.6 billion euros) from the federal government to avoid its bankruptcy. The political decision makers managed to convince the supervising bodies to invest some of these resources to support economic restructuring and urban regeneration rather than using it entirely for debt repayment.

Photo 1: *Universum Science Center in Technology Park in Bremen, Located in proximity to the university*

Photo by Jörg Plöger

Leaders in several cities used the work of scholars on urban or regional development to inform their policy approaches. In Leipzig, economic development policy focused on the identification of viable clusters. Here, as elsewhere, the work of economist Michael Porter was a main source of inspiration. Richard Florida's ideas about the importance of the so-called creative class and the three T's (talent, technology, tolerance) for attracting it was picked up eagerly in many cities. Saint-Etienne, for example, supports a local gay pride parade and focuses on its fashion design sectors. Manuel Castell's idea of nodes and networks in a globalized world informed the strategic vision of Bilbao to become a major regional hub. In Belfast, renowned academics and policy advisers have repeatedly been involved in producing strategy papers outlining the future development, such as Michael Parkinson's involvement in the production of the *State of the City* report.

New Modes of Governance

Since the 1990s, the urban public sector underwent a process of restructuring in many countries. This can be understood as a direct consequence of trying to be more competitive in a context of globalization and the need to adapt to rapid change. Neoliberal policy approaches introducing market principles to formerly state-controlled sectors and downsizing of state functions were widely applied.[18] In Germany, older industrial cities are chronically underfinanced and have amassed huge debts.[19] Forced to balance their budgets and to reduce debts, they responded by privatizing city services (for example, utility companies) or even leasing them to foreign corporations, selling city-owned land, buildings, and infrastructure, and reducing the number of public employees.

Partnerships between the public and the private sectors became more common, with an early example being urban development corporations in Sheffield and Belfast. A further step was the formation of publicly owned agencies operating as private companies to carry out defined tasks such as economic development or project development. Although they are essentially public-sector bodies, they operate at arm's length from core government. An interesting example representing the new project-based approach in urban regeneration is Bilbao Ría 2000.

This not-for-profit public-public partnership was set up in 1992 by local, provincial, regional, and national governments to act as a project developer for major redevelopment sites formerly in harbor, railway, or industrial use in and around Bilbao. The complex constellation of powers was necessary because decision making is located at different administrative levels, for example, urban planning by local government, fiscal power by provincial government, and ownership of the land often by central government authorities. For political reasons, it was agreed that the Basque and national government entities would each hold half of the shares (Table 2). The start-up funding to finance the operations of Bilbao Ría came from central and regional governments and the EU.

Table 2: *Bilbao Ría 2000 Shareholders*

National Gov.	*50%*	*Basque Gov.*	*50%*
SEPES (land management company)	25%	Regional gov.	15%
Port Authority	10%	Provincial gov.	15%
FEVE and RENFE (railway companies)	15%	City of Bilbao	15%
		City of Barakaldo	5%

The public landowners contributed land to the company's portfolio. In return the port authority was compensated by receiving permission to extend its harbor facilities at the river's mouth. The railway companies were compensated by assistance to modernize their infrastructure elsewhere. After taking control of the land, Bilbao Ría 2000 carried out redevelopment activities in designated 'opportunity zones'. The most well-known of these redevelopment sites is Abandoibarra on the river Nervión, famous for the landmark Guggenheim Museum (*Photo 2*).

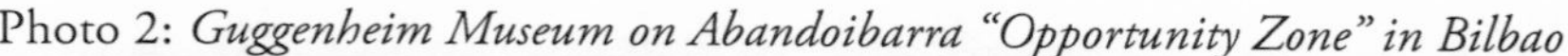

Photo 2: *Guggenheim Museum on Abandoibarra "Opportunity Zone" in Bilbao*

Photo by Jörg Plöger

Bilbao Ria 2000 plans the sites and changes the designated land-uses with the intention of increasing the land value before the land is sold to developers, with profits reinvested in further urban regeneration. The financial autonomy of its operations is considered highly significant for Bilbao Ria 200's success, and due to the prime locations of the opportunity zones, its activities have been self-financing so far. Its responsibility for major redevelopment projects and its access to land have led Bilbao Ría 2000 to become the major planning and regeneration body in Bilbao.

Large Scale Projects

To galvanize external and internal support for the turnaround of places, city leaders had to present a powerful vision for urban renaissance. To put the city "back on the map," as some of the policymakers expressed it, they looked for projects that would stand out. Their intention was to create anchors for further development, to rebuild trust in the city as a location for investment, and to gain public support. *Table 3* mentions some of the more visible projects developed in the cities.

Table 3: *Selected Large-Scale Projects*

Transport Infrastructure	*Flagship Projects*
New metro (Bilbao) Modernized airport (Bilbao)	Guggenheim (Bilbao) Winter Garden (Sheffield) Trade Fair (Leipzig)
Redevelopment of Water/Riverfront	*Events*
Overseas City (Bremen) Abandoibarra (Bilbao) Titanic Quarter (Belfast)	Winter Olympics (Turin)
Redevelopment of Fomer Industrial Land	*New Functions*
Transforming open-cast mines into lake landscape (Leipzig) Laganside (Belfast)	Retail developments (Belfast) Renewable energies (Bremen)

Many of these projects, however, were controversial. The famous Guggenheim Museum in Bilbao was a very risky investment due to its high costs and uncertain outcome.[20] Leipzig attempted to revive its traditional function as a location for trade fairs. After reunification, the city immediately started to build a brand new trade fair complex to replace the old one. Several cities also tried to gain attention by attracting major events. Turin managed to host the Winter Olympics in 2006, which was accompanied by heavy investment in infrastructure and facilities. In Bilbao, the objectives of acessibility and connectivity resulted in large-scale investments in the transport infrastructure, including the new metro, designed by Norman Foster.

Neighborhood Renewal

U.S. cities like Baltimore, Philadelphia, and Pittsburgh are changing their neighborhood renewal approaches. Resource allocation is shifting toward more focused investment in neighborhoods that are showing signs of distress yet are also considered to be "savable" if supported. The nature of investment in the most distressed areas has included large amounts of low-income housing and social service provision, which— while arguably improving living conditions for the residents—has done little to confront socio-economic and racial segregation. It reflects insufficient public funding for all neighborhood renewal needs, even if including the resources provided by local nonprofit organizations and foundations. It also reflects the more recent pressures to measure the effects of policy approaches. The rationale behind this is that improvements might be achieved more easily in "neighborhoods in transition", thus justifying policy decisions.

In Europe, cities have been heavily reliant on public funding streams. Different layers of government, such as EU, national, regional, and local, offered funding for neighborhood renewal approaches, enabling a long-term commitment to certain areas and preventing neighborhood decay to the extent of the situation in the United States.

Several of the cities studied here (for example, Bilbao, Bremen, Leipzig) have implemented monitoring systems that are regularly fed with data on social, economic, demographic, and housing-related issues. Monitoring has become an important tool to measure local development, plan resource allocation, and design specific area-based approaches.

In European cities, we can usually distinguish two types of residential areas that are most likely to be affected by decline:

- Traditional working-class neighborhoods in inner-city locations that were most affected by the consequences of economic restructuring. They are often characterized by a low proportion of people in secure employment, lack of amenities, physical decay, housing vacancies, concentrated deprivation, a bad image, the out-migration of middle-class households, as well as often-fragile community relations between long-term residents and—mostly migrant—newcomers. Examples include Gröpelingen in Bremen, East Leipzig, North Belfast, and the left-bank industrial communities in the Bilbao metropolitan area.
- Large mass-housing estates built between the late 1960s and early 1980s, mostly in unfavorable locations on the urban periphery. They are often badly connected to public transport and are characterized by a concentration of disadvantaged groups and vacancies. Tenever in Bremen, Grünau in Leipzig, and Otxarkoaga in Bilbao fall into this category. In many cases, the size of such estates has been reduced through partial demolition.

In Bremen, the main rationale behind supporting disadvantaged neighborhoods is social cohesion. The city used an interesting approach to neighborhood renewal. First, it identified the most deprived areas and decided to allocate the available resources to them, including funding through the federal and regional government program Soziale Stadt. The city then added further resources through its own program WIN (German acronym for Living in Neighborhoods). Apart from investments in the physical infrastructure and the built environment, this also supports events, educational courses, and neighborhood management. Due to particularly great population decline in the 1990s, the main objective in Leipzig was to attract and retain residents. Interventions thus focused on the physical upgrading of the existing housing stock and the creation of new housing options. Due to a lack of examples elsewhere, the city designed several innovative instruments and projects, such as those indicated in *Table 4.*

Photo 3: *Temporary Neighborhood Park Created After Demolition of Derelict Buildings in East Leipzig*

Photo by Jörg Plöger

Confronting the Skills Mismatch

In some cities, the industries that declined have not completely disappeared. Many companies—sometimes with public-sector support—managed to adapt older skills to more advanced types of manufacturing. In Saint–Etienne, a specialist optic–lenses cluster has emerged on the site of the former arms factory. It is building on the earlier experience in arms manufacturing, particularly the precision engineering used for the production of gun lenses. In Sheffield, health-related engineering (for example, laser technologies) builds on former expertise in stainless steel, knife making and metal processing technologies.

Table 4: *Urban Renewal Instruments and Projects Used in Leipzig*

Instruments / Projects	*Aim*	*Description*	*Impact*
Townhouses	Creation of attractive housing options; competing with the suburbs for families.	Construction of owner-occupied, semi-detached townhouses in attractive inner-city locations	By 2007: 100 houses built; but: developers often prefer suburban locations (less regulation, larger sites)
Tenant refurbishment incentive	Stopping decline of the housing stock	Tenants receive financial assistance to refurbish semi-derelict buildings	Limited success: housing market already offers wide choice of inexpensive renovated housing
Self-user program	Provision of inner-city housing for middle-classes (vs. suburbanization) Consolidation of older housing stock	City helps organizing and advising "owner groups" for buildings	2001-2007: ~300 families
Guardian houses	Symbolic intervention in areas with high vacancy rates Stop further dereliction of housing stock Side-effect: low-cost housing option for creative groups (e.g., students, artists)	Temporary rental-free lease of decaying buildings in strateic locations Occupiers required to make necessary repairs	Small-scale: only a few dozen buildings
Interim use of private properties as public space (see photo 3)	Adding public spaces, increasing quality of life Solution during weak real-estate/land market	Intermediate solution Contract between city and landowner: city allowed to temporarily (usually 10 years) use vacant private land as public space; particularly after demolition of derelict buildings Owner responsible for demolition and clearing of site, but exempt from property taxes and site security.	1999-2005: ~100 contracts

Source: Adapted from Plöger (2007).

Yet new jobs in the service economy or the advanced manufacturing sector require a skillset different from that required for previous manufacturing jobs. The inability of some of the unemployed to gain access to new jobs is attributed to this skills mismatch. In most of the cities, this was considered a major problem. On the one hand, city leaders became worried about their working-class population,

Table 5: *Selected skills programs*

Project (City)	*Initiated / run by*	*Funding*	*Target group*	*Aim*	*Tasks / services*	*Results*
Lan Ekintza (Bilbao)	City Council (1998)	City Council, regional Basque government, EU and others	Unemployed Low-skilled Migrants	Linking unemployed to labor market	Information Help in creating small enterprises Linking people to jobs	Mediation of ~2,000 jobs, assisting ~100 business creations per year
JobMatch & JobNet (Sheffield)	JobMatch run by City council and private construction companies	JobMatch: Private construction companies (2/3), Decent Homes and Housing Market Renewal (UK government) (1/3), minor EU funding Total: ~2 mio. GBP	Women Minorities Long-term unemployed	Attracting companies Linking deprived neighborhoods to labor market Training hard-to-reach groups	JobMatch: Free human resources consultancy to inward investors JobNet: Drop-in centers in 15 neighborhoods Employment advice Linking to jobs offered by JobMatch	Trainees: 100 (city), ~500 (city-region)
Gasworks Employment Matching Scheme (GEMS) (Belfast)	City Council and South Belfast partnership (2002)	Mixed funding from local gov., Laganside Corporation, central gov., EFRE (EU) and others 1.2 mio. Euros	Low-skilled, unemployed in deprived wards of East and South Belfast Migrants	Linking deprived neighborhoods to nearby new jobs at Laganside redevelopment	Training of job-market skills Job application skills Linking jobs with people Promoting corporate responsibility	Assisted ~2,000; into employment: ~1,000; 800 completed training courses
Personal services to businesses (PUUL) (Leipzig)	City Council; more independent now with City Council still major shareholder	2001-2005: 2.5 mi. euros (2/3 by city council) Since 2006: 60% private companies, 40% city council	(Long-term) unemployed	Linking (long-term) unemployed with labor market Service to new inward investors	Not associated with particular neighborhoods Employment agency for large investors (e.g. BMW, DHL, amazon) intending to locate in city/ region (e.g., workforce pre-selection) Supporting relocation of higher-up professionals	Channeled more than 3,000 into new jobs (~50% formerly unemployed)

Information collected in 2007-2008

Adapted from Power, Plöger, and Winkler (2010).

which was increasingly losing access to the labor market. Improving skills was regarded as way of strengthening community cohesion under difficult circumstances. On the other hand, the cities needed qualified workforces as a key asset in order to attract potential investors. As a result, they implemented several skills initiatives and programs, often supported by different layers of government. As

Table 5 illustrates, the individual design, objectives, and target groups of these programs varied from city to city. Their tasks include training, information about job opportunities, recruitment, or supporting self-employment.

Recovery and New Challenges

Assessing Recovery

The data clearly suggests that most of the cities are recovering, as reflected by population growth and unemployment rates. During the period from 1990 to 2000 all of the European cities were still losing population, as were the three U.S. cities. After several decades of population decline, five out of the seven European and two out of the three American cities gained population during the following decade (*Figure 9*). Although these growth rates were modest in most cases, they nevertheless mark a trend reversal.

Figure. 9: *Population Change, 1990-2010 (in %)*

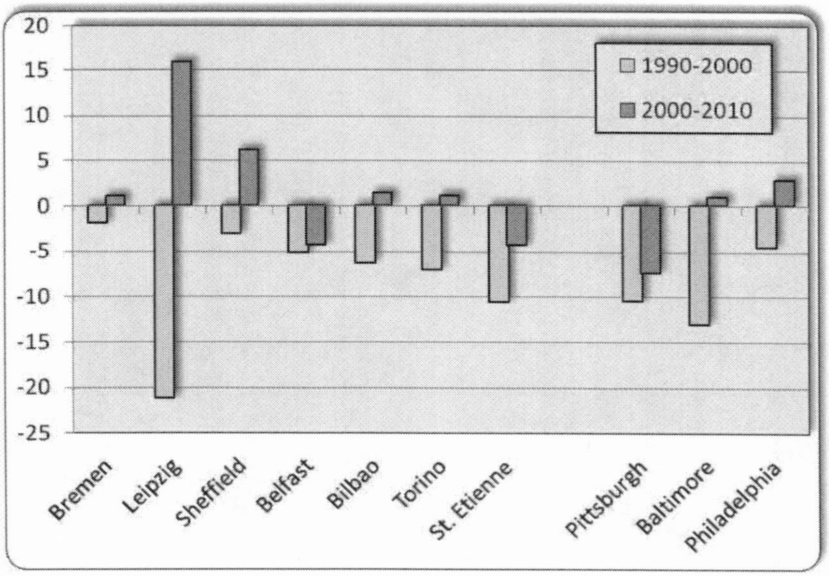

Source: Official statistics from national, regional, and city offices.

Unemployment rates also dropped from their high 1990 level in most cities. Some cities such as Turin, Bilbao, Sheffield and Belfast even saw their unemployment rates cut more than half (*Figure 10*). In Bremen and Saint-Etienne, unemployment remained relatively stable. The only case of an extreme increase in unemployment is Leipzig, which is explained by the particular situation after German reunification. Interestingly, most of these cities that were once characterized by severe social problems now show unemployment rates below their respective national average.

As an in-depth analysis of both quantitative and qualitative data has shown, these cities have reached different stages of recovery. [21] Assessment of a set of fourteen quantitative indicators on topics such as population change, unemployment, qualification levels of residents, employment, GDP, and sprawl for the period between 1990 and 2008 illustrates this. Bilbao shows the greatest progress, according to the data. Bremen, Sheffield and Turin performed relatively well also. The remaining cities, Leipzig, Belfast, and Saint-Etienne, still confront major challenges and thus have not been able to recover to the same extent.

Figure 10: *Unemployment Rates, 1990-2005 (in %)*

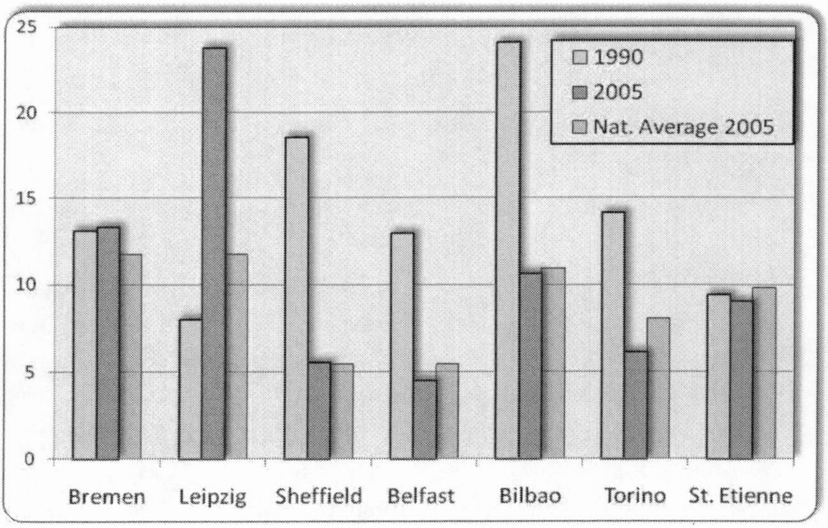

Source: Official statistics from national, regional, and city offices.

Statistical information can be misleading, however, and comparisons between countries of the EU are difficult to make due to a variety of factors. We thus decided to support the analysis with qualitative information on a number of different themes, including evaluating important projects, approaches and other interventions whose outcome may be difficult to measure in quantitative terms.[22] This information is based on personal observations during the field work, analysis of policy documents, literature review, and interviews with key experts and policymakers. Interestingly, the results show a slightly different order of the ranking. Bremen scores highest, followed by Leipzig and Turin. Sheffield, Belfast, and Bilbao are medium performers, with Saint-Etienne holding the lowest rank.

As we have seen, different factors have shaped the trajectory from decline to recovery in the cities studied. The following conclusions can be reached:

Competitiveness: the main rationale behind urban-recovery actions; competition not only for investors and companies but also increasingly for high-skilled people.

Deindustrialization: a fact, but the process is not finished yet and varies from city to city. Depending on its ability to constantly adapt and focus on advanced technologies and innovation, the sector remains an important economic driver.

Economic Restructuring: in many cases, former functions inform future options (for example, rediscovery of traditional roles; building on former strengths); service sector employment in most cases does not yet compensate for losses in manufacturing..

Recovery Strategies: can be considered an important tool; they are widely used to provide a common vision for the future.

Urban Regeneration Projects: often resemble one another; they are often costly, with uncertain outcomes, and few outstanding examples of really successful projects are apparent.

Social Cohesion and Neighborhood Renewal: on the agenda in all cities, but resources are limited; characterized by small-scale, sometimes innovative programs and interventions.

Regional Cooperation: some initial cooperation is present but usually at a low level of formalization; considered important (for example, suburbanization, regional public transport, planning) but often problematic due to conflicting interests.

Local Remits: varying degree of devolution across Europe; local autonomy enables more customized approaches; needs to coincide with availability of funding.

Political Leadership: important to initiate certain processes, yet not necessarily decisive.

Citizen Involvement: the successful implementation of recovery actions is dependent upon citizen support; in many cases participatory measures are thus used to involve the population.

Accountability of Actions: measuring outcome of policy-making; improving resource allocation; used by several cities.

The global financial crisis of 2007 and 2008 and the subsequent economic crisis have had significant consequences on the urban level. They have added a new layer of problems to the ongoing struggle to overcome urban decline and are potentially detrimental to the progress achieved so far. This time, however, they do not result from outdated modes of production or growing economic competition, but from risky speculation and bad decision-making in the financial sector, which was previously considered to be a driving force for innovation and economic growth.

Older industrial cities have been reliant on external funding during their transformation process. In many countries, governments have assisted the economic restructuring through large-scale intervention. These funding streams have also arrived in cities, of course. The cities have gained substantial experience in dealing with decline, which certainly has created a valuable skillset for crisis intervention, guaranteeing at least some level of resilience.

Due to many unresolved problems as well as external factors out of their control, the development of these cities continues to be fragile, however.[23] They still lack sufficiently differentiated economies with a larger share of innovative sectors. Evidence from Britain and Germany suggests that regional inequalities are likely to increase further, which limits the ability of cities with structural disadvantages to remain competitive. The economic recession is felt more profoundly in cities with a prevalence of fragile labor markets characterized by increasingly insecure labor conditions and low-skilled employment. Their financial resources to respond are very limited, however. In Germany, for example, many cities—and cities in weak regions in particular—are facing severe budgetary crises. They are often overburdened with debts, while austerity measures further limit their ability to actively frame local development patterns.

Notes

1. Power, Plöger, and Winkler (2010).
2. Western Europe here refers to the countries with market-economies and democratically elected governments as opposed to the former Eastern Bloc countries which had socialist regimes and state-controlled economies. The label Western Europe thus also includes Southern European countries such as Spain and Italy.
3. Hohenberg and Lees (1985).
4. Power, Plöger and Winkler, (2010).
5. Roberts and Steadman, (1999).
6. Clark, Feldman, and Gertler (2000).
7. Amin (1994).
8. Daniels (1993).
9. Power, Plöger, and Winkler (2010).
10. Turok and Mykhnenko (2007).
11. Poblan (1996).
12. Nuissl and Rink (2005).
13. The research for the project was carried out between 2006 and 2008. More recent developments, particularly the impact of the financial and economic crisis, are part of a current second project phase.
14. Paddison (2001).
15. Winkler (2007).
16. Plöger (2007).
17. Educational policy is determined at the state-level in Germany. Being a city-state, Bremen is thus able to design its own higher education strategy.
18. Heinz (2008).
19. Jungfer (2005).
20. Plaza (2007).
21. Power, Plöger, and Winkler (2010), p. 280.
22. Ibid. p. 283.
23. Kunzmann (2010).

Bibliography

Amin, A., ed. 1994. *Post-Fordism. A Reader*. Cambridge, MA: Blackwell.

Clark, G., M., Feldman, and M., Gertler, 2000. *The Oxford Handbook of Economic Geography*. Oxford: Oxford University Press.

Daniels, P. 1993. *Service Industries in the World Economy*. Cambridge, MA: Blackwell.

Heinz, W. 2008. *Der große Umbruch: Deutsche Städte und Globalisierung*. Berlin: Difu.

Hohenberg, P. and L., Hollen Lees 1985. *The Making of Urban Europe, 1000-1950*. Cambridge MA: Harvard University Press.

Jungfer, K. 2005. *Die Stadt in der Krise: Ein Manifest für starke Kommunen*. Bonn: Bpb.

Kunzmann, K. 2010. "After the Global Economic Crisis: Policy Implications for the Future of the European Territory." *Informationen zur Raumentwicklung* 8: 601-612.

Nuissl, H. and D., Rink 2005. "The 'Production' of Urban Sprawl in Eastern Germany as a Phenomenon of Post-Socialist Transformation." *Cities* 22, no. 2: 123-124.

Paddison, R., ed. 2001. *Handbook of Urban Studies*. London: Sage.

Plaza, B. 2007. "The Return on Investment of the Guggenheim Museum in Bilbao." *International Journal of Urban and Regional Research* 30, no. 2: 452-467.

Poblan, J. 1996. "Processes of Suburbanization and its Effects on the Finances of Cities in West Germany: The Example of Bremen and the Surrounding Communities." *Environment and Planning C: Government and Policy* 14 no. 1: 25-37.

Power, A.J., Plöger and A. Winkler 2010. *Phoenix Cities:The Fall and Rise of Great Industrial Cities*. Bristol: Policy Press.

———. 2008. "Transforming Cities Across Europe: An Interim Report on Problems and Progress." *CASE Report* 49. London: LSE.

Roberts, G. and P., Steadman 1999. *American Cities & Technology:Wilderness to Wired City*. London: Routledge.

Turok, I. and V., Mykhnenko, 2007. "The Trajectories of European Cities, 1960-2005." *Cities* 24 no. 3: 165-182.

Appendix

Reinventing America's Legacy Cities

Strategies for Cities Losing Population

Report of the 110th American Assembly

Disclaimer

At the close of their discussions, the participants in the 110th American Assembly, "Defining a Future for America's Cities Experiencing Severe Population Loss" at the Westin Book Cadillac Hotel in Detroit, Michigan, April 14-17, 2011, reviewed as a group the following statement. The statement represents general agreement, however, no one was asked to sign it. Furthermore, it should be understood that not everyone agreed with all of it.

> *From time to time in American history—in Detroit as the automotive industry forces closures, in New Orleans after Hurricane Katrina, in various cities after economic crisis or natural disasters—there has been speculation that an American city has been lost, that the right course is to give up on it. But as Americans we don't do that. This is a matter of principle. But it is also practical. Even our damaged cities have immense value and essential parts to play in the nation's future.*
>
> Henry G. Cisneros, Executive Chair, CityView

> *A great city should not be confounded with a populous city.*
>
> Aristotle

I. Introduction

The global knowledge economy favors cities because their density and infrastructure support the knowledge spillovers and innovation that flow from concentrated economic activity. Increasing demand for energy efficiency, too, favors the proximity and walkability found in cities' dense urban development patterns. Perhaps most importantly, cities continue to offer a unique opportunity for living well together in dense, dynamic communities where diversity and democracy flourish. In the United States people continue to move to metropolitan areas and before the Great Recession were increasingly returning to central cities, a trend expected to continue as the economy rebounds.

Approximately 84 percent of Americans live in metropolitan areas, and in the past two decades many of the central cities within them have begun to see their populations rebound. But despite favorable trends in some American cities, others—largely concentrated in the Midwest and parts of the Northeast—have continued to lose residents and jobs for over a half century or more. Some have argued that this turn of events is the outcome of historic processes of economic and demographic change, and that we should therefore write off these "legacy cities" and let others absorb the nation's growth. For the United States to follow this course would be a strategic and costly mistake. America's legacy cities and their assets deserve attention for equity and sustainability reasons, but equally important, their revitalization is critical to our national economic competitiveness. As a purely economic proposition, the enormous value of the physical infrastructure, civic institutions, and human capital embedded in these cities should be supported and exploited for the common good. The country needs them as much as they need the support of the country.

America's legacy cities are vital places with living histories. If they can reinvent their economic and land strategies, they can be desirable places to live, to work, and to raise families. These cities may not have the same numbers of residents and jobs as in the past, but they can be authentic and economically efficient urban areas where residents can feel safe, workers can find and sustain quality employment, and children can thrive in strong neighborhoods with high quality schools. To these goals legacy cities can and should aspire.

The United States needs to understand the global stakes in the decisions it makes. Our competitors in China, India, and Europe are not allowing their cities to disintegrate. Even as China builds new cities to accommodate its expanding economy and population, it is investing heavily in high speed rail and transit-oriented development in its older communities. India and Europe, too, are focusing resources on their existing cities and metropolitan regions. We will be at a global competitive disadvantage if we disregard the urban gems we have cultivated over the past two centuries. We cannot afford such wastefulness as a matter of national policy.

Legacy Cities Have a Complex Mix of Assets and Challenges

In an era when the American economy was driven by manufacturing, the industrial cities of the Heartland were the engines of the nation. Vibrant and dynamic, they epitomized the energy of a growing country. That changed after World War II, when urban disinvestment swept the United States. Suburban flight, deindustrialization, and automobile-oriented sprawl triggered massive population and job losses in the cities that had once led America's growth. While some older cities began to rebound in the 1990s, others are still losing population and jobs. These include large cities such as Detroit, Cleveland, St. Louis, Buffalo, and Pittsburgh, as well as many smaller cities such as Youngstown, Scranton, Saginaw, Trenton, and Utica.

As the population of these legacy cities has declined, so too has demand for their buildings and land, creating a new urban landscape rife with vacant lots and abandoned structures. Even in relatively more stable neighborhoods boarded-up houses are scattered among the blocks. But the impacts of population loss are not purely physical: As affluent residents have left, legacy cities have become poorer, with barriers of race and class impeding access to opportunities. Such long-standing challenges have been made worse by the Great Recession, the mortgage crisis, and the tumult in the automotive industry, which have hit many of these cities with particular force. Trapped behind rigid municipal boundaries, today legacy cities face growing fiscal crises, making it increasingly difficult for them to provide public services and maintain their infrastructure.

Yet this is only part of the picture. Legacy cities contain assets that are important for their own futures and for those of their states, regions, and of the United States as a whole. These assets include business clusters, manufacturing plants, and Fortune 500 headquarters, along with major hospitals and universities, large nonprofit organizations, arts institutions, and foundations. These cities contain rich resources of historic buildings, gracious tree-lined neighborhoods, and beautiful lakes and riverfronts. Above all, they contain valuable human capital—the leaders and ordinary citizens working in businesses and government, nonprofits and neighborhoods, who are committed to making their cities better places in which to live and work.

Across legacy cities, however, conditions vary considerably in both nature and degree. And areas of both strength and weakness can be found in each, with vital neighborhoods adjacent to areas that have been largely abandoned and thriving downtowns just blocks from acres of empty factory buildings. As such, cities are already developing strategies and tools that will work best to address their unique challenges: Philadelphia has begun to stabilize its population, for example, while Pittsburgh, although still losing residents, has begun to rebuild its economy around new technologies. Moving forward, the strategies that will restore America's legacy cities must be thoughtful and nuanced, reflecting both the differences between cities and those within them.

Building a Framework for Change

Understanding that one size does not fit all places, in this report attendees of the American Assembly lay out the following recommendations for fostering transformative change in cities that have lost substantial portions of their population:

1. Develop a creative vision for the future of the city, grounded in a thorough understanding of the city's economic geography, the role it plays in its region, and its function in the global economy
2. Rigorously and objectively analyze the city's assets, understanding both opportunities and constraints
3. Design strategies tailored to areas and opportunities with the greatest market potential, informed by social, environmental, and other values
4. Recapture surplus land for public uses in areas where private markets are not functioning
5. Build the city's ability to execute complex revival strategies by:
    - Strengthening governance and leadership
    - Growing financial capacity
    - Investing in information infrastructure
6. Forge supportive partnerships among federal, state, and local governments by:
    - Targeting resources
    - Revisiting regulatory policies
    - Incentivizing regional collaboration

Though this report focuses on actions that legacy cities should undertake, it emphasizes that state and federal governments also have crucial roles. States need to conserve financial resources, environmental amenities and previous investments in the built environment and, thus, states should give strong preferences to already-developed areas in funding transportation, sewer, water and other infrastructure, state facilities, and restoration of previously used sites in a coordinated fashion. The federal government should similarly support these state initiatives through its allocation of transportation funding, incentives for meeting environmental regulations, and stimulation of regional planning efforts that recognize the costs of sprawl. Change will not come easily nor will it come quickly. Cities, states, and the federal government need to commit to long-term strategies and follow them consistently and aggressively not for years, but for decades. Change is possible, and it is worth our effort.

II. Develop an Informed Vision Through a Broad, Inclusive Process

Reinventing legacy cities commences with crafting a vision built on the collective understanding of the reasons for their losses, an acceptance of current conditions, and a realistic assessment of an achievable future.

Informing a city's vision must be data that describe the regional economic geography in which the city exists, and provide a socioeconomic portrait of each of the city's neighborhoods. It must present its assets, including residents, land, legacy industries, newly emerging business clusters, anchor institutions, history, and infrastructure. And it must document its liabilities, including high crime rates, failing schools, a limited tax base, low labor force participation, vacant and distressed properties, the fiscal burden of pension obligations, and an overall loss of confidence in the city. While a vision needs a fact-based foundation, capturing more intangible attributes—the "soul of the city"—through qualitative or local knowledge is also essential. In sum, a vision, grounded in facts and shared values, expresses community hopes and expectations for a city's future.

Developing such a vision is complex. For some cities, it may include a period of mourning the past, passing through the stages of denial, anger, bargaining, and depression to acceptance. For others, it may include the reconstruction of the history of how things came to be by confronting longstanding racial and class divisions. However it begins, the visioning process must move toward developing a new construct for the city, one that focuses on substantive issues, envisions a future in which each participant can see a role for him or herself, and which is realistically aspirational. Recognition that a city can be smaller and still be a good place to live, work, and gather enables a community to turn a psychological corner and begin addressing its concrete challenges. Cities can rally around new opportunities to produce turning points. These may be inspired by a new leader, landmark projects, or civic processes to generate a new consensus. The object is to create targets and deadlines to pursue milestone initiatives together.

Developing a shared vision in a legacy city requires much more than the routine forms of citizen participation because the consensus built must be strong enough to power a long and arduous implementation process. Five principles should guide the process of developing a vision:

1. it is inclusive and substantive;
2. it is conducted in trust, based on honest and transparent discussion;
3. it is fact-driven, grounded in market realities that can inform a plan for action that will follow;
4. it factors in both current residents and potential newcomers;

5. it produces a vision that is creative, internally coherent, has integrated elements, and provides the specifications and community values to be embodied in the reimagined city.

III. Develop Strategies Based on Market Realities

If legacy cities are to build sound and healthy futures, they must base their decisions on a clear, objective understanding of the realities of their market conditions, with deep knowledge of the city's assets and liabilities and where it fits within the broader regional economy. While some parts of these cities retain varying degrees of market strength, other areas may be extensively abandoned and no longer capable of generating market activity. Cities must recognize this bifurcation, making investments that are reality-based, and that ultimately link spatial development plans with regional and local economic development strategies.

Youngstown's 2010: A Plan for a Smaller City

When Youngstown, Ohio lost its last steel mill, its leaders realized that the city had hit rock bottom. Over thirty years, Youngstown had lost tens of thousands of jobs and more than half its population; the hoped-for revival of manufacturing had vanished. But this last plant closing was a wake-up call. It energized the mayor and the president of Youngstown State University to start a broadly inclusive planning process that first yielded a vision to guide the plan, Youngstown 2010, and finally led to its adoption in 2005. Crafting the vision involved extensive community engagement and resulted in a simple, compelling statement of four principles:

1. Accepting that Youngstown is a smaller city: Youngstown should strive to be a model mid-sized city.
2. Defining Youngstown's role in the new regional economy: Youngstown must align itself with the realities of the new regional economy.
3. Improving Youngstown's image and enhancing quality of life: Making Youngstown a healthier and better place to live and work.
4. A call to action: An achievable and practical plan to make things happen.

See **www.youngstown2010.com**

1. Principles for Market-Supporting Areas

Market-supporting areas are those where the market still continues to function, although in many cases low prices may mean that public subsidies may initially be needed to make new projects feasible. In order for local economic development approaches to capitalize on market opportunities and reuse land productively, they should be informed by and linked to regional economic activity and growth strategies. (Some of these approaches were highlighted in The American Assembly's earlier report, Retooling for Growth). Neighborhood assets need to be connected and deployed into economic markets that are nearly always larger than the neighborhood, and that are frequently regional in scope. A key goal is to build practical, operational economic linkages between the people, businesses, land uses, and marketplaces of the neighborhood with this broader activity: connecting workforce to emerging sectors, entrepreneurs to supply chains, land to migrating people and businesses looking for sites. These connections not only restore local economic vitality, but also build the practical foundation for institution and relationship building that helps align interests and generates more deliberate collaboration between central cities and their suburbs.Some key principles for redevelopment in market-supporting areas include:

Build from strength

Areas with relatively strong market activity should be targeted for investment, with the goal of increasing demand, strengthening property values, and rebuilding confidence in the community. Focusing resources on these places—which may include residential neighborhoods, commercial districts, and/or downtowns—can motivate existing property owners to reinvest in their properties, and encourage people to buy in the area. Anchor institutions such as universities can make a major contribution by providing financial assistance to employees to buy homes in surrounding neighborhoods, as well as by strengthening neighborhood amenities such as local public schools.

Building from Strength in Baltimore

The Baltimore Healthy Neighborhoods Program targets neighborhoods with market conditions strong enough that a combination of neighborhood marketing, slightly discounted mortgage loans, organized residents, and modest community improvements have resulted in an increase in both home prices and community confidence.

See **www.healthyneighborhoods.org**

Change the investment climate

Public investments need to change the climate so as to leverage private financing. Approaches include making strategic infrastructure investments, eliminating deterrents to investment, creating an entrepreneurial environment that builds on existing businesses, focusing on clusters that leverage the city's economic assets, and growing export-oriented firms. Under some circumstances cities can benefit from import-substitution strategies oriented around major anchor institutions—like Cleveland's Evergreen Industries—which, when executed well, can have a positive effect on local economies.

Invest in human capital

Racial and poverty concentrations are a distressing by-product of sustained population loss in legacy cities. Improving schooling at all levels and connecting workforce training to regional job growth can help integrate the city's human capital with surrounding economic opportunities. Advancing public policies that promote equity is essential for overcoming these cities' histories of race and class disparities. Other opportunities can be provided by drawing immigrants to legacy cities, which can help repopulate neighborhoods and schools, and revitalize business districts.

Changing the Investment Climate in Cleveland

The city of Cleveland and the region's transit agency constructed the nation's first bus rapid transit line (BRT), the Health Line, on Euclid Avenue. The $200 million transit investment has triggered over $4 billion in investment in the teeth of a brutal recession. The line connects the traditional downtown to its arts and culture center six miles away. Downtown is turning into a residential neighborhood with a 92 percent occupancy rate. Cleveland State University invested $500 million to reconnect to the city and support a residential campus. The Cleveland Clinic is supporting a global presence with investments in clinical and research facilities. University Circle, Inc. is evolving from a traditional community development corporation to a community service organization. In-fill development is occurring all along the line. The BRT investment proved to be to be catalytic in triggering institutional and market-responsive investment.

See **www.rtahealthline.com**

Promote density

Evidence is growing that demand for city living is greater when there are dense, walkable neighborhoods. Even in legacy cities with a surplus of land, growing nodes of density can be an effective strategy to strengthen the city's residential and commercial areas. Where appropriate, strategies should focus on increasing densities to help support healthy residential neighborhoods, strong downtowns, and effective public transportation systems.

As they focus on encouraging neighborhood density, cities should offer a variety of housing types for people of all incomes. In order to support a balanced workforce, cities must include affordable and upscale housing in for-sale and rental buildings, townhouses, and detached homes in safe neighborhoods. Given low prices in most legacy cities, however, building markets and increasing home values should be a priority.

Nevertheless, planning for areas with market strength is not just about economic development and housing. Successful communities need safety, access, and in the case of residential neighborhoods, good schools and quality of life amenities. Public sector and nonprofit strategies must address these issues, while building community engagement and cohesion.

2. Principles for Weak- and Non-Market Areas

Many legacy cities contain areas where widespread abandonment has taken place, where market demand is limited to few but low-end speculators, and where vacant buildings and lots predominate. Approaches to these areas must be radically different from those areas where there is market strength.

Some key principles for redevelopment in these non market-supporting areas include:

Get land under public control
Cities should build their capacity to assemble, hold, and maintain vacant land, clear title, and dispose of property for non-market uses. Cities—enabled by their states—should employ land assembly tools including the aggressive use of tax foreclosure.

Incentivize responsible property stewardship
Property owners have responsibilities as well as rights. States should enact measures such as vacant property registration fees and aggressive code enforcement that press owners to restore vacant properties to productive use, maintain them responsibly, or relinquish them to others. At the same time, cities should provide incentives for owners willing to restore properties to use.

Encourage alternative land uses
Strategies for non-market areas should be designed to ensure that surplus land enhances the city's stronger neighborhoods and economic development strategies. Vacant land can be used for a wide range of both interim and permanent uses, including productive landscapes for environmental remediation, storm water management, habitat and wetland restoration, community gardening, recreational and cultural activities, and contemporary forms of homesteading.

Encourage relocation where necessary
In implementing their land use strategies, cities may seek to encourage residents and businesses left in largely vacant areas to relocate to more populated neighborhoods with better amenities and services. This raises difficult issues, as many people, particularly older individuals, may be reluctant or unable to afford to move. Rather than forcing people to leave their homes and businesses, cities should provide sensitive, thoughtful incentives and support that enable them to relocate to communities that

may offer a better quality of life or more viable business location. The critical goal is to offer residents and businesses choices, rather than impose "solutions" on them.

All of these strategies—for market-supporting and non-market areas—are difficult to execute and slow to show results. Cities were originally built lot by lot, block by block, and restoration proceeds in the same way. Cities and their partners in regeneration—neighborhood organizations, community development corporations (CDCs), foundations, anchor institutions, developers and realtors—must not only have patience, but must be willing to chart a course and stick with it for the long haul.

IV. Develop New Civic and Governance Capacity

Legacy cities have been described as a size 40 man wearing a size 60 suit. Though apt, this metaphor misses the fact that this man is not just smaller, but undernourished in a multitude of ways. In addition to economic and social challenges, legacy cities suffer from weakened political, social, and civic structures; profound fiscal stress; and a lack of the data and information needed to successfully develop and implement their respective vision and strategies—and, ultimately, restore their overall economic health and vitality. As such, it is essential that cities take innovative, entrepreneurial approaches to building or rebuilding the robust governance structures, financial capacities, and information infrastructure needed to successfully implement their vision and strategies.

1. Construct the New Governance for the Next Economy

The places best poised for economic success forge governance structures that encourage nimble, cross-sectoral activity, engage firms and citizens in the work of government, welcome newcomers, and tolerate risk. To prosper in the next economy, then, legacy cities need not just improved government, but better governance, which encompasses the entire civic and institutional infrastructure that drives economic activity. These cities need to cultivate and lift up leaders who can garner widespread support for their city's vision and strategy, and have the ability to inspire the human and financial capital to implement it. They need the civic and governmental capacity to undertake the day-to-day work required to foment real change. And they need organizational structures suited to 21st century economy functions.

Cultivating New Forms of Leadership

In their heyday, groups of corporate civic elites—together with city hall—played a major leadership role in the development and governance of their respective cities.

The power and influence of these leaders, and elite business organizations of which they were a part, has waned considerably in recent decades, however, and has been reduced by the forces of economic restructuring, corporate reorganization, and deregulation.

In many American cities today, leadership is different, both in terms of its composition and how it wields its influence. This leadership emerges from several different spheres, including government and business, as has always been the case, but also the nonprofit sector, anchor institutions, neighborhood organizations, and a range of other groups—from networks of young professionals to parent advocates— that have declared a commitment to the city.

But these groups may not always fully exercise their leadership, nor always work together in productive and successful ways around a defined set of common goals. True leaders must self-identify as such; be so recognized both among residents and their peers as worthy of trust and confidence; and be willing to commit their time and energies over the course of many years. Most importantly, they must engage with one another in consistent, durable partnerships oriented around the strategies described herein.

Building Stronger Civic and Governance Capacity

Cultivating a new leadership regime must be coupled with aggressive efforts to rebuild the basic functional capacities—both in the public sector and the broader civic fabric—that allow a city to provide the basic services and amenities that residents and businesses expect and depend upon.

In the public sector realm, this begins with ensuring that government has the necessary competencies in such basics as planning, budgeting, procurement, and hiring, and can provide quality services in key domains such as education and safety. It also means that the public sector has the capacity to tackle complex matters of economic development and land management that are marked by the uncertainty and constrained resources characterizing legacy cities. Finally, city governments need the capacity to substantively and authentically ensure citizen engagement in the development and certification of strategies and plans.

External philanthropic resources used to augment staffing, import technical expertise, support strategy development and convening, and a range of other assistance can support such public sector capacity building through stand-alone grants, ongoing partnerships, or enduring training programs. For example, philanthropy, in partnership with local universities, could establish formal training institutes designed to provide rigorous education and skill building for both new and incumbent public employees in legacy cities.

Cities' broader civic capacity must also be cultivated at all levels. Whether through the development of new intermediary structures or through the coalescing of existing efforts, legacy cities must have formal, organized, and representative civic leadership that cuts across sectors and coalesces around large-scale problem solving. Such a macro-level civic platform is essential to driving large-scale consensus building, but it is also important as a mechanism for leveraging resources, aligning efforts, and providing the necessary continuity for the long-term efforts required to turn these cities around.

Neighborhood-focused leadership, for example, is critical to ensuring that city-wide strategies are responsive to on-the-ground realities and that large-scale plans can actually take root in neighborhoods. Such leadership, particularly through the work of formal associations, is essential to organizing and executing the detailed and labor-intensive efforts needed to sustain neighborhoods through the difficult transitions faced by legacy cities, ranging from reclaiming abandoned land to marketing neighborhoods and welcoming new neighbors. Wherever possible, cities should strive to link neighborhood associations to one another in order to ensure resource and solution sharing, promote cooperative efforts, and develop a clear sense of how each neighborhood fits into the city's future.

Finally, legacy cities must also participate in or catalyze regional civic formations. Such regional relationships are vital to ensuring that city interests—in matters of emergency response, transportation planning, economic development, talent attraction, and other critical areas—are represented in the broader regional context.

Detroit Works

The Detroit Works Project is a process to create a collective vision for Detroit's future at the neighborhood, city, and metropolitan scale. Envisioned as an extended process of community engagement and planning, the work is led by a fifty-five-member Advisory Task Force, representing residents, community members, faith-based and nonprofit organizations, city council members, the business and foundation communities, and civic leaders. The Mayor's Interagency Task Force, made up of key city departments and local government agencies, works to ensure that all elements of the plan are achievable and able to be implemented as part of a shared vision.

See **http://detroitworksproject.com/**

Creating 21st Century Organizational Structures

Public sector workers at all levels have made positive contributions to the success of American cities, and will continue to be critical to their renewal. However, over the last fifty years in the United States, a new governmental entity has been created, on average, every eighteen hours. Such proliferation and fragmentation of government has too often resulted in fiefdoms, self-serving bureaucracies, and inefficiencies in taxation, allocation of resources, and provision of public goods.

To make matters worse, these trends move us in exactly the wrong direction for the next economy. Today's economic boundaries and political boundaries no longer even remotely coincide. Indeed, while we have city, state, and national governments, the geography of the economy is increasingly neighborhoods (where assets reside and are developed and connected to larger systems), regions (where assets are deployed into regional economic systems), and global markets. Government needs to be reoriented towards this new economic geography.

To do so, government functions need to be focused where they can best enable economic activity. Some of the functions of city government, like transportation and fire protection, need to move "upstream" to counties and regions—not necessarily through consolidation, but through deliberate coordination. Other functions need to move "downstream"—to neighborhoods, where local institutions more readily know and can support their assets, and/or through tax increment financing districts (TIFs), business improvement districts, community service corporations, local development authorities, or other entities. Such entities can tailor services more closely to neighborhood needs, achieve economies of scale, and raise resources from non-governmental sources.

The George Washington Project

The Certified Public Manager (CPM) Program is designed to provide District of Columbia government managers the tools to be more effective leaders. The nationally accredited CPM program is administered by the District of Columbia Department of Human Resources. Academic rigor is brought to the program through strategic partnerships with The George Washington University.

See **www.gwu.edu/~cepl/regional/pemm.html**

2. Chart New Directions in Municipal Finance

With rising costs and declining revenues, governments at all levels are facing severe financial stress. This is a particularly difficult challenge in America's legacy cities, which have fewer and poorer taxpayers and reduced industrial and commercial activity, at the same time they face the growing costs of maintaining aging infrastructure, meeting payroll and retiree benefit obligations, and managing a landscape strewn with empty houses and vacant lots. Any responsible approach to these challenges will demand hard choices, choices that will force state and local leaders to rethink the very nature of the services they provide and how they will be funded.

Traditional methods of funding municipal services assumed that sales, income, and property tax revenue were aligned with city boundaries. That is no longer the case, however, as revenue-providing wealth is now generated across cities' respective regions, often out of cities' reach. No legacy city can rebuild if it

Flint's Tax Foreclosure Model

Rather than selling tax liens to speculators, Genesee County (Flint), MI internalizes tax enforcement revenues by issuing delinquent tax anticipation notes (DTANs) for unpaid taxes and by providing full funding of anticipated taxes to all local governments. The county then collects delinquent taxes, retiring the note and foreclosing on unpaid properties. This process creates significant arbitrage earnings – money that once flowed to tax lien speculators. The result has been $1.6-$2.1 million per year of new revenue to a fund dedicated to management, remediation, and redevelopment of tax-foreclosed properties. Taking title to and selling foreclosed properties has raised additional revenue previously lost to speculators.

See **www.thelandbank.org/aboutus.asp**

cannot provide essential services. As such, cities must explore every available avenue to raise revenues and reduce costs. There are a number of approaches worth considering, many of which may require changes in state law. These include:

Seek new dedicated revenues beyond traditional sources:

- *Reform the property tax collection system, a major source of revenue for most cities.* Most cities—working under antiquated state laws—enforce property tax collections in ways that effectively transfer delinquent tax fees and the value of foreclosed properties to speculators. By reforming state tax foreclosure systems, cities and counties can reap significant new revenues and retain the ability to direct the reuse of abandoned properties in ways consistent with local needs. Coupling such reforms with local or regional land banks offers a new source of both revenue and land control for legacy cities.
- *Employ new models of tax-increment financing (TIF).* TIFs have proved an effective way of directing revenues to cities experiencing large-scale abandonment. In Michigan, for example, brownfield TIFs allow for regional, scattered site, cross-collateralized plans that generate regional revenues to fund redevelopment in distressed areas that could not otherwise attract investment.
- *Implement user fees and other tax methods of cost recovery such as vacant property registration fees.* Such fees can be an effective method by which to raise resources to manage problem properties.
- *Explore regional revenue sharing models.* While difficult to enact, revenue sharing, such as that employed in Minneapolis/St. Paul and in the Allegheny Regional Asset District, is an equitable method of tax revenue distribution that recognizes the critical role cities play in a region's economic health.

Increase efficiency to achieve better financial performance and stabilize the tax base:

- Reduce the negative financial consequences of mortgage foreclosures by reforming state foreclosure laws. This includes requiring recordation of all foreclosure filings with local government, and allowing local government to enforce codes on vacant properties in foreclosure against lenders.
- Reform state laws governing shared service agreements. Many existing laws, while allowing such agreements, are overly restrictive and thus can thwart successful intergovernmental cooperation.
- Realign public services at the appropriate neighborhood, city, or regional level, as discussed in the preceding section.

Generate new tax revenue by stimulating urban reinvestment:

- Maintain business and development tax credits for urban investment, rather than reduce or eliminate them, as is currently occurring.
- Develop investment funds to support business expansion and transformative real estate development projects. Such funds should include money derived from public and union pension funds.
- Develop a federal and/or state infrastructure bank. Such a bank can help finance the rebuilding of essential infrastructure, as well as the development of transformative new urban reinvestments such as high-speed rail and modern public transit systems.

Despite the best efforts of responsible local officials, some legacy cities may continue to face insolvency, a problem that most state systems aren't adequately equipped to manage. Thus, in addition to the tools described above, states may also need to consider emergency measures—including state financial distress programs—as a means of instituting lasting financial reforms.

3. Create a Robust Information Infrastructure

Data and analytics are central to governance activities and constitute the lifeblood of economic activity. As such, establishing a grounded vision and detailed strategies tailored to place, enabling excellent execution, and restoring market activity all depend upon rich and interactive information resources. Such resources should include a range of knowledge from expert to novice, and should be comprised of raw data, sophisticated analytics, and social engagement. They should also include state-of-the-art interactive tools that enable transparency and easy use—particularly by the private sector—and a qualitative assessment of local knowledge and expertise.

Information resources serve several key purposes with respect to the special challenges and opportunities of legacy cities:

Developing strategies tailored to place

Strategies for each neighborhood—and even for each asset, such as a parcel of land—have to be tailored to their particular challenges and attributes. This requires rich information and analysis to understand neighborhood assets and markets, and where they fall on the spectrum from strong (where market-based strategies are most fitting) to weak (where alternative uses are more appropriate). It also demands knowledge of how local neighborhoods and assets connect to the unique opportunities of the larger metropolitan economy: What clusters of economic activity are emerging in the city and region? And which local labor force, supplier, and land assets can strengthen and grow with these emerging clusters? Such fine-grained information is vital to public development agencies', community-based organizations', and private developers' ability to appropriately and strategically allocate their resources.

Intelligent Cities

From the next generation of "e-government" technologies that improve value for customers while reducing cost and complexity to a wide array of applications made possible by wireless broadband, mobile devices, social media, and other Web 2.0 developments, technology is taking the promise of "intelligent cities" well beyond the basic information infrastructure emphasized in the main text. Such developments include infrastructure and buildings that "talk" to locals and visitors alike, providing real-time information through smartphones, pad computers, or other devices; homes and workplaces that provide real-time energy consumption feedback to their occupants; interactive tools for public education and "e-democracy;" and compact mini-vehicles that are available for short-term, cross-town rentals just like luggage carts in the airport. Innovations are no longer just premium products for the highest income communities. In more and more cases, they provide lighter weight, lower cost ways of meeting the public's needs while engaging the public in supporting and continuously improving what gets delivered, by whom, and how. Intelligent Cities, a collaborative project by the National Building Museum, TIME magazine, IBM, and the Rockefeller Foundation, is highlighting a wide range of innovative technologies already in use and shining a light forward, too—on cutting-edge efforts to change our conception of what is possible in cities and how to make it accessible to as many communities as possible.

See **www.nbm.org/intelligentcities**

Undertaking inclusive market-based development

More accurate credit data enables lending to new people and places. Accessible data on local expenditures enables expanded retail services. And better data and tools on human capital and labor demand make labor markets more efficient and inclusive. Rich information resources, in short, can help expand market-based neighborhood strategies so that they include under-deployed neighborhood assets, align neighborhood and regional development, and ultimately foster more inclusive prosperity, which is better for both.

Promoting sustainable development informed by market trends

More accurate data on market trends also supports sustainable and forward-looking development by helping disparate parties—including public agencies, CDCs, and private developers to coalesce around a common strategy for revitalizing communities. Sustainable neighborhood development strategies depend on accurate information to enable appropriate and strategic allocation of public and private capital by public development agencies, community-based organizations, and private developers. Neighborhood and city-level institutions are uniquely situated to analyze information and ensure that development strategies foster an inclusive and equitable prosperity.

Improving governance

Government and local communities are primary sources of the key information resources necessary for developing market-based improvement strategies. Effective governments in the next economy will use their information resources to further engage citizens and firms in the work of government. These resources must thus be transparent, providing clear and readily accessible information that can help forge new partnerships. Well-conceived government partnerships can be important tools for cultivating and reinforcing change, and providing support for new policy and practice reforms.

Information resources can also vastly improve the efficiency of government itself: They are critical to fact-based government planning, as well as to monitoring performance and on-going operational evaluation and improvement. "Government 2.0" could reduce the costs to both government and governed, by more efficiently enabling transactions with government, from obtaining business licenses to reporting building code violations.

Developing the information infrastructure described above entails a cultural shift towards valuing transparency and engagement, and an ongoing commitment to continuously building capacity. Modern computer-based data mining, modeling, Geographic Information System (GIS), and other platforms, such as community meetings, provide continuing opportunities to enrich information resources and expand their use. These tools should allow for the collection and analysis of well-organized, accurate, and accessible data on land use and the status of parcels; activity in residential housing markets; nature and performance of neighborhood businesses; labor demand and supply characteristics; and much more. Advanced tools for amassing and using this data for the varied purposes described above range from The Reinvestment Fund's PolicyMap to NEO CANDO's data for planning and monitoring to RW Ventures' "Dynamic Neighborhoods" database and tools for evaluating markets and interventions.

Advanced data management tools

The Reinvestment Fund's PolicyMap (**www.policymap.com**) is a fully web-based online data and mapping application that provides access to over 10,000 indicators related to demographics, housing, crime, mortgages, health, jobs, and more. NEO CANDO (**www.neocando.case.edu**), Northeast Ohio Community and Neighborhood Data for Organizing, is a free and publicly accessible social and economic data system of the Center on Urban Poverty and Community Development at Case Western Reserve University. RW Venture's "Dynamic Neighborhoods" database (**www.rw-ventures.com/publications/n_analysis.php**) provides sophisticated tools for analyzing neighborhoods and the impacts of interventions.

V. Forge Supportive Government Partnerships & Strategies

To leverage the strategies suggested above, legacy cities, their counties, regional entities, neighboring communities, states, and the federal government need to forge new partnerships with one another, aligning their efforts both vertically and horizontally. Government must also engage in effective cross-sector partnerships with anchor institutions (such as colleges and hospitals), businesses, foundations, and other organizations.

1. Partner With State Governments

In an era of broad fiscal challenges, rising energy costs, and environmental concerns, states can no longer afford to facilitate low-density, high-cost development at the metropolitan fringe while its older communities continue to decline. Instead, states need to conserve financial resources, environmental amenities, and previous investments in the built environment, including their legacy cities.

One key way states can accomplish these objectives is to give strong preferences to already-developed areas in funding transportation, sewer, water, and other infrastructure, as well as state facilities, in a coordinated fashion. The federal government should similarly support these state initiatives through its allocation of transportation funding, incentives for meeting environmental regulations, and stimulation of regional planning efforts that recognize the costs of sprawl. Both federal and state infrastructure support should encourage rehabilitation, repair, and maintenance of existing infrastructure and should incentivize a life-cycle budgeting and finance plan.

States should also reexamine other policies and programs. Many states have tax policies, resource allocation formulas, business location incentives, and other policies that historically have disadvantaged legacy cities. These include, for example, policies and approaches that encourage cities, suburbs, and exurbs to compete against one another for new business and economic development rather than cooperate for the benefit of their metropolitan area. States could better position legacy cities to compete in the next economy through numerous reforms and innovations. In the first place, state agencies themselves could take a more coordinated approach by breaking down program silos and by exhibiting sustained commitments that transcend political cycles and jurisdictional boundaries. In this spirit, states could also provide tools to support the new governance framework outlined above, including legislation allowing permissive local government mergers, or modernizing antiquated planning statutes. Other innovative state tools might include supporting approaches that pool regional resources to pave the way for regional economic development, such as creating a regional revolving loan fund for infrastructure and development projects, and incentivizing and directing investments to places where anchor institutions are aligned with cluster development. States might explore how they can reform and expand state tax increment financing laws, and provide incentives for TIF-supported projects and areas. And they should create incentives for legacy cities to better concentrate resources by prioritizing assistance toward areas the city has identified as strategic targets for intervention.

Working Together in the Denver Area

The Metro Denver Economic Development Corporation (Metro Denver EDC) is a full-scale regional economic development entity in which many area economic development groups have joined together to represent, and further, the interests of an entire region. Its partners include seventy cities, counties, and economic development organizations in the seven-county Metro Denver and two-county Northern Colorado region. These entities have signed a no-compete agreement, in which they prohibited themselves from using financial incentives to lure businesses across jurisdictional lines via the use of financial incentives.

See **www.metrodenver.org**

Finally, states should reform outmoded laws and regulations that thwart legacy cities' efforts to acquire, manage, dispose, and/or redevelop vacant and abandoned land and buildings—and to prevent vacancy and abandonment in the first place. Cities are creatures of the state. As such, state laws, regulations, and policies establish the ground rules for what cities can and cannot do and set the stage for how and where development occurs. States need to consider, for example, major overhauls in such basic systems as the property tax foreclosure system (to finance new land banks and eliminate sale of tax liens); code enforcement (to provide for priority "superliens" for cities); mortgage foreclosure (to address the responsibilities of mortgagees and shift from non-judicial to judicial procedure); and the municipal finance tax structure.

Ohio Hubs of Innovation

The Ohio Hubs of Innovation are regional economic development initiatives that build upon leading assets in urban centers to accomplish three major goals:

1. Propel innovation through cutting-edge, market-driven applied technology and knowledge spillover;
2. Foster the opportunity for job creation and retention; and
3. Catalyze the formation of new companies in the region, while at the same time helping to ensure that Ohio's existing industries retain their competitive advantage in the global marketplace.

See **www.development.ohio.gov/Urban/OhioHubs.htm**

2. Partner with the Federal Government

While the federal government plays a more limited regulatory and institutional role than state government, it can leverage its financial resources and, in so doing, exert strong influence over how states use their legal powers and discretionary funding, and how local governments pursue revitalization activities.

Jumpstarting the process by which legacy cities develop their economies and reconfigure their physical landscapes demands better alignment of federal and state policies with the aim of bolstering local practices—a goal that must be pursued systematically and intentionally. For instance, if state and federal governments can align in making strategic and targeted funding decisions, both the public and private sectors can leverage their respective investments with greater potential for success. For its part, the federal government can better support legacy cities in three primary areas: (1) stream-lining and making existing programs more flexible, especially the Department of Housing and Urban Development (HUD)'s Community Development Block Grant Program; (2) designing "race to the top"- like qualifications for funding allocations that would require specified state reforms to enhance a city's ability to deal with vacant land, such as faster property transfer in the face of tax delinquency or code enforcement liens; and (3) expanding cross-departmental cooperation in crafting incentive programs to enhance regional cooperation in planning and economic development.

Two new Obama Administration initiatives exemplify these approaches.

First, through the new Partnership for Sustainable Communities, the Environmental Protection Agency (EPA), Department of Housing and Urban Development (HUD), and Department of Transportation (DOT) have together developed overarching "Livability Principles" to guide the collaborative allocation of grants and technical assistance, including: HUD's $150 million in Sustainable

Communities grants for local and regional planning that integrates land use, transportation, and economic development; DOT's $600 million in Transportation Investment Generating Economic Recovery (TIGER II) grants for innovative, high-return transportation projects; and EPA's technical assistance for local sustainability efforts tied to water quality, infrastructure investment, housing, and other sustainable development priorities.

Second, the Economic Development Administration (EDA), Department of Education (DOE), Small Business Administration (SBA), and Department of Labor (DOL) have joined forces through the Task Force for Advancing Regional Innovation Clusters (TARIC) to coordinate the goals and allocations of competitive grant programs and technical assistance, with a focus on promoting regional competitive advantage. TARIC's priorities include coordinating and leveraging federal resources to support the growth of existing regional business clusters—for example, through federal research and development investments and efforts to commercialize technological innovations—and promoting the establishment of new ones. TARIC aims to monitor market trends, coordinate federal staff in regional offices, and thereby facilitate a more unified federal response to requests from regions for assistance related to economic development, education, workforce, and entrepreneurship. Two more agencies with important economic development functions—the Department of Agriculture and HUD—are now joining the effort.

VI. Conclusion

This report focuses on how America can help legacy cities stem their losses, uplift their communities and their institutions, and harness their assets to help move the nation toward success in the next economy. This American Assembly has focused particularly on the challenge of recalibrating the economic strengths, human capital abilities, and physical attributes—land, buildings, and infrastructure—of these valuable cities to new roles and functions. The Assembly has offered recommendations about rational land use strategies, creative financing approaches, improved civic capacity, and stronger partnerships. These recommendations proceed from the conviction that our nation gratefully acknowledges the historic contributions of these cities, and that the immense value in skills, institutions, and hard resources that these cities hold are a key asset for America's future. The smartest course for America is to put them back to work.

Project Leadership

Co-Chairs

The Hon. Henry G. Cisneros
Executive Chairman
CityView
Former Mayor
City of San Antonio
San Antonio, TX

The Hon. Gregory S. Lashutka
Consultant
Findley Davies
Former Mayor
City of Columbus
Columbus, OH

Co-Directors

Paul C. Brophy
Principal
Broaphy and Reilly LLC
Columbia, MD

Elliott D. Sclar
Professor of Urban Planning
School of Architecture & Planning
Columbia University
Director
Center for Sustainable Urban Development
Earth Institute
New York, NY

Participants

Frank S. Alexander
Sam Nunn Professor of Law
Emory University School of Law
Atlanta, GA

Richard Barnes
Board of Governors
Society of Innovators
Ivy Tech College
Gary, IN

Aaron Bartley
Executive Director
PUSH Buffalo
Buffalo, NY

Robert A. Beauregard
Professor of Urban Planning
Graduate School of Architecture, Planning and Preservation
Columbia University
New York, NY

Laura Berman
Columnist
Detroit News
Detroit, MI

Matthias Bernt
Senior Researcher
Leibniz Institute for Regional Development and Structural Planning
Erkner, Germany

Paul Beyer
Director of Smart Growth
New York State Department of State
Albany, NY

The Hon. David Bing
Mayor
City of Detroit
Detroit, MI

Eugenie L. Birch *
Nussdorf Professor of Urban Research and Education
Department of City and Regional Planning
University of Pennsylvania
Philadelphia, PA

Austin Black II
Broker/President
City Living Detroit
Detroit, MI

Lavea Brachman § **
Executive Director
Greater Ohio Policy Center
Non-Resident Senior Fellow
Brookings Institution
Columbus, OH

Michael J. Brady, Jr.
Legal and Policy Director
Community Legal Resources
Detroit, MI

Andre Brumfield
Principal & Director of Urban Design and Planning
AECOM
Chicago, IL

Valentino Castellani §
President
Unimanagement
Former Mayor
City of Torino, Italy
Torino, Italy

Don Chen
Senior Program Officer
Metropolitan Opportunity Unit
Ford Foundation
New York, NY

Matthew Clayson
Director
Detroit Creative Corridor Center
Detroit, MI

Engelbert Lutke Daldrup §
Professor & CEO
Urban Stakeholder Consulting
Berlin, Germany

The Hon. Chris Doherty
Mayor of the City of Scranton
Scranton, PA

Mike Emmerich §
Chief Executive
New Economy
Manchester, UK

Sylvie Fol
Professor
University Paris 1 Pantheon, Sorbonne
Institut de Geographie
Paris, France

Gus Frangos
President & General Counsel
Cuyahoga County Land Reutilization Corporation
Cleveland, OH

John Gallagher
Journalist
Detroit Free Press
Detroit, MI

George Galster
Hilberry Professer of Urban Affairs
Department of Urban Studies and Planning
Wayne State University
Detroit, MI

Presley L. Gillespie
Executive Director
Youngstown Neighborhood Development Corporation
Youngstown, OH

Kim Graziani
Director
Neighborhood Initiatives
Office of Mayor Luke Ravenstahl
City of Pittsburgh
Pittsburgh, PA

Toni L. Griffin
Adjunct Associate Professor
Harvard Graduate School of Design
New York, NY

Robin Hacke
Director, Capital Formation
Living Cities
Washington, DC

Marvin Hayes
Former Director
Office of Urban Development & Infrastructure
Office of Ted Strickland
Former Governor of Ohio
Cleveland, OH

Edward W. Hill
Dean
The Maxine Goodman Levin College of Urban Affairs
Cleveland State University
Cleveland, OH

Eric A. Johnson
Executive Director
University Park Alliance
Akron, OH

Curt Johnson
President
Citistates Group
Minneapolis, MN

The Hon. William A. Johnson, Jr. §
Distinguished Professor of Public Policy
Rochester Institute of Technology
Former Mayor, City of Rochester
Rochester, NY

Daniel T. Kildee §
President
Center for Community Progress
Washington, DC

Alicia Kitsuse
Program Officer
Charles Stewart Mott Foundation
Flint, MI

John Kromer
Senior Fellow
Center for Community Progress
Philadelphia, PA

Lillian A. Kuri
Program Director
Architecture, Urban Design and Sustainable Development
Cleveland Foundation
Cleveland, OH

Diana Lind **
Editor at Large
Next American City
New York, NY

Teresa Lynch
Senior Vice President, Research
Initiative for Competitive Inner City
Boston, MA

Alan Mallach *
Non-resident Senior Fellow
Brookings Institute
Senior Fellow
Center for Community Progress
Roosevelt, NJ

The Hon. Hannah McKinney
Vice Mayor
City of Kalamazoo
Kalamazoo, MI

Kurt Metzger
Director
Data Driven Detroit (D3)
Detroit, MI

Mark Morante
Senior Vice President
Policy, Governmental Affairs, and Strategic Planning
Michigan Economic Development Corporation (MEDC)
Lansing, MI

Hunter Morrison §
Director
Campus Planning and Community Development
Youngstown State University
Youngstown, OH

Susan T. Mosey
President
University Cultural Center Association
Detroit, MI

Kristen Mucitelli-Heath
Executive Director
Upstate Caucus
New York State Senate
Syracuse, NY

Mary Mulligan
Brownfields Specialist
Department of Environmental Affairs
City of Gary
Gary, IN

Tom Murphy
Senior Fellow
Urban Land Institute
Washington, DC

Michael A. Pagano
Dean
College of Urban Planning and Public Affairs
University of Illinois-Chicago
Chicago, IL

Jörg Plöger
Research Fellow
ILS—Research Institute for Regional and Urban Development
Dortmund, Germany

Eric W. Price
Executive Vice President
Housing Investment Trust
AFL-CIO
Washington, DC

Richard Rapson §
President and CEO
The Kresge Foundation
Troy, MI

Chris Ronayne
President
University Circle Inc.
Cleveland, OH

Joseph Schilling
Interim Director
Metropolitan Institute
Virginia Tech
Alexandria, VA

Mark C. Schneider
Principal
Fourth River Development LLC
Pittsburgh, PA

Terry Schwarz
Director
Cleveland Urban Design Collaborative
Kent State University
Cleveland, OH

Eric Scorsone
Assistant Professor
Department of Agricultural Economics
Michigan State University
East Lansing, MI

Tamar Shapiro
Director of Urban and Regional Policy
The German Marshall Fund of the United States
Washington, DC

Scot T. Spencer §
Associate Director for Advocacy and Influence
The Annie E. Casey Foundation
Baltimore, MD

Sarah Szurpicki
Director
Great Lakes Urban Exchange (GLUE)
Detroit, MI

Vickie B. Tassan
CRA Executive
Global Compliance and Regulatory Affairs
Ally Bank
Washington, DC

June Manning Thomas
Centennial Professor of Urban and Regional Planning
Taubman College
University of Michigan
Ann Arbor, MI

Steve Tobocman
Director
Global Detroit
Lansing, MI

Laura Trudeau
Senior Program Director
The Kresge Foundation
Troy, MI

Marian Urquilla § *
Director, Program Strategies
Living Cities
Washington, DC

Jennifer S. Vey **
Fellow
Metropolitan Policy Program
The Brookings Institution
Washington, DC

Aundra C. Wallace
Executive Director
Detroit Land Bank Authority
Detroit, MI

The Hon. Dayne Walling §
Mayor
City of Flint
Flint, MI

Orson Watson
Advisor, Community Revitalization
The Garfield Foundation
Boston, MA

Oliver Weigel §
Head of Urban Development Policy Division
Federal Ministry of Transport, Building and Urban Development
Berlin, Germany

Robert Weissbourd *
President
RW Ventures, LLC
Chicago, IL

Thorsten Wiechmann §
Professor
Department of Spatial Planning
TU Dortmund University
Dortmund, Germany

The Hon. Jay Williams §
Mayor
City of Youngstown
Youngstown, OH

Hal Wolman
Director
George Washington Institute of Public Policy
Professor of Political Science
Washington, DC

Observer

Charles R. Henderson
CSR Philanthropy Manager
Bank of America
Norfolk, VA

Legend
* Discussion Leader
** Rapporteur
\+ Delivered Formal Address
§ Panelist

U.S. Government Employees

U.S. Government employees attended the Assembly convening but take no stance on the report:

Raphael Bostic §
Assistant Secretary
Office of Policy Development and Research
U.S. Department of Housing and Urban Development
Washington, DC

Xavier de Souza Briggs
Associate Director
General Government Programs
Office of Management and Budget
Executive Office of the President
Washington, DC

Erika Poethig
Deputy Assistant Secretary for Policy Development
U.S. Department of Housing and Urban Development
Washington, DC

Media Representatives

Media representatives observed the Assembly as individuals:

Matthew Dolan
Reporter
The Wall Street Journal
Southfield, MI

Rosemarie Ward
New York Correspondent
The Economist
New York, NY

Steering Committee

Frank S. Alexander
Professor of Law
Emory University School of Law
Atlanta, GA

Robert A. Beauregard
Professor of Urban Planning
Graduate School of Architecture, Planning and Preservation
Columbia University
New York, NY

Judith Bell
President
PolicyLink
Oakland, CA

Lavea Brachman
Executive Director
Greater Ohio Policy Center
Non-Resident Senior Fellow
Brookings Institution
Columbus, OH

Paul C. Brophy
Principal
Brophy and Reilly LLC
Columbia, MD

Ruth Clevenger
Vice President and Community Affairs Officer
Communications and Community Development
Federal Reserve Bank of Cleveland
Cleveland, OH

Margaret Dewar
Emil Lorch Professor of Architecture and Urban Planning
Taubman College of Architecture and Urban Planning
University of Michigan
Ann Arbor, MI

The Hon. Chris Doherty
Mayor
City of Scranton
Scranton, PA

Kathryn A. Foster
Director
University at Buffalo Regional Institute
The State University of New York
Buffalo, NY

Toni Griffin
Adjunct Associate Professor
Harvard Graduate School of Design
New York, NY

Edward W. Hill
Dean
The Maxine Goodman Levin College of Urban Affairs
Cleveland State University
Cleveland, OH

The Hon. William A. Johnson, Jr.
Distinguished Professor of Public Policy
Rochester Institute of Technology
Former Mayor
City of Rochester
Rochester, NY

Dan Kildee
President
Center for Community Progress
Washington, DC

Alan Mallach
Non-resident Senior Fellow
Brookings Institute
Senior Fellow
Center for Community Progress
Washington, DC

Hunter Morrison
Director
Campus Planning and Community Development
Youngstown State University
Youngstown, OH

Michael Pagano
Dean
Department of Public Administration
University of Illinois-Chicago
Chicago, IL

Richard Rapson
President and CEO
The Kresge Foundation
Troy, MI

Joel Ratner
President & CEO
Neighborhood Progress
Cleveland, OH

Elliott D. Sclar
Professor of Urban Planning
School of Architecture & Planning
Columbia University
Director
Center for Sustainable Urban Development
Earth Institute
New York, NY

Tamar Shapiro
Director of Comparative Domestic Policy
The German Marshall Fund of the United States
Washington, DC

Jennifer Vey
Fellow
Metropolitan Policy Program
The Brookings Institution
Washington, DC

Robert Weissbourd
President
RW Ventures, LLC
Chicago, IL

The Hon. Jay Williams
Mayor
City of Youngstown
Youngstown, OH

Tom Wolfe
Executive Director
Northeast-Midwest Institute
Minneapolis, MN

The American Assembly

The American Assembly, founded by Dwight D. Eisenhower in 1950, is affiliated with Columbia University. The Assembly is a national, non-partisan public affairs forum that illuminates issues of public policy through commissioning research and publications, sponsoring meetings, and issuing reports, books, and other literature. Its projects bring together leading authorities representing a broad spectrum of views and interests. Assembly reports and other publications are used by government, community, and civic leaders, and public officials. American Assembly topics concern not only domestic and foreign policy, but also issues that include arts and culture, philanthropy, health, business, economy, education, law, race, religion and security.

The Center For Sustainable Urban Development

The Earth Institute, Columbia University

The Center for Sustainable Urban Development (CSUD) engages in and fosters education and research for the advancement of physically and socially sustainable cities. To fulfill its mission, CSUD undertakes interdisciplinary analyses of the linkages between urban transport and land use to economic development, demographic shifts, population health and climate change. It collaborates with faculty, students and researchers across Columbia University, but its work stretches far beyond the university setting. Affiliates work on the ground with CSUD, both locally and internationally, with a variety of stakeholders including local universities, officials and community-based organizations to develop policies and plans to meet their goals for sustainable urban-based social and economic development.

The Center For Community Progress

The Center for Community Progress was launched in 2010 with a mission to revitalize America's cities and create vibrant communities through the reuse of vacant, abandoned, and problem property—to transform the systems that affect how the community development, government, and private development fields repurpose these properties and communities. This national organization supports the development of new policy approaches at the federal, state, and local levels and works directly with local officials and practitioners to develop new strategies and capacity to implement meaningful reforms. With offices located in Flint, Michigan; New Orleans, Louisiana; and Washington, DC; Community Progress seeks to connect policymakers at the national and state level with its hands-on work in the cities and towns of America.

Board of Directors

Index

Page numbers in *italics* refer to illustrations.